PHASERS ON STUN!

PHASERS ON STUN!

How the Making (and Remaking)
of Star Trek Changed the World

RYAN BRITT

PLUME

PLUME

An imprint of Penguin Random House LLC

penguinrandomhouse.com

LIBRARY OF CONGRESS CATALOGING-IN-PUBLICATION DATA
has been applied for.

ISBN 9780593185698 (hardcover)
ISBN 9780593185704 (ebook)

Printed in the United States of America
1st Printing

Interior art: Speed lines © pixssa / Shutterstock

BOOK DESIGN BY KRISTIN DEL ROSARIO

For Mary

CONTENTS

Contents

AUTHOR'S NOTE

The bulk of this book was researched, written, revised, and edited between the summer of 2020 and the early months of 2022. However, I have been writing professionally about science fiction since 2009, and, as such, have interviewed people associated with Star Trek for well over a decade. When an interview subject is quoted prior to 2020, the interview was probably conducted for one of the following publications: Tor.com, Clarkesworld, Inverse, SyFy Wire, or Den of Geek. In all cases, anecdotes or quotations appear in entirely different forms than they did in those publications and, just as often, are quotations that did not appear in the final versions of those pieces at all. That said, I strongly encourage the reader to patronize the publications listed above.

Also, in all cases, interview subjects were made aware they were speaking to me in a journalistic capacity. This book has been researched to the best of my ability and fact-checked by independent sources. That said, what you hold is a work of creative nonfiction, and if there are objections, disagreements, or "errors"—subjective or otherwise—they are mine alone and not the fault of my editors, publishers, or the hundreds of people interviewed in these pages.

Finally, because this book was completed during the airing of

Star Trek: Prodigy Season 1 and prior to the airing of at least two new seasons of different Star Trek series—*Picard* Season 2 and *Strange New Worlds* Season 1—a few aspects of the franchise will, naturally, have changed. All parts of Trek change the whole, which, as I hope you'll see in the following pages, has always been a beautiful and inspiring tradition.

RYAN BRITT

PORTLAND, MAINE, JANUARY 2022

PHASERS ON STUN!

On a cold afternoon in February 2018, I looked out at the New York City skyline from my apartment in Queens as I held my sleeping nine-month-old daughter on my shoulder. I had to adjust her just right, worried I was going to wake her up. In about twenty minutes, my wife would be back from work, but the subway was delayed, and this important phone call was going to happen before that. If my baby woke up during the interview, the person at the other end would just have to deal with it.

My phone vibrated and as I answered the call, I wished I'd still had a flip phone. The voice at the other end of the phone was that of Captain Kirk. "This is Mr. Shatner," the voice said. Reflexively, because I'd watched *Star Trek* since I was six years old, I began calling him "sir" immediately.

I was interviewing William Shatner, briefly, for an article, mostly because of some voiceover work he'd done in a children's film called *Aliens Ate My Homework*. Weirdly, this movie was based on a series of children's chapter books that I'd read in grade school, around the same time I'd become obsessed with Trek. As a journalist, I'd interviewed famous people before, but Shatner was different. He was the captain. I was nervous, and my sleeping baby had started to squirm. I launched into my first question: I asked Shatner about his unique cadence, that famous, halting Captain Kirk thing he . . . does . . . SO . . . well.

"People who have some characteristic way of speaking, to my knowledge, don't assume it. It's just there, and slowly they become aware of the fact that they may talk in a pattern that is uniquely theirs. In fact, even now, I have to turn to my wife and say, is he imitating . . . me?" This struck me as both totally honest and bizarrely out of touch with reality. I laughed nervously. Shatner pretending like he doesn't know about how he talks is like if Kareem Abdul-Jabbar said: "I've never noticed I'm tall. How strange of you to notice."

Shatner and I talked a little bit about the science of plants and whether we'll ever be able to communicate with flowers directly. Around this time, my daughter woke up and started crying. Loudly. "That's the cry . . . of . . . hunger . . ." William Shatner said, suddenly the authority on my entire life. "You must feed her now." Yeah, no kidding, Kirk. Thanks for the tip!

Although I obviously was recording the call, I don't actually *remember* the rest of the phone call that well. I have Shatner's words and mine, but what I was doing with my baby while trying to talk to Captain Kirk is less clear. I do know that as I struggled with a bottle, Shatner continued to give orders, becoming an on-the-spot parenting coach over the phone. Time began to blur, and I think for a moment I was caught between dimensions, kind of like Kirk was in "The Tholian Web." On the one hand, I was on the phone with my childhood; on the other hand, I was holding my child.

From 1990 to 1992, I was Spock for Halloween three years in a row. I was never Captain Kirk because I never really identified with him. I loved Kirk, but to me, Kirk was like somebody's dad. Spock felt closer to a friend, a cipher for ways I could deal with whatever emotional trouble the universe threw at me. During my Shatner call, at some point I walked to the living room and noticed a faded photograph of myself in third grade, dressed as Spock. I'm not smiling in this picture. No way. I'm Spock. My mom has wedged the store-bought plastic Vulcan ears to the sides of my head as best she can. She's penciled on the requisite upswept eyebrows—which look great on Spock, but just make a little kid look like a permanently angry *Peanuts* character. She's dyed my blond hair midnight black, but Mom didn't have to worry about doing the Spock haircut. I'm a third-grade kid in 1990, so I've got that bowl cut anyway. In Star Trek's only true Halloween episode, 1967's "Catspaw," Captain Kirk says Spock would be a "natural" for "trick or treat," accidentally predicting a go-to costume not only for me, but for millions of people for over five decades. We never found out what Spock really thought about the human holiday of Halloween, but my third-grade self believes he'd be down to study the strange human rituals from the ground level. Spock finds this stuff comforting because experiencing human banalities just reaffirms that he's above all that shit.

In this photo, I see my plastic trick-or-treat pumpkin sitting at my feet because I'm clasping my hands behind my back. That's the way Spock holds his hands in one of the famous photographs I had tacked up in my bedroom. He's pictured standing like this on the covers of so many of the dog-eared paperbacks that dominate my childhood home library. He stands this way in my favorite movie at the time—*The Wrath of Khan*—usually when he's about to say something awesome, like "The needs of the many outweigh the needs of the few." Little kids with nervous energy never know what to do with their hands. Spock taught us all how to relax, or more accurately, to *look* like we're relaxed. What Spock taught me, and millions of others, was a badass version of fake it 'til you make it.

But Star Trek isn't just an adult version of *Care Bears*. Its fictional world is about more than fluffy clouds and hope. Star Trek's power is in its humanist *strategy*. In order to live long and prosper, we must admit we're flawed. "We are what we are," Captain Picard says in the 1987 debut episode of *Star Trek: The Next Generation*. "But we're doing the best we can." This sentiment describes all of us, from people struggling to get through the day, to the quest to find the perfect balance of mental health and the achievement of personal goals, to those of us holding babies, to those of us who just want justice and peace in our time. The world is not easy, but the heroes of Star Trek constantly provide us new tactics to rethink not just how we can succeed, but sometimes to alter the way we define that success.

As a piece of journalism, my 2018 phone call with William Shatner may have been a failure, but it was a victory in another way. I remembered that my professional life and my childhood love of Star Trek were connected. Something that was once a place for imagination and intellectual refuge was now a building block of my life. My daughter's life literally couldn't have existed without William Shatner, without Star Trek. In *The Wrath of Khan*, Kirk says, "I don't believe in the no-win scenario," positing the notion that failure may not exist if we reframe the conditions of the test.

In 2020, speaking to the official Star Trek podcast, *The Pod Directive*, Stacey Abrams pointed out that her inspiration in politics came from an episode of *The Next Generation*, called "Peak Performance." In it, the android Lieutenant Commander Data (Brent Spiner) plays a complicated (and silly-looking) strategy game called Strategema. Although Data is a superintelligent android, he still is bested by his alien opponent in this game. Captain Picard (Patrick Stewart) comforts Data, saying: "It is possible to commit no mistakes and still lose. That is not a weakness, that is life." Abrams said she drew "great inspiration from this episode," because Data is "compelled to investigate how he frames winning."

"Data wasn't going to play by the general notion of defeating the other person, but he was playing to stay in the game," Abrams said. "That was the responsibility I had as Democratic leader. We weren't going to always win. But we had to stay competitive."

Star Trek's famous catchphrase—"Live long and prosper"—doesn't evoke a belief in magic or a quasi-religious faith in a mystical energy field controlling your destiny. It's more about staying in the game. "Live long and prosper" is shockingly simple in its brazen sweetness: Hello, my name is Star Trek, I'd like to encourage you to stay healthy, and while you're doing that, to have your life be as thoughtful and fulfilling as possible.

For me, a world in which Star Trek never existed is a timeline where my childhood collapses like dried Play-Doh. Mr. Spock and Data weren't just cool space superheroes to me as a kid, they were beacons of resilience. Kids can relate to Star Trek heroes without feeling like they're being talked down to. Adults can relate to Star Trek heroes because unlike the perpetual coming-of-age stories that dominate everything from Harry Potter to Luke Skywalker, the Trek heroes are, for the most part, functioning adults.

The love of Star Trek isn't about trying to recapture youthful adventure, it's an interest in stories that take place over entire lifetimes. Living long and prospering doesn't just mean getting older and not dying. It means embracing change.

In the 1969 *Star Trek: The Original Series* episode "Let That Be Your Last Battlefield," Spock says, "Change is the essential process of all existence." In the context of that story, he's talking about racism on the alien planet Cheron, and how they need to cut it out. Like all aspects of Trek, this is a process. Spock didn't tell the Cherons: "Eradicating systemic racism on your planet will be fun," he told them that if they don't change their racist ways, eventually they'll cease to exist. "Let That Be Your Last Battlefield" doesn't have a happy ending, proving that Star Trek's dance between optimism and cautionary tales is perpetual, and constantly in flux.

But how does change begin? In the episode "Return to Tomorrow," Captain Kirk drops a stirring speech that concludes with "Risk is our business!" Kirk is trying to encourage Spock, Scotty, and Bones to go along with something pretty dangerous: voluntarily getting possessed by formless alien spirits in order to give said aliens time to build new, robot bodies. This is a little less relatable than Spock talking about the Cherons' racism, but thematically, these things are intertwined: Change is necessary for survival and those changes often involve some risky business. In Star Trek's fictional history, James T. Kirk was the youngest person to become a starship captain in the twenty-third century, but in our world, William Shatner became the oldest person to fly in space at ninety years of age. After returning from Blue Origin's brief *New Shepard* spaceflight on October 13, 2021, the man who originated the role of Captain Kirk said: "I am overwhelmed. I had no idea." After flying in space, William Shatner was, at least at first, at a loss for words, an outcome that *nobody* expected. When I got the chance to speak to Shatner about the experience during a Zoom call late in 2021, he seemed to look deep into my eyes and said, "Never forget, Yuri Gagarin told us, 'My god, it's blue!' Our *perspective* on the planet is all we have."

The history of Star Trek's making is an epic story about hundreds of people, perhaps the most dynamic and shocking story in the history of film and television. From a vague idea in the mind of creator Gene Roddenberry, to *The Next Generation*, to the J. J. Abrams films, to the explosion of new streaming Trek shows, to, yes, William Shatner flying in a real rocket, this long trek is not only bold, but improbable. The fact that Star Trek endured for so long and has been so *different* in its various incarnations is both profound and life-affirming. But this history also has various points of view, its gospels arising from the perspectives of the different players: the Gospel of Roddenberry, the Gospel of Shatner, the Gospel of J. J. Abrams, and literally thousands of other outer space apostles. It also has its Dead Sea Scrolls and apocrypha and, of course, its Trekkie myths that often obscure what passes for "truth" when we're talking about science fiction. The details of these stories vary. But through the entire story of Star Trek, there's one evolutionary feature that explains its shocking longevity: Radical metamorphosis of the final frontier is the way it lives long, prospers, and alters our present world for a better future.

Star Trek's future tells us that a brighter day begins on April 5, 2063, when a pioneer named Zefram Cochrane (James Cromwell) invents faster-than-light travel, causing a race of friendly, chess-loving stoics called the Vulcans to take notice, and drop by to say hello. This might sound awesome, but there is a huge catch: In the Star Trek timeline, World War III will wipe out half of Earth's population before space cozy time can happen. As we inch closer toward

First Contact Day in the twenty-first century, will Star Trek revise this aspect of its backstory, and let us defer doomsday a little longer? The answer is almost certainly yes, and that's because Star Trek's whole deal—both in its fictional world and behind the scenes—is about changing its own story to make the real future feel like a day worth living for.

So, which is it? Is Star Trek a cozy story about a utopian future where everyone lives happily, living long and prospering? Or maybe, is Star Trek a complicated piece of fiction—an art form—with hundreds of authors and artists, all with competing visions for how to make mediative science fiction into something gripping, suspenseful, and, yes, *commercial* enough to be viable for decades? Spock would say the story of Star Trek's constant revisions and changes is "fascinating." Kirk would say it "sounds like fun." Both are right. Neither is right. The story of Star Trek's making and re-making isn't binary. Like in the stories of Trek itself, the heroes and villains aren't always so clear-cut. Unlike other kinds of pop sci-fi, the power of Star Trek isn't only escapist. "That's the beauty of Star Trek," *Star Trek: Discovery* star—and *The Shape of Water*'s sexy fish-man—Doug Jones told me in 2020. "We can fly off our own planet and see how others do it. And once we turn the TV off, we're more empowered to face what's ahead of us in our real lives." He's not wrong. For almost six decades, Star Trek's little starships have taken us boldly through the looking glass, to find ourselves. The making and remaking of Star Trek isn't just about complicated business decisions made in Hollywood. That's a part of it. But the profound aspect of Star Trek is in its willingness to radically change so often. It's the story of human survival, and human triumph.

But let's cut Captain Kirk a break—it's fun, too.

CHAPTER 1

SPOCK STOLE HIS OWN BRAIN

The creation of Star Trek: The Original Series

You might think the alien worlds in the original *Star Trek* look fake. You might think the blinky lights on those old sets are silly. You might not love those oh-so-tight 1960s velour uniforms. But nobody thinks Spock's pointed ears look bad. The ears are legit. It's one of those classic Hollywood tricks that should be hugely impressive but somehow isn't praised enough. Whether the stoic Vulcan is played by Leonard Nimoy, Zachary Quinto, or Ethan Peck, the applause for the most famous fake alien ears is mostly absent. And that's because the ears work. Praising Spock's ears would be like praising James Bond's tailor; you *expect* Spock to look that way. The believability of Spock's ears allowed the characters—and by extension the earliest *Star Trek*—to prevent the entire series from becoming, as Leonard Nimoy had worried in 1964, "a bad sci-fi joke." According to him, the total cost to produce the first "acceptable" pair of Vulcan ears worn on-screen was roughly "six hundred dollars." Despite countless millions poured into filming over eight hundred hours in the Star Trek franchise, spread across almost six decades, all the money and time spent on Spock's ears in the 1960s is possibly the most crucial investment the franchise ever made. Spock's ears weren't quite right at first, because Spock himself didn't arrive fully formed. And neither did Star Trek. From 1964 to the present day, Star Trek was created through trial and error, blessed with the occasional solar flare of true genius.

In the dynamic story of Star Trek's constant reinvention, the origin of these iconic ears is just one pointed tip of a very large dark matter iceberg. The pivotal character of Mr. Spock may never have become a pop culture icon without several radical revisions to both his appearance and personality. Even before Nimoy was cast as Spock, and before anyone was worried about creating durable and believable rubber alien ears, the original Spock, at least on paper, was an outer space reincarnation of Satan.

In 1963, a year before *Star Trek* began preproduction, its creator, Gene Roddenberry, was already a veteran of TV writing. In fact, he was running a series—the peacetime military drama *The Lieutenant*, which starred future *Star Trek* guest star[1] Gary Lockwood. A former pilot and police officer, Roddenberry's early professional scripts in the 1950s found him writing what he knew: cop shows. "They were very bad shows," Roddenberry recalled in 1968, referencing work for the production company Ziv, specifically the shows *Mr. District Attorney* and *Highway Patrol*. But it was also during this time, in 1955, that Roddenberry tried to sell a story to a series owned by Ziv, *Science Fiction Theater*. This early pitch was called "The Transporter," which was essentially about a "device

---

1 After his role as Gary Mitchell in "Where No Man Has Gone Before," Gary Lockwood would become even more well-known as the co-star of the 1968 film *2001: A Space Odyssey*.

which creates an artificial world for the user." Imagine if *The Matrix* was a story about iPhone addiction, and you've got the gist. *Science Fiction Theater* didn't buy the story because, perhaps, the world wasn't ready for *Black Mirror* just yet. But Roddenberry's determination to do a new kind of TV storytelling stuck.

With his pitch for *Star Trek*, Roddenberry sought to reinvent what an episodic TV show could be. It was his dream project, a place where he could push boundaries of what audiences expected of television, to challenge the status quo and ruffle the feathers of the white, conservative American public. In order to make a statement against the Vietnam War, or campaign for racial equality, Roddenberry believed "that if I had similar situations involving these subjects happening on other planets to little green people, indeed, it might get by."

Roddenberry wanted all those things, and more. But he also wanted some job stability. "In television, the only way to get that security is to own a piece of the action . . . to own a series . . ." At the same time he was pitching *Star Trek* in 1964, Roddenberry was also working on a different pilot for a TV series called *Police Story*, which starred future *Trek* actors DeForest Kelley and Grace Lee Whitney. Was Roddenberry's idealism about *Star Trek* merely the product of decades of revisionism? It's tough to say. Had *Police Story* been picked up and *Star Trek* not, we'd be living in a very different world, but almost certainly, a much worse one. Even if Roddenberry retroactively played up his idealistic notions for creating *Trek*, the result is the same. The world got *Star Trek*, not another tired police procedural.

A self-identifying humanist later in life, Roddenberry was frustrated with more than just played-out TV genres. He disliked the dogma of Christianity intensely, saying in 1991, "I reject religion.

I accept the notion of God . . . I don't humanify God." These independent notions about religion make his early sketch of a devilish version of Spock explicable. In an early 1964 series outline, Roddenberry wrote that Spock looks "so satanic you might also expect him to have a forked tail." This very early draft of Spock was an alien, but Roddenberry hadn't really decided what kind. Spock's visage was "frightening" because he was "probably half-Martian" with red skin. Devil Spock is not the guy who became the spokesperson for a hopeful, progressive, pro-science conception of the future. Instead, Roddenberry's first character sketch of Spock seems so burdened by '40s pulp science fiction clichés of bug-eyed monsters that it's almost laughable.

And yet, buried in Spock 1.0 was the germ of a great idea. "Mr. Spock's quiet temperament is in dramatic contrast to his satanic looks." Okay, so, this guy might *look* like the devil, but you're only afraid of him because of your prejudices against devils. From the pizza-looking rock monster the Horta in "The Devil in the Dark" to the overgrown friendly Tardigrade named Ripper in *Star Trek: Discovery*, misunderstood monsters are the stars of many of Trek's most lauded installments, and Mr. Spock was, arguably, the very first misunderstood monster of them all. If there's one moral imperative in all of Roddenberry's rules about how Star Trek should play out, it's the idea that the heroes of the story don't really encounter villains but, rather, life-forms that are mirrors of ourselves. For Roddenberry, what was "wrong" with filmed science fiction up until that point was "whenever a monster was used . . . nobody ever asks 'why?'" Imagining Spock as a nice devil is the first and most critical step *Trek* takes toward creating a context for attacking all kinds of other biases and stereotypes.

Although Leonard Nimoy did perform at least one screen test

with red facial makeup, the idea that Spock looked just like the devil never made it into a final shooting script. Devil Spock only existed in Roddenberry's original outline for *Star Trek*, which is what he showed Desilu Studios producer Herb Solow in April 1964. By the '80s, Roddenberry had downplayed these first drafts, saying he only recalled them "vaguely." The only remnants of Devil Spock in actual *Star Trek* episodes exist as jokes. In the episode "Charlie X," Uhura playfully sings to Spock: *All around the Starship Enterprise / there's someone who's in Satan's guise.* At the end of "The Apple," after reminiscing about original sin, Bones and Kirk pace around Spock like they're doing some improv comedy, "yesAND"ing the shit out of each other, and saying, "Is there anyone on board who resembles Satan?"

The idea that Nimoy's Spock—and by extension the Vulcans and the Romulans—appears "devilish" is, in truth, more of an inside joke that *Star Trek* likes to have about itself. Yes, NBC and Desilu were concerned that Spock's visage could get them in trouble with Bible Belt viewers, going so far as to airbrush Spock's eyebrows and ears to look more human in one set of press materials. But, once *Star Trek* was on the air in the late '60s, the biggest instances of angry Christians crying foul had little to do with Spock's looks. Usually, these reactions were more hung up on Kirk willingly letting his body be possessed by alien intelligence in "Return to Tomorrow," or the ghost of Jack the Ripper making Scotty stab a belly dancer in "Wolf in the Fold." Considering the latter episode was written by Robert Bloch, the same guy who wrote *Psycho*, you can kind of see their point. If you look for some creepy witchcraft shit in the original *Star Trek,* you will find it.

So, who really talked Gene Roddenberry out of Spock, the Sympathetic Space Devil? Everybody wants credit for that one.

From the writer of "Where No Man Has Gone Before," Samuel Peeples, to Desilu producer Herb Solow, there was pressure on Roddenberry to "humanize" the Spock character to avoid phasering the entire show in the foot. But, thanks to some early revisions on the page, Spock wasn't ever the focus of a satanic panic about *Trek*, because Roddenberry decided to take the character in a different direction. He considered casting a Black man as Spock. He considered a dwarf. He even, somewhat infamously, tried to get future *Mission: Impossible* star Martin Landau. According to Trek historian and author Marc Cushman, Roddenberry approached Landau during the time that the various proposals for *Star Trek* were being written. "Gene told Landau, 'I'm putting this thing together, I'm getting ready to shop it around, there will be a great part in it for you,'" Cushman tells me. "But Martin Landau turned him down because he found it to be 'too limited of a role.' He didn't see the potential for the nuances that Nimoy put into it."

Roddenberry even mentioned the role to an actor he'd worked with before, DeForest Kelley, then famous for playing bad guys in westerns. Kelley turned him down flat, but as fate would have it, would end up spending the rest of his career famous for arguing with Spock in his iconic role as Dr. Leonard "Bones" McCoy throughout the entire *Original Series*, six films, and one memorable cameo in the first episode of *The Next Generation*. "I don't think DeForest Kelley was ever a serious consideration," Cushman tells me. "I think that was more Gene teasing Kelley, because Kelley, at that time, had a reputation for playing villains in westerns."

Still, what if Kelley had said yes, and held Roddenberry to the offer? What if Martin Landau had changed his mind? Could the first Spock have become the Spock we know without Leonard Nimoy?

The answer is almost certainly *no,* or perhaps, as Spock would say, *negative.* The person who gets the most credit for creating Spock is, correctly, not Roddenberry, but a gifted Bostonian actor named Leonard Nimoy. Roddenberry had worked with Nimoy on *The Lieutenant,* and upon the urging of Gary Lockwood and script editor Dorothy Fontana, got Nimoy to audition for the role. Once cast, it was time to figure out how to make the Spock of the page become the Spock of the screen. Before those fancy six-hundred-dollar ears, a much cheaper attempt had been slapped on Nimoy's head. Designed by Lee Greenway and made from "papier-mâché and glue," the first set of ears made Spock look more like a "jack-rabbit" than a slick alien from the planet Vulcan. Because Desilu was run by Lucille Ball, the first test footage of Leonard Nimoy as Spock happened on the set of *The Lucy Show.*[2] Nimoy said this footage is "ludicrous," and if film archivists never discover it, it could be because Nimoy himself vowed to "burn it." The thirty-three-year-old actor was about to embody and create another TV icon. But if nobody took the character seriously, Nimoy knew *Star Trek* couldn't fly. For the actor, being filmed on the empty set of a popular sitcom was a formative moment. Nimoy "felt alien," and started "building up defenses" because he knew that the "mere humans" operating the cameras would surely mock him once the screen test was over. Nimoy was merging with Spock, even before the shooting script for the first episode had been finalized.

After seeing the terrible footage of Nimoy in the first set of

---

2 *The Lucy Show* was Ball's follow-up to the mega-famous series *I Love Lucy.* By 1964, Ball and Desi Arnaz had divorced and Ball was running the studio they'd created—Desilu—alone. She was the only woman running a TV studio at the time.

ears—and talking Nimoy out of quitting the show altogether[3]—Roddenberry quickly replaced Greenway with a more experienced makeup artist, Fred Phillips, who had previously worked with *Trek* producer Robert H. Justman on the sci-fi anthology series *The Outer Limits*. Phillips realized that the first set of ears was too generic and made from flimsy foam rubber. Phillips made several attempts, but the studio had wanted this done on the cheap, resulting in a one-size-fits-all condom approach to pointed alien ears. Not only did the ears stick out and look fake, but they also didn't fit. Phillips knew the only way to make the ears look good was a custom job, bespoke for Nimoy's actual ears. What Phillips needed wasn't just a piece of rubber designed to be pulled on and off like a cheap monster mask; he wanted a molded cast of Nimoy's extra ears. But to do this would have required Desilu Studios to search for "an outside appliance maker," and the cost of that contract was six hundred dollars. This wasn't in Fred Phillips's budget, but as Nimoy later recalled, "Fred put his job on the line. He could have been fired for spending the money without authorization." Phillips got the outside contract for Nimoy's ears from Charlie Schram, the head of makeup at MGM, and one of the people responsible for innovative latex prosthetics on *The Wizard of Oz*, a film Fred Phillips had also worked on. Nimoy and Phillips took a drive to MGM, Schram and Phillips had a brief *Oz* reunion, and the mold of Spock's ears was born. Although tape was needed to hold back Spock's new ears, this mold worked. Without Fred Phillips taking a risk of getting fired and simultaneously calling in favors within the Hollywood makeup world of the 1960s, there's every reason to believe *Star Trek* would have died right there.

---

3 Leonard Nimoy threatening to quit Star Trek would happen a lot during his forty-nine-year association with the franchise.

Nimoy had many collaborators who helped make Spock into the intellectual hero he became. Fred Phillips and Roddenberry were among the first. But make no mistake. In the beginning, Spock belonged to Nimoy. Presciently, at a very early stage, Nimoy and Spock seemed to merge. Over the years, Leonard Nimoy made various attempts to embrace his Spock persona—and also paradoxically distance himself from it, too. But in terms of his control over the role, the boundary between Nimoy the person and Spock the character is unclear. "He was our contribution to method acting," co-star Walter Koenig said of Nimoy's performance. "I mean he was always Spock." Nimoy himself copped to his total immersion in the role, saying, "I was Spock all day long. I really was."

On December 12, 1964, the first pilot for *Star Trek*—"The Cage"—began filming. Nimoy counts this as Spock's birthday. Everyone involved knew what Spock looked like by that point, but it was still unclear how he behaved. Roddenberry's notes still described him as "catlike," but what did that mean? Spock learned to move because Nimoy happened to catch Harry Belafonte perform in a Los Angeles nightclub in the '60s. In 2019, actor Ethan Peck, the incumbent Spock for *Star Trek: Discovery, Star Trek: Short Treks,* and *Star Trek: Strange New Worlds,* told me that he internalized the Belafonte connection in his own performance. "Belafonte started on stage singing, standing utterly still for about twenty or thirty minutes. And then in the crescendo of the music, he raised his hand suddenly. And for Nimoy, seeing that contrast between stillness and this great gesture inspired Spock's control."

Even in the earliest scene in "The Cage," Spock's movements reflect this concept of body control. But Spock's personality is decidedly not the Spock we know. This *Enterprise* has just recently recovered from a huge battle. Some characters—like helmsman

Tyler (Peter Duryea)—are still wearing bandages on their wrists. When Spock beams down to the planet Talos IV, he's limping. Despite myths that suggested Nimoy was injured in real life, the actor refuted this claim many times and said that Spock limps on Talos IV because "Gene Roddenberry told me to limp." Infamously, Nimoy was also told by director Robert Butler to *smile* when Spock touches the ethereal singing plants with Captain Pike.

In "The Cage," the Starship *Enterprise* doesn't have Captain Kirk yet. The ship is commanded by Captain Christopher Pike (Jeffrey Hunter), with Spock as the science officer. This smiling, limping Spock may not be an energy-eating red devil, but he's not the cold, calculating Sherlock-Holmes-in-space that we're familiar with, either. Instead, Pike's second-in-command is the coldly logical, stoic, and deadly serious officer only referred to as "Number One." Like a secret agent, this nickname was intended to hide her true name, but later, in *The Next Generation* and all the series following, we learned "Number One" was a term of friendly endearment that a starship captain bestowed on their first officer. Number One was played by Majel Barrett, who, after this role became Nurse Christine Chapel on *Star Trek*, the voice of every single *Enterprise* computer up until her death in 2009, and Counselor Deanna Troi's hilariously overbearing telepathic mother Lwaxana Troi in *The Next Generation* and *Star Trek: Deep Space Nine*. By 1969, she'd also be Gene Roddenberry's wife. However, in 1964, Majel Barrett was *not* Gene Roddenberry's wife, but she was his mistress.

"She would have never been cast had she not been his girlfriend," Harrison Solow, widow of *TOS* producer Herb Solow, tells me. "It's nothing against Majel. I knew Majel in the years before Gene died. She loved Gene completely. And he loved her."

Like the stories of John and Yoko, or Carl Sagan and Ann

Druyan, we tend to forget that some legendary romances between influential and smart people begin as affairs. Before marrying Majel after *Star Trek* was canceled in 1969, Gene Roddenberry's first wife was Eileen Anita Rexroat, who he had been married to since 1942. Both of Gene's children with Eileen, Darlene and Dawn, appear in the early episode "Miri" as inhabitants of a planet populated only by children, doomed to die when they hit puberty. In the larger Trek legend, Eileen Rexroat's relationship to the creation of the Star Trek franchise is similar to the way a casual Beatles fan thinks about John Lennon's first wife, Cynthia. That is to say, Trek fans think of Eileen Rexroat hardly at all. Was Roddenberry right to cheat on his wife? Was John Lennon? What about Carl Sagan?

"I think when my father entered into Hollywood, he was con-sumed by the Hollywood lifestyle," Gene Roddenberry's son, Rod Roddenberry, tells me. "Whether it was women, alcohol, late nights, hard work, I mean, legitimate things, but also extracurricular things. And I think that had a huge impact on his first wife. I don't mean to say anything negative about her whatsoever. I don't even know her, but I know she didn't fit into that lifestyle. The rift grew. And even-tually, he met my mother [Majel Barrett]. I think that really harmed the daughters and that previous family. I think he had so many re-grets about it, because when I was a child, he was there."

As the younger Roddenberry alludes to, there's a lot of dirty space laundry we shove out the airlock, but the simple fact is, like John Lennon writing "Beautiful Boy," Roddenberry's infidelity in his first marriage led not only to the eventual birth of Rod with Majel but, perhaps more crucially for Trekkies, his love of Majel directly led to the rebirth of Spock.

Let's make one thing totally clear: In "The Cage," Majel Bar-rett's Number One is a much bigger character than Spock, because, at this point, she *is* Spock. When Captain Pike is abducted by big-brained telepathic aliens called Talosians, the person in charge of the ship is Number One. She's the one with the nerves of steel and the superintelligence. Despite Nimoy's subtle performance, Spock, as a character, is just kind of *there,* hanging out. Viewed in isolation, Spock's presence in "The Cage" is *Star Trek* trying for casual sci-fi realism: Oh, we just happen to have this alien crew member, it's not a big deal. In this way, "The Cage" oddly undersells Spock by not having him be more central, and by extension undersells *Star Trek*. Like most of this first pilot episode, this is a rough draft for *Star Trek* and a dourer vision than the colorful, buoyant series that was to come. This isn't to say the "The Cage" is bad. The illusionary powers of the Talosians make them some of the greatest Trek aliens in the canon. Pike is a stiff yet basically likable captain, and his relationships with Dr. Boyce (John Hoyt) and Number One are unique enough to make us wonder what this version of *Star Trek* might have looked like had it become the *only* version of *Star Trek*.

In early 1965, Desilu presented NBC with the "The Cage," and they rejected it. They didn't want to make a show with this cast, citing the overall concept of the telepathic alien world of illusion as "too cerebral" for average TV viewers. Purists might say that NBC was forcing Roddenberry to dumb *Star Trek* down, but the truth is, if they hadn't, it's hard to believe the cast of "The Cage" would have found their way into the hearts of viewers the way the eventual cast of *Star Trek* did. So, the pilot went away, or at least it did for several decades. Unless you caught a screening at a sci-fi convention in the '60s, you couldn't watch "The Cage" in its entirety until 1986. Outside of Spock and Pike, the other characters in "The Cage" were mostly entirely erased from Star Trek history. Specifically, Number One, Star Trek's first feminist icon, and one of the characters NBC wanted removed from the show. According to co-producer Robert Justman, "The character of Number One tested badly with the sample audience, especially among women." According to Justman, this test audience didn't mind women in the show in subordinate roles, but Number One had too much power.

But is this legit? Turns out, the idea that Majel Barrett's Number One was *too* feminist and *too* progressive for NBC is almost certainly a myth perpetuated by Roddenberry himself. "Did he believe NBC was sexist in asking him to remove the character of Number One?" Star Trek historian Mark A. Altman says. "Well, for four decades Gene Roddenberry would peddle the story of how a sexist NBC didn't want Majel in the show because focus groups would ask, 'Who the hell does she think *she* is?' As in most things with Star Trek, the truth is somewhat more nuanced and complicated. It's far more likely—as others have stated—that the network didn't like the fact that Gene cast his mistress as one of the leads of the show."

This viewpoint is backed up by Herb Solow, too, who was shocked when one NBC executive had to gently tell him that "you know she's his girlfriend, right?" The story Roddenberry later told was that the cold, rational Number One was too feminist, and she was too much for the suits at NBC. Altman believes there "may be some modicum of truth" to this, but it's hard to ignore the fact that other strong women manifested in other ways in the version of *Star Trek* NBC eventually committed to. If NBC had been composed of sexist men who didn't want a strong woman on *Star Trek*, it seems they would have objected to the character of Dr. Elizabeth Dehner (Sally Kellerman), the no-bullshit starship psychiatrist, who wore pants, killed her space-happy former lover, and saved the *Enterprise* in the second pilot episode, "Where No Man Has

Gone Before." Either way, one thing is clear: Roddenberry's love for Majel Barrett led to him giving her a job in *Star Trek*, and that decision ultimately painted him into a corner, leading to the most pivotal decision in creating *Star Trek*. "No one else but Majel was even considered for the part," Harrison Solow tells me. "He was clearly trying to help her get acting work. But that also meant NBC had something on him."

NBC gave Roddenberry a choice. He could either lose Spock or lose the powerful, stoic, female command officer with the secret-agent-sounding name. Roddenberry made the hard call and cut Number One. In capitulating, he did something nuts as well: He took her entire personality and gave it to Spock. Nimoy described it as "absorbing much of Number One's cool, reserved demeanor." Roddenberry admitted that he "combined the two roles into one," making Spock the new second-in-command to the captain, but now with a "computer-like, logical mind, never displaying emotion." Roddenberry later joked that he "kept the Martian and married the woman," but this simple decision led to the creation of Spock as we know him. "In a way, Number One had to die so Spock could live," Altman tells me.

If you can call compromises strokes of genius, then this was the most brilliant compromise in all of pop culture. Spock is the Darth Vader of Star Trek insofar as there is no way Star Trek exists and becomes a world-shaking pop phenomenon without him. The shouting, smiling Spock in "The Cage" is, for many fans, not *really* Spock. True, you couldn't see "The Cage" in its *entirety* until the '80s, *but* when you watch the run of the regular series, you'll find most of "The Cage" inside of the episode "The Menagerie," which retroactively establishes that Spock served on the *Enterprise* with Pike and Number One thirteen years prior to the "present" of *The Original Series*. Relative to Spock's backstory and the existence of Number One, Roddenberry's reappropriating 1964 footage from "The Cage" and turning it into a backstory for "The Menagerie" in 1966 changed everything. When Roddenberry stuck in "The Cage" footage as a retroactive flashback in "The Menagerie," Number One ceased to be a rough draft of Spock, but instead, a character who vaguely existed in *Star Trek*'s backstory. "The Menagerie" established that Spock had a life before Kirk and Bones, and that he had a slew of adventures on the *Enterprise* with Number One and Captain Pike when he was a little younger. In 2009, Captain Pike (Bruce Greenwood) reappeared in two of the rebooted J. J. Abrams films. Nobody mentioned Number One. That is, until 2019.

———————

"There might not be another character quite like Number One in any other fandom, that I can think of," Pulitzer Prize–winning novelist and *Star Trek: Picard* co-creator Michael Chabon told me over the phone in late 2019. "The subject of how to treat her canonicity is a subject that could probably only interest fans. I mean, you have to be more than a slightly casual fan to even know about her up until the second season of *Discovery*."

Starting in 2017, the CBS All Access (later Paramount+) streaming series *Star Trek: Discovery* positioned itself as a soft prequel to *The Original Series*, beginning in the year 2256, roughly a decade before the more familiar adventures of Kirk and Spock. But this also weirdly put *Discovery* (or *DISCO,* as the cool kids call it) smack-dab in the timeline of "The Cage." (Or "The Menagerie" flashbacks, depending on how you look at it.) This timeline thing not only necessitated a new Captain Pike (Anson Mount) and a new Spock (Ethan Peck) but also, for the first time since 1964, a new Number One, played by Rebecca Romijn in *Discovery* Season 2 (2019), the short anthology series *Short Treks* (2019), and the ongoing episodic Paramount+ series *Strange New Worlds* (2022). The new Number One is a little more sarcastic than Majel Barrett's icy version, but she's also just as reserved and no-nonsense as the character was originally conceived. Consequently, she's no longer a character who exists in ill-defined flashback. In the twenty-first century, Number One, the original female version of Spock, is suddenly a full-fledged Star Trek character who appears in new installments regularly. So, how does the female rough draft of Spock coexist alongside Spock?

In 2018, Chabon attempted to sort it out by writing the *Short Treks* episode "Q&A." Eventually airing in October 2019, the brief episode depicts Spock's (Ethan Peck) very first day on board the USS *Enterprise*, in which he's accidentally trapped inside of a turbolift (space elevator) with his new boss, Number One (Rebecca Romijn). Turns out her name is Una, and she and Spock both share an interest in musical theater, specifically the works of Gilbert and Sullivan. After being stuck together for a long time, and asking each other endless questions, Spock and Number One get a little slaphappy, and that's when the singing starts. Chabon's episode cleverly takes the complex real-world reasoning behind Number One's erasure, and her semi-melding with Spock, and tries to infuse it with fannish meaning.

"In the extra-fictional sense, Spock took over Number One's personality. And if we're going to really plunge into them and they're going to be coexisting with each other, we need to account for that," Chabon tells me. "But I wanted to tackle what happened outside of the extra-fictional and take that and put it into the fiction itself—and to show how Number One had this influence over Spock; sort of having her say, 'If you want to be a commander, that to a degree, you're going to have to sacrifice yourself to duty and responsibility.'"

In Chabon's officially sanctioned "fan fiction" (as he calls it), Number One becomes Spock's role model. The reason he acts super logical and colder throughout the rest of Star Trek is only partly because of his cold Vulcan heritage. In this newly revised version, Spock isn't just Spock because he's an alien trying to balance an emotional side with a logical side. He becomes the tightly controlled person we know because he's worried the world may not accept him otherwise. In Chabon's revision of Number One, Spock's Spockishness is still his armor, but that armor was given to him illicitly by his secret best friend. From red space devil, to confused child, to the Zen'd-out logistician he became, the patchwork construction of Spock requires us to not only jump back in time to before "The Cage" was filmed, but also check out the 1991 film *Star Trek VI: The Undiscovered Country*, in which Spock drops the famous Sherlock Holmes quote, "When you eliminate the impossible, whatever remains, however improbable, must be the truth." Spock attributes this quote to "an ancestor of mine," implying Spock is related either to Sir Arthur Conan Doyle or Sherlock Holmes[4] on his human side. The director of *The Undiscovered Country*, Nicholas Meyer, tells me he prefers thinking of this ancestry as coming

---

4 Or Watson? Or a duplicate Vulcan Holmes? Or a Vulcan author who met Conan Doyle via secret space travel? In 2021, I had a delightful exchange with a Wikipedia editor (who shall remain anonymous) in which we figured out there are like fifteen different ways you can reconcile Spock's "real" connection to this Holmesian quote. The jury is still out, but all we *really* know is that Spock *attributes* this quote to *someone* he was related to. Vulcans don't lie!

directly from Sherlock Holmes. Both Chabon and Meyer have written their own Sherlock Holmes novels, and both shaped Spock's biography, and the way his mind works, well after the character had existed for decades.

Back in 1965, *Star Trek* was recast *twice* after NBC gave Desilu its mandate to change things up. The director of "The Cage," Robert Butler, says the directive from NBC about giving Desilu another shot at Trek was: "We like it, we believe it, we don't understand it. Do it again." The only character who remained from "The Cage" was Spock. After "The Cage" was rejected, the second pilot became "Where No Man Has Gone Before," directed by James Goldstone and written by Samuel Peeples. The network selected this episode from a list of synopses of several other stories. It was the episode that sold the show, and in the last scene, Spock mentions that he "felt" for Gary Mitchell. His new captain—Captain James T. Kirk—turns to him and says, "Mr. Spock, there may be hope for you yet."

Kirk was, of course, played by William Shatner, a Canadian actor who at the time was probably best known for *The Twilight Zone*; famously, he's that passenger hassled by a monster hanging out on the wing of the plane in the 1963 episode "Nightmare at 20,000 Feet." But immediately before being cast as Kirk in *Star Trek*, Shatner starred as a do-gooder lawyer in a legal drama called *For the People* which also starred a pre-fame Jessica Walter, as his wife.

Right out of the gate, Shatner completed the *Star Trek* puzzle. Even though Kirk and Spock feel a little *off* in "Where No Man Has Gone Before," watching this pilot right after you've watched "The Cage" is like having a cup of coffee after someone has given you warm milk for an hour. In "Where No Man Has Gone Before," the friendly bickering between Kirk and Spock over a game of chess opens the episode and washes *Star Trek* in a buddy-comedy bubble bath. Right there, in the first scene of the "real" *Star Trek*, it's about two friends giving each other shit over a spacey chess game. As *Seinfeld* actor Jason Alexander said, the brilliant thing about Shatner's portrayal of Kirk is that Shatner decided that Kirk likes to "fuck with Spock." Instead of a show about Captain Pike—a distant and removed starship captain who is drinking teeny-tiny martinis in his quarters, bitching about how he wants to quit his job—Captain Kirk is screwing with his science officer and making weird jokes about Spock's family tree in *literally* the first thirty seconds of the show. *Star Trek* wouldn't have worked without Nimoy's Spock, but Shatner's Kirk—a *second draft* necessitation—became the human glue that made Spock's ears stick. Spock without Kirk in *TOS* would have been like Paul McCartney singing "We Can Work It Out" without John Lennon. This John/Paul feeling between Spock and Kirk isn't a direct analogy (which one is which?) but if you think about their energy or look at just one photo of Spock and Kirk standing next to each other, it's clear that they are totally the John and Paul of classic *Trek*.

This idea is so ingrained into the mythos of the characters that for the 2009 reboot film *Star Trek*, screenwriter Roberto Orci said outright that "one of the inspirations for the Kirk/Spock relationship was the friendship between Paul McCartney and John Lennon." Other than perhaps Sherlock Holmes and Dr. Watson (again, not a clean analogy) there are few duos in pop fiction who seem to need each other narratively as much as Kirk and Spock, so much so that we tend to look toward *real people*, like the Beatles, for parallels.

Spock could not have existed without Number One's personality, but the entire mood of Spock and, by extension, the swagger and confidence of *The Original Series* needed Captain Kirk to bring it all together. In one interview, Nimoy admitted to Shatner, "When you came on board, with your energy, and a sense of humor and twinkle in your eye, I was able to become the *cooler* Spock." The contrast between Spock and Kirk—a super-buttoned-up alien and a flippant braggart with a shit-eating grin—is classic fictional juxtaposition. Spock is the straight man and Kirk is the guy who is there to mess with him. As the series progressed, DeForest Kelley's "Bones" McCoy became the character who more famously challenged Spock's ultra-logical and cold opinions. But whereas Kirk was messing with Spock, he's also not *the* opposite of Spock. Bones is the other extreme; he, like Spock, passionately believes he is always right, too. Kirk kind of thinks they're both just adorable, and pretty much gets off on watching them bicker. He doesn't have a dog in any of Bones's or Spock's arguments; he's got two dogs in the fight, and he loves them both. *Star Trek*'s script editor for the first two seasons, and the writer who would shape both Spock and Kirk in incalculable ways, was Dorothy Fontana. In 2016 she told me: "These two men grew up in totally different backgrounds and had to learn to trust each other and rely on each other. They are friends, and that is important—but *more important* is that Kirk and Spock are officers who know their jobs, execute their missions with great skill, and know they can count on each other in dangerous situations."

Standing on the deck of the Intrepid Sea, Air & Space Museum in 2016, I shamelessly asked George Takei to tell me his favorite Star Trek captain, and he floored me by proclaiming, "Captain Kirk was my favorite captain. Kirk was an inspiration for Sulu. He loved his problem-solving, his command leadership, and his decisiveness." Like many Star Trek cast members, Takei has some beef with William Shatner here on Earth, but keeps some warm feelings reserved for Kirk. Even Jason Isaacs, who was briefly blocked by

William Shatner on Twitter (many are) told me that Captain Kirk was "the man" and an "absolute hero to me."

And yet, it is Spock—the second-in-command of the Starship *Enterprise*—whose legacy launched the *Trek* mania. This is easy to prove now: Everyone is aware of Spock's customary greeting; it's even an emoji on your phone. It's easy to dress as him for Halloween. But Kirk's popularity is slippery insofar as it's *connected* to Spock's. And this was never truer than it was during the run of the original *Star Trek*. Metrics of popularity in the 1960s could be weighed using pounds of mail, and Leonard Nimoy got *a lot* more fan mail than William Shatner. This pissed Shatner off royally. Shatner was the star of the show, but that wasn't just a status thing, it was a *money* thing. William Shatner made $5,000 an episode. Nimoy made $1,250 an episode. Shatner also had equity in *Star Trek*, and at that point, pretty much none of the rest of the cast did. Shatner wasn't just Captain Kirk on the Starship *Enterprise*; he had a pretty big influence on how the series played out, and Nimoy, and everyone else, were beneath his pay grade, literally. Harlan Ellison, onetime *Star Trek* writer and winner of many science fiction literary prizes, claimed Shatner always counted the number of lines he had in a script, and often lobbied to have lines taken away from supporting actors and rewritten to be delivered by Kirk. Who backs up this claim? Nearly every single cast member of *The Original Series,* with the notable exceptions of Leonard Nimoy and DeForest Kelley, who, after the ending of *The Original Series,* never publicly spoke out against their captain.

During the first season of *The Original Series* (September 1966—April 1967), some might say that the personality and mainstream charm of *Star Trek* wouldn't have worked without Bill Shatner's Captain Kirk. It's hard to know what people who didn't write fan mail thought of Kirk and Spock, but the people who *did* take the time to write letters wrote to Nimoy by hundreds and thousands of times more than to Shatner. If this had remained an in-house secret between NBC and Desilu, no big deal. But, according to Herb Solow, the problem was that the fan mail figures had been "leaked to the entertainment consumer press." Shatner flipped his lid, which yes, even then, was a toupee.

In contemporary interviews, Shatner still admits that he was jealous of the Spock popularity at first. But the version of the story he tells now is that Gene Roddenberry simply told him that "if Spock is successful, then we're all successful." This isn't exactly true, but it's not exactly a lie, either. The larger truth is that Roddenberry knew that Spock's popularity could possibly eclipse the show's, and then his creation would be superdependent on one actor, rather than an entire cast. Roddenberry recognized the power Nimoy had, but also resented it. On top of that, he resented Shatner's prima donna antics but didn't know what to do about any of it.

So, he turned to a friend. In this case, the writer Isaac Asimov. Roddenberry and Asimov's friendship had a bizarre origin. When Roddenberry first had "The Cage" screened for a science fiction convention in 1964, Asimov rudely talked through the opening scenes. Roddenberry shushed the hell out of the famous inventor of the word "robotics" and, basically, the two ended up becoming best friends. A divisive figure in literary science fiction history, with a troublesome reputation for arrogance and misogyny, Asimov was initially disparaging of *Star Trek*. He published a caustic review in *TV Guide* mocking some of the real-life space science. Roddenberry must have initially been annoyed, but later reached out to Asimov to ask for help in making things more realistic on the series.

Asimov obliged. The man known as much for his muttonchops

as his writing never wrote an episode of *Star Trek*, but in 1987 his laws of robotics were programmed into Data in *Star Trek: The Next Generation*. And in 2020, in *Star Trek: Picard*, when Dr. Jurati (Alison Pill) is browsing Jean-Luc Picard's bookshelf, the first book she gravitates toward is *The Complete Robot* by Isaac Asimov. In 2021, *Star Trek: Lower Decks* creator Mike McMahan told me: "If you go back far enough, it's like Isaac Asimov wrote for *Star Trek*." For better or worse, the legacy of Asimov's strange friendship with Roddenberry is in the bones of the series, and literally in the skeletons of many of the franchise's artificial life-forms. But Asimov's biggest contribution to *Star Trek* might be that he helped Roddenberry save the Kirk-and-Spock relationship—on-screen and off. Roddenberry's girlfriend's career had already taken a hit thanks to the power of Mr. Spock, and now, with Shatner furious and Nimoy becoming the biggest sci-fi heartthrob of all time, the *Trek* creator was worried he was going to lose control of *Star Trek* to a family feud between his creations.

Asimov's advice to Roddenberry was simple, but the clarity of the idea changed everything, or at least it seemed to in Roddenberry's mind. "I promised to get back to you with my thoughts on the question of Mr. Shatner and the dilemma of playing lead against such a fad-character as Mr. Spock," Asimov wrote in July 1967. "It might be well to unify the team of Kirk and Spock a bit, by having them actively meet various menaces together with one saving the life of the other one on occasion. The idea of this would be to get people to think of Kirk when they think of Spock."

This suggestion has a dubious place in history. In 1967, the show was very much under way, and there were several episodes *already aired* that had established Kirk and Spock as a team. Did this piece of advice from a titan of the print science fiction world really change the way *Trek* was made? Did it resolve the spat over money and the spotlight between Nimoy and Shatner? Marc Cushman says that "you see the Kirk-Spock camaraderie and humor in the later part of the first season, in 'City on the Edge of Forever,' and so forth. But they didn't really go to town with it until the second season. So, what Isaac's letter did for Roddenberry is that it helped him accept the humor a bit more, but it also helped him accept that it was like a dual protagonist. It might sound like a minor thing, but it was a big enough nuance that it really helped change the way Gene was looking at these two characters."

In later years, Roddenberry repeated the Asimov anecdote enough to change it from nuance to revelation. In 1991, Roddenberry told Harrison Solow that there is a "fair amount" of Asimov's influence on *The Original Series*. In 2021, writers Ben Robinson and Ian Spelling even asserted that Roddenberry drew direct "inspiration from Isaac Asimov's *Foundation* novels." Meanwhile, Herb Solow and Bob Justman, two *Trek* producers who both openly criticized Roddenberry after his death, *also* cite the Asimov Kirk-Spock "team" idea as a turning point, or, at the very least, a Band-Aid.

Throughout *The Original Series*, Kirk and Spock do save each other's lives quite a few times. But, thanks to outer space spores, Vulcan mating rituals, and various forms of space madness, they also end up punching each other all the time, too. In these fight scenes, it's easy to imagine that Nimoy and Shatner thought they were *really* fighting each other, especially in episodes like "Amok Time" when, you know, Spock chokes Kirk to death. But, whenever Kirk and Spock wrestled around, or grabbed each other out of harm's way, the people watching all saw the same thing: two men who needed each other, embracing.

CHAPTER 2

SPACE COWBOYS

The writing of *The Original Series*

The story of *Star Trek* seems endless because it lacks a beginning. Even with two pilot episodes tucked into its velour waistband— "Where No Man Has Gone Before" and the rejected first pilot "The Cage"—by the summer of 1966, *Star Trek* still hadn't become the series we think of now. With its ruminations about ESP mutations leading to corruptible and evil human beings, the dark, cautionary vibe of "Where No Man Has Gone Before" didn't as yet embody the more upbeat and straight-up fun feeling of the rest of the series. In this episode, sarcastic helmsman Gary Mitchell gets zapped by an energy barrier at the edge of the galaxy, gains telekinetic and tele-pathic powers, and basically turns into a huge asshole who consid-ers himself a god and the crew of the *Enterprise* lesser beings he can destroy with a simple thought. In the end, Kirk has to murder his old friend, first with a phaser rifle, and when that doesn't work, with a giant boulder that buries Gary alive. Gary Mitchell is like if Han Solo turned into an evil mutant from the X-Men—it's sad, disturbing, and dark. If this cautionary accidental-Frankenstein story truly embodied the rest of the show, *Star Trek* would have never become timeless.

When *Star Trek* is reassessed by contemporary critics, it tends to be judged by its best moments. In 2020, *Rolling Stone* ranked the fifty best science fiction shows of all time, awarding the top spot to *Trek*, claiming that "its muscular, humane cold-war liberalism still holds up." This isn't wrong, but to pretend like *Star Trek* was always a TV series with a political agenda is to misunderstand how it was written. *Star Trek* was usually about big ideas, but it also delivered those ideas with a pulpy punch line.

Here's a good example: The premise of the episode "Shore Leave"—written by award-winning science fiction author Theodore Sturgeon—concerns an amusement park populated by bespoke robots, all designed to do whatever the visitor wants—fight, play, maybe (definitely) have sex with said robots. This premise also happens to describe the HBO TV series *Westworld*,[1] which has entire seasons of "Shore Leave"–esque storylines, but deadly serious. *Star Trek* knocked out this premise in fifty minutes, had one of the robots be the White Rabbit from *Alice in Wonderland*, and, after the robots calmed down, everybody laughed off the whole thing. If the *Westworld* people had been doing classic *Trek*, we might have had to endure an entire season where Captain Kirk has a love affair with a robot rabbit.

---

1 Funnily enough, the original 1973 film *Westworld*, written and directed by Michael Crichton, co-stars none other than Majel Barrett Roddenberry. In the film, Barrett plays an android madame named Miss Carrie who runs a saloon in Westworld. In the HBO show, Thandie Newton's character Maeve is loosely based on the character originated by Barrett.

What *Westworld* spends entire years exploring, the classic *Star Trek* threw over its shoulder. This flippancy and diversity of different story ideas is one part of why *Trek* is timeless. But the *reason* that happened is because the talent pool spanned several generations and points of view. The oldest person who wrote for *The Original Series*, Barry Trivers ("The Conscience of the King"), was born in 1907, and the youngest, David Gerrold ("The Trouble with Tribbles"), was born in 1944. Roddenberry was born in 1921. Keep these generation gaps in mind the next time you feel like classic *Trek* is either beautifully prescient or hopelessly outdated. The collection of people who wrote for *Star Trek*—which ranges from the novelist who wrote *Psycho,* Robert Bloch ("Wolf in the Fold," "Catspaw," "What Are Little Girls Made Of?"), to Shari Lewis ("The Lights of Zetar"), the woman who created the puppet Lamb Chop (really!)—were never all in the same room together. And if you could cross space and time and put all fifty classic *Trek* writers in one place, it's very possible they'd have a huge fight over what *Star Trek* was really about, anyway. The search for writing talent on *Star Trek* in the '60s feels a little like an edgy ice cream truck owner deciding to buy a bunch of different flavors of ice cream, but also throw in some frozen hamburgers just to see if people will buy them. Tonally and thematically, different episodes of *Star Trek* have almost nothing in common. What does an episode about Jack the Ripper's ghost ("Wolf in the Fold") have to do with a pizza-shaped alien ("Devil in the Dark") trying to protect its babies? Our minds have tricked us into believing there is a typical episode of *Star Trek*, but when you actually watch the series, episode by episode, what you'll find is that the only consistent thread is the characters.

"They [the *Star Trek* characters] were developed with enough personality, but not so much to damage their ability to reappear the following week," tribble inventor David Gerrold said in 1973. He followed it up by noting that *Star Trek* got its whole schtick across to TV audiences not with a bunch of exposition, but cumulatively. "The sum total feeling after viewing five or six episodes is that these are *real* people."

Real people. It seems like a weird brag now, particularly if you're not a fan and you can't really get over the brightly colored pajamas. But if you ask a random stranger on the street who Scotty is, there's at least a fifty-fifty chance they can do the requisite bad Scottish accent and blurt "I'm giving it all she's got!" (Like William Shatner, Scotty actor James Doohan was Canadian, not Scottish.) Ask the same stranger on the street who Spock is, and 80 percent of people will flash you that live-long-and-prosper Vulcan salute without thinking. Trek characters—from *The Original Series* to *The Next Generation* to *Discovery* and beyond—have become fictional friends for countless millions. In a letter addressed to Gene Roddenberry in 1967, a young child gushed: "I like *Star Trek* because Spock has green blood and I like the names."

Roddenberry may have given Spock his name and pumped green blood into his veins, but he didn't really do much as a writer to make Spock or the crew of the *Enterprise* change and grow. Casual fans tend to think that the classic *Trek* was simply written by Gene Roddenberry, but when it comes to the actual scripts of the '60 series, very few actually have his name on them. Yes, Roddenberry *rewrote* or altered many of the scripts to make the stories "more *Star Trek*," but a mosaic of eclectic and varied talent—from amateur fans to famous authors—all contributed to making the characters who they eventually became. The narrative engine that drove the series was brazenly innovative and represented a massive shift in two areas of fiction writing: TV and science fiction. It accomplished these innovations through the "series bible,"[2] a shorthand literary approach to characterization never attempted by TV shows before. *Star Trek* took sci-fi writing seriously and hired eccentric writers to make it happen. But, when a TV show isn't on the air yet, writers have to write a show they haven't seen. So, what the hell did Roddenberry tell his writers that *Star Trek* was even about?

"Just by looking at the series bible, I can tell you that it was only one step beyond the westerns that were on the air," Judy Burns—writer of "The Tholian Web"—tells me. "I didn't get there until the third year, but I think that morality-tale style of the westerns of the time was ingrained in Gene, and into the series format." Burns has a point. In George Clayton Johnson's "The Man Trap," the first episode of *Star Trek* ever seen by the public, the mission of the *Enterprise* isn't scientific discovery at all, but about bringing some lonely space colonists supplies out there on the edge of the frontier.

In nearly every documentary about *Star Trek*, you'll hear someone (often Roddenberry himself) say that the series was pitched as "*Wagon Train* to the Stars." I've been in a lot of rooms where people just kind of nod solemnly when this is mentioned, and I gotta say, I'm willing to bet a million bucks that most living TV watchers have never seen *Wagon Train*, nor do they give a warp-speed fuck what *Wagon Train* even is. Further, *Star Trek* was not in any way, shape, or form like a science fiction version of a story about westward expansion. I mean, come on. If *Star Trek* had just been a "*Wagon Train* to the Stars," then it would have been racist *by default*. The

---

2 The screenwriting term "TV series bible" may come from *Star Trek*. Though it wasn't until the second season when D. C. Fontana coined "the writers bible" to describe the guidelines given to prospective writers of the show.

mission of the *Enterprise* wasn't some jingoistic manifest destiny crap, it was (eventually) all about peaceful contact. On top of that, the crew weren't looking to *settle* the final frontier, they were looking to visit it and learn from it. The crew of the *Enterprise* didn't leave Earth to find a new home. They left Earth because it was their job.

Now to be fair, in most all of his actual pitch documents, Roddenberry did call *Star Trek* "a Wagon Train" concept. I'm not saying he never said it. He did. A lot. But according to Harlan Ellison, Roddenberry lifted this phrase from *Star Trek* writer Samuel Peeples, and used the coinage as his own. Roddenberry calling *Star Trek* "*Wagon Train* to the Stars" was an elevator pitch *only*. Roddenberry defended it as such, later telling historian Marc Cushman that the *Wagon Train* thing "was about finding a means for *them* [the studio] to see that it wasn't impossible to tell those kinds of stories." This is like if you pretend that George Lucas pitched *Star Wars* in 1977 by saying, "It's like *Flash Gordon*, but it doesn't suck." Still, despite Roddenberry repeating this catchphrase in the years that followed—and several documentaries fixating on the phrase—it wasn't even uttered in the final pitch meeting to NBC that sold the series. Roddenberry's producer, Herb Solow, the guy who Lucille Ball hired to make the show happen for Desilu Studios, thought the *Wagon Train* analogy didn't click. "Gene's pet metaphor for *Star Trek*, '*Wagon Train* to the Stars,' came from a very successful television series about a wagon train moving from St. Joseph, Missouri, to Oregon, during the nineteenth century," Solow explained. "But that was a time and event most viewers knew from school or from the movies, and accepted it, because it had already taken place." In the 1964 pitch meeting in which NBC executives Grant Tinker and Jerry Stanley greenlit *Star Trek*, Roddenberry didn't mention *Wagon*

Train at all. There's also no indication that Lucille Ball—who proudly supported *Star Trek*'s early ratings success with a letter of congratulations to Gene Roddenberry—thought of the series as "*Wagon Train* to the Stars," either. In terms of *Trek* getting over the finish line with NBC, according to Jerry Stanley it was all Herb Solow's "tenacity" and "presentation" that convinced them to write the check.

———————

Still, if you only look at the way *Star Trek* was workshopped (not sold!) early on, you might think it was just a western in space, populated by a bunch of space cowboys, riding around in the lawless frontier, bringing morality and order to random towns (planets) whenever they could. And in the '50s and early '60s, westerns, especially on TV, were still the most popular format for adventure fiction. Roddenberry cut his teeth writing for the series *Have Gun— Will Travel*, starring Richard Boone as the gun-for-hire Paladin, a deeply ethical gunslinger who is essentially Kirk, Spock, and Bones wrapped up into one person. In a Roddenberry-penned episode called "Alice" (1962), Paladin says, "The quickest way to bring out the worst in a man is make certain it's there." Roddenberry liked flawed heroes, but there's nothing cynical or angsty about the writing of *Have Gun*. Instead, Paladin scans like an early *Star Trek* character: moral, stoic, and formidable. If Roddenberry had been down with referencing a show he actually wrote for, he may have just pitched *Star Trek* not as "*Wagon Train* to the Stars," but instead, as "*Have Gun—Will Travel* in Space, with Non-Lethal Guns and More Heroes."

Because *Star Trek* was loosely formatted as a space western, there are many episodes in which the *Enterprise* isn't boldly going anywhere, but instead, seemingly just rolling into town on a random planet. Turns out, the actual mission of the *Enterprise*, and the idea for Kirk's logs, were invented retroactively. This happened with two narrative devices: the captain's log and the famous opening voice-over narration. The captain's log was invented first, primarily by Herb Solow, as a relatability shortcut for the audience. Instead of explaining that *Star Trek* was happening in the future, Solow suggested that "the voyages of the *Enterprise* had already taken place." Both Roddenberry and Solow were inspired by Jonathan Swift's *Gulliver's Travels*, so much so that at one point, Solow suggested that *Star Trek* become a full-on *Gulliver* homage, even to the point that the captain could be called "Captain Gulliver." Obviously, Solow was very wrong about the Gulliver thing, but very right about the captain's log framing, which is simultaneously the most down-to-earth thing about classic *Trek* and the most outrageous. We rarely see Kirk literally recording his captain's log,[3] but based on the voice-overs, we're forced to assume that Kirk is punching up these stories after the fact. The captain's logs are full of cliffhangers and pieces of information that only an omniscient godlike narrator could know. The Kirk who narrates the captain's logs already knows what is happening in the episode because, presumably, he recorded this stuff after the fact. But did he? Sometimes it feels like he's taking a break to record a captain's log in the middle of the action, like a half-assed space-age LiveJournal.

The narrative impossibility of the captain's log creates a veneer of plausibility in the classic *Star Trek*, partly because it vaguely

---

3 Throughout all of Star Trek, scenes of people actually recording the captain's log are rare, but in the *Deep Space Nine* episode "In the Pale Moonlight," Captain Sisko frames the entire episode with a log recording, speaking directly to the audience while he does so. And then . . . he deletes it! So, even when the logs are explicitly recorded, they're still unreliable.

suggests a truer narrative might be lurking beneath what we see in any given episode. In "Where No Man Has Gone Before," we see Kirk telling Spock that he's going to falsify his logs about what happened to Gary Mitchell and Elizabeth Dehner, which implies his voice-overs could be viewed as a Nabokovian unreliable narrator. In "City on the Edge of Forever," when Kirk says: "Captain's Log, Stardate: Unknown," he narrates the predicament in present tense. If he recorded this shit later, why the dramatic "Stardate: Unknown" shtick? We know the real-world answer is that the captain's log thing is like a rim shot, punctuating the story of each episode for the viewer. If we look for an in-universe answer, it's clearly that Kirk is a drama queen.

Speaking of drama, imagine if the prosaic opening narration to *Star Trek* had gone something like this early draft: *This is the story of the United Space Ship* Enterprise. *Assigned a five-year patrol of our galaxy, the giant starship visits Earth colonies, regulates commerce, and explores strange new worlds and civilizations. These are its voyages . . . and its adventures.*

How excited are you to watch a show about a spaceship that regulates commerce?! What next? Will Scotty do your taxes? The various drafts of the opening narration of *Star Trek* happened very late in the production process and it wasn't recorded until August 10, 1966, during the filming of the sixth episode ever made (tenth aired), "Dagger of the Mind," in which the *Enterprise* visits a goofy space penal colony. Hardly seeking out new life there! Neither pilot episode viewed by Desilu or NBC had the famous voice-over, so, "to boldly go where no man has gone before" had no part in selling the show. Between August 2 and August 6, 1966, one month before *Star Trek* made its September 8 TV debut (one day earlier in

Canada), producer John D. F. Black, Bob Justman, and Gene Roddenberry exchanged a flurry of memos about the exact wording of the teaser narration. In addition to regulating commerce, the mission of the *Enterprise* is maybe about finding "exotic people"; at other times, the ship will be out in space to "enforce intergalactic law"; and sometimes the words "a star trek" are spoken at the end of the narration.

Now. There's no question that William Shatner could have sold the lines "where no man has gone before . . . on . . . a star trek!" He could have. For sure. But it wouldn't have been cool. What's perfect about Roddenberry's final version of the opening narration is that it doesn't need to tell you that the show is called *Star Trek*, because the narration is too cool to say the title. After Kirk says, "to boldly go where no man has gone before!" the *Enterprise* wooshes by and deposits the words "Star Trek" on the screen.

The phrase "where no man has gone before" was not written by Gene Roddenberry. Instead, he lifted it outright from the title of the Sam Peeples script of the same name, which, a year and a half prior, had been the script that finally got the series greenlit by NBC. Besides "The Cage," the only classic *Star Trek* episode that was not initially edited with the "where no man has gone before" opening narration was, ironically, the episode titled "Where No Man Has Gone Before." Here's why: Although "Where No Man Has Gone Before" sold the series, it wasn't until a year later that the regular episodes began filming, starting with "The Corbomite Maneuver." For the first half of *TOS*, many of these episodes aired out of order, mostly because NBC wanted to lead with what it perceived to be the most accessible. This is why "The Man Trap," an episode seemingly about a bug-eyed space monster, was aired first. At the time, it felt the most like what sci-fi felt like at the time. Like many things about *Trek*, the opening narration was applied retroactively and underwent several revisions before it became the canonical thing we all know today.

The narration was also down to the wire: Just minutes before William Shatner was set to record the lines, Roddenberry gave the final version one last pass, emphasized the word "starship," and tightened up the entire thing. The brilliance of the opening *Star Trek* narration is that it has a poetic quality insofar as it builds as it goes along. Kirk's litany about what the ship does slowly gets more interesting, until he's just straight-up shouting. This is something you only notice when you apply some *Mystery Science Theater 3000*–style commentary to Shatner's vocal conations. So, let's do that!

Space . . . The final frontier Matter-of-fact, but also casual and extemporaneous. It's like he's making this up as he goes along.

These are the voyages of the Starship **Enterprise** More confident, but still bullshit. Kirk's in a corporate pitch meeting.

Its five-year mission, to explore strange, new worlds Is "strange" his favorite word ever? Is that warm delivery of "new" intoned that way to make us think he's kind of a horndog?

To seek out new life and new civilizations Now it's like he's coaching Little League. Get those nine-year-olds fired up! Also, it seems like he wants you to be impressed that he knows the word "civilizations."

To boldly go where no man has gone before! Suddenly he's yelling! Also, and most critically, we tend to forget how fast he says this part. It's sooooo fast. This phrase is nine words long, it's a mouthful. But, somehow Shatner makes it feel like he's said two words. The amount of time it takes to read it on paper feels a hundred times longer than how fast Shatner says it. It's a true vocal special effect. Though, to be fair, sound mixer El-den Ruberg did add a reverb sound effect to Shatner's voice. But reverb or not, it's impossible to invent William Shatner's cadence.

Luckily, when narration was retroactively inserted into all the episodes, Shatner's performance worked because the Kirk in 1965 is the same Kirk in 1966 and 1969. And, at the end of the day, Shatner's *Star Trek* opening monologue is great, even if the "man" part of the last sentence (is it a sentence?) is hopelessly sexist and outdated. But, for the purposes of framing the show, the monologue sets the tone—Kirk is the sheriff in these here parts, and these parts are, well, nearly anywhere the show wants to go. Kirk and the gang don't pack six-shooters, but like Paladin, Kirk draws his phaser more often than he doesn't. By the climax of "The Man Trap," as Kirk and Spock hunt down Dr. Crater (Alfred Ryder) to get some answers about the shape-shifting salt-sucking monster loose on their ship, we learn what kinds of gunslingers they really are. They put their phasers on "stun."

It's a pretty famous sci-fi innovation, so famous in fact that *Star Wars* just lifted the idea outright in 1977 when two stormtroopers apprehend Princess Leia by saying quickly, "Set for stun!" It took *Star Wars* exactly forty years, until *The Last Jedi*, to remember their guns had a nonlethal setting, but for *Star Trek*, this small detail is what elevated the western style of the show's format into something more complex. Sure. These might be space cowboys, but what if their guns don't kill? What if their guns just kind of knock somebody out for a while? Although Captain Pike packed a "laser" in "The Cage," after consulting with physicist Harvey P. Lynn at the RAND Corporation, Roddenberry was convinced lasers were obviously scientifically outdated, so he invented something unassailable: "phased energy." Although the lightsaber in *Star Wars* purports to be an "elegant weapon for a more civilized age," it's hard to figure out what's civilized about cutting people up into pieces. Lightsabers do not have a tranquilizer mode, but phasers do. Walter Koenig tells me that he loves phasers because they "prove that maybe we don't have to kill each other after all."

In *TOS*, the crew might be the literal embodiments of space law out there on the lawless final frontier, but they've all got some restraint about using violence. In the episode "The Enemy Within," written by Richard Matheson of *Twilight Zone* fame, Nimoy took this pacifist-in-combat notion a step further. In Matheson's script, when confronted with the evil version of Captain Kirk, Spock was supposed to knock him out with the butt of a phaser. Nimoy didn't like this, and told Roddenberry, "Gene . . . Spock is involved in a fight, but I think he would find a way to avoid violence." Roddenberry didn't buy it. And owing to his roots as a writer of cop shows and westerns, he believed his action-adventure show—however progressive it might be—still needed fistfights. Nimoy didn't care about Kirk beating the shit out of people on the show, but he did take offense to Spock throwing punches. And so, in "The Enemy Within," Nimoy convinced director Leo Penn[4] to let him try

---

4 Sean Penn's father!

something. He pinched William Shatner's shoulder—and invented the Vulcan nerve pinch. "He's the one who sold it," Nimoy later joked of Shatner's performance, a moment where evil Kirk cries out in pain and then slumps over, asleep. The cowboys of the *Enterprise* could set their six-shooters to stun, but Spock, the embodiment of *Star Trek*'s intellectual tenor, could make his hands into nonlethal weapons, too.

The broad popularity of Spock, and the nuances in his character in *The Original Series*, can largely be attributed to choices made by Leonard Nimoy, various one-off screenwriters, and writer-producer Gene Coon. Even Joseph Sargent, who, while directing the first non-pilot, regularly filmed episode of *TOS*—"The Corbomite Maneuver," which was aired ninth—suggested that Spock should convey a sense of awe and intelligence in the face of an immensely dangerous alien spacecraft. "Don't act uptight about what you see on the screen," Sargent told Nimoy. "Instead, when you deliver your line, be cool and curious, a scientist." Nimoy describes this as a moment when "something inside me clicked, he [Sargent] had just illuminated what it was that made this character unique and different . . ." Nimoy also maintained that the filming of "The Corbomite Maneuver," on May 25, 1966, counts as yet another moment when Spock was "reborn." But after Spock's various rebirths, who actually raised the character? In the fictional world of Trek, Spock's parents are a human woman named Amanda Grayson and a Vulcan man named Sarek. But the person who invented Spock's backstory was, arguably, the most influential writer on *The Original Series*, Dorothy Fontana, known by her writing credit at that time, D. C. Fontana.

Fontana's career on *Star Trek* began as secretary for Gene Roddenberry, and she helped shape the series from the very beginning.

Fontana had written for Roddenberry's military series *The Lieutenant*, which also starred many actors who would later appear in *Trek*, including Nimoy, Nichelle Nichols, and Gary Lockwood. Her influence on the entirety of the Trek franchise cannot be overstated. She wrote some of Trek's most famous episodes, and not just on *The Original Series*—Fontana's credits extended to *The Next Generation* in 1987, and even *Deep Space Nine* in 1993. In a sense, she helped launch *three* different Trek TV series.

Fontana describes her ascension like this: "Roddenberry told me: 'If you rewrite this script to my satisfaction and NBC's satisfaction, you will become my story editor.'" The script she was asked to rewrite was Jerry Sohl's "The Way of the Spores," which had been pitched as a love story for Mr. Sulu. But Fontana saw it differently. "I said no, this is a love story for Mr. Spock." The result was "This Side of Paradise," an episode where we learn that Spock not only has feelings, but once had a human girlfriend named Leila (Jill Ireland), and, as it turns out, is a deeply passionate person. Nimoy was "scared" that the episode would ruin everything he'd been working to build with Spock, but by the time the cameras rolled, Nimoy had told Fontana that "it turned out to be a lovely story." Fontana's rewrite earned her the script editor position on *TOS*, and at twenty-seven years old she was, at the time, the youngest script editor in Hollywood.

"Spock was always a favorite character for me and the fans," Fontana told me in 2016. "And I felt he deserved the exploration of character allowed by 'This Side of Paradise,' and also 'Journey to Babel.' I feel equally proud of [having written] both episodes because they offered a deep look into Spock, his emotions, his relationship with his parents, and the traditions and ethics that drove him."

D. C. Fontana may have given Spock his family and his soul, but writer Theodore Sturgeon gave Spock his libido. In the episode "Amok Time," we find out that Spock has to "mate" every seven years of his adult life or he will die. This episode—the debut episode of *Trek*'s second season, is the first time the *Enterprise* visited the planet Vulcan, and the first time that Spock says, "Live long and prosper," accompanied by that famous Vulcan hand greeting. Again, like the neck pinch, this was something Nimoy invented *on the spot*. He said he based the gesture on a Hebrew blessing he had witnessed as a child. "I saw the priests enrapt in religious ecstasy, their heads and faces hidden by shawls, pressing their arms over the congregation. As they invoked the essence of God, their hands were fixed in representations of the letter *shin*. So it was that, when I searched my imagination for an appropriate gesture to represent the peace-loving Vulcans, the *Kohanim*'s symbol of blessing came to mind."

The authorship of the characters of Star Trek is very much connected to the actors who play them, a tradition that continues well into *The Next Generation* and the contemporary series. But, outside of the "in-house" writers of *The Original Series*, and the brilliance of Dorothy Fontana, *Star Trek* did something TV series usually *never* did. Roddenberry actively recruited novelists and short-story writers, popular in the science fiction literary field, to pitch episodes. Again, "Amok Time," that pivotal Vulcan episode, was written by Theodore Sturgeon, an eccentric science fiction writer who was the real-life basis for Kurt Vonnegut's infamous *fictional* sci-fi writer Kilgore Trout. Sturgeon. Trout. Get it? Both fish? There's even a line in "Amok Time" where Spock compares the mating cycles of Vulcans to salmon swimming upstream. "But you're not a fish, Mr. Spock!" Kirk says. "Nor am I a man," Spock retorts. "I'm a Vulcan."

This deeply alien flavor of *Star Trek* could only come from actual science fiction writers, who, up until that point, were only known in the insular circles of the science fiction literary world. Science fiction, in a mainstream sense, didn't exist. Yes, there were B movies featuring alien invasions, and everyone had heard of *War of the Worlds*, but the idea that mainstream science fiction could be something other than cheap monster movies was rare. There were cinematic exceptions like *Forbidden Planet*, but after the end of *The Outer Limits* in 1965, science fiction on TV was still very much a niche interest. The crossover into everyday culture simply hadn't happened yet—because it was *Star Trek* that made it happen.

"Science fiction writers in general owe an awful lot to *Star Trek*," Norman Spinrad, writer of the episode "The Doomsday Machine," tells me. "Without *Star Trek* there would have never been a *Star Wars*. Sure, the first year, ratings were supposedly lousy. But what they considered lousy ratings was 21 million people a week! So, what that did is it made all the tropes of science fiction now a part of general culture. It opened up a narrow science fiction field into the main thing."

But in order to make this happen, Roddenberry needed not only the talent of "real" science fiction writers, but also their support. Above all, he wanted the show to reach people who did not consider themselves science fiction readers, but he also knew he couldn't piss off the gatekeepers, either. Like George Lucas a decade later, Roddenberry realized that he needed the convention devotee as much as he needed the less nerdy suburban families.

"*Star Trek* was conceived as a type of show that needed a specific pool of hard science fiction writers," Alec Nevala-Lee tells me. "Roddenberry recruiting contemporary and famous science fiction writers was totally pragmatic—the show couldn't have existed otherwise. And this move goes a long way toward explaining everything else. It meant that the series appealed to hard-core science fiction fans in a way that no other show ever had."

In Nevala-Lee's excellent book *Astounding*—a detailed (and astounding!) history of the so-called Golden Age of print science fiction—he points out that influential magazine editors in the field, specifically Joseph Campbell, began to notice the power balance of science fiction shifting away from the pulp magazines and books and toward TV. The gravitational pull behind this sea change was certainly Roddenberry, and the thing he was attracting was science fiction writers who were respected within the community. Prior to *Star Trek*, the only other markets for science fiction writers to sell teleplays were *The Twilight Zone*, *The Outer Limits*, or *One Step Beyond*, none of which were on the air by the time *Star Trek* went into production. Roddenberry knew that without the assistance of this tiny literary community, he wouldn't be able to make the show into what he was promising he would make it into: serious science fiction for grown-ups.

"Gene went to science fiction conventions to promote the thing to get it made in the first place," Norman Spinrad tells me over the phone. "He met people. He knew people. I don't think he wanted to take people's short stories and make them scripts. He wanted science fiction writers who could write scripts." Spinrad, a former president of the Science Fiction Writers of America (SFWA) and a celebrated author of numerous novels, jokes that he is mostly known "as the guy who wrote 'The Doomsday Machine'." That's the one where the *Enterprise* is nearly swallowed by a giant planet killer shaped like a cornucopia from hell. "I had never written a script," Spinrad says with a laugh. "When Gene asked me to write my episode, I had to ask Harlan Ellison, 'Can you show me what a script is?'"

Of all the science fiction writers of the 1960s, the one most likely to be the subject of a Quentin Tarantino movie is, easily, Harlan Ellison. Forever immortalized in the Gay Talese 1966 *Esquire* profile, "Frank Sinatra Has a Cold," Ellison is the guy who Sinatra tries to have thrown out of a club for wearing boots Sinatra doesn't like. With pool cue in hand, Ellison acts like he's going to stand his ground against Sinatra, but kind of loses the moxie war and ends up leaving the club anyway. As the story goes: "Three minutes after it was over, Frank Sinatra had probably forgotten about it for the rest of his life—as Ellison will probably remember it for the rest of his life." But Harlan Ellison's impact on *Star Trek* is the reverse: *Star Trek* can never get over Ellison, yet Ellison spent (nearly) the rest of his life complaining about the show. The episode Ellison wrote—which was extensively rewritten by several others, including Roddenberry and, later, D. C. Fontana—is called "City on the Edge of Forever," and is generally considered to be the best episode of Star Trek, ever. Curiously, like many of Trek's most lauded installments, it would be a *terrible* episode to watch if you'd never seen the show before, since it in no way represents what the show is like. The story involves time travel to the year 1930, Kirk falling in love with a social worker named Edith Keeler (Joan Collins), Spock wearing a beanie, and everybody worried about an accidental alternate reality in which the Nazis will win World War II. If you took out the Star Trek-y framing of the episode, the script could easily pass for a pretty solid *Twilight Zone*.

Saying "City on the Edge of Forever" is the best Star Trek episode ever is just like saying "A Day in the Life" is the best Beatles song ever or that Heath Ledger's best movie is *The Dark Knight.* Saying this isn't wrong—but the story is also a giant bummer. "City on the Edge of Forever" is the rare episode in which the crew doesn't gather on the bridge for their customary exchange of zingers. At the end of "City," after having to let the woman he loves die in a car accident, Kirk just says, "Let's get the hell out of here,"[5] and everyone solemnly gets beamed up to the *Enterprise* in depressing silence.

Ellison was an iconoclast in the SF field, and before *Star Trek* he was probably best known for his short fiction and the groundbreaking *Outer Limits* episode "The Demon with the Glass Hand," a gripping episode of sci-fi TV with a climax that will remind you more than a little bit of the ending of 1982's *Blade Runner.* Like the time travel that was central to so many of his plots, Ellison's reputation seemed to precede his actual writing, and like much of the history of *Star Trek,* an unsolvable the-chicken-or-the-egg paradox swirls around Ellison and many of the writers who contributed to *The Original Series.* And that's because Ellison was significant in *Star Trek* history not just for writing "City on the Edge of Forever." In fact, it's possible, even likely, that had he *never* written a script for *Star Trek,* his impact on the series would have been just as important. By his own account, it was through Ellison that Roddenberry was able to recruit many big-name science fiction writers not only to write for Trek, but also to advocate for the TV series in general.

"I was one of the first guys to even introduce Roddenberry to

---

5 Clearly, "Let's get the hell out of here" is a less iconic catchphrase than "Beam me up, Scotty," even though Kirk never says that *exact* phrase in any Star Trek thing, ever. Kirk used various versions, like "Scotty, two to beam up." Or "Beam me up." But never, "Beam me up, Scotty." At some point, in one of the newer shows or movies, it's bound to happen.

the community," Ellison told me over the phone in 2011. "I guess Isaac [Asimov] can take some of the credit, but I'm the one who got all the other big names on board." Some of these names included *Dune* author Frank Herbert and Arthur C. Clarke, and although neither would end up writing for the series, they did, at least once in an open letter to NBC, because of Harlan Ellison's prodding, publicly support the series.

I interviewed the cantankerous Harlan Ellison three times before his death in 2018, and each time the phone call was exactly the same: He would answer the phone suspiciously, assume that I was some kind of cretin who had obtained his phone number through nefarious means, and then by the end of the call, it felt like we'd been friends for life or that I'd just reconciled with an unhinged, estranged uncle. Ellison's boast about being an early supporter of *Star Trek* and funneling science fiction writers to Roddenberry wasn't just limited to what he told me. In 2016, he was quoted saying, "I was very optimistic about *Star Trek* . . . I showed the first pilot the first time it was shown to the science fiction community . . . That was how Roddenberry came to hire Ted Sturgeon and the others, because of my intercession."

Eventually, like feuding rock stars, Roddenberry and Ellison would have a huge falling-out, mostly over the fact that Roddenberry rewrote (and assigned rewrites) to "City on the Edge of Forever," which fundamentally changed what Ellison had wanted. In Ellison's version, there was a drug dealer on the *Enterprise,* and his addiction set into motion the chain of events that led to an accidental leap through a time portal. In the final episode, this concept was changed to Bones accidentally injecting himself with an overdose of a life-saving drug which, in high quantities, makes him go bonkers. This is just one of several changes. In 1995, Ellison literally wrote an entire book about the experience, which also contained his original script. Responding to the final aired version of the episode, Ellison wrote, "I hated it."

Does this mean other famous science fiction writers had huge dustups with Gene Roddenberry over getting rewritten? Not Norman Spinrad. "I used to have a lot of parties in those days," Spinrad tells me. "I invited Gene to one of the parties. I told him that Harlan was going to be there too. And I told Gene I have two rules at my parties: no fisticuffs and no puking. They didn't really screw around with my script too much. I got along with Roddenberry. We were not best friends, but we were pretty good friends. I admired Gene. He was a sincere guy and he really believed in what he was doing."

Ellison's experience writing for *Star Trek* is totally the most infamous, but his (possible) legacy as the initial ambassador between the SF lit community and the series itself is a subtle asteroid impact in both literary and television history. Robert Bloch (*Psycho*) wrote three episodes, George Clayton Johnson (*Logan's Run*) wrote one, Jerome Bixby wrote "Mirror, Mirror," and of course Ted Sturgeon wrote "Amok Time." Did the science fiction community rejoice? Not exactly. "Some people were jealous of that, I suppose," Spinrad tells me. "But some people who never wrote for it still got good things from it."

If you pick up any nonfiction book about the history of science fiction, and that book was published before 1977, before George Lucas's *Star Wars*, you'll see the doth-protest-too-much attitude from the gatekeepers of the old guard of SF. In most books like these, what you'll find is a bunch of chapters about the history of the genre of science fiction books and magazines ("SF" for the print purists), and then at the very end, like one chapter squeezed in about TV science fiction, which, back in the day was called, pejoratively, "sci-fi." In James Gunn's *Alternate Worlds: The Illustrated History of Science Fiction*—published in 1975—the *only* sci-fi TV series to be given more than one sentence is *Star Trek*. But Gunn, like many of his fellow SF critics, felt that *Star Trek* and TV "sci-fi" in general was an "alternate world of science fiction." Even within the genre, *Star Trek* was met with resistance from hard-core SF people, partly because of crankiness from famous authors like Ellison. But, more obviously, because *Star Trek* made science fiction really and truly popular. Anyone who says they liked a band before they sold out knows how this goes.

"Roddenberry had politics points in the stuff he was doing. He was sophisticated in a certain way," Spinrad says with a sigh. "If other SF writers didn't get the money from *Star Trek*, I can see why they were jealous. But what he did was like when Bob Dylan played an electric guitar. Roddenberry opened up something that was narrow, and he opened up science fiction to the larger culture."

Thanks to the huge viewership of *Star Trek*, the science fiction times of the late '60s were a-changing. Despite the general feeling that *Trek*'s ratings were poor, by today's metrics that wouldn't be true. As historian Marc Cushman points out, nearly 47 percent of American homes watched "The Man Trap," the debut episode of the series. *Star Trek* may have made science fiction mainstream, and done so very successfully, and rapidly, even if the SF writers of the time didn't admit it right away. In the middle of its run, in 1968, the show was still very much on its own, and it was about to face its own rolling stones, social controversies, and political gambits. And of course, huge Styrofoam boulders hurled by lizard-men.

CHAPTER 3

INFINITE DIVERSITY, FINITE GENES

The progressive politics and diversity of *Star Trek* in the '60s

In May 1965, wearing a light pink Chanel jumpsuit, Nichelle Nichols walked into the Desilu offices and transformed Spock into a Black woman. Perfectly content touring Europe with a troupe of singers and dancers, Nichols had never chased TV fame. She'd been pulled back to the states by her agent, begging her to read for a series she'd never heard of called *Star Trek*. Unlike her current limited gig, her agent told her, this was a steady job. Nichols liked the promise of stability even if she thought the medium of TV was bogus. "Working in television was not that pleasurable for me," she said. "I thought my career would be in musical theater, before *Star Trek* interrupted my career." Like many things that accidentally clicked about the OG *Trek*, the creation of Uhura was the result of an actor taking thin writing and stuffing it with artistry and intelligence. But whereas Spock evolved from Space Devil to shouty weirdo to the coolly rational Vulcan, Uhura evolved from Nichols having to read Spock's dialogue and imagining what he'd be like if she was him. Before she walked into that audition, Uhura literally didn't exist.

"They handed me a script and apologized, saying the part I would be playing would be a communications officer," Nichols recalled. The assembled group of men, including director Joseph Sargent and Gene Roddenberry, told her the role was changing, but that the pages they were giving her were "probably close" to what her character might be. The idea that Spock was a male character wasn't made clear at first, so Nichols innocently wondered, "What's she like?" And in that moment, the souls of Spock and Uhura were joined forever. Could Nichols have replaced Leonard Nimoy as a female Black Spock? Probably not. And yet, Nichols said at least one person present asked that somebody "phone the contracts department" to see if Nimoy had put pen to paper. Because of the way history played out, it's hard to really believe that Roddenberry would have fired Nimoy after fighting for his inclusion after "The Cage." But over the years, Nichols, Sargent, Roddenberry, and others each repeated the story of her audition with very little variation, which makes a solid case that at least one person (probably Sargent) was taken with the idea that Spock as a Black woman might have worked.

More than any character in the entire Star Trek pantheon, Uhura is unique because *everything* was created by the actress, including the character's name. During her audition, Nichols had a book tucked under her arm; the 1962 novel *Uhuru* by Robert Ruark—a fictionalized account of the Mau Mau uprisings against landowners in Kenya in the 1950s. In Swahili, the word "Uhuru" means "freedom." Once it was settled that Nichols was taking the part of the new communications officer, Roddenberry suggested taking the name Sulu away from Mr. Sulu, but Nichols insisted that

"Uhuru" be Uhura. Pundits and historians love to talk about how Nichelle Nichols and William Shatner participated in the first kiss between a Black person and a white person on American network television,[1] but far more progressive and interesting is the casual introduction of the Swahili language into the homes of millions of Americans. In the first episode of *Star Trek* ever aired—"The Man Trap"—Uhura speaks Swahili, never mind that she's talking to a shape-shifting alien salt vampire in disguise! Jim Kirk's backstory had him born in Iowa, but Uhura was from the future-facing United States of Africa. Kirk was a throwback white-male-hero archetype. Uhura, like Spock, wasn't an archetype at all. For American TV, she was something new.

The connection between Spock and Uhura wasn't just the result of random pages thrown at a young actress. In the first season of *Star Trek*, it's totally clear that Uhura and Spock have a *relationship* that exists outside of what we see on the screen. As Nichols developed the character with Roddenberry, she decided that "Spock was my mentor" and that Spock "inspired [Uhura] mentally and professionally," which, in the 2022 series *Strange New Wolds*, Celia Rose Gooding's newest Uhura has already expounded upon.

Other than Kirk and Bones, Uhura is the only character in *The Original Series* who openly fucks with Spock and gets away with it. In "The Man Trap," she shamelessly flirts with Spock, saying, "Tell me how your planet Vulcan looks on a lazy evening when the moon is full." When Spock says, "Vulcan has no moon," Uhura quips, "I'm not surprised." In "Charlie X," she sings that joke song we talked

---

1 That episode is "Plato's Stepchildren." Although this episode is often celebrated as a progressive moment for classic *Trek*, you really have to wonder if people have actually watched it recently. In the story, Kirk and Uhura are *forced* to kiss by hedonist telekinetic "gods." Any way you slice it, a Black woman being *forced* to kiss a white man isn't exactly progress.

about in Chapter 1, where Uhura implies Spock is like a hot version of Satan. In both instances, Spock takes it because he clearly thinks she's great. Just like Spock stole his personality from Number One, Uhura tapped some of Spock's steely competence. Nichols also felt that most of the episodes on *The Original Series* that dealt with racism directly were the stories written for Spock. "*Star Trek* explored storylines concerning his mixed heritage," Nichols recalled. "[Roddenberry] might have made exactly the same points in writing the same stories with Spock being the human child of a Black parent and a white parent living in the sixties."

As a Black woman, in 1965 Nichols had good reason to roll her eyes at the thought of becoming a TV actor: In 1964, blatant racism had prevented her last guest spot on a TV series from ever airing. Sure, she'd been paid, but nobody had seen her. Over a year before her fateful meeting at Desilu, Nichols had been cast in what would become the final episode of the 1963–1964 military drama *The Lieutenant*, "To Set It Right," co-starring with Don Marshall, Gary Lockwood, and Dennis Hopper. The story focused on the racial conflicts between Corporal Devlin (Hopper) and Private Cameron (Marshall) with Lockwood's titular Lieutenant William Tiberius Rice[2] acting as the de-facto moderator. Nichols played Norma, Cameron's girlfriend, who consoles him about the racism he faces within the Marines. *The Lieutenant* was created and produced by Gene Roddenberry, and when NBC and the Pentagon opposed the airing of an episode about racism in the armed forces, Roddenberry called the NAACP for an assist. NBC pulled the plug and the Marines said

---

2 Gary Lockwood would go on to play Gary Mitchell in "Where No Man Has Gone Before," and then later, Frank Poole (not Dave, the other guy) in *2001: A Space Odyssey*. And yes, his character's middle name, "Tiberius," in *The Lieutenant* was later given to James Tiberius Kirk.

they'd stop cooperating with the production of the show. "My problem was not the Marine Corps; it was NBC, who turned down [the episode] flat," Roddenberry said. "I went to the NAACP, and they lowered the boom on NBC." It didn't really work. The entire series was canceled, and Roddenberry was, righteously, furious.

"He was certainly trying to get back at them for what they did to him on *The Lieutenant*," Judy Burns tells me. "But I don't think he was out to make a giant statement [with *Star Trek*] to begin with. I don't think he thought about changing the planet or changing racial considerations—although I do think he understood it. And that's one of the reasons he hired George [Takei] and Nichelle. I think he understood the ramifications. But I also think he was just trying to get a show on the air."

Like Uhura, the character of Mr. Sulu was barely "a sketch" when Roddenberry offered the role to George Takei. By the time his agent encouraged him to audition for Roddenberry, Takei had already had an extensive career in TV and film. With guest spots on *Perry Mason* and *The Twilight Zone* and a film career that included *An American Dream*, plus voice-over work in several *Godzilla* films, Takei was young, but no amateur.[3] But right at the start, Takei saw what Nichols saw: a loosely sketched character that he could utterly create, and that also would give him a steady job. For actors of color in the 1960s, roles that were not limited to guest spots were just not that common. Pervasive racism in casting is crushingly still prevalent in Hollywood today, but there's no question that it was much worse in 1965. Takei's struggle was to make sure that the roles he

---

3 Takei's film career grew while he was on *Star Trek*; during the show's second season in 1967, Takei took a part in the John Wayne film *The Green Berets*, which took him away from the *Star Trek* set for several episodes. This is why Sulu is missing from famous episodes like "The Trouble with Tribbles." He was busy!

took weren't stereotypical and admitted to having "lost" parts because of offensive depictions of Asian men as "buffoons" or "menaces."

So, when Roddenberry told him the part of Sulu wasn't completely defined, Takei wasn't offended, he was pumped. "This producer [Roddenberry] was sheepishly apologizing for the best opportunity I had yet come across . . . as sketched already, this character was a breakthrough role for Asian Americans." As conceived by Roddenberry and Takei, Sulu's background was "pan-Asian," meaning he didn't specifically represent any one nationality. Correlatively, in 1986's *The Voyage Home*, we learned that Sulu was born in San Francisco, and in 2009, when it was announced that Korean-born John Cho would take the role of Mr. Sulu for the J. J. Abrams *Star Trek*, Takei defended the casting decision, pointing out that Sulu wasn't necessarily Japanese. He also revealed that Abrams had consulted him before giving the part to Cho, which Takei endorsed by saying, "To me, so long as the character remains Asian-American, that would be all that matters."

During the filming of "The Naked Time," Takei also pushed back on explicitly depicting Sulu as having exclusively Japanese interests. When the writer of "The Naked Time," John D. F. Black, initially wrote the script, his idea was that Sulu would lose his mind and then run around the ship swinging a Samurai sword. Takei liked the idea, and Sulu, famously, runs around the *Enterprise* shirtless, swinging a sword. But, in the final episode, it's not a Samurai sword, it's a fencing foil. And that change was Takei's idea. "Sulu is a twenty-third-century guy. He would see his heritage as much *broader* and larger than just ethnically confined," he explained in 2020 in an interview with Wil Wheaton. "I didn't play Samurai as a kid. I played Robin Hood." Sulu, as conceived by

Takei, was a futuristic swashbuckler, endearing himself to every-one in those famous sword-swinging scenes. Spock, in a rare, back-handed joke, refers to Sulu as "D'Artagnan" adding to the myriad layers of multicultural references. When I asked George Takei why Sulu didn't go shirtless more often in *Star Trek*, he laughed and said, "I don't know, but I think we all know people wanted to see more of it."

As Burns says, Roddenberry may not have been trying to eradi-cate racism with a Westernized sci-fi series, but in casting Takei and Nichols for the regular series—and giving them room to de-velop the characters themselves—he did bring aspects of a much older passion to life. Before there was the diverse crew of the Star-ship *Enterprise*, Sulu, Uhura, and Kirk might have flown a giant steampunk blimp. Roddenberry's close friend Christopher Knopf recounted a story several times that during a baseball game at Dodger Stadium in 1963 Roddenberry enthusiastically described the premise of a TV series that he thought was a "winner." It would be set at the end of the nineteenth century and feature the crew of a dirigible "full of mixed races, who travel to places no one has discovered before." Knopf said this pitch was clearly the "philo-sophical forerunner to *Star Trek*." But, roughly a year later, around the exact same time Roddenberry was trying to sell *Star Trek*, he had also produced a western pilot called *The Long Hunt of April Savage*, all about a man on a revenge-murder quest. On top of that, he was also trying to sell a dry police procedural called, uninspir-ingly, *Police Story*. The ill-fated *Police Story* pilot episode starred future *Star Trek* actors DeForest Kelley and Grace Lee Whitney. Neither Kelley's Bones McCoy nor Whitney's Yeoman Rand would have ended up on *Star Trek* if *Police Story* had become on ongoing TV show. And what if *The Long Hunt of April Savage* had been picked up? In fact, what if *The Lieutenant* hadn't been canceled in the first place? Without all these other false starts, and competing projects, could Roddenberry's random notion of a steampunk crew flying in a dirigible have solidified into a groovy woke sci-fi show? *Star Trek* may be the creation that Roddenberry loved most, but it was also the only TV series he ever managed to sell.

Still, *Star Trek* has a nuanced perspective on idealism, and where it comes from. In 1991's *Star Trek VI: The Undiscovered Country,* the Klingon chancellor Azetbur (Rosanna DeSoto) gives her peace-loving progressive (and dead) father a backhanded compliment, noting that if a certain moon hadn't exploded, "his idealism may not have found expression." In 1996's *Star Trek: First Contact,* thanks to time travel, the *Next Generation* crew are disappointed to learn that the inventor of warp drive, Zefram Cochrane (James Cromwell), is a drunk horndog who mostly created a new kind of spaceship for the dough. "Dollar signs. Money . . . That's Zefram Cochrane. *That's* his vision." Trek fans the world over insist that the overriding philosophy of Star Trek is connected to the Vulcan philosophy of IDIC—Infinite Diversity in Infinite Combinations—which first appeared casually, represented by a piece of jewelry worn by Spock in the episode "Is There in Truth No Beauty?" But, just like Zefram Cochrane hoped that inventing the warp engine would make him heaps of money, Roddenberry wasn't exactly running a nonprofit. He was an artist, and like many artists, he was trying to make money off of his art in any way that he could. The famous IDIC pin worn by Spock in "Is There in Truth No Beauty?" was slipped into the script by Roddenberry because he had already been producing replicas of the same pin to be sold by his side hustle, the start-up company known as Lincoln Enterprises. Leonard Nimoy was so disgusted by Roddenberry's obvious attempts to sell some merch through his character, he briefly threatened not to shoot the episode. So, which one is the real Gene Roddenberry? The one who developed the ideal of the IDIC, or the one who sold the pin?

Roddenberry is lauded with casting Nichelle Nichols and George Takei in the roles of Uhura and Sulu, but it's not like the *first* pilot—"The Cage"—was populated by any people of color, even as background characters. Had that version of *Star Trek* been picked up for a series run, would Roddenberry have still thought to bring on a more diverse cast? Just like the fusing of Spock's personality with Number One's, the progressive notion of "infinite diversity" seems to be retroactive and, perhaps, born of necessity. Accurately, *Star Trek* is often lauded for presenting a multiracial crew working together in a distant future without any signs of racism. And yet, there are no documents in the series bible that indicate that the original *Star Trek* would have, at its core, a political philosophy of racial and gender diversity. An early bible for the series describes it as "action adventure," in which characters visit worlds that have a "similar social evolution as our own."

On the business side, the progressive political philosophy was not a stated goal of *Star Trek,* but it was a result. By 1968, two years after the show was on the air, Roddenberry's more forward-thinking version of the series had taken shape, at least in the interviews he gave. "Intolerance in the twenty-third century? Improbable!" he told Stephen E. Whitfield, the first author to write a book about *Star Trek.* "If man survives that long, he will have learned to take a delight in the essential differences between men and between cultures . . . this is part of the optimism we built into *Star Trek.*" Roddenberry was clearly serious about what he believed, but he wasn't consistent. In fact, the first Black actor who worked on *Star*

Trek—Lloyd Haynes, who played Lieutenant Alden in the second pilot, "Where No Man Has Gone Before"—Roddenberry fired. Lieutenant Alden hadn't spoken a lot but, unlike Kelso (Paul Carr), Gary Mitchell (Gary Lockwood), and Dr. Dehner (Sally Kellerman), he'd survived several explosions, lightning bolts, and one strangulation. Unlike the frightening Hollywood cliché of killing off Black men in adventure narratives, Alden was alive, and ready to boldly go another day—and Kirk even recommends a commendation for Alden in the captain's log at the end of the episode. By 1966, Roddenberry was "bored" with the character and got rid of him, eventually replacing him with Nichelle Nichols.

Some of the Trek faithful have deified Roddenberry as a great progressive ideologue, pushing for diversity and representation in *Star Trek* and breaking boundaries as a result. They're not wrong. Gene Roddenberry clearly did care about these things, but it didn't always come from an ideologically pure place, as Nichelle Nichols revealed to the public in 1994, three years after Roddenberry's death. In both *TV Guide* and in her memoir, Nichols recalled that he'd often joke that if Nichols had "played her cards right" she would have become Mrs. Gene Roddenberry. Nichols's response? "Yeah, right, Gene."

"Our relationship was long over before *Star Trek*," Nichols wrote in 1994. "And few knew we had even met before." Nichols maintains that their affair was over way before *Trek*, and never resumed. Whatever stupid things he'd say about her "playing her cards right" was drunken talk that Nichols blew off. Although she relied on him for her initial *Star Trek* paychecks, Nichols was in control of Gene Roddenberry, not the other way around.

In *First Contact*, we learn that the inventor of warp drive had a copilot, a Black woman named Lily Sloane (Alfre Woodard). Before their big night, Lily pulls Zefram Cochrane away from the bar, saying, "Z! Z! You've had enough!" If you're looking for a fictional representation of who Nichelle Nichols and Gene Roddenberry really are within *Trek*, there they are. In "The Man Trap," Sulu says, "May the Great Bird of the Galaxy bless your planet." Just like Ernest Hemingway became Papa, from 1966 onward, after this line (which originated with producer Bob Justman), Roddenberry was given the nickname "the Great Bird of the Galaxy," which he fucking loved. His one and only book of fiction, the novelization of *Star Trek: The Motion Picture,* trumpets his reputation with this nickname on the front cover. This single detail about Roddenberry almost tells you everything you need to know about him. Anyone who enthusiastically cultivates the nickname "the Great Bird of the Galaxy" totally *is* the Great Bird of the Galaxy.

There are many ways to look at Roddenberry. Was the Great Bird an early social justice crusader who just happened to be a TV producer? Was he a half-assed humanist sci-fi philosopher? A sleazy, career-minded opportunist with delusions of godhood? Like many pivotal historical figures, Gene Roddenberry can't be defined by just one trait. The creation of the idealistic United Federation of Planets sometimes feels as important as the signing of the Declaration of Independence. As an American, I'm thankful that George Washington existed, but I'm also aware that George Washington owned slaves. Roddenberry wasn't as bad as all that, but you can see where this is going. He was the founding father of the science fiction country of dreams called *Star Trek*. And in creating *Star Trek*, Roddenberry unwittingly created a new art form, one that spans several types of media and will likely last for at least a hundred years. He was also a deeply flawed, and apparently problematic, human being.

But, when it came to building the humanitarian ethics of *Star Trek*'s progressive future, Roddenberry wasn't the only founding father of *Trek*. If Roddenberry is the George Washington in the saga of *Star Trek*'s early days, then the Alexander Hamilton of *Trek*'s early days is another Gene—Gene L. Coon.

"Gene Coon had more to do with the infusion of life into *Star Trek* than any other single person," William Shatner said in 1991, shortly after Roddenberry's death. In 2008, he doubled down, writing, "After the first thirteen episodes, writer/producer Gene Coon was brought in . . . after that, [Roddenberry's] primary job seemed to be exploiting *Star Trek* in every possible way." Shatner isn't alone in his praise for the Other Gene. Dorothy Fontana called Coon "half of *Star Trek*'s Genes." Russell Bates, Coon's protégé and writer for *Star Trek: The Animated Series*, said, "Coon was like Nikola Tesla. He wasn't interested in credit." Like Roddenberry, Coon was an ex-cop and an ex-pilot who had turned to TV writing. Both men also shared liberal-leaning views, and desperately wanted to distance themselves from their racist fathers.

After John D. F. Black left *Star Trek*, Roddenberry hired Coon as the show's new story editor, the equivalent of what we would call a "showrunner" today. Coon was a fast writer and rewriter. Like the Beatles playing all-night shows in Hamburg, totally high on pills, some of Gene L. Coon's speed at the typewriter was the result of taking speed. Ande Richardson, Coon's secretary, recalled buying "jars of amphetamines" for Coon. According to her, Coon would stay up all night writing and she would go out all night dancing. Richardson has been called "the real Uhura" insofar as she was a Black woman who worked on *Star Trek*. Before her gig with Coon, she had worked with both Malcolm X and Martin Luther King Jr. and said that "working with Gene [Coon] was as normal as working with them." In 2016, she said that she put Gene Coon in the same category as Malcolm X and MLK. But not Roddenberry. She attended Gene (Roddenberry) and Majel's wedding in 1969 but maintained that Gene Coon "was my heart." Richardson encouraged Gene to attend Black Panther rallies, too, which she and others credit with the development of *Star Trek*'s moral and ethical tone. "We would talk about politics . . . and then I would see all of that in *Star Trek*."

The so-called noble purpose of *Star Trek* can be attributed to Gene Roddenberry for creating the whole thing, but for most of the people who were there, the execution of that purpose comes from Other Gene. "The Devil in the Dark"—the best episode about a misunderstood monster *ever*—was written by Coon in just four days, high out of his mind on those pills his young secretary scored. His output and impact on the political nature of *Trek* is unparalleled. In the twenty-sixth episode of *Star Trek*'s first season, "Errand of Mercy," Coon created the Klingons and promptly turned the story into an antiwar parable. If you've never seen *Star Trek* before, and you're watching the classic shows in order, getting to "Errand of Mercy" will blow your mind. The war with the Klingons is coming. You can feel that the show is about to change. And then . . . the episode isn't about turning *Star Trek* into *Star Wars*, because "Errand of Mercy" is all about aliens telling us to stop trying to blow each other up with ray guns, or, in this case, Kirk and Spock's homemade bombs.

The strength of "Errand of Mercy," and several of Coon's other episodes, is a flourish reminiscent of *The Day the Earth Stood Still*. You look at the movie poster for *The Day the Earth Stood Still*, and you think it's about a flying saucer and an invading robot coming to destroy the world, à la *War of the Worlds*. But the movie is really about an alien demanding that Earth disarm, or else. Kirk and the rest of the crew in the classic *Star Trek* aren't much different. They appear on planets and try to fix problems. But, if the planet hasn't hit certain milestones in technological and cultural advancements, Starfleet is forbidden to interfere. Essentially, the number one rule of *Star Trek* is that the good guys out there boldly going are not racist colonizers. Starfleet doesn't displace alien cultures in favor of humanity's bold expansion. If it's not appropriate and the time isn't right, Starfleet avoids first contact with aliens and lets the planet evolve at its own pace. It's called the Prime Directive, and it was invented by Gene Coon. Basically, Coon invented a rule for the United Federation of Planets that was the opposite of colonial racism. If the Prime Directive existed in real life, would Indigenous peoples globally likely still have their land? Would the transatlantic slave trade or apartheid have been prevented altogether?

"What made the show compelling was the metaphors," George Takei told me in 2016. "We dealt with the Civil Rights movement while it was happening in the '60s. There were some obvious ones. People with faces with black on one side, and white on the other." Takei refers to the third-season episode "Let That Be Your Last Battlefield,"[4] in which the crew meets two aliens from the planet Cheron—Lokai (Lou Antonio) and Bele (Frank Gorshin)[5]—each

---

4 This episode was cowritten by "Lee Cronin," a pseudonym of Gene Coon. In the third season, Coon had left as a producer, but still wrote freelance for the series and used a pen name for his episodes at that time. This is mostly because Coon had a new deal with Universal and was hiding his *Trek* writing from that other gig.

5 Frank Gorshin was famous for his role as the Riddler on the '60s Biff-Pow version of *Batman*. The fact that he's in one of the most famous episodes of *Star Trek* is simply not talked

with face makeup that makes them look like a black-and-white cookie. Although the crew is baffled at first, Commissioner Bele reveals that he is from the population of Cherons who are "black on the right side," while Lokai is descended from an "inferior breed" of people who are "white on the right side." This sounds silly, and it mostly is. (My right, or your right?)

But the heart of classic *Star Trek* is very much in the right place in this one. Spock, the victim of racism both veiled and obvious, makes the case that it doesn't matter what colors appear on either side of anyone's face. "The obvious visual evidence, Commissioner, is that he is of the same breed as yourself." This isn't to say that the episode pushes for any "color blindness," because the *Enterprise* crew overall sympathizes with Lokai, the renegade, who is from an oppressed racial group. The episode might seem like it's saying, "It don't matter if you're right-black or right-white," but it's not. Even in this simplistic allegory, *Star Trek* still points out that there are oppressors and victims. In "The Day of the Dove," an energy alien that feeds off of hate and racial conflict goads the crew of *Enterprise* into fighting (with swords!) an endless battle with the Klingons. Under pressure, and after receiving fake propaganda through tricky telepathy, our supposedly enlightened human crew slips into racist attitudes quickly. The Klingons didn't *really* attack that Earth colony, but because Chekov, Bones, and Scotty have all been brainwashed to think that's what happened, suddenly our heroes are in favor of genocide. This racism swings back toward Spock, since he's the only nonhuman on board.

In "Balance of Terror," the crew learns that their deadly

---

about enough. He's also fantastic, and the episode would not work without his tremendous talent.

enemies, the Romulans, look exactly like Vulcans.[6] One crew member, Lieutenant Stiles (Paul Comi), whose ancestors fought in a war against the Romulans a hundred years before, immediately suggests that Spock is a spy for the Romulans because he has pointed ears. Before the racism boils over into paranoia, Kirk grabs Stiles's chair, spins him around, and shouts, "Leave any bigotry in your quarters. There's no room for it on the bridge."

In "Space Seed," Spock notes that "insufficient facts always invite danger," and time and time again, *Star Trek* presents an information gap—what we would call fake news—as the source of racism, war, and death. In "Day of the Dove," Chekov is convinced he suffered a family atrocity that never occurred—the death of a brother that Sulu points out never existed. In Gene Coon's "Devil in the Dark," Federation miners are determined to kill the Horta before it kills them, all before Spock learns that the Horta is a mother protecting her unborn baby Hortas. Unlike on our own planet, Spock can "mind-meld" with other people and life-forms, which in the case of the mother Horta means that he cries out ("PAIN!!"), experiencing the anguish of the Horta as though it were happening to him.

"There are so many people in pain, in real life. And they are living lives of quiet desperation," Walter Koenig—who famously played the young Russian navigator Mr. Chekov—tells me over the phone. "So, that anger can boil to the top, and they're looking for

---

6 The first Romulan, in "Balance of Terror," was played by Mark Lenard, who more famously went on to play Spock's father, Sarek, in "Journey to Babel"; three of the Trek films; and two episodes of *The Next Generation*. The Vulcan/Romulan schism was later explored in excellent detail in the Spock-centric *TNG* two-parter "Unification" (1991); the *Enterprise* three-part story starting with "The Forge" (2005); the *Star Trek* 2009 reboot film; all of *Star Trek: Picard* Season 1 (2020); and the *Discovery* episode "Unification III" (2020). The latter explores what happens when Vulcans and Romulans try to reintegrate their societies after centuries of segregation.

avenues to express it. We're not genetically predetermined to hate, but as a consequence of circumstances, angry people can embrace [the] culture of hate and misinformation, and then you've got people breaking windows and storming the Capitol."

If someone had never seen an episode of *Star Trek* before, having them watch only "Let That Be Your Last Battlefield" or "Day of the Dove" could convince them that this show was just a series of heavy-handed old-timey after-school specials written by white people on drugs. Which, through a certain microscope, is *exactly* what '60s *Star Trek* was. But the power of classic *Trek*'s diversity politics can be easily misunderstood if you try to pick out one great episode. Takei felt it was all about metaphors, but Walter Koenig thinks the representation itself was more impactful than specific plotlines.

"I think more than any story that we told, it was more about those seven faces on the bridge," Koenig tells me. "A Japanese American. An African American. The Russian, there, while the Iron Curtain was in place. Some stories we told were just action stories. Some had something to say about humanity. But the fact that we saw those faces, every week, I think that was settled into our consciousness simply by the fact that we *saw them*. And that they worked together and had each other's back. I think that's the greatest gift we gave the world, without actually having to tell a story."

Koenig, the son of Russian immigrants who Americanized their real name "Königsberg," grew up in New York and affected an over-the-top Russian accent for the character of Pavel Chekov. His casting was the result of a supposed letter Roddenberry received from Russian fans who had allegedly watched the first season of *Star Trek* and felt slighted by the lack of representation from the USSR. Whether or not such a letter truly existed is up for debate. *Star Trek* was a new show that American audiences were struggling to connect with, so it feels strange that Soviet-era Russian TV watchers were getting bootlegs of the classic show. Did Roddenberry invent the letter? Other critics point to Koenig's casting as a stunt to attract younger viewers who might be obsessed with the Monkees, since Chekov's hair was reminiscent of the mop-tops popularized by the Beatles, and in the late '60s by the Monkees' short-lived TV series. D. C. Fontana supported this claim, and said, "The Beatles were hot, of course; they were still at that point and Gene Roddenberry decided 'we need a young character.'" Still, if the move had been entirely cynical, then it seems like Roddenberry would have just had Koenig do a bad English accent. If the point was to capture British Invasion–obsessed teens, why bother making the character Russian?

"He didn't have to do that," Norman Spinrad tells me. "Putting a friendly, heroic Russian character right there in the crew, that was a big deal back then." Over the years, Koenig has poked fun at the relative progressivism of Chekov, later recalling that his character was mostly just there to "scream" or deliver jokes about how "everything was invented in Russia." But, these days, Koenig has settled into a more generous view of Chekov. "There are some very pragmatic reasons for making the show the way we did," he tells me. "We had to compete in the world of entertainment, so that meant we had to have action, we had to have over-the-top jokes. Even now, if you don't have that stuff, your movie or TV show isn't going to make money. I think those early shows do contain some idealism, but we were also just trying to stay on the air."

Because it was a network television show, *Star Trek* made a lot of compromises to keep going. And, if a script was going to be shortened, or a scene cut, the first characters to lose lines or moments were always Sulu, Chekov, and Uhura. "We were the moveable furniture," Koenig said. While Nichols wrote that D. C. Fontana had penned several "wonderful scripts" that focused on Uhura and made her character more central, all of those scripts were "decimated."

Nichols recalled that while the studio was giving "lip service" to the idea of racial equality, people of color were still not being given equal time on the show. Her role, and the roles of Sulu and Chekov, were greatly diminished by the time cameras rolled. Other Black characters appeared only in a handful of episodes, like a *second* doctor who works on the *Enterprise*, Dr. M'Benga, played by Booker Bradshaw in just two episodes, "A Private Little War" and "That Which Survives." Seemingly, M'Benga is not only as good as Bones, but, in many ways, better. He knows more about Vulcan physiology than Bones seems to, enough to know that slapping Spock in the face *hard* is the only way to save his life. In the 2022 series *Strange New Worlds*, M'Benga is now played by Babs Olusanmokun, and is a series regular. But why wasn't M'Benga in more episodes of *TOS*? Technically, just like Scotty, he's not part of the main cast, just a special guest star. M'Benga isn't killed off or anything, either. Booker Bradshaw simply wasn't featured as much as other actors who weren't Black.

Meanwhile, Nichelle Nichols also was the victim of racism on the Desilu lot. Though she wrote that it never happened "on the set," she was harassed at the gate, simply for trying to drive into work. On top of this, Nichols's fan mail was being *withheld* from her. Nichols never got to the bottom of *why* this happened, but the assumption is that it was a mix of racism and the fact that *technically*, she wasn't a full-time cast member, merely a reoccurring day player. Due to the kindness of two mail room attendants, Nichols finally was able to open bags and bags of mail, all addressed to her, almost all overwhelmingly positive. Contrary to popular myth, racist viewers did not mount a letter-writing campaign to remove Nichols from the show. Instead, the racism came from within, from, as Nichols wrote, "the studio's front office," who perceived that white audiences weren't ready to see more of Uhura. The paper trail, though, reflects the simple fact that viewers liked her more than the studio or the network.

In "The Naked Time," when Sulu is running around with his shirt off, believing he's some kind of swashbuckling hero, he grabs Uhura and says, "I'll protect you, fair maiden!" Without missing a beat, Uhura says, "Sorry, neither!"[7] She's neither fair, nor is she a virginal maiden. It's a line that you can almost miss the first time you hear it, but it's suggestive of the larger potential of underused characters on the classic *Star Trek*, and Uhura in particular. "Sorry, neither" is the real Uhura talking, the unheard Uhura, the Uhura who had better story lines written for her, but that we never got to see because of pervasive racism and fear. Women are not automatically "fair" and they're not automatically good people because of patriarchal standards. It's one line from an iconic character who pushes back against systematic white supremacy. The word "fair" also reinforces oppression of beauty that derives from racist viewpoints. Uhura's rejection of the label "fair maiden" rejects systematic racism and entrenched sexism, too.

By the end of the first season in early 1967, fed up with rewritten scripts, harassment, and open racism, Nichelle Nichols didn't

---

7 There's a pervasive myth that suggests that Nichols ad-libbed this line. It's not true. Nichols loved playing the scene and gushes about it in her memoir *Beyond Uhura*, but the line was in the script, as written by John D. F. Black.

just *think* about quitting *Star Trek*, she quit outright. Roddenberry begged her not to leave, but she was done. The night after her resignation from *Star Trek*, Nichols attended "an important NAACP fundraising event." At one point, she was asked to do a meet-and-greet with someone who was a self-professed *Star Trek* fan. That fan turned out to be Dr. Martin Luther King Jr.[8]

When King met Nichols, he said that he and his daughters "adored" Uhura and that they watched the show "faithfully." Nichols then gave him the bad news that she had quit. King told her that she couldn't, and begged her to reconsider. "Remember you are not important there in spite of your color. You are important there *because* of your color." A week later, Nichols returned to *Star Trek*. Did Martin Luther King Jr. really love *Star Trek* as much as Nichols, Roddenberry, and the rest of us have been told? When it comes to projecting optimism about the future and anti-racist attitudes, the Trek franchise is a full-time PR machine for itself, which occasionally means the uglier bits of that progress are overlooked.

"Uhura's role in hindsight reads like tokenism, technically," writer and scholar Syreeta McFadden tells me. McFadden is a contemporary critic known for her writing on race and pop culture, and is perhaps most famous for her essay "Teaching the Camera to See My Skin," in which she elucidates the racist history of film technology. Specifically, the notion that Kodak and other film companies calibrated their film specifically to favor white skin. Interestingly, Nichelle Nichols notes that in the early days of *Trek* conventions, she'd occasionally meet a fan who had only ever seen the show on black-and-white TV and was unaware she was Black.

---

8 In April 2012, history would repeat itself. This time, Nichelle Nichols would meet *Star Trek* fan President Barack Obama at the White House, where he admitted that as a kid, he'd had a "crush" on Uhura.

"She, and the others, were set pieces. Sure, it was ground-breaking, but it was kitschy groundbreaking," McFadden explains. "What matters more is the timing. Coming at the end of the Civil Rights movement in the '60s, having that visibility was big. I'm not sure MLK believed *Star Trek* was a great show, but compared to what was out there, it was the only thing on mainstream TV that was friendly to representing different races and gender identities without a bunch of stereotypes." She then adds, with a laugh, "I mean, I think MLK was like 'this is *huge*. There's something huge manifesting on this not-so-great show.'"

The classic *Star Trek* will always have a tenuous place in the history of racism and pop culture. On the one hand, it was light-years ahead of its time. On the other hand, there are dudes painted half-white, half-black, and the messaging is ham-fisted and, sometimes, racist on accident. *Star Trek* was considered feminist at the time it was made, but the "strong" roles for women that Rodden-berry promised with the character of Number One are few and far between. "Everything about the '60s was different," Harrison Solow tells me. "It's hard to really judge the first *Star Trek* by today's standards because it will fail every time. No matter how many times you tell people this, they can't hear it because of what it became." What *Star Trek* was in the '60s and what it came to represent aren't the same. Was it a progressive antiracist show conceived by a visionary humanist? Or was it a populist action-adventure show that conveniently had a moral and political conscience in the writers' room? As Uhura might say, the answer is clearly: Sorry, neither! When it comes to diversity and representation, the holistic intention of the original *Star Trek* is hard to pinpoint, partly because we'll always be looking at it from the perspective of improvement.

Competing intentions show the history of *Trek*'s early representation as filled with contradictions. But then again, Scotty needed contradictory elements to power the *Enterprise*, too. Without matter and antimatter banging against each other, the *Enterprise* would never fly.

CHAPTER 4

THE TROUBLE WITH TREKKIES

The death of *The Original Series* and the birth of Star Trek fandom

Sitting in his room in the Americana Hotel in Midtown Manhattan, DeForest Kelley was drinking a full quart of orange juice. Whether the OJ was spiked with vodka or Saurian brandy is unclear. Like most people who have just checked in to their hotel in New York City, DeForest Kelley wanted to get outside, walk around, and buy some stuff. Specifically, he wanted a new pair of shoes. While finishing his orange juice, Kelley realized that leaving the Americana Hotel without getting mobbed on Seventh Avenue was going to be tricky. He certainly did not say: "Damnit, Jim, what the hell's the matter with these Trekkies!?" But he was considering donning "a false beard and nose," created on the fly by original *Trek* makeup artist Fred Phillips. On February 18, 1974, Dr. Leonard "Bones" McCoy could not just stroll the streets of Manhattan, at least not while the third-ever *Star Trek* convention was in town.

If you switched decades, genders, age brackets, and fictional universes, the debacle of DeForest Kelley in the Americana Hotel in chilly early 1974 isn't unlike Carrie Bradshaw in a random epi-sode of *Sex and the City*; shoe-buying problems that scan as simul-taneously faux-tragic and glamorous in a kitschy way. Like the Beatles running from their fans in *A Hard Day's Night,* it's not relat-able at all, and yet, the story of any human trying to regain their anonymity is ultimately relatable, especially if we're talking about Bones and the City. In 1974, DeForest Kelley was not a twenty-something heartthrob. He was a fifty-four-year-old heartthrob. *Star Trek* had been canceled five years prior, in 1969, and in 1968, Kelley had complained to *TV Guide* that he'd felt "left out" by the writers and producers of *Star Trek*. In the early days of the Star Trek fan phenomenon, Kelley and his co-stars were not only more famous than ever; they were famous, seemingly, *forever.*

While plotting to make Bones's escape into the streets of NYC, convention organizer Joan Winston and DeForest Kelley turned on the TV to check out local news coverage of the 1974 *Trek* conven-tion, which was already in progress. The news broadcast failed to mention most of the actors who were in attendance. Kelley was left out of the spotlight again. To press, the stars of the show were the Trekkies.

Or was it Trekkers? Since 1968, people have been trying to make "Trekker" happen, claiming it's the less pejorative term of the two. "Trekkie" sounds like the love child of a "groupie" and a "hip-pie," and not in a good way. "It's the difference between the people who go overboard and the people who don't," early *Trek* superfan Jacqueline Lichtenberg said in 2004. But, with all apologies to Lich-tenberg, "Trekkie" is the term that stuck. And here's why: The first generation of Trekkers worked their assess off so the next genera-tion of Trekkies—and every other type of fan of *anything*—could inherit the earth.

Before the conventions, and one year before *Star Trek* was canceled by NBC, Brooklyn College student Devra Langsam was making a zine. In the summer of 1967, from her apartment in Crown Heights, Brooklyn, Langsam became patient zero for all the organized, competent, and influential Trek fans who would follow. Black and white, with a neatly stapled spine, her zine, *Spockanalia #1*, was adorned with fan art, including a striking ink portrait of Spock on the cover by fan artist Kathy B. Sanders, credited with her artist moniker "Bush." This zine, the first *Star Trek*–themed publication *ever*, also boasts a foreword by Leonard Nimoy, who, like Roddenberry, was an early adopter of the underground power of fandom. Holding *Spockanalia #1* is like holding the lost ark of all *Trek* swag, but what makes it so freaking cool is that the cover doesn't have any words, just some moody Spock art. Curated by Langsam, featuring work from several contributors, *Spockanalia #1* has poems, short stories, and more than one rigorous essay speculating about what Vulcan emotions are *really* like.

Spockanalia also contains a written-out song called "The Territory of Rigel," by another fan contributor, Dorothy Jones. In the Vulcan language, Jones says, this pseudo-libretto is a "Ni Var," which means "two forms." The dualistic nature of Spock—half red-blooded human and half green-blooded Vulcan—is alluded to within the "Ni Var," an idea later Trek writers liked so much, it was added to the official canon.[1] In 2002, the prequel series *Enterprise* introduced a Vulcan starship called *Ni'Var*, and in 2020, in the

---

1 Tragically, not everything in early zines got picked up by the writers of Star Trek. In Langsam's essay, "Thoughts on Vulcan Culture," she writes: "Those who support the theory of feline Vulcan ancestry have suggested that catnip might have an invigorating, if not to say, intoxicating, effect on them." Contemporary Star Trek writers have never incorporated this idea into a Trek film or TV series, which means we've all been robbed of scenes featuring Zachary Quinto or Ethan Peck furtively doing lines of catnip.

episode "Unification III," *Discovery* established that in the far future, the entire planet Vulcan is renamed Ni'Var after those naughty pointed-eared Romulans return home to form a more peaceful union. *Discovery* writer and *Picard* co-creator Kirsten Beyer told me renaming the planet Vulcan Ni'Var was one hundred percent because of the first *Star Trek* zine ever, and that she felt the idea of Ni'Var "was beautiful."

Speaking of beautiful, Spock's sex appeal as the match that lit the gasoline that set the *Trek* fandom on fire cannot be understated. It also can't be overstated. Langsam's game-changing zine wasn't called *Kirk-a-palooza* or *Bones Bones Bones*, it was called *Spockanalia*. Remember when Roddenberry accidentally created Spock's personality because of a conflict of interest? The result, surprisingly, was the explosion of the world's most powerful and enduring fandom. While this may be less true now, at the beginning, it was always Spock. Kirk is the bro who boasts about getting laid all the time. Spock is the person who is above all that, and sexier because of it.

"He was a tremendous lure. I mean, he's a pretty good-looking guy," Devra Langsam tells me. Although she was a college student at the time she crafted *Spockanalia*, Langsam essentially created a career out of being a professional fan. She eventually even started her own small publisher, Poison Pen Press, and although semi-retired, she continues to write to this day. "Spock's a challenge. He's interesting. Fans would think: *I could make him melt.* The networks, for the longest time, seemed to think that all the fans were teenage boys with pimples who lived in their parents' basements and collected buttons. They seemed to ignore the fact that seventy percent of the fans were women, with, um, *normal*, uh, *interests*. And they, we, were attracted to these people because they were interesting and challenging."

At the beginning of fandom, the love of *Star Trek* cannot be separated from the love of Spock, or, more precisely, the *lust* for Spock. Although the five handmade issues of *Spockanalia* aren't overtly erotic, some of the zines that followed, by other authors, were. The result of this phenomenon is the emergence of the world-altering Kirk/Spock fan fiction, in which the characters were depicted by the fans as lovers. This is the origin of what is now called "slash fanfic," in which fans "ship" certain couplings of fictional characters in all sorts of fandoms, not even remotely limited to *Star Trek*. Infamously, *Fifty Shades of Grey* was a retelling of *Twilight* in a different setting with different character names. This is now often called "alternate universe fanfiction," and here too, *Star Trek* fans basically invented it. At the same time, and throughout the early '70s, Jacqueline Lichtenberg, along with Sondra Marshak, created the alternate fanfic universe of *Kraith*, in which the lives of Spock and Kirk are explored through emotional dramas, with many of the stories focusing on Kirk deprogramming from a human-centric (read: racist) view of the universe. *Kraith* stories weren't slash, but Kirk was Spock's emotional subordinate, and not the other way around. So, you know, *kinky*.

Della Van Hise, one of the most prominent writers of hot and heavy Kirk/Spock fic, would later land a mainstream book deal with Pocket Books, a division of Simon and Schuster that has published the officially licensed Star Trek fiction from 1979 to the present day. Zine writers Myrna Culbreath and Sondra Marshak also wrote several novels[2] featuring *very* close relationships between Kirk and Spock, eventually published as officially licensed Star

---

2 *The Price of the Phoenix, The Fate of the Phoenix* (both Bantam), and later, *Triangle* (Pocket Books). Marshak and Culbreath also edited anthologies called *Star Trek: The New Voyages* (Bantam), the second of which featured a short story, written by the editors, called

Trek books, too. Van Hise's alternate universe novel *Killing Time* was perceived as so racy that Paramount asked Simon and Schuster to pull the original print run and replace certain scenes—including Kirk enjoying the "warmth" of Spock's hand—with watered-down versions.[3] When I corresponded with Van Hise in 2017, she told me that she felt the legacy of slash fic and *Killing Time* specifically had embedded itself so strongly into fandom, that aspects of her story were casually borrowed for the 2009 J. J. Abrams reboot film. In *Killing Time*, an alternate universe is created by the Romulans in which Kirk is, again, Spock's subordinate. "Captain Spock. Ensign Kirk. Sound familiar?" Van Hise said. "It did to me."

If you've heard about the racy fanfic before, what gets left out of the discussion is just how mainstream the themes became; specifically the idea that Spock is always topping from the bottom. Van Hise might not be right about Alex Kurtzman and Roberto Orci cribbing *Killing Time* for their 2009 script, but what she is right about is the larger impact of Star Trek fan fiction on "official" Star Trek.

As a grade-schooler in the '90s, I got the novel *Black Fire* (1983) from my local library. It is a very real mass-market Star Trek

---

"The Procrustean Petard" in which the gender of every single *Enterprise* crew member is reversed. That is, Kirk becomes a woman, Uhura becomes a man.

3 Legend has it that Van Hise's original manuscript of *Killing Time* featured Spock actually ejaculating. She tells me this is one hundred percent untrue. Basically, what Paramount was mostly worried about was too many descriptions of warm hands. To be clear, Van Hise *did* write slash fic before getting the book deal to do *Killing Time*, but that hardly means anything. Sam J. Jones, the dude who played *Flash Gordon* in the 1980 movie version, was a former *Playgirl* centerfold, and that fact was certainly partly why he was cast. But that doesn't mean there's a suppressed version of the *Flash Gordon* where Flash flashes. Right?

paperback book in which Spock becomes a sexy space pirate.[4] In 2015, when I asked *Black Fire* novelist Sonni Cooper why she and other writers made Spock so overtly sexualized in their fiction, she said: "Spock always denied his human side and sublimated it as much as he could. It seemed right, and ultimately amusing, to make him an object of sexual interest and therefore even more uncomfortable about dealing with his duality."

If you go looking for old '70s Kirk/Spock slashfic on eBay, you will find it. If you Google Kirk/Spock fan art, you will see what you'd expect to see. However, while it's fun to snicker at the proliferation of zines where Kirk and Spock would fuck, the truth is, the vast majority of zines were more restrained. The super-raunchy-sounding novella *Spock Enslaved!* (by Diane T. Steiner)—which features cover art of a bare-chested Spock standing in manacles (drawn by Karen Flanery)—is not actually that overtly sexual. In fact, there's not a ton of sex in *Spock Enslaved!* at all, and Steiner's writing is pretty damn good. The tonal differences between *Spock Enslaved!* and the professionally published *Black Fire* are largely superficial. I prefer *Black Fire* because I like space pirates, but that's me.

Even if the myth of all-dirty *Trek* fanfic were true, it's not like these people were just coming up with this material on their own. The '60s *Star Trek* was an overtly sexual series, but because it was the '60s, it was a repressed one, too. In the first regularly filmed episode of *Star Trek* in 1966, "The Corbomite Maneuver," and the last episode ever, filmed in 1969, "Turnabout Intruder," Kirk takes his shirt off and hits a miniature gym in sickbay while Bones

---

4 Named Black Fire. In this guise Spock wears a transformative cape and robe that make him look like a walking field of stars. Spock also wears a black jeweled earring. This book kicks so much ass.

watches, making sure his bod is still up to Starfleet specs. In "Amok Time," Spock is only broken out of a Vulcan mating drive when he thinks he's killed Kirk. In "Shore Leave,"[5] Kirk actively believes that Spock is giving him a back massage. "Dig in there, Spock!" Kirk says. But then, he acts disappointed when he realizes Spock is standing on his left, and it is actually Yeoman Barrows rubbing his back. In Jean Lisette Aroeste's scripts for "Is There in Truth No Beauty?" and "All Our Yesterdays,"[6] Spock's emotionalism and romanticism are not just passing jokes, but essential to the plots, the latter of which involves Spock hooking up with a cavewoman. Even in *Trek*'s troubled final episode, "Turnabout Intruder," we get fifty shades of Kirk/Spock heat. When Kirk swaps bodies, *Freaky Friday* style, with an angry ex-girlfriend named Janice Lester (Sandra Smith), the only person who buys it is Spock. After mind-melding with "Janice" and realizing Kirk is in her body, Spock's tenderness toward a *female* Kirk is played up big-time. Overall, this episode is hopelessly sexist, and shoddily written (by Gene Roddenberry!) but, blink-and-you'll-miss-it, there's Spock holding Janice's hand *after* he knows it's really Kirk's hand. Yep! The final episode of the classic *Star Trek* has Spock holding Kirk's hand like Kirk is his girlfriend.

"Turnabout Intruder" wasn't aired until June 3, 1969, but it was filmed in January. Although *Trek*'s third and final season ran in the first half of 1969, "Turnabout Intruder" was the only episode filmed that year. Visiting the set and snapping as many photo-

---

5 Both of these episodes were written by Theodore Sturgeon, who also wrote the foreword to Sonni Cooper's *Black Fire*.

6 Jean Lisette Aroeste was one of six woman writers on the original *Star Trek*. The other five were Judy Burns, Shari Lewis, Joyce Muskat, Margaret Armen, and of course, Dorothy Fontana.

graphs with her Instamatic camera as possible was Joan Winston, a New York–based TV studio publicist *who did not* work for NBC, but rather for their competitor, ABC. Out of all the pivotal early *Star Trek* influencers, Winston is remarkable because she wasn't a science fiction convention-goer or a college student. She was a talkative, well-connected industry insider who "knew everyone" and just *happened* to be a superfan. Winston was a native New Yorker who never learned to drive and, during the fateful filming of "Turnabout Intruder," befriended DeForest Kelley, who offered to drive her around town. She was ostensibly visiting Los Angeles on business for her bosses at ABC, but as she recounted in the book *Star Trek Lives!,* Winston didn't see much of LA because she spent nearly all of her time soaking up the last days of *Trek*. While driving Winston to the *Star Trek* set, DeForest Kelley could not possibly have known that five years later, their situations would be reversed, and Winston would be showing him around her town, New York City.

———————

For the past five decades (and counting), various Star Trek retrospectives have tended to paint the grassroots nature of *Trek* fans in the '60s and '70s as a kind of cutesy cultural curiosity. Like the hive-mind Borg from *The Next Generation*, Trekkies are all lumped in together in these narratives. Writing for the *Los Angeles Times* on January 8, 1968, Jerry Ruhlow mused, "Students at Caltech have found little time for demonstrations, protests and draft card burnings rampant on many of the nation's campuses . . . In what some observers suggest may be the emergence of the college's social conscience, the enraged students voiced opposition to rumored canceling of NBC's science fiction series *Star Trek*." Ruhlow was writing about a famous in-person demonstration on January 6, 1968, and the most visible part of the "Save Star Trek" campaign to get the show renewed for a third season. Funnily enough though, at the Burbank offices for NBC, many of the executives actually favored renewing *Star Trek* for a third season, so the protest was, according to Bob Justman, closer to a "love-in." Everybody grokked Spock.[7] Everybody thought Sulu was groovy. From January 1968 to March 1968, NBC received somewhere between 12,000 and 114,667[8] letters, all telling them the same thing: Give *Star Trek* a third year. It worked. Thanks to massive *Trek* fan outcry, *Star Trek* lived to have one more season, before getting canceled the following year.

But there were two questions Ruhlow's reporting (and the rest of the media) failed to ask. First, who organized the protesters? Second, why did the New York suits at NBC want to cancel *Star Trek*? These oddly enough have easier answers, all of which have been made unnecessarily complicated over time.

Who organized the protesters? Gene Roddenberry! Roddenberry was a hundred percent behind both the protesters and the letter-writing campaign. He used several proxies of motivated fans, notably, superfans Bjo and John Trimble. This couple was en-

---

7 "I Grok Spock" was a slogan found on various fan-made buttons of the time. The word "grok" means to deeply understand something and make that thing a part of you. It's like you telepathically comprehend something really hard. It comes from Robert A. Heinlein's infamous 1961 science fiction novel *Stranger in a Strange Land*. Heinlein had briefly toyed with suing *Star Trek* in 1967 after the airing of "The Trouble with Tribbles," noticing how similar the tribbles were to furry creatures called "flat cats" in his short story "The Rolling Stones." Heinlein dropped the suit and eventually became friendly enough with Gene Roddenberry to write him a letter congratulating Roddenberry on the *novel* version of *Star Trek: The Motion Picture*.

8 There's debate—online and in other books—about the exact number of letters. Unsurprisingly, Roddenberry claimed it was a million. Nimoy says 100,000. Alan Baker, an NBC publicist at the time, said it was closer to 12,000. But, getting more than 2,000 letters about *anything* during a three-month period was *a lot*. In 2020, *Star Trek: Discovery* actress Rachael Ancheril told me, "My mom was one of the people who wrote a letter to tell NBC not to cancel the original *Trek*!" So, maybe thank Rachael's mom?

trenched in the literary science fiction community and was adept at organizing letter-writing campaigns. Roddenberry not only hired the Trimbles, but he also funneled money into the "Save Star Trek" campaign and even wrote off his expenses. There's a paper trail of Roddenberry doing this, which, any way you slice it, is gutsy as hell. Roddenberry rented the Trimbles offices to mount their campaign. He also flew a fan named Wanda Kendall from LA to NYC to give Joan Winston a box of "Spock For President" bumper stickers. Winston slapped these on the cars of everyone who worked at NBC in New York. Roddenberry later filed an expense report to Desilu for the creation of the bumper stickers and the plane ticket for Wanda Kendall. During the January 6, 1968, protests, Roddenberry was chilling on his motorcycle, dressed "all in leather" like a Hell's Angel, watching the protesters march.

Why did NBC want to cancel *Star Trek*? Because it had bad mainstream ratings and it was expensive as hell. There are A LOT of arguments about this. Roddenberry claimed both the network and the studio just didn't "get" the show, and that the show's intelligence was just too much for them. He and others have also pointed out that the Nielsen ratings at the time weren't accurate, insofar as the individual demographics weren't taken into account. This is similar to Langsam's point that the studios were looking too broadly and not noticing the specific demographic of women between the ages of nineteen and fifty-five. But, the Nielsen ratings—based on the metrics of the time—were "bad," and by the time *Star Trek* was stuck in a Friday-night slot for the third season, there were literally just not enough people watching it to make the show economically viable. Some contemporary historians—specifically Marc Cushman—have argued that the ratings for *Star Trek* were actually better than we've been led to believe, and compared to ratings today, 60 million is a lot of people. But this might be a game of false equivalences. *Star Trek* was hard to make on a budget, and by whatever metrics NBC and Desilu-Paramount were using, it wasn't giving them a return on their investment. Cushman also points out that Roddenberry was hard to work with. There's plenty of evidence here: *Star Trek* also had a lot of turnover among the writers and producers. By the third season, both Gene Coon and Dorothy Fontana were no longer involved day-to-day. Even Roddenberry relinquished control to producer Fred Freiberger in Season 3, supposedly out of protest against the bad time slot NBC had given *Trek*, though some think that Roddenberry just didn't want to stay with a sinking ship. The bottom line: If *Star Trek* had been a secret runaway hit, NBC wouldn't have canceled it. It got canceled because the metrics used by the Neilsen ratings showed the show wasn't competitive enough with other mainstream shows *and* it was costly. This reveals more about the way people watched TV in the '60s than anything else. There were only three networks, so finding its niche audience in prime-time TV was tricky simply because TV channels had yet to proliferate and alternate metrics like syndication and cable were in their infancy.

This isn't to say *Star Trek* didn't make *any* money. It did. It just sometimes didn't make money directly for the studio and the network. If you think the colorful look of *The Original Series* is a little over-the-top now, consider this: This was one of the *very* first TV shows made specifically with color TV in mind. In 1966, during the first season, Nielsen research "indicated that *Star Trek* was the highest-rated color series on television." Now, NBC was founded and still co-owned by TV maker RCA at the time, which means there was some incentive to create shows that could sell more color TVs. However, NBC wasn't exclusively in the business of selling

TVs; like everyone else, they made their money through advertisers, which meant they needed the most eyeballs to win.[9]

Still, when you set aside the myths and all the Hollywood inside-baseball stuff, the fact is the Trekkers—the people who organized the letter-writing campaign (Bjo and John Trimble), and the people who made zines and got the word out to other fans (Devra Langsam, Joan Winston, Jacqueline Lichtenberg), and the protesters who marched—all succeeded in gifting the entire world with the status quo of pop culture as we know it. Today, studios and brands kind of go out of their way to provide "fan service" or listen to "fan feedback." This simply didn't exist until the Trekkers/Trekkies demonstrated the power of organized fandom. *Star Trek* fandom's birth is significant because nothing *quite* like it had ever happened in the history of the world[10] and entire new worlds were created because of it. Countless journalists, authors, vloggers, Instagram cosplay models, social media influencers, and the person writing this sentence all benefit directly from the twenty-first-century media industry of "geek" fandom. And the most popular fandoms in the world—from Marvel to anime to Star Wars—all orbit around love for media brands.

What made the early efforts of *Star Trek* fans different, and

---

9 Imagine some new Netflix/streaming show driving up the sale of a certain kind of smartphone or laptop. Unless Netflix (or whoever) had a deal with that hardware, there's no way that metric actually means people are watching your show. This is why the big studios charge subscription fees for their streaming channels these days, including Paramount+ (formerly CBS All Access), the current home of the new Star Trek shows. If NBC and Desilu could have created a subscriber-only version of *Star Trek* in 1968, they would have. *Star Trek* was like the canary in the mineshaft for niche TV. This niche audience–based model basically describes all TV now.

10 Prior to 1966, other than comic book fandoms, the only other mainstream fandoms around fictional characters that even came close to *Star Trek* were Sherlock Holmes and daytime soap operas.

bonkers, was the near-perfect blend of hyperprofessionalism and adorable naiveté: a love for a media brand that wasn't actively being sold to them. The first generations of *Star Trek* fans were scrappy and were good at playing behind the eight ball. The modern geek world—and its unique embrace of kitsch lifestyles—does not exist without the explosion of *Trek* fandom in the late 1960s and throughout the 1970s. The birth of Trekkies isn't just about the appreciation of a certain kind of sci-fi TV art form, it's about the remapping of the culture. Before Trekkies, to love kitsch meant that you loved a thing—art, books, film, or TV. After the birth of Trekkies, loving kitschy things could be applied to an entire subculture. This essentially is the beginning of a new way of finding a name for identity. And it caught on quickly. In 1970, only 300 people attended the first San Diego Comic-Con. The first *Star Trek* convention in 1972 at the Statler Hilton had a whopping 3,000. The 1974 convention at the Americana Hotel had 15,000.

This doesn't mean that other geeks were nice to the earliest *Trek* fans. Just the inverse: the science fiction establishment was outright hostile, which is how we got the word "Trekkies."

"There was a snobbery within literary SF circles well into the seventies and eighties," Star Trek historian and archivist Larry Nemecek tells me. "It was the old guard lit people acting like you couldn't be at a science fiction convention unless you've read your Heinlein and your Asimov." Despite some of the street cred of various science fiction authors writing for *Star Trek*, in the 1960s, the institution of science fiction, at least in America, was still firmly rooted in the printed word. Pre-*Trek*, science fiction conventions—specifically the long-running Worldcon, in which the coveted Hugo Awards are doled out—were never going for populism. (They still aren't.) SF fandom, as defined before *Star Trek*, was focused on novels, short stories, fanzines, and other things you could read. After trying to hand-sell her zine at the 1967 Worldcon[11] in New York City (also known as Nycon 3), Langsam tells me that much of the science fiction and fantasy establishment was dismissive. "At Nycon, [renowned fantasy novelist] Anne McCaffrey bought one copy of *Spockanalia*!" Langsam remembers. "But she made sure to say it was for *her son* like it was juvenile or something."

So, the Trekkers decided to create their own conventions. While there were several nonpublicized gatherings—like Devra Langsam and Sherna Comerford hosting a *Star Trek* night at the Newark Public Library—the first New York City convention, January 21–23, 1972, was the event that sent a clear signal to the world: Whatever was going on with *Star Trek* was not small. It was very big. "We did it," Joan Winston wrote in 1977. "Our January 1972 convention did it. We lit the fuse and the fandom burst into flame. Up until that time, *Star Trek* fandom had been underground."

Again, the first "Star Trek Lives!" convention at the Statler in NYC (the Hotel Pennsylvania today) had 3,000 people show up. Here's the funny thing: The only *Star Trek* actor who attended the first convention was Majel Barrett. The other guests of honor were Gene Roddenberry, D. C. Fontana, and science fiction writers Isaac Asimov and Hal Clement, neither of whom *ever* wrote for *Star Trek*. So, in the winter of '72, 3,000 people in New York City crashed a huge hotel across from Penn Station to see Nurse Chapel, the creator of *Star Trek*, the story editor of *Star Trek*, and a couple of other guys who were there to say nice things. To put things in perspective, at Nycon 3 in 1967, a convention that was thought to represent the

---

11 "Worldcon" is the collective name given to an annual science fiction (SF) convention which tends to take place in a different city every year; hence "Nycon" for the New York City convention in 1967.

entire world of science fiction, you only had 1,500 people. This is how niche science fiction fandom was before *Star Trek*: only 1,500 people in all of NYC showed up for Worldcon but double that showed up for the first *Star Trek* convention. By the second NYC convention in 1973, there were 6,200 attendees who came out to meet George Takei and James Doohan. But, not to be outdone by Sulu and Scotty, Spock himself, Leonard Nimoy, made a surprise guest appearance at this convention. Other than paid airfare and room and board, the former stars of *Star Trek* weren't getting any real compensation. Even by 1974, when DeForest Kelley was chilling with Joan Winston in his hotel room, he was getting paid in free meals. One anonymous source tells me that Kelley also figured out a way for the hotel to "eat the bill," and not have anyone pay for it. At a certain point at the 1974 convention (attendance: 15,000) Kelley decided to not worry about the mob, posted himself up in the hotel bar, and bought drinks for anyone wearing a badge that identified them as a convention volunteer. The Americana paid the tab.

Nineteen seventy-six was the last of the first run of "Star Trek Lives!" NYC conventions spearheaded by mastermind Joan Winston. Langsam and Lichtenberg tell me that the end of that era was bittersweet. They helped create the fandom, but once Nimoy, Shatner, Kelley, Nichols, Takei, Doohan, Koenig—and, yes, Roddenberry—all realized they could charge a speaker's fee, there was no turning back. The industry part of fandom was born right alongside the fandom itself.

"At the very beginning, the first couple of conventions, I was so shocked and thrilled that they came," Devra Langsam tells me. "We paid their hotel rooms and they were amazed. But then after a while they realized 'this is my livelihood. This is how I earned my living. I cannot afford to give it away.'"

In the 1970s, the *Star Trek* cast and creators became rock stars, able to ask for huge sums of money just for personal appearances. This single fact alone may explain why "Trekkie" became more dominant than "Trekker." If the crew of the *Enterprise* were legit rock stars, then perhaps the "Trekkies" were the (figurative) groupies at the concert (convention).

Still, which term *should* be used—"Trekkie" or "Trekker"? Although the coinage of "Trekkie" is hard to pin down, most give SF author and editor Arthur W. Saha the dubious credit when, in 1967, he told journalist Pete Hamill that "Trekkies" wearing pointed ears had started to invade the literary SF scene. But, because this term seems to have come from the anti-*Trek* SF establishment, it makes sense that early fandom pioneers would hate it, at least at first.

"I am a Trekker. Not a Trekkie," Jacqueline Lichtenberg said in 2004. "'Trekkie' is the put-down."

"I used to say that 'Trekkies' are the kids who run down the aisle screaming 'SPOOCK!'" Joan Winston said. "But I'm a 'Trekker.' I *walk* down the aisle."

Winston's sense of humor about the debate is the essential answer. Her joke about walking versus running implies that everyone is still *screaming*. This hints at the key element to Star Trek fandom that everyone forgets: We know Trek is a little silly, but if you ask us about it, we'll tell you it's the most fucking intellectually important thing of all time. From where I sit, the word "Trekkie" embodies that dichotomy in a way "Trekker" doesn't. A "Trekkie" sounds funky and friendly, and above all, it's a word that embraces the kitsch and camp that make the coziness of Star Trek popular.

Notice I didn't say "relevant." Star Trek is *popular* because it blends a colorful, campy sci-fi quality with specifically ethical storytelling rules. That ethical storytelling part is generally called

"the philosophy of Star Trek." That's IDIC. That's the Prime Directive, et al. That's Star Trek's *relevance*. It's not, however, the sole
reason Star Trek is popular. Star Trek is also popular because it's
goofy as hell. In his book *Fargo Rock City*, Chuck Klosterman ar-
gues that "goofiness" doesn't disqualify significance, but instead,
"expands the significance, because the product becomes accessible
to a wider audience." Klosterman was writing about Mötley Crüe,
but the point stands. Star Trek is just as popular for its goofiness as
it is for its various profundities. To me, calling yourself a Trekkie
means you *love* that spandex uniform on Kirk's dad bod. You know
that it's a little embarrassing, but that's also the point. The word
"Trekkie" contains that juxtaposition: Captain Kirk is like a philosopher king, but he's also goofy as hell. The word "Trekker," I
feel, is someone who suspects the greater platonic form of Captain
Kirk is *less* goofy, and that he's only made to be goofy in our world
so that people will pay attention. "Trekker" sounds more serious,
and rejects the kitsch, which jettisons some of the fun.

For all the compliments Star Trek receives about its hopeful
view of the future and progressive agenda, one of the core reasons
it has survived for so long is that it mixes in all of those high-
minded sci-fi ruminations with silliness. This is what a huge swath
of cultural assessments of Star Trek has gotten wrong for almost
six decades. When asked why Star Trek is *popular*, people tend to
answer with the reasons why Star Trek is *good*. But this conclusion
skips a step. It's like saying the invention of trains was only important because it got stuff from one place to another. You can't leave
out the train whistle, the tracks, or the fact that riding on a train is
just freaking *fun*.

The argument that Star Trek has survived because its philosophy was unique and progressive in a vast sea of intellectual TV laziness is true. The layered cultural relevance of Star Trek is its historical legacy. But the ethics of Star Trek don't *exclusively* explain its popularity. This is similar to the over-intellectualization of why Star Wars is so lauded. Pundits say that Star Wars is relevant because George Lucas mined the Jungian archetypes and adhered to Joseph Campbell's monomyth concept of the hero's journey. But the larger truth is, people also like lightsabers because lightsabers are cool. Ditto Star Trek and beaming, warp drive, Vulcan neck pinches, phasers on stun, and nearly every main character from *The Original Series*. In Star Wars, the only person winking at the camera was Han Solo. In the classic *Star Trek*, pretty much every character gets their Han Solo moments of genuine, and hilarious, humanity.

"*Star Trek* softened up the entertainment arena so that *Star Wars* could come along and stand on its shoulders," George Lucas said in 2013. But what was he talking about? The moral and ethical philosophies of Starfleet? The progressive political nature of the Federation? Gene Roddenberry's hopeful vision of the future? Star Wars contains virtually *none* of these things, and yet, because game recognizes game, George Lucas noticed that Star Trek fandom made it easier for Star Wars to exist.

In 2009, talking to Gene Roddenberry's son, Rod Roddenberry, Rob Zombie said, "Everyone has their reasons . . . like the dreams of tomorrow or whatever. But I think it's just a *good show*. Everybody seems *cool*. William Shatner's cool. Leonard Nimoy's cool."

Some of the most popular episodes of *The Original Series* are also the most outrageous. Sure, *Star Trek* can be unintentionally funny (for example, anytime Shatner writhes around, pretending like an alien has taken over his body), but it's really at warp 9 when everybody is in on the joke. For decades, the most popular (again not *best*) episode of *Star Trek: The Original Series* was "The Trouble with Tribbles." Even someone who has never seen an entire episode of *Star Trek* (like my young child) understands what a tribble is and why they're hilarious. Before the cuddly Ewoks, *Star Trek* introduced adorable purring fuzzballs that forever perfected the mash-up of science fiction and slapstick. One furry tribble isn't a big deal, but when you dump a mountain of them on Captain Kirk? That's hilarious. Written by David Gerrold—who, yes, was a frequent guest at the first conventions—"The Trouble with Tribbles" doesn't only excel at physical comedy, it's witty as hell. In the entire run of the show it's hard to find an episode where Kirk gets better one-liners. When the *Enterprise* is diverted from its important work to guard a shipment of space grain, Kirk treats the bureaucrats responsible to a never-ending buffet of jabs and insults. When one official accuses Kirk of "taking this entire matter lightly," Kirk deadpans back, "No, it is you I take lightly."

Kirk, Spock, Uhura, Chekov, Sulu, Bones, and Scotty and the crew are *important* because of what Koenig told me: It wasn't about the stories they told, but the unity the characters represented. But those characters were also *fun*, and each of them had the potential to be a comedy gold mine. In "By Any Other Name," Scotty tricks an alien into a drinking contest to get control of the ship. Chekov is constantly pretending like everything was invented in Russia. Uhura is throwing shade at Spock, Kirk, and everyone else. Bones is weaving incredible analogies—"What am I? A doctor or a moon shuttle conductor?" And there's no one with a drier line delivery than George Takei as Sulu.

Because of pervasive media bias, and the politically groundbreaking nature of *The Original Series,* we've undervalued the raw charm. When *Star Trek* is good, it will make you think, but when *Star Trek* is *great,* it will also make you laugh. The political relevance of *Star Trek* was certainly a huge factor in the early formation of the fandom, but to pretend like it was the only factor strangely undersells the impact of *Trek* on the culture at large.

The ability to be smart and funny simultaneously is the basic definition of cool. President Barack Obama said it in 2014: "Long before being a geek was cool, there was Leonard Nimoy." *Star Trek* fandom didn't happen because Trekkies were serious, although that didn't hurt. It really happened because *Star Trek* is cool.

CHAPTER 5

AN ALMOST TOTALLY NEW ENTERPRISE

The Animated Series and the fusion of Star Trek and NASA

In the summer of 1977, when artist Matt Jefferies was rehired[1] to update the look of the famous starship *Enterprise*, he decided that the "engines could easily be changed," while the basic hull of the *Enterprise* should remain the same. This is why the *Enterprise* had cigar-shaped engines in *The Original Series*, but in *Star Trek: The Motion Picture* and the feature films that followed, the newer engines were boxier, like freight cars adorned with giant blue neon engine grilles. Though not intended by Jefferies, the *Enterprise* engine swap analogously describes nearly every major alteration, paradigm shift, revision, addition, or erasure in the Trek pantheon after 1969. In *The Original Series*, the *Enterprise* had one set of creative engines, but after 1969, the driving forces behind Star Trek

---

1 Jefferies drew and designed the classic *Enterprise* in 1964. Weirdly, it seems like his original idea was for the *Enterprise* to "sit" in the opposite orientation than what we're used to, that is, "upside down." In every single iteration of Star Trek, starships have little crawl spaces called "Jefferies tubes," named in honor of Matt Jefferies.

began to shift. The 1970s set the stage for fiercely competing visions of Trek that wouldn't be fully reconciled until the 1990s. The '70s were a decade where Star Trek changed the course of real-life spaceflight history, but it was also a time when it changed itself, radically and irrevocably.

"NBC actually did *Star Trek* a favor by canceling it," William Shatner recalled in 1994, adding that *Star Trek* "would be remembered fondly as a great show that got screwed by the network, rather than a good show that got worse over time." Shatner's point is well taken, but there's some revisionism in the legend of Trek's rise from the ashes. The common story is that *Star Trek* was canceled and left for dead, and then Trek was gradually rebuilt for almost a decade, until late 1979, when it was reborn as a movie franchise, starting with *Star Trek: The Motion Picture.*

From the perspective of the people making Star Trek, this perception is mostly correct. But in no way does that journey describe what the public experienced. This single dichotomy describes the biggest chasm in nearly all retellings of pop culture phenomena. By the nature of studying a TV series or a film series or rock band, the critic (or documentarian) has to look at what the insiders believed, otherwise we're not doing our job. But sometimes, the point of view of the general public matters more. The 1970s wasn't exactly Star Trek's comeback tour, because for the vast majority of living humans, it was the beginning.

"The myth is that the '70s was a 'dormant' period for Star Trek. It really wasn't," the *Animated Series* writer Howard Weinstein tells me. "At the start of the '70s, all we had were the reruns, and Paramount had to be pleased with those huge syndication ratings." Weinstein was nineteen years old when he sold a spec script to Star Trek called "The Pirates of Orion." In the animated episode that resulted, Kirk fights one of those titular pirates on the surface of an asteroid in order to get a very specific drug that will save Spock's life. It's one of the only times someone has a hand-to-hand brawl in the vacuum of space within Star Trek *without* the aid of a traditional space suit. Instead, Kirk rocks a glowing force field, which emanates from a "life support belt," which is basically just a gold outline around him. It's the sort of comic-book special effect that is exactly the kind of thing a teenage writer would invent. Weinstein's story is, perhaps, the story many of us wish could have happened to us—to submit a story to their favorite TV show and have the TV show say yes. He was the first Trekkie-turned-Trek-writer, but he wasn't the last. "I went to that very first New York City convention in '72 as a college-kid fan—and four years later, I went back in '76 for my first appearance as a professional Star Trek writer after I sold 'The Pirates of Orion' to *The Animated Series*."

In 1972, before Weinstein made that leap, and before *The Animated Series* materialized, a bigger audience, one not yet part of the "fandom" but better known as the *mainstream public*, was just getting introduced to *Star Trek* for the first time. By the end of 1969, because the entire show was running five days a week in syndication, it became the '70s equivalent of a binge-worthy hit. As soon as *Star Trek* was "dead," it was like a sprinting zombie, already coming back to life. As early as 1967, while *The Original Series* was still on the air, Kaiser Broadcasting executive Dick Block made a "handshake" deal with Desilu-Paramount[2] to buy the syndication rights to *Star Trek*, meaning that had the show not gotten the third season, the 55 episodes that made up Seasons 1 and 2 could have

---

2 Desilu Studios was absorbed by Paramount Studios around the end of *Star Trek*'s second season.

still been run on Kaiser-owned stations. One month after "Turn-about Intruder" ended *Star Trek*'s first run on NBC, on July 12, 1969, *Star Trek* reruns began airing on the BBC with a black-and-white version of "Where No Man Has Gone Before" in a time slot previously reserved for *Doctor Who*.[3] As academic Trek scholar Sherilyn Connelly points out, "That [*Star Trek: The Original Series*] was a major hit in syndication has always been baked into the [fan] mythology, but the fact that it happened so fast—and that the wheels had been turning since before the series was canceled—tends to be overlooked."

Because the first "Star Trek Lives!" convention in 1972 put Gene Roddenberry in the same room with one of his old NBC bosses, Oscar Katz, the space dominos were set in motion to relaunch a new version of *Star Trek* only a couple of years after it went off the air. Instead of spending a bunch of money on sets and special effects and guest actors, *Star Trek: The Animated Series* could be made on the cheap. And so, on September 8, 1973—exactly seven years to the day after *The Original Series* had debuted on NBC, *Star Trek* returned as a half-an-hour Saturday morning cartoon with the debut episode "Beyond the Farthest Star."[4] Other than the fact that

---

3 I've never heard of UK fans counting July 12, 1969, as the British birthday of *Star Trek*, but it's a fun idea. If you were a UK sci-fi fan in 1969, *Star Trek* was probably an awesome way to distract you from a huge *Doctor Who* cliffhanger. On June 21, 1969, the BBC aired the last part of "The War Games," in which the second Doctor (Patrick Troughton) was forced to regenerate (turn into a new actor) and was exiled to Earth forever. Unlike most famous "regenerations" on *Doctor Who*, fans had no idea who would play the "new" Doctor until Jon Pertwee fell out of the TARDIS in January 1970 in "The Spearhead from Space," the first *Who* episode in color. So, in between two very different eras of *Doctor Who*, UK fans could have literally watched the entire seventy-nine-episode run of *Star Trek* from July 1969 to January 1970. Imagine getting all of *Star Trek* as a "bonus" while you waited for new *Doctor Who*.

4 "Beyond the Farthest Star" was written by Sam Peeples, the same writer who penned the second *TOS* pilot, "Where No Man Has Gone Before."

it was a cartoon, *Star Trek: The Animated Series* wasn't really marketed differently than *The Original Series*. In fact, it wasn't even called "The Animated Series." Script editor D. C. Fontana remembered that Gene Roddenberry "insisted that this animated series would be *Star Trek*." NBC even co-opted a popular convention t-shirt featuring the *Enterprise* with the phrase "Star Trek Lives!" on the front and "On NBC on Saturday mornings" on the back.

Produced by Filmation, most of the episodes were directed by color-blind animation guru Hal Sutherland,[5] who later went on to produce *He-Man and the Masters of the Universe*. With Dorothy Fontana acting as showrunner and scripts from *TOS* veterans like David Gerrold, Margaret Armen, Stephen Kandel, Marc Daniels, David P. Harmon—and one script from award-winning science fiction writer Larry Niven—the creative pedigree of *The Animated Series* was very similar to *TOS*, but with 22-minute episodes instead of hour-long stories. To this day, many fans consider *The Animated Series* as the fourth season, and therefore chronologically toward the end of the "five-year mission"[6] of the *Enterprise*. This is largely

---

5 Sutherland's color blindness has led to a pervasive myth about the preponderance of pink in *The Animated Series*. The tribbles in *The Animated Series* were bright pink. The uniforms worn by the Klingons had a lot of pink. The uniforms worn by the hostile cat-people called the Kzinti in "The Slaver Weapon" were pink. *The Animated Series* is the pinkest Trek. And because Sutherland was color-blind, and pink looked gray to him, this has often been the explanation for all the pink; that it was an accident. BUT in 2020, *TAS* artist Bob Kline said this wasn't entirely true. Yes, Sutherland was color-blind, and that might have led to more pink. But apparently, colorist Irv Kaplan really loved the color pink. So, the pink on *The Animated Series* wasn't entirely an accident. At least some of that pink was on purpose. Which makes it way better.

6 Chronologically, Kirk's five-year mission of the *Enterprise* is supposed to be from 2265 to 2270. *TOS* and *TAS* occupy 2266–2270. Weirdly, the only classic-era TV episode to take place in 2265 (Kirk's first year as captain) is "Where No Man Has Gone Before." Most of the Trek timeline stuff is retroactive, but if you don't count the animated series, we only ever got three years of that five-year mission. This gets super hilarious when you're supposed to believe that *The Motion Picture* is only supposed to happen a couple years after 2270, even

true, but despite having a bunch of the same writing talent (plus an openness to newcomers like the young Weinstein), *The Animated Series* was different from *The Original Series* in one surprising way: Because it masqueraded as a kids' show, it was more consistent with its ethical messaging than its live-action predecessor. *The Animated Series* has none of the edgy sex-and-violence vibe that, for better or worse, defined the flavor of the classic series. If you truly believe that the intent of *Star Trek* was always about portraying a progressive, egalitarian, peaceful future, *The Animated Series* makes that case fifty percent better than *The Original Series*. While the '60s show would affect an after-school-special vibe, *The Animated Series* leaned into that model even harder. What's quietly groundbreaking is that *The Animated Series* wasn't written *for kids,* it was just a (mostly) clean-cut animated show that kids could watch. Although Mister Rogers buried his dead goldfish in 1970, it was *Star Trek*, in the 1973 animated episode "Yesteryear," that became the first children's show in which a child copes with the death of a pet on-screen. With all respect to Fred Rogers, watching young Spock comfort his giant living teddy bear I-Chaya[7] as the poor thing dies is way more hard-core than a fish dying. "Yesteryear" isn't even about a pet dying, but at the very end, when Spock mentions the trauma, Kirk irately dismisses the death of a pet as trivial, to which Spock replies, "It might matter"—and then looking at the kids in the audience—"to some."

---

though everyone looks ten years older and, relative to their cartoon counterparts, like they've been drinking heavily, too.

7 The fact that Spock had a pet *sehlat*, which resembled "a giant teddy bear with fangs" was described by Spock's mother Amanda in the *TOS* episode "Journey to Babel." Both that episode and "Yesteryear" were written by Dorothy Fontana. We didn't get to see the big furry *sehlat* that Amanda described until "Yesteryear."

The Animated Series was also super well reviewed from the beginning. On September 10, 1973, in his review for the *LA Times*, critic Cecil Smith wrote:

"Don't be put off by the fact it's now a cartoon . . . [*Star Trek*] is fascinating fare, written, produced and executed with all the imaginative skill, the intellectual flair and the literary level that made Gene Roddenberry's famous old science fiction epic the most avidly followed program in TV history, particularly in high I.Q. circles. NBC might do well to consider moving it into prime time at mid-series."

In *The Animated Series*, the action-adventure-fisticuffs component of the *Star Trek* brand softened, which highlighted some of the raw, message-oriented politics. Kirk didn't beat people up as often, and the bulk of the stories reminded viewers that life was sacred and disrespecting nature made you an asshole. Two episodes are *Horton Hears a Who*–esque stories, reminding us that size is relative in the circle of life. "The Terratin Incident" is *Honey I Shrunk the Star Trek Crew*, while "One of Our Planets Is Missing" casts humans as relatively tiny life-forms because a giant planet-eating intelligent space cloud hardly knows we're buzzing around. Even David Gerrold's tribble sequel, "More Tribbles, More Troubles," has a slightly clearer message[8] about ecology, ecosystems, and genetic tampering than its *TOS* progenitor. In *TAS*, there are rarely overtly

---

8 Sort of? The entire tribble thing is pretty muddled when you try to decide how we're supposed to feel about them. In "The Trouble with Tribbles," it's unclear what the original tribbles ecosystem was supposed to be like before Cyrano Jones poached them. In "More Tribbles, More Troubles," the big pink tribbles AND a tribble predator critter called a Glommer are both genetically engineered by Jones and the Klingons. In the 2019 *Short Treks* episode, "The Trouble with Edward," starring H. Jon Benjamin as Larkin, the Dr. Frankenstein of tribble lore, we retroactively learn that the "original" tribbles were *also* genetically manipulated to multiply rapidly; and that these original tribbles, pre-DNA splicing, bred *slowly*. In "Trials and Tribble-ations," Worf basically says the Klingons classify tribbles as "an enemy of the Empire." Bottom line: Trek canon tells us tribbles have been genetically modified

bad guys or monsters. Every villain is misunderstood, every monster a victim of circumstance and prejudice. Sympathy for the space devil returns in "The Magicks of Megas-Tu," when Kirk defends a dude who looks like Satan. Very reminiscent of Roddenberry's early concept for Spock, this guy's name was Lucien, and he was an alien who just *happens* to look like the devil. When he and his buddies visited Earth back in the 1700s, they all got burned at the stake for being witches. But Kirk and Spock aren't having it. Just because other people have labeled this guy a demon, Kirk defends his right to be whoever he wants to be and bases his assessment only on what Lucien has done lately. "I loved Kirk," episode writer Larry Brody recalled. "He defended everybody."

Essentially, "The Magicks of Megas-Tu" is like Mark Twain's *Letters from Earth* (a novel about the devil), twisted to make Satan into an alien, and then, deftly, turned into a Saturday morning kids' show. Remember when everyone thought the 2015 movie *The Witch* was super edgy because it made you kind of want to get down with Satan? Well, I'm not saying "The Magicks of Megas-Tu" is a better piece of art, but because it was an episode of a children's program in which Spock drew a pentagram and did some magic because it was *useful* to do so, it feels way more transgressive than *The Witch* and slightly more punk rock than *Hocus Pocus*. If you count Spock's love of a black cat in the *TOS* episode "Assignment: Earth," and that time Kirk gets accused of being a witch in "All Our Yesterdays," "The Magicks of Megas-Tu" seems to reaffirm that Kirk and Spock are low-key witches. Take that, Agatha Harkness! Turns out it was Kirk and Spock all along!

---

at least *twice* and nearly hunted to extinction at least once. The real trouble with tribbles is clearly that nobody leaves them alone.

Spocky witchcraft aside, unlike the wildly uneven (and border-line schizophrenic) *Original Series, The Animated Series* is a much more consistent and steadier Star Trek product. Except for Spock's childhood time-travel tale "Yesteryear," the highs of *The Animated Series* are never as high as in the classic show, but crucially, the lows are never as low. *The Animated Series* does have some meh episodes, but if you like *Star Trek* already, none are as painfully hard to watch as "Spock's Brain" or "Turnabout Intruder." *The Animated Series* is flawed, but it's rarely terrible. It might have only one home run ("Yesteryear"), but it almost never strikes out, either.

Once, drunk at a bar in Brooklyn, I tried to convince a bartender to keep a repeat episode of *The Animated Series* playing in the background. His argument was that *TAS* was "bad *Star Trek*," and my argument was that even "bad *Star Trek* is better than a good version of anything else." I wasn't right, exactly, partly because I don't think *TAS* was bad *Star Trek*, though relative to the classic show, or *TNG*, I can see why someone would say that. The real crime of *TAS* is that it felt somewhat bland, mostly due to that absence of home runs. "The Magicks of Megas-Tu" isn't better than that episode of *The Sopranos* where Christopher sits on the dog, but I do think the former leaves you with more to think about, and that those thoughts probably push you closer to being a better person. If pop culture stories are brain food, then Trek—even meh Trek—tends to be like vegetables. Even when it's cooked poorly, looks gross, and doesn't taste good, it's still good for you. Star Trek episodes tend to stick out next to episodes of other TV shows in the same way a poem sticks out in the middle of the *New Yorker*. It's just a slightly different art form. Even when it's not brilliant, it's very clearly playing by a totally different set of rules.

The only real critical proof that *The Animated Series* is a little bit better than its reputation is that of all the Star Trek series, it was the only one to win an Emmy for "Best Series." In 1974, *Star Trek: The Animated Series* was awarded "Best Outstanding Children's Program." This is the Emmy that *Sesame Street* has won thirty-three times and *Reading Rainbow* won ten times. *TAS* was also nominated in 1973, which means even though it was only on TV for two years, the show was nominated for an Emmy during its entire run. Does this mean that, had *The Animated Series* continued past 1974, it might have cleaned up yearly as a prestige kids' show? Maybe?

The original cast of *Star Trek*—including William Shatner, Leonard Nimoy, DeForest Kelley, James Doohan, George Takei, Majel Barrett, and Nichelle Nichols—were all in a recording studio together for only *three* of the twenty-two episodes of *The Animated Series*. The rest of the time, they recorded their parts remotely, and mailed the cassette tapes over to Filmation. Walter Koenig's Chekov was conspicuously absent from *TAS* because Roddenberry wanted more far-out aliens on the bridge and replaced the navigator position with a three-armed alien named Arex. Uhura also got a relief communications officer named M'Ress, a cat person, who often purred her lines. Other than a few notable guest stars, any other character on *TAS* who was not one of the main cast members was voiced either by James Doohan, Nichelle Nichols, George Takei, or Majel Barrett. At first, Roddenberry wanted to save money by not even having Takei and Nichols back. His original plan was just to have Doohan do the voice of Sulu *and* Scotty and have Barrett do Uhura. Leonard Nimoy learned of this cheapskate scheme and threatened to quit if Roddenberry didn't at least rehire Takei and Nichols. "I was lost in the shuffle," Walter Koenig tells me of Chekov's omission from *TAS*. "But I did get to write one episode." Koenig's script, "The Infinite Vulcan," featured a giant, twenty-foot-tall clone of Mr. Spock, who is totally left alive on the planet Phylos.[9]

But in 1974, the better-than-nothing return of *Star Trek* to TV was already over. Although *The Animated Series* brought *Trek* back as a weekly TV series, even the insular niche fandom publications of the day—like *The Monster Times*—didn't exactly give it glowing reviews. In a September 1973 issue, columnist Mark Evanier made it clear that there was no way "any animated product could ever satisfy the most zealous 'Trekkies.'" Roddenberry had "mixed" feelings about the series anyway, and due to that fact, combined with poor ratings and a decidedly *meh* reaction from the hard-core fan base, NBC decided not to renew *The Animated Series* after its first season. This resulted in an abbreviated second season of left-over episodes. In what became the series finale episode, "The Counter-Clock Incident," a reverse universe turned the crew back into babies, as though *Trek* itself was getting self-conscious about growing up and growing older.

By 1976, back in the real world, another massive *Trek* fan letter-writing campaign[10] to President Gerald Ford convinced him to

---

9 In 2020, in the episode "Veritas," the animated adult comedy *Star Trek: Lower Decks* made an overt reference to the "giant Spock on Phylos." And then again, in the 2021 Season 2 episode of *Lower Decks*, "Kayshon, His Eyes Open," we see what appears to be the *skeleton* of giant Spock Two, deceased in the twenty-fourth century, during a time that regular Spock was still around.

10 Yep. There's another debate about how many letters were written! Was it 10,000? Two thousand? Again, it doesn't matter. People were writing the president of the United States letters about a *Star Trek* spaceship and he listened to them. Gerald Ford is nobody's favorite president, but the fact that this happened at all is magical.

change the name of the first NASA space shuttle from *Constitution*[11] to *Enterprise*. The president noted he was "partial" to the name "Enterprise" anyway and called Gene Roddenberry with the good news. At least one report from the magazine *Starlog* noted that, contrary to popular myth, Roddenberry initially opposed this name-changing campaign because he had hoped the first NASA space shuttle would not be named for a "military ship." In January 1977, *Starlog* also reported that "the *Enterprise* will probably make its first space flight sometime in 1983." Spoiler alert: It didn't. Although OV-101 (orbiter vehicle *Enterprise*) was intended to be given proper shuttle engines later in its life, NASA redesigned the space shuttle's heat shield substantially enough that it suddenly made more sense to build a whole new shuttle rather than refit *Enterprise*, and *Enterprise* never made a space mission.

Still, for the entire original series cast (plus Roddenberry, minus Shatner), attending the unveiling of the Space Shuttle *Enterprise* was a once-in-a-lifetime moment. "The roll-out of Orbiter 101 [the *Enterprise*] remains my keenest *Star Trek*–aligned memory," Walter Koenig wrote in 1980. None of the assembled cast had any idea that the US Air Force Band was going to play the Alexander Courage *Star Trek* theme as the space shuttle was presented. But then, "The spacecraft was approaching to the theme music of *Star Trek*," Koenig remembered. "I felt close to tears and wasn't the least embarrassed by it."

In various montages of early spaceflight featuring the rollout of the *Enterprise*, you'll see snippets of this footage; specifically in the opening credits of both *Star Trek: Enterprise* (2001–2005) and

---

11 For what it's worth, the *TOS* USS *Enterprise* was a "Constitution-class starship," and one of the possible names for the *Enterprise* that Roddenberry had before he settled on *Enterprise* was *Constitution*.

the contemporary (2018–2021) Netflix reboot of *Lost in Space*. At the time, in 1976, Paramount Pictures was so pumped by the free publicity that they used the existence of the Space Shuttle *Enterprise* to promote the upcoming Trek feature film with print ads in *Time* saying:

WELCOME ABOARD...
SPACE SHUTTLE ENTERPRISE

Paramount Pictures and the thousands of loyal fans of Star Trek are happy that the United States of America's new space shuttle has been named after Star Trek's starship, The Enterprise. (It's nice to know that sometimes science fiction becomes science fact.) Starship Enterprise will be joining the Space Shuttle Enterprise in its space travels very soon. Early next year, Paramount Pictures begins filming an extraordinary motion picture adventure—STAR TREK. Now we can look forward to two great space adventures.

Neither of these "two great space adventures" happened. The Space Shuttle *Enterprise* never flew in space, and the specific film that Paramount was touting in 1976 was not the same film that was eventually released in 1979. But we'll get to that in a second. Instead, let's linger on the *image* of a space shuttle named *Enterprise*, and how for five decades that single event has always been cited as the most obvious connection between actual spaceflight and *Star Trek*. But, obviously, it was far from the only one.

In 2012, along with a handful of comrades who worked for a prominent science fiction book publisher, I climbed a ladder that led to the roof of the Flatiron Building. The Flatiron is the oldest "skyscraper" in Manhattan, and while working in a small office on the very top floor, writing about science fiction, it cozily felt like the bubble of a steampunk alternate reality. From the prow of the Flatiron's roof, it feels like you're on the deck of an oceangoing ship, and the skyline of Manhattan above 23rd Street is a crowded and rocky ocean. When you turn to face downtown Manhattan, the view is slightly less crowded, and because in 2012 One World Trade Center was still under construction, this view of the city had an unfinished feeling, full of scaffolding and cranes, reminiscent of orbital dry dock for the USS *Enterprise* in *Star Trek: The Motion Picture*, or the grounded starship construction yard Chris Pine drives his motorcycle to in the 2009 Trek movie.

We were gathered on the roof to witness a historic flyby. The shuttle *Enterprise* was being flown on a special 747 from Washington, DC, to a new permanent home at the Intrepid Sea, Air & Space Museum. And, from the roof of the Flatiron, we were going to get an amazing first look at the *Enterprise* flying in, coming to its new home in New York City. All of the retired shuttles were going to different museums around the country, and of course NYC was going to get the *Enterprise*. Like New York itself, the Space Shuttle *Enterprise* is both very real and kind of fake at the same time. There's the illusion and glamour of New York—very intoxicating when you're taking in the view from the Flatiron roof—and then there's the cold reality of New York: expensive, unwieldy, undying, diverse, and complicated—kind of like the history of Star Trek. Watching a real spaceship that didn't fly in space and that was named after a fictional spaceship piggyback on an airplane, and then navigate the NYC skyline, is literally the most New York thing I've ever experienced. These streets will make you feel brand-new. Star Trek will inspire you.

What I didn't know at the time was that the Star Trek impact on NASA was much more tangible than a nonfunctioning space shuttle with a familiar name. The fact that a real-life space shuttle was given its name because of Trekkies is the most visible example of Star Trek's impact on spaceflight history. It's also superficial. The more profound Star Trek–NASA connection isn't the *Enterprise* naming thing at all. Just like the beauty of New York looks amazing from up high, the symbolism of the Space Shuttle *Enterprise* has, up until very recently, eclipsed the much more meaningful impact Star Trek had on the space program. Because after that rollout of Orbiter 101, Nichelle Nichols decided that just getting a space shuttle with the name "Enterprise" wasn't enough. If there was going to be a *real Enterprise,* ushering in a new fleet of spaceships, Nichols wanted to make damn sure the people on those ships represented all of humanity.

Throughout the 1970s, one of Gene Roddenberry's closest allies at NASA was Dr. Jesco von Puttkamer. Like the infamous German-American rocket scientist Wernher von Braun, Puttkamer emigrated to the US from Germany with the hopes that his aerospace skills would be put to better use at NASA. Starting in 1962, Puttkamer was working on the Apollo program, and by the '70s was, in many ways, one of the very public faces of NASA. He was also a huge Trekkie, and was a frequent fixture at Star Trek conventions and crossover events where NASA would hitch its wagon to Trek. Eventually, Puttkamer would become the science consultant on *Star*

Trek: The Motion Picture, in which he helped devise a new warp drive effect and also refined the concept of the *Enterprise* going through a wormhole, leading to one of the trippiest slow-motion scenes in all of science fiction. Throughout the decade, the *Trek* cast became friendly enough with Puttkamer that DeForest Kelley nicknamed him "Jessie," and Nichelle Nichols attended a ton of his lectures. But, as inspired as Nichols was by all the advances made by NASA, including the game-changing space shuttle program, she was horrified that the entire astronaut corps was still very much white and exclusively male.

"There was no one in the astronaut corps who looked anything like me," Nichols wrote in 1994. "There were no women. No Blacks, no Asians, no Latinos." And so, through her connection to Puttkamer, Nichols decided to do something about it. If the United States was really going to send representatives into space, Nichols decided the diversity presented in *Star Trek* needed to start immediately. In 1977, Nichols snagged a seat on the board of directors of the National Space Institute, at which point she started to publicly shame NASA and the government for their utter failure to attract astronaut candidates who were either female or non-white. In January 1977, she addressed a council meeting in Washington, DC, where she asserted that by having a history of all-white, all-male astronauts, NASA was sending a message to women and non-white communities that they shouldn't apply.

John Yardley, the head of NASA's Office for Manned Spaceflight, took her point seriously. Women and non-whites needed to be actively recruited by someone who they could trust. If the space shuttle program was going to represent America, Nichols believed that if she *personally* was part of the recruitment drives, things would change. And, after agreeing to team up with NASA to help with recruitment, Nichols also made it clear how high the stakes were, saying: "If I put my name and my reputation on the line for NASA, and I find qualified women and minority people to apply, and a year from now I still see a lily-white, all-male astronaut corps, I will personally file a class action lawsuit against NASA."

For five months in early 1977 Nichelle Nichols toured the country, spreading the message that had never been spread: NASA wants qualified Black and female astronauts to apply NOW. She also underwent astronaut training, proving that Nichelle Nichols, not Lieutenant Uhura, could indeed fly a real spaceship. In simulators, Nichols was able to successfully land the space shuttle. She never had reason to do this in real life, but much like the Space Shuttle *Enterprise* never went to space, she could have, in theory. In some kind of *Armageddon*-style emergency, Nichelle Nichols *could* have flown a space shuttle. "I wanted to do the training for real," she said.

Nichols's efforts were wildly successful. "When Nichelle started her campaign, NASA had very few Black or female applicants," documentarian Todd Thompson tells me. "I'm not saying zero. But Sally Ride and Ron McNair; yes, they were there as a direct result of her campaign with NASA." Thompson is the director of the 2020 documentary *Woman in Motion*, which takes its name from a company called Women in Motion, founded by Nichelle Nichols in 1975 to help support working women through financial aid and educational assistance.

In 2021, the wide release of Thompson's documentary created shock waves. Although Nichols's involvement in NASA was a historical fact, for some reason Trekkie pundits and historians have tended to glaze over it. The photographs of the *TOS* cast with the Space Shuttle *Enterprise* have been in every Star Trek coffee table book and documentary for decades. But, the fact that Sally Ride and Ron McNair—and the first Black man in space, Guion Stewart Bluford Jr.—might not have even been in NASA if it weren't for Nichelle Nichols, has never really been given its due. Nichols's leaving acting behind in the '70s to pursue social change through her influence with the space program is singular. There is no other example of a celebrity so perfectly aligning the thing they are famous for with a real-world application. Nichols *successfully* recruiting women and people of color into the space program would be like if Jerry Seinfeld gave up comedy and became a social activist, intent on reforming the customer service practices of fancy soup places in New York. It's so on the nose that it can't even be fictionalized. It sounds made-up, which is why it's so revolutionary.

"Could it have happened without her?" Thompson asks me over the phone in 2021. "Well, the only way I can answer that question is that those applicants reached out for a reason. If we'd already had the diverse Trek universe up there in space, there probably wouldn't have been a need for Nichelle to, you know, go on a rampage and rally NASA."

The legacy of Star Trek's progressive influence on NASA continued well beyond the '70s and '80s. On September 12, 1992, Dr. Mae Jemison became the first Black woman in space. She was among the first round of new NASA recruits in 1987, following the *Challenger* disaster, which claimed the lives of many of Nichelle Nichols's recruits, including Ron McNair. Upon joining NASA, one of the influences Jemison cited was Nichelle Nichols and Star Trek specifically. In 1993, Jemison appeared in a *Next Generation* episode called "Second Chances," bridging the gap between science fiction and real life. Up until that point, NASA folks like Puttkamer were only really a part of Trek behind the scenes. Jemison's historic shuttle flight in 1992—during the heyday of *The Next Generation,* and the same year she appeared on the show—brought the Trek-NASA connection full circle.

The long overdue fight for representation in all areas of American culture wasn't exclusively won because of Nichelle Nichols and Star Trek. But, as Thompson points out, it's hard to imagine history unfolding the way it did without her intercession in early 1977. Ron McNair, Sally Ride, Guion Stewart Bluford Jr., and Mae Jemison were out there in the world, of course. They could have joined NASA at some later time, through a different recruitment drive. But here in this universe, in this timeline, that's how it happened.

In 2020, NASA announced its intention to put a woman on the moon by 2024, as part of the Artemis program. Right alongside this proposal NASA also outlined the Artemis Accords, an extension of the Outer Space Treaty of 1967. The basic tenets of the Artemis Accords are strikingly similar to the peaceful rules of the United Federation of Planets in Star Trek. Both make it clear that you can't make war in space, and that the exploration of space and the pursuits of peace are essentially the same thing. The text for the Federation charter was based, in part, on the charter of the United Nations. But, in June 2020, NASA specifically said in a press release that "via the Artemis Accords, we hope that the future will look a lot more like 'Star Trek,' and a lot less like 'Star Wars' by getting ahead of these issues."

At that time, I reached out to NASA to see if they were pulling our leg. Was the mention of Star Trek just a clever PR thing? Or is the Trekkie wisdom of peace and cooperation in space actually baked into the core of NASA?

"Star Trek has always been an inspiration for many of us in the space field," NASA acting associate administrator for the Office of

International and Interagency Relations Mike Gold told me. "It's also fair to say that the principles described in the Artemis Accords were developed to create the peaceful future filled with awe, wonder, and adventure that is depicted in Star Trek. Star Trek is the dream that the Artemis Program and the Artemis Accords can transform into reality."

Mike Gold stopped short of promising that NASA would seriously consider naming a new spacecraft *Enterprise* before the end of 2029. And if you think about it, it's totally shocking that Blue Origin didn't name the capsule that took William Shatner into space *Enterprise*. Then again, all our existing spacecraft here on Earth don't quite have the long-term space probe abilities of the *Enterprise*. Maybe when you can comfortably wear a velour shirt without a space helmet while smoothly riding into orbit, the various space agencies of the world will consider the name *Enterprise* for a real spacecraft. It's as though in holding off in naming another spaceship *Enterprise*, the people of Earth feel, somehow, we haven't quite earned it yet.

CHAPTER 6

KILLING SPOCK

The Motion Picture, The Wrath of Khan, and the mainstreaming of Trek

While on the set of *Star Trek: The Motion Picture* in 1978, Walter Koenig listened intently as Nichelle Nichols regaled him with her whirlwind adventure of recruitment for NASA. Writing in his 1980 memoir *Chekov's Enterprise*, Koenig said he was "deeply impressed by Nichols," and worried that his character's influence on history wouldn't be quite as aspirational. While Nichelle Nichols's actions with NASA might send some dominos falling that could eventually result in "the first person on Saturn," Koenig worried that misguided fans of Mr. Chekov would write him letters claiming: "Because of you, I won't drink anything but vodka."[1]

Whether or not anyone really started drinking vodka because of Mr. Chekov, a lot of people were drinking heavily, or being driven to drink, in the years and months leading up to the release

---

1 In the 2016 film *Star Trek Beyond*, Kirk (Chris Pine) and Bones (Karl Urban) raid Chekov's (Anton Yelchin) locker and steal his booze. They are both shocked to discover scotch, assuming Chekov was more "of a vodka guy." It's a good joke.

of *Star Trek: The Motion Picture*. In 1979, associate producer on *The Motion Picture* Jon Povill went to see the final film with Gene Roddenberry and right afterward, he said, "We all got drunk." To be clear, Povill getting drunk after watching *The Motion Picture* wasn't a celebratory kind of drunk. This was a drinking-away-the-pain kind of drunk. Because it was released on December 7, 1979, calling *The Motion Picture* a '70s movie is technically correct; it was made in the '70s, and those tracksuit Starfleet uniforms definitely date the film. But the majority of *The Motion Picture*'s theatrical run happened in the early months of the '80s, a decade that was destined to change Star Trek more than any other. If '60s Trek was a groovy party you had to kind of know about to know about, and '70s Trek was like a coked-up night at the discotheque, the '80s is where Star Trek truly grew up and moved out of its parents' house. And by parents, I mean specifically Gene Roddenberry's influence. The story of Star Trek growing up in the '80s and finding greater acceptance in the mass culture is specifically connected with the franchise distancing itself from Roddenberry.

As a brand, as an idea, and as an artistic medium for unique pop culture stories, the '80s was the do-or-die moment for Trek. And with the making and release of *The Motion Picture*, it almost died. In Simon Pegg and Jessica Stevenson's excellent comedy series *Spaced*, several characters employ the phrase "skip to the end" to prevent someone from continuing with a long and boring story.[2] The making of *Star Trek: The Motion Picture* is the sole subject of at

---

2 Devoted Simon Pegg fans will also remember that in *Spaced* Pegg's character Tim says, "I mean, it's a fact, sure as day follows night, sure as eggs is eggs, sure as every odd-numbered Star Trek movie is shit." *The Motion Picture*—an "odd-numbered" Trek film—was the start of this curse/superstition. Pegg would later go on to play Scotty in the 2009 film *Star Trek*, technically the *eleventh* Trek film at that time, making it an odd-numbered entry. Pegg also cowrote *Star Trek Beyond* in 2016—the thirteenth Trek film.

least four traditional books and one coffee table book[3]; but I'm gonna skip to the end and spoil the one consistent piece of information you will glean from everything experts will tell you about *The Motion Picture*: It was not a fun movie for anybody to make, and most everyone agrees that fact shows in the final product. It's the *Let It Be* of Star Trek movies, and nearly broke up the franchise forever.

The Motion Picture is a film that was poorly reviewed and failed to connect with the fan base. And there are good reasons for that. The actors all hated the script, and even the writers who worked on it—Harold Livingston and Alan Dean Foster to name two—found the experience of writing and rewriting painful. In 2017, Alan Dean Foster (who has story credit on *TMP*) told me: "The reason you don't see very nice things written about Gene Roddenberry is because he had a tendency to take credit for other people's writing . . . I worked with both Gene Roddenberry and George Lucas . . . one of them was the most professional and genuine person I ever met in Hollywood. The other was Gene Roddenberry."

That said, the high cost and chaos of making *The Motion Picture* was not entirely Gene Roddenberry's fault. Here's the quick timeline for why *The Motion Picture* spiraled out of control, at least on the money side.

---

3 These books include: *The First Star Trek Movie* (2019), an academic deep dive by Sherilyn Connelly; *Return to Tomorrow* (2014), a super-detailed oral history by Preston Neal Jones; *The Making of Star Trek: The Motion Picture*, by Susan Sackett and Gene Roddenberry (1980); *Chekov's Enterprise* (1980), a journal/memoir written by Walter Koenig on the set of the film; and *Star Trek: The Motion Picture: Inside the Art and Visual Effects* (2020), by Jeff Bond and Gene Kozicki. There are probably more. All of these are good books, but if you want to read something that feels like Larry David on the set of a Star Trek movie, read *Chekov's Enterprise*.

1973: Concurrent with the run of *The Animated Series*, Roddenberry met with Herb Solow about a Star Trek feature film with the working title "A Question of Cannibalism." The story was about the *Enterprise* encountering a race of intelligent aliens being raised and slaughtered like cattle.[4] This idea did not get picked up, and Solow and Roddenberry quarreled over how much Roddenberry should be paid. They never spoke again, and the project quietly died.

1975: Paramount green-lights a Star Trek movie. Roddenberry gives them a script called "The God Thing" (really!!). It is a thing about God. Kirk fights a fake Jesus at some point. Everyone hates it.

Also 1975: Paramount hires director Philip Kaufman and British screenwriters Allan Scott and Chris Bryant. Kaufman would eventually be famous for movies like *The Right Stuff* (1983) and *Quills* (2000), not to mention the 1978 remake of *Invasion of the Body Snatchers*, starring none other than Leonard Nimoy. But in 1975, his biggest movie was a western, *The Great Northfield Minnesota Raid*. Screenwriters Scott and Bryant come up with "Star Trek: Planet of the Titans," in which, via time travel, the crew become the Titans of ancient mythology and Captain Kirk invents fire. Everyone hates it,[5] but not right away.

---

4 Interestingly, forty-four years later, the character of Saru (Doug Jones) on *Star Trek: Discovery*, comes from a species called Kelpiens, who, when first introduced, *are kept as cattle* by another alien race called the Ba'ul.

5 The aesthetic legacy of "Planet of the Titans" can be found in Ralph McQuarrie and Ken Adams's designs for a new Starship *Enterprise*. Because the script for "Planet of the Titans" would have seen the *Enterprise* get some far-future upgrades, the design of the ship looked pretty different, notably sporting a big old triangle section in the middle. This design is very

1976: Paramount runs that ad about the real *Enterprise* and the new feature film. They're still thinking about "Planet of the Titans."

1977: "Planet of the Titans" is over. But now, Paramount is set to launch their own TV network and the first show on the network will be a new Star Trek TV series, which is generally known as "Star Trek: Phase II." Several scripts are written, including a pilot by Alan Dean Foster called "In Thy Image." New characters are created, and entirely new sets are built for a revamped *Enterprise*. Leonard Nimoy decides not to return. A full Vulcan named Xon (David Gautreaux) is created to replace Spock.[6]

Also 1977: *Star Wars* and *Close Encounters of the Third Kind* slay at the box office. Paramount decides an expensive TV series is a bad call, and everything should just be thrown into developing a Star Trek feature film. Xon is out. Paramount is desperate to get Nimoy back as Spock.

The total cost of all these projects, plus the cost of *The Motion Picture* itself, was all rolled together to the tune of $44 million. To

---

similar to the USS *Discovery* from *Star Trek: Discovery*, and the idea of a ship getting tons of upgrades in the far future eventually did happen in 2020, during *Discovery*'s third season. Back in 2016, *Discovery* co-creator Bryan Fuller acknowledged the obvious design similarity between the Starship *Discovery* and the Ralph McQuarrie concept art for this *Enterprise*. McQuarrie is much more famous to Star Wars fans as the concept artist who designed *everything* in the galaxy far, far away. His *Enterprise* redesign (which lives on as the USS *Discovery*) is fly as hell.

6 David Gautreaux later had a very small part in *The Motion Picture*, as a Starfleet officer named Commander Branch. The non-canonicity of Xon was referenced in the comedy series *Lower Decks* when Mariner said she considered Boimler's role "more of a Xon"; perhaps the most inside-baseball Star Trek joke of all time.

put this in perspective, the original *Star Wars* was made for $11 million. Even though *The Motion Picture* became a huge box office hit ($139 million) the cost of making the movie made Paramount executives see red.

In an attempt to control the messaging and make a little extra money on the side, Gene Roddenberry also published a novelization of *The Motion Picture*, written by him, essentially adapting a screenplay by Harold Livingston into a short novella. This is the wildest piece of any Star Trek prose you'll ever encounter, far stranger than any fan fiction, partly because Roddenberry writes about Kirk's semi-erections *several* times, and in one scene late in the book, Spock hits up a part of the *Enterprise* where crew members apparently go to bone each other in like an outer-space swingers' club. Because of its misplaced free-love horndog style, the book also feels slightly closer to the tone of *The Original Series* insofar as it's a little bit trashy.

Smartly, Roddenberry also creates a kind of Watson-Holmes relationship between himself and Captain Kirk: the novel begins with an introduction by Kirk, explaining why he wanted this specific story written down as an old-fashioned book. Then, there's an introduction from Roddenberry, but still written from this Watsonian perspective, that in the Star Trek universe, "he" was one of the people who chronicled the various adventures of the *Enterprise* for mass consumption in the twenty-third century. To Roddenberry's credit, this was clever. With this strange nested narrative framing of his novel *Star Trek: The Motion Picture*, Roddenberry suggested a deeper and truer canon of Star Trek beneath the versions we've seen. This point-of-view shift, and the allusion to in-universe twenty-third-century dramatizations (hologram shows? Telepathic TV?) of the *Enterprise* gestures at the idea that within the world of Star Trek, there is some media version *of* Star Trek,[7] presumably being consumed by civilians, or even other members of Starfleet. According to Roddenberry, people in Star Trek, apparently, watch Star Trek.

———————

In the final version of the film, we meet a giant machine intelligence called V'ger, which is an immense space cloud of pure energy and mind; kind of like if God didn't know it was God. It is both a living spaceship and an appropriated NASA space probe, the fictional *Voyager 6*. For half the movie, V'ger is also *presented* in the form of actress Persis Khambatta, who has taken the form of Ilia, a nice bald woman that V'ger killed. Like V'ger, *The Motion Picture* had an identity crisis. If you watch the original theatrical trailers for the film, you can actually see what the studio was going for: *2001: A Space Odyssey* prestige. Narrated by Orson Welles (who had *nothing* to do with the movie!) the trailer for *The Motion Picture* feels serious and grim, as though this version of Star Trek has more in common with *Solaris*[8] than Star Wars. It's a half-assed attempt to be a "serious" science fiction film that somehow disappointed hard-core science

———————

7 In 2020, *Lower Decks* showrunner Mike McMahan told me that "people on Star Trek watch Star Trek." This concept is explored in various ways on that series, indicating that throughout the Federation, the exploits of more famous Starfleet officers are translated into other media, but mostly holographic simulations.

8 Few have compared *Star Trek: The Motion Picture* to *Solaris* (either the wonderful Tarkovsky film or the novel by Stanislaw Lem), which is really weird because the plots, tones, and visual aesthetics have superficial similarities. Both deal with a giant alien consciousness that is hard to talk to. On top of that, the alien consciousness conjures a simulacrum of a main character's dead lover in both stories. Had Ilia committed suicide off camera before the movie began, it would have basically been the same thing. The fact that I'm comparing *The Motion Picture* to *Solaris* is a compliment, but it's also kind of like comparing a slice of pizza to lasagna. Lasagna is good, but if I'm comparing your pizza to it, it means you failed to make a convincing pizza.

fiction people and also left Star Trek fans cold. Remember how fun and kitschy *The Original Series* was? *The Motion Picture* had never heard of a tribble.

The saving grace is easily Jerry Goldsmith's wonderful score. In addition to having the dubious distinction of being the first motion picture adapted from a TV series, *The Motion Picture* was one of the last major features to have an overture play before the main credits. In several screenings, as you headed to your seats, "Ilia's Theme" played, and then, on an all-black screen, with white text, *The Motion Picture* began with that now familiar bah-bup-bup-bah-bup-bup-bah. This new main theme—a total departure from the quirky TV theme—was so good that Roddenberry reused it just eight years later, as the opening music for *Star Trek: The Next Generation*. For aging millennials like me, this means many '90s Trek fans encountered the music the other way around: When I saw *The Motion Picture* on VHS in the '90s, it seemed like it was ripping off the theme music from *The Next Generation*. This is both factually incorrect and spiritually right on the money. *The Motion Picture* feels like a rip-off of all of Star Trek, possibly because the essential plot—a space probe merging with an alien consciousness and then going on a murder spree—had already been done in a tighter, more interesting sixty-minute version in *The Original Series* called "The Changeling."[9] Spock even mind-melds with the alien/robot probe in both stories!

There's a joke Paul McCartney has made over the years that his

---

9 "The Changeling" was written by John Meredyth Lucas. In fairness, the basic story for *The Motion Picture* came from the Alan Dean Foster treatment for a pilot episode called "In Thy Image." Foster later admitted he wasn't aware of the similarities to "The Changeling," because he'd never seen it. But Gene Roddenberry, who helped adapt "In Thy Image" to *The Motion Picture*, certainly had seen "The Changeling" more than a couple times.

father told him to change the lyrics "Yeah Yeah Yeah" in "She Loves You" to "Yes Yes Yes." *Star Trek: The Motion Picture* is like if Paul McCartney had done that. There are a few light moments ("Will you PLEASE sit down!"), but the movie is stodgy and slow, imitating the glacial pace of *2001: A Space Odyssey*. Director Robert Wise is the same guy who did *The Day the Earth Stood Still* and *The Sound of Music*, so his work on *Star Trek: The Motion Picture* looks freaking beautiful. For the first several scenes of the film there's almost no (human) dialogue. Goldsmith's music carries the movie so much, you kind of get disappointed when humans (and Klingons) start talking. If you were to watch *Star Trek: The Motion Picture* with ONLY the score, it would probably be just as good. This is both a backhanded compliment and a huge problem for something that's not supposed to be a silent movie.

In his 1979 review of *The Motion Picture*, Roger Ebert gave it three stars and noted what he felt the essential flaw in the film was: The *Star Trek* characters didn't really work with this kind of "big" sci-fi story. "There are ways in which our familiarity with the series works against the effectiveness of this movie. On the one hand we have incomprehensible alien forces and a plot that reaches out to the edge of the galaxy. On the other hand, confronting these vast forces, we have television pop heroes. It's great to enjoy the in-jokes involving the relationships of the *Enterprise* crew members and it's great that Trekkies can pick up references meant for them, but the extreme familiarity of the *Star Trek* characters somehow tends to break the illusion in the big scenes involving the alien ship."

Ebert was right, and oddly more prophetic than he could have known. For classic *Star Trek* to survive in cinema, it needed to move *away* from prestige art house sci-fi and move *toward* the characters. It needed to feel like *Star Trek*, but more so. Ebert wasn't suggesting this, exactly, and in fact, his review sort of indicates the opposite: that maybe Star Trek would be better off with new characters lacking the baggage. That would happen, of course, but Ebert's offhand observation did predict a cycle that Star Trek narratives tend to be locked into to this day: The stories either go really hard on nostalgia for the characters, or an entirely new set of characters is introduced to create breathing room for new ideas. In the film that followed, *The Wrath of Khan*, the movie is ONLY about the characters, doubling down on the "familiarity" everybody feels with them, but this time, taking them in a new direction. As much as *The Motion Picture* tried to play with Kirk's angst and Spock's journey of self-discovery, the movie ended up back at the status quo, having killed off the only two new characters—Stephen Collins's Commander Decker and Ilia—who might have had the chance to grow and change.

From 1975 to 1977, the zigs and zags the first Trek film took are dizzying. For a certain kind of fan, this creates an endless hall of mirrors leading to myriad alternate dimensions of pop culture. If you've got one friend who goes on and on about *Jodorowsky's Dune* or people who are really into the minutiae of the Beach Boys' unfinished *Smile* album, then let me tell you, you've only scratched the surface of a certain corner of Trek fandom's obsession with the creation of *The Motion Picture*. I'm not knocking this obsession. I'm just noting it exists. I am also not one of those people. To me, the long and winding road called *The Motion Picture* had one historical end point: It resulted in Paramount freezing out Gene Roddenberry from having influence on the sequel. On some level, Roddenberry might have been a scapegoat; it wasn't his fault that Paramount wanted to turn the movie project into a TV show and then back to a movie. That wasted time and money, for sure. But had Gene Roddenberry stayed in control of Star Trek, the film franchise could never have become mainstream. By the mid-1970s, in the mind of Gene Roddenberry, the notion of what Star Trek *should be*, versus what it *could be*, from a commercial point of view, were incongruous. Whereas *The Original Series* benefited from a diversity of various writing talents, *Star Trek: The Motion Picture* was hobbled by Roddenberry hammering the concepts of a few other writers into a more rigid and decidedly less *fun* version of Star Trek.

"The world is filled with examples of what I call the Moses-Joshua theory," *Star Trek II: The Wrath of Khan* director Nicholas Meyer tells me over the phone. "You got people who are charismatic creators. Who, out of nothing, manage to conjure universes into being where none existed before. Having done this, they strangely prove unequal to the secondary tasks of *managing* what they've brought into being. And Moses is the classic example. Moses creates the Hebrews, and *then*, when they finally get to the River Jordan, God taps Moses on the shoulder and says, 'I'm giving you this gold watch, but you're not getting to cross the river. Joshua will take it from here.' And Joshua is not a charismatic character. He's a general. He's a closer. He's a can-do man. It's a different kind of thing. It may be that Roddenberry falls into this kind of messianic profile of somebody who manages—God knows how—to bring this *Star Trek* thing to life. And for a while, all the wandering-in-the-desert years—he and Gene Coon or whatever—but *then*, when it came time to do the first feature [*The Motion Picture*], things went a bit wobbly. And I don't criticize the first feature. But maybe it took a flatfoot like me to follow in the wake of all that to say, 'hang on a second, this needs some serious rethinking.'"

The Star Trek film series needed new writers, producers, and directors. It needed outsiders to solve the problem Ebert noticed so expertly: How do you make a movie about these people, but make the movie for *more* than just a Star Trek audience? The answer was to kill the one character who was the definition of Star Trek. To save Star Trek, Spock had to die.

Spock's death in *The Wrath of Khan* is the ultimate paradox within the history of Star Trek's evolution. If the movie had not been a massive *crossover* hit, Star Trek would have died in 1982. Killing Spock may have been the only way to keep the franchise alive, and that's because the movie needed to create stakes for someone who didn't really understand who Spock was.

"Our picture wasn't just a Star Trek movie," *Wrath* producer Bob Sallin tells me over the phone. "It was just a good movie. The first film was so focused on the sci-fi elements. But I'll tell you, you can't cry over a machine." If the failure of *The Motion Picture* was a lack of emotion, then *The Wrath of Khan*'s agenda was to get you to cry. A lot. Nobody shed a tear for the machine intelligence of V'ger, but everybody was going to lose their minds when Spock died.

Early in the production process of *Star Trek II*, as the death of Spock became the thrust of the film, Bob Sallin came home to a message on his answering machine. The voice warbled, but its meaning was clear: "If you kill Spock, we'll kill you." This is certainly the most specific and horrifying voice mail a person could ever receive, especially if they are one of four people directly responsible for killing Spock.

Today, the idea that someone could be moved to make such a call feels ludicrous because Spock's death and eventual rebirth are, in some ways, his defining traits. If you've never seen *The Wrath of Khan*, Spock dying at the end, while rasping, "I have been and always shall be . . . your friend . . . Live long and prosper," is likely one of two things you know about this movie. The other thing is, of course, the part where Kirk screams "KHAAAAAN!" at the top of his lungs like a maniac.

I'd love to tell you that you need to know more about *The Wrath of Khan* than these two things, but Spock's death and people yelling are the correct microcosms. If these are the only two things you know (or remember) about *The Wrath*, you have correctly understood it. That said, even among hard-core Trek fans, the lasting influence of its success is strangely underestimated. Even if you do somehow dislike *The Wrath*, it's hard to debate the most important thing about it: Killing Spock allowed Trek to live. But the weirdest thing about Spock's death is that everyone knew about it for a year before the movie came out.

From late 1981 to early 1982, Leonard Nimoy, director Nicholas Meyer, and producer Harve Bennett received handwritten letters, typed letters, and even in-person harassment. The message was clear: Killing Spock was going to cause them some serious problems. But, along with Sallin and the rest of the cast, they all collectively believed that killing Spock was an "artistic" decision.

In his second memoir, *I Am Spock*, Nimoy stops short of saying he had the death of Spock written into his contract, but every version of the story (including Nimoy's) makes it plain he was excited about doing the film because he was promised "a great death scene." Before the cameras started rolling on *The Wrath*, this death was intended to be permanent, which meant future *Treks* would have boldly gone on without Spock. Then, by the time the movie wrapped, Nimoy and Bennett had a change of heart, and were already hatching a plan to bring him back to life.

In the year before the film came out, the idea of Spock's resurrection was not a foregone conclusion. As far as the angry fans knew, Spock's death meant, in effect, Star Trek was about to go out with a whimper. On September 24, 1981, a fan named Laura Leach—the spokesperson for "The Concerned Supporters of Star Trek"—published an ad in *Hollywood Reporter* titled "Why Is Paramount Deliberately Jeopardizing 28 Million in Revenues?" In it, she referred to a 22-page (self-conducted) survey called "Analyses of the Impact of Killing Spock in the New Star Trek Movie," which concluded, among other things, that fans would boycott the film, and, more specifically, even if they did see it, that they'd refuse to ever see it again because "the reaction to the idea of killing Spock was overwhelmingly negative." This fuzzy math was probably best debunked by Leonard Nimoy himself: "It's like standing outside a record store and a person goes in to buy an album they haven't heard yet, and you say, 'How many times are you going to listen to that?' Of course, they don't know until they hear it."

Nimoy's album analogy is fun, but there's a big difference between knowing about music before it's out and hearing about a movie or TV show before it's released. If you're given a plot detail about a piece of narrative, you possess information that *could* facilitate outrage. But this isn't true in other media: If someone just tells you Thom Yorke is using a theremin on his next album, it's kind of meaningless until you hear it. With Star Trek, even talking about the colors of the uniforms in a new series or films matters because, on some level, that's a story decision. Narrative art can (bizarrely) be discussed before it's seen or read, and anyone who has pretended to have seen a movie they haven't really seen knows why this is true. In other words, you can't have a "spoiler" for an album, or, if you could, it wouldn't "ruin" the album. The argument against spoilers is that knowing something about the plot—out of context— ruins the surprise inherent in the experience of narrative fiction.

This is debatable, and there are at least three studies I'm aware of that have tried to prove that spoilers *don't* spoil people's enjoyment of fiction, but that's not really what I'm talking about. Because we can all agree that the only thing spoilers actually *do* (regardless of how you feel about them) is that they remove context.

Out of context, the death of Spock—in advance of its "happening"—was a fairly big scoop. Star Trek was planning on killing Spock in *Star Trek II* and suddenly it was the talk of the town. The *Hollywood Reporter* ad was picked up by the *New York Post* and the *Wall Street Journal*, and boom—the biggest spoiler in all twentieth-century geek film history had hit the mainstream press: Spock is going to die. Nobody thought the leak was a lie, by the way. Paramount didn't even try to deny it. The *Post* and other tabloids were jazzed, and for a hot second, they acted like Spock's death was the best dumpster fire since Studio 54 got shut down. Leonard Nimoy discovered the leak by reading the *Journal* while he was shooting a Marco Polo miniseries in China. If the death threat letters were any indication, the fans were going apeshit bananas. Spock wasn't just dying. He was getting *killed*.

But how did the Concerned Supporters even know? Short answer: Gene Roddenberry, who had been assigned the role of "executive consultant" and essentially stripped of all control, creative or otherwise, after the failure of *TMP*, told them. Scurrilous? Maybe. In violation of his agreements with Paramount about confidentiality? Almost certainly. The behind-the-scenes creation of *The Wrath of Khan* is the most sacrilegious moment in the entire history of how Star Trek was made. This is the moment the gospel of Trek was created almost exclusively by outsiders. Neither Bennett nor Meyer had been Trek fans before taking on the project, but by the end of making the movie, they'd redefined how people felt about

Trek, and in terms of the critical response, the movie was perceived as a return to form, even if the form had been radically altered. Janet Maslin's review of the movie in the *New York Times* began with the words, "Now that's more like it." But more like what?

The Wrath represents the first time a Star Trek project was created against the vast majority of Roddenberry's wishes, and the success of the finished product proved Roddenberry wrong and the interlopers right. The Concerned Supporters' concern was misplaced. Not only was killing Spock a good call, it gave the movie actual weight, and made Star Trek *realer* than it had ever been before. In the twenty-first century, internet trolls tend to attack new Star Trek projects by reaching for a cudgel labeled "Roddenberry's Star Trek." Even in 2016, George Takei was filmed watching a trailer for *Star Trek Beyond*, reacting with disgust to spaceship explosions, and saying, "This is not the peaceful vision of the future Gene Roddenberry created." Now, Takei is a wonderful and smart person, but even he still leans into the false narrative that all good Star Trek comes from Gene Roddenberry's vision and all bad Star Trek is made by hacks.

And that's simply not true. There are pieces of evidence prior to *The Wrath of Khan* (everything Gene Coon made), but if you want to quickly win a debate with someone who is using the Roddenberry defense to attack any aspect of new Star Trek—from *Discovery* to the reboot films to individual episodes of *Picard* or *Strange New Worlds*—all you have to do is say this: Roddenberry hated *The Wrath of Khan* and did his best to sabotage the movie by leaking the biggest plot twist in the movie to the world.

"You have to understand, Roddenberry felt like he had to save face with the fans," historian Larry Nemecek tells me. Nicknamed Dr. Trek, Nemecek is, without a doubt, one of the world's most knowledgeable Star Trek historians and experts. Over three decades, he's written several officially licensed Trek books (like *Star Trek: The Next Generation Companion*) and worked as an archivist to research and preserve original documents connected to the making of all of Trek, which he often discusses in his podcast, *The Trek Files*. If you want to actually see what Laura Leach's ad in the *Hollywood Reporter* looked like, calling Larry Nemecek is like going to the microfiche section of the library and finding that the librarian has already organized all the material for you and found the exact piece of information you need. Nemecek's Trek research predates the game of telephone caused by the twin influences of time and Wikipedia. Not only is he the person who supplied me with scans of these original articles and documents, but he also put the material into context relative to how fans felt at the time. Back then, there was no internet, but there was a lot of correspondence in fanzines.

"After Paramount gave him the consulting title, and effectively took Star Trek away from him, Roddenberry knew he had to make sure the fanzines still saw him as the Great Bird of the Galaxy. From his point of view, if the fans no longer associated him with Star Trek, he was finished," Nemecek explains. "Now, at the time, it's important to remember this. Just because we have evidence of fanzines and a threat of a boycott of *Star Trek II*, that does not mean most people were ever thinking of actually boycotting it. What it was, is that back then, we had something called 'BNFs' or 'Big Name Fans,' and if those fans started saying one thing or another, sometimes that could influence other people. There's every reason to believe the biggest reason the survey was conducted was because some of the fans were worried they were losing the subject of their fan fiction."

Nemecek doesn't think you can prove that *all* the Concerned

Supporters were readers of erotic Spock fan fiction, but he also says that at least a few of them were writers of it. In this way, the goal of the boycott wasn't about canonical Star Trek media at all, but rather, the concern that you might not get as much mileage out of your fanfic if everyone's favorite sexy Vulcan was deceased. Still, the goals of these fans and the goals of Roddenberry briefly aligned.

Roddenberry had a lot of quibbles about the details of *The Wrath of Khan*, but the thing he publicly claimed to be against was the death of Spock. Late in the game, when the movie was complete, Roddenberry seemed to shift some of this blame to Nimoy, saying, "Leonard seems to want to move on," but while the movie was being made, Roddenberry and his secretary, Susan Sackett, were the people who Laura Leach *specifically* cited as her source for where she got the information. Bennett was told by the studio that he could mostly ignore Roddenberry, and when he discovered it was Roddenberry who leaked early script pages to the fanzines, he vowed not to get even, but to simply rethink the way these movies were going to go in the future.

Roddenberry's power was gone, despite the fancy "executive consultant" title, and in this way, twenty-third-century art imitates twentieth-century life. Roddenberry's status as an emperor with no power is exactly the place James T. Kirk finds himself at the beginning of *The Wrath of Khan*. Kirk has become an admiral and is no longer able to command starships. The difference is that in *The Wrath*, Kirk returns to command the *Enterprise*, but for Roddenberry, that didn't happen for another six years, with the launch of *The Next Generation*. The Roddenberry era of Trek—at least as far as the original cast is concerned—largely ends with the success of *The Wrath of Khan*. He had to go make a new TV series—with all new characters—to get creative control of Star Trek back. If Roddenberry was Brian Jones and Star Trek was the Rolling Stones, the making of *The Wrath* is the moment when the Stones kicked him out of the band. This analogy also requires Mick Jagger to fake his own death, but you get it.

Did Roddenberry truly dislike the idea that the movie was going to kill Spock, or did he just leak the info because he was pissed? Probably a little bit of both, and it doesn't matter, because on some level, it was Nimoy's decision, anyway. But Roddenberry knew certain folks would hate it, so it seems that to get the fans frothing at the mouth, he leaked Spock's death because he could. Roddenberry had other complaints about *The Wrath*, all of which, in a vacuum, sound reasonable. He disliked the violence. He didn't like the new uniforms. He thought a film that focused on Kirk having a midlife crisis was a mistake. He objected to Kirk killing the eel that emerges from Chekov's ear without first thinking about studying it. He didn't like that the movie was about revenge. All of these conflicts are compelling, but really, Roddenberry's problem with *The Wrath of Khan* can probably be boiled down to cigarettes.

Nicholas Meyer wanted to make the future of Starfleet more "cramped" and "dirty" than the style he'd seen in *TOS*, and to that end, he tried to include more naturalistic production elements: recognizable exit signs, buttons and belt buckles on the Starfleet uniforms, space booze that looked like real booze, a hardcover copy of *A Tale of Two Cities*. But the synecdoche for these conflicts was Meyer's decision to include a "No Smoking" sign on the bridge of the USS *Enterprise*. Roddenberry hated it because he claimed nobody in the future would smoke. Meyer thought Roddenberry was naive. On this point, Bennett intervened to pacify Roddenberry, and eventually the "No Smoking" sign was removed. That said, you can still see it in the very first scene of the movie, in which Spock is standing on a simulator version of a starship bridge, and not the real thing, as we later learn. The "No Smoking" sign behind Spock in the scene is the ultimate compromise between Roddenberry's vision for Star Trek and nearly everyone else's. In Roddenberry's vision of the future, nobody has vices. But, in Meyer's version, some people still do, they just do their best not to take those vices into space.[10]

This first scene is also the first time Spock dies in the movie. In the context of the film, the idea is that all these Starfleet cadets—specifically young Saavik (Kirstie Alley)—are undergoing a test of character. This test requires the students to face a "no-win scenario" in which there's no way to save their starship. The characters are in on the fact that this is all a test, but the audience is not. In the first five minutes of the film, *every* major Star Trek character dies in this simulation sans Kirk and Chekov, who aren't there. And this happens the way it does because Bennett and Meyer were trying to mess with all the fans who thought they knew the truth about Spock's death.

As Meyer revealed in his 2009 memoir, *The View from the Bridge*, it was during a marathon of screening old episodes of *Star Trek* that he and producer Harve Bennett landed on the idea about creating a fake-out version of Spock's death to throw off the angry fans. Meyer told Bennett: "We'll kill him in the simulator right at the beginning." Bennett was thrilled. The fans who hated the idea of killing Spock would be less worried, and that way, when Spock

---

10 If you do some mental gymnastics and accept that this "No Smoking" sign only exists at Starfleet Academy, you can convince yourself that Starfleet is only concerned about its *students* smoking on a fake starship bridge but are less concerned about the actual spacefaring officers smoking on a real one. In this way, you get to have it both ways. Roddenberry is right: Grown-ass adults tend not to have such terrible vices, but the kids still have to learn.

died for real at the end of the film, it would stick. So, in a sense, Meyer and Bennett collaborated with angry fans and with Gene Roddenberry. They changed the structure of *The Wrath of Khan* to acknowledge what was happening in the fanzines and the mainstream press. They successfully regained control of the out-of-context spoiler of Spock's death, and made it work for them. Instead of the spoiler of Spock's death being a problem, Meyer and Bennett made it part of the movie. To really drive this home, after Kirk and Spock chat about Kirk's birthday present (that hardcover of *A Tale of Two Cities*), Kirk says, "Aren't you dead?" Meyer was worried that this was laying it on too thick, but Bennett talked him into it. They faced the angry mob of Trekkies, and by making a clever joke, lived to tell the tale.

In October 2016, at the Star Trek: Mission New York convention, I watched Meyer face down another crowd of anxious Trekkies. This was a year before the debut of *Star Trek: Discovery*, during which, in its first season, Meyer served as an executive consultant. Fans at this convention (and now) still have complaints and questions about the direction or darkness of this particular *Trek*. Is this Gene Roddenberry's *Star Trek*? After cantankerously fielding audience questions in the vein of "How much will this connect to the other films?" Meyer said this:

"Art is not a democracy. There are only two kinds of art: good art and bad art. You don't make good art by taking a vote. Good art is not made by a committee."

This idea is almost certainly Meyer's personal credo. Before this convention appearance, he'd said that exact phrase to me on the phone earlier that year as we were discussing *The Wrath of Khan* and his position on *Discovery*. He's also quoted saying something like this in an official "making of" book about *The Wrath of Khan* published in 1982. He's also said this relative to how he writes his Sherlock Holmes novels. He's probably saying it right now, having just emerged from a crucible of not giving a shit about what you or anyone else thinks.

And yet, it's not like *The Wrath of Khan* is some kind of performance art piece where Nicholas Meyer is sitting alone in Spock makeup, staring at the audience for 113 minutes, willing his conception of *Star Trek* into existence through pure artistic integrity. "The perception of the whole when you see the picture does not include rivulets of disagreement between seventeen people for how it should be," Bennett said in 1982. "The assumption is that one intelligence guided it, which is not true."

Bennett is clearly right. Although he received no screenwriting credit at the time, Nicholas Meyer rewrote the screenplay for *The Wrath of Khan* using material culled from five separate drafts written by five different writers. Because the movie was so behind schedule, Meyer heroically did this in only twelve days, but even that script, which he created alone, existed because of previous failed drafts. Interestingly, the one narrative aesthetic that Meyer emphasized repeatedly in his rewrite was to give the world of Star Trek a more nautical influence. Meyer tells me that he "loved the C. S. Forester Horatio Hornblower novels when [he] was a kid." In rewatching the classic *Trek*, Meyer noticed that Kirk reminded him of Hornblower and, so, added as much nautical flair to the film as he could muster. Ironically, despite their disagreements on the film, Meyer later learned that Roddenberry had *also* been inspired by Forester's Hornblower books in the creation of *Star Trek* in the 1960s. This fact remained such an integral part of Star Trek's foundation that Patrick Stewart would later recall that in 1987, when he asked Roddenberry about the character of Captain Picard,

Roddenberry gave him a stack of Horatio Hornblower books and said, "There's your man." To put this in perspective, *The Wrath of Khan* hit theaters just five years before *The Next Generation* debuted on TV.

So, by borrowing from C. S. Forester for *The Wrath*, Nick Meyer accidentally mined one of Roddenberry's inspirations for Trek. This proves that Star Trek is made by committee, even unintentionally.

The idea of killing Spock was not Meyer's. It was Bennett's and Nimoy's. Finally, the way *The Wrath* was shot was influenced by producer Robert Sallin, who infamously suggested that Kirk's entrance in the simulator scene be backlit, making it one of the most iconic entrances of a Trek hero ever. When you add in the way the fans influenced Meyer and Bennett's thought process about *when* Spock should die, you've suddenly got a very big committee that successfully made very good art.

That said, I think we all know what Meyer means. Even though there were rumblings about Paramount forcing Meyer to shoot an alternate ending where Spock doesn't die, there's no evidence then or now that that ever happened. The filmmakers stuck to their photon torpedoes about Spock dying and did not back away from that bold decision, showing they were not afraid of Roddenberry or of what Trekkies might think. So, in that way, Meyer's statement could be easily amended: You *can* make good art by committee, but at the end of the day, just like on the Starship *Enterprise*, only one or two people are going to make the final decision.

The decision to kill Spock never wavered throughout the making of *The Wrath of Khan*, but the decision to bring him back to life happened late in the process. Just before Spock puts himself into the dilithium reactor chamber to manually repair the ship's warp engines, he must do the Vulcan nerve pinch on Dr. McCoy, who is *not* about to let him sacrifice himself. After Spock peacefully renders McCoy unconscious with the nerve pinch, he then places his hand on McCoy's cheek and says, "Remember." The implication is that Spock has mind-melded with McCoy and put *something* in his mind. (Spoiler: It's his whole soul!)

Against Meyer's protests, Bennett had asked Nimoy to come up with *something* that could indicate that Spock could come back in a future installment, and this is what Nimoy came up with— "Remember." In 1994, William Shatner attributed this inspiration 100 percent to Nimoy, making it seem like this ad lib happened entirely without Meyer and Bennett's knowledge. Nimoy's memoir splits the difference, taking credit for what he did, but not quite calling it an ad lib. Meyer's memoir claims he wasn't crazy about Spock doing anything in the death scene to indicate he was going to come back to life, but he does admit that the later scene, which shows that Spock's casket had safely landed, was shot without him. He briefly threatened to quit the film over the scene's inclusion.[11] And best of all, at different times, both William Shatner and Leonard Nimoy have accused Meyer of cosplaying as Sherlock Holmes just to fuck with them while filming the death of Spock.

---

11 To his credit, Meyer admits that today, the fact that Spock's resurrection was telegraphed strongly in *The Wrath of Khan* no longer bothers him. Some of this might have to do with the fact that Meyer got to work on two more Trek movies, or simply because, looked at objectively, the ending of the movie works. The scene featuring Spock's casket having safely landed on the Genesis Planet is the only scene in *The Wrath of Khan* shot outside. The rest of the movie was shot on a sound stage, and either took place inside a starship, a space station, an asteroid cavern, or the barren wasteland of Ceti Alpha V. The ending sequence, featuring the lush surface of the Genesis Planet, was shot in Golden Gate Park. Two movies later, in *The Voyage Home*, the crew traveled back in time and hid their commandeered (stolen) Klingon ship in the exact same place.

Meyer denies dressing up as Sherlock Holmes while shooting Spock's death scene in *The Wrath of Khan*, though he does cop to wearing not-his-normal-clothes: "I had opera tickets that night; I was dressed for the opera. I've never dressed as Sherlock Holmes in my life."

This is a small bummer. A second-time movie director[12] dressing as Sherlock Holmes to film the death of Spock is so batshit crazy, that even when it's shot down as apocryphal, you just want it to be true. But the truth is, in terms of myths and legends about this scene, the death of Spock itself was pretty much exactly the way the actors, the director, and the producers wanted it. Meyer wanted some green blood on Spock's hand, but because of an error made by the makeup department, the green blood had turned out more like green foam. This is probably for the best. Imagining Spock's "live long and prosper" hand with green blood on the palm is kind of neat, but it's hard to think of the scene made any other way. In real life, William Shatner has always had a difficult time performing the Vulcan salute, but here, it would have been weird if Kirk had done it back. The fact that Kirk's open palm just lingers there is what makes this scene feel real. It's what makes the scene hurt. Our alien hero, who represents the best of all of us, has died nobly, and Kirk really looks like he's going to pass out.

The thing is, he probably was. Meyer's trick to get a naturalistic performance out of William Shatner was to do so many takes that, eventually, Shatner was so worn-out that he stopped being his

---

12 Meyer's first director's credit was the time-travel movie *Time after Time* (1979). That film starred Malcolm McDowell as H. G. Wells, and David Warner as Jack the Ripper. McDowell later played Dr. Soren on *Star Trek: Generations* (1994), better known as the guy who killed Captain Kirk. David Warner later appeared in Star Trek *three* times: as a cigarette-smoking, disillusioned ambassador in *Star Trek V: The Final Frontier* (1989), as the Klingon chancellor Gorkon (who Kirk is accused of killing) in *Star Trek VI: The Undiscovered Country* (1991), and finally, as the Cardassian Gul Madred, who tortures Captain Picard in the *Next Generation* episode "Chain of Command" (1992).

over-the-top Shatner self. As Meyer said: "The more tired he got, the more he became Kirk." For most of the movie, Shatner is fairly low-key, which is part of what makes it so endlessly watchable; Kirk's not clowning around. Meyer mentions that he "never had to give Nimoy a note," but to sell the audience on Kirk in this movie, he had to do a gazillion takes. This is why the KHAAAAAN!!! scream is so significant. It's actually the only time in the movie that Kirk raises his voice and the only moment that reminds us of the scenery-chewing William Shatner persona that made him famous.

But there's a small detail everyone forgets about this scene.

Kirk is acting. Not Shatner. The character Admiral James T. Kirk is *pretending* to be angry beyond all reason in this scene, and he's doing it for Khan's benefit. Just prior to this scene, Kirk had been contacted by Spock, and Spock told him *in code* that the *Enterprise* would be able to beam them back in two hours. The audience doesn't know this yet, and Khan (who is eavesdropping on their communications) doesn't know this yet. Kirk knows that Khan is spying on them. And Kirk knows Spock is going to pick them up real soon. Kirk knows that when Spock says "partial restoration may be possible in two days," he means two hours. So, when Khan gives his "buried alive" speech, and Kirk screams "KHAAAAAN!!!" Kirk actually knows he'll be getting out of there in two hours. The "Khan" scream is to make Khan feel like he's won, and for the audience to think Kirk is really out of control, but the character of Kirk has never actually lost control. In this small way, Kirk is actually like Spock. He's only acting like he's lost his cool, but deep down, he's still stoic as fuck.

Because Spock dies at the end of *The Wrath of Khan*, the movie briefly makes you think that Star Trek has been about James T. Kirk all along. Though this is the movie where Spock dies, Spock himself is not the main character. But, just like Spock became the focus of *The Original Series* in the '60s, the second life for Trek films in the '80s also became Spock-centric. After Spock's death in *The Wrath of Khan*, Leonard Nimoy played Spock in six more Star Trek films from 1984 to 2013. In 1994, William Shatner's Captain Kirk died in *Star Trek: Generations*. Guess how many appearances Shatner had as Kirk after that? Yup. You're right. It's zero.

Star Trek II: The Wrath of Khan is a legit classic, and was a huge box-office hit. Its success proved, as Sallin tells me, "that the audience was much bigger than just the hard-core fans." Today, new fans are often encouraged to *start* with *The Wrath of Khan*, and for many casual fans, their entire conception of *The Original Series* cast comes from the feature films starting with *The Wrath*. While *The Wrath* is, by nature, a comeback of Ricardo Montalbán's villainous Khan, anecdotally, the number of people who have loved this movie and have also seen Khan's origin in "Space Seed" is not even close to a one-to-one ratio. Khan's return in *The Wrath* is more famous than Khan's first appearance by literally every possible metric. *The Wrath of Khan* was Trek's *Empire Strikes Back* moment, made even more impressive because you didn't need to have seen the previous installments at all.

In the summer of 1982, ambitious science fictions like *Blade Runner* and *Tron* struggled to connect with mainstream audiences. Those movies starred Harrison Ford and Jeff Bridges, respectively. A Star Trek movie blew them both away. The character-oriented approach to Star Trek worked. The death of Spock was a big enough scandal for people to check in and see what all the fuss was about. In the end, the leak worked to everyone's advantage. The faithful and the Trek-curious alike all came out in droves. It was Star Trek's biggest audience of all time. "Star Trek is a little bit like a church,"

Bob Sallin tells me. "Some people are part of the congregation every Sunday. Some people show up only for the holidays. Some people haven't gone in a very long time."

What *The Wrath of Khan* proved was that Spock was immortal in a way the other characters were not. When he transferred his soul into McCoy's brain, a very literal precedent was set. If Spock could be reborn in other bodies, then very soon, he—and the rest of Star Trek—might not even need Captain Kirk. And after Gene Roddenberry's failed coup to stop, or at least disrupt or ruin, the movie, it appeared Star Trek might not need its creator anymore, either.

CHAPTER 7

COLORFUL METAPHORS

The Search for Spock and
The Voyage Home, and Star Trek of the 1980s

Kirk teaching Spock how to swear in *Star Trek IV: The Voyage Home* is adorable. In the most ecologically progressive Trek movie of all time, Spock clumsily says "damn" and "hell" on purpose while he tries to master the human art form of cussing: "colorful metaphors." After time-warping back to 1986—in a Klingon ship ripped off from none other than Christopher Lloyd[1]—Spock notices Kirk's "language has changed since our arrival" and Kirk's excuse is that unless you "swear every other word," nobody will take you seriously in the gritty '80s. Hilariously, Kirk doesn't really know how

---

1 One year before his role as Doc Brown in *Back to the Future*, Christopher Lloyd played Kruge, the crazed Klingon commander who attacks the *Enterprise* in *Star Trek III: The Search for Spock*. Lloyd has the strange distinction of being the first actor to wear the bumpy Klingon foreheads who *also* spoke in English in the same film or episode. In *TOS*, all the Klingons were smooth-headed, and the first lobster-headed Klingon in *The Motion Picture*, played by Mark Lenard, who also played Spock's father, only spoke *in* Klingon. In terms of the way we think about the Klingons, Christopher Lloyd isn't given nearly enough credit for basically reinventing them. And of course, it's only appropriate that the crew would use his ship to travel back in time.

to swear either, because when a cab driver calls him a dumbass, Kirk stammers back with befuddlement, "double-dumbass on you!" The bigger joke underneath this is sweet: The crew of the *Enterprise* are such loveable squares that they don't even know how to pretend to be raunchy. Huey Lewis's "Hip to Be Square" was a hit the same year, but, tragically, is not on the film's soundtrack.

Taken together, the three most prominent Trek films of the '80s—*The Wrath of Khan* (1982), *The Search for Spock* (1984), and *The Voyage Home* (1986)—made Star Trek relevant to a mainstream moviegoing public in a way *The Original Series* never could. And for good reason. While varying in relative critical quality, the Trek films of the 1980s packaged the series in a breezy and confident style insomuch as each movie was a nostalgic family reunion. Like the "monster maroon"[2] Starfleet uniforms worn by the crew in these films, the Star Trek of the '80s was like a chunky holiday sweater. While it's true that these films altered and shook up a lot of Trek traditions—the *Enterprise* was destroyed, Kirk's son David was murdered, and Spock came back to life thanks to mysticism rather than science—you'd be hard-pressed to call these films edgy. On paper the films look risky because of the actual events

---

2 Starting with *The Wrath*, the color-coded spandex of *The Original Series* was swapped for a much more militaristic uniform design that irked Gene Roddenberry and a large portion of the fan base. Nick Meyer based these uniforms loosely on costumes from the 1937 film *The Prisoner of Zenda*. The phrase "monster maroon" comes from Trek cosplayers, who have found these intricate uniforms difficult to replicate. Despite initial objections, this uniform style stuck around for a while both in real life and in the fictional Trek chronology. In various flashbacks in *The Next Generation*, Picard and Jack Crusher are glimpsed rocking this uniform style with some variations, indicating that it lasted for at least five decades after the classic films ended in the late twenty-third century. In *The Original Series*, the notion that someone wearing a red shirt would die a horrible death was a well-known joke. After the monster maroon uniforms took over, there was a subtle clue sent to the audience: Now that everyone was wearing red, anyone could die. Even by *TNG*, this red/burgundy/maroon color was chosen as the color to represent the command division of Starfleet, a tradition that more or less continues to this day.

contained within. But the reason why these movies connected to such a broad audience is that they *feel* laid-back. Stylistically, this is the Jimmy Buffett period of Star Trek: comfortable, crowd-pleasing, and cozy.

After *The Wrath*, the mainstreaming of Trek is mostly thanks to Leonard Nimoy, who both directed *Star Trek III* and *IV* and crafted their stories. Nicholas Meyer, the maestro of *The Wrath*, had a hand in co-writing *Star Trek IV*, but, creatively, the man who helped kill Spock was opposed to bringing him back to life.

"I was offered to write and direct *Star Trek III*," Nicholas Meyer tells me. "And I said, 'What will that be about?' And they said, 'It will be about bringing Spock back to life.' Rightly or wrongly, I said, 'Gee, resurrection, I don't, I don't know how I feel about the possibilities of resurrection. I don't think I know how to do that.' At the time, I didn't want Spock coming back to life. I just thought that was unforgivable. As I was coming to understand, he meant so much to people, *so much* that the idea of sort of dry hustling them, I just thought was really bad. And I fought this. I fought it hard and I was overruled. Perhaps I was right to be overruled."

Along with co-producer Robert Sallin (who shot the scenes for *The Wrath* that teased Spock's comeback), Meyer declined to be a part of *Star Trek III*. As Spock later said in the 1991 Nicholas Meyer–directed film *The Undiscovered Country*, "nature abhors a vacuum." Somebody needed to sit in that director's chair.

Before Star Trek, *Wrath of Khan* producer Harve Bennett had had a long career with Paramount as a TV producer. In 1980 he was hired to produce a *Star Trek* sequel film on a much tighter budget than *The Motion Picture*. The point is, Bennett wasn't initially hired to be the creative guy. He was hired to make sure Trek didn't bleed money. By hiring Nick Meyer and Bob Sallin and turning *The*

Wrath of Khan into a tighter project, Bennett essentially won the keys to the Starship *Enterprise*. To extend Meyer's analogy, he was another can-do man. Another Joshua to Roddenberry's Moses. Still, because Gene Roddenberry had been sidelined, Bennett needed to find a director for the sequel to *The Wrath of Khan*. He needed someone with a vision for not only continuing the new style laid down by the previous film, but also someone who understood what Star Trek fans—diehard convention-goers and casual viewers alike—wanted out of these stories. That person was Leonard Nimoy. Although both Nimoy and Shatner had wanted to direct episodes of *The Original Series*, they had been, as Nimoy remembered, "turned down flat." But now, things were different. The success of *The Wrath of Khan* suddenly made Nimoy a focal point, at least in the eyes of the studio, to the success of Trek. Nimoy's directorial experience was limited, but he had directed an episode[3] of the sci-fi TV series *The Powers of Matthew Star*, produced by none other than Harve Bennett. From experience, Nimoy knew the Trek franchise was never going to be *2001* and he also knew it was never going to be Star Wars. He also figured that if *The Wrath* had one flaw, it was that beyond Kirk, Spock, and Saavik—and a surprisingly expanded role for Chekov—the rest of the "supporting" crew had very little to do. As scripted, Sulu was supposed to have been promoted to captain, a scene that never made it into the final film,[4] while Uhura

---

3 The episode was called "Triangle." Incidentally, Walter Koenig wrote an episode of *The Powers of Matthew Star* called "Mother." Harve Bennett clearly took care of his (adopted) Star Trek children.

4 This scene exists in the novelization of *The Wrath of Khan*, written by science fiction novelist Vonda N. McIntyre. In her previous original Trek novel, *The Entropy Effect* (1981), McIntyre also gave Sulu his first name, Hikaru. In the film *Star Trek VI: The Undiscovered Country* (1991), both things would be true: Sulu's first name would be heard on-screen *and* he'd be given his own starship to captain, the USS *Excelsior*.

and Scotty, and even Bones, have very little screen time. Because the bulk of *The Search for Spock* lacked Spock himself, Nimoy wanted to prove this film "fully used the Star Trek family." To this end, Nimoy "worked very consciously . . . to define special moments for each of the *Enterprise* bridge crew." Ironically or not, he learned the best method for pulling this off was to pretend like Star Trek was an episode of *Mission: Impossible*, a series he'd starred on from 1969 to 1971 as the master-of-disguise agent Paris the Great.

"I think I was influenced by my experience in *Mission: Impossible*, where each character had a specific job to complete in any given adventure," Nimoy explained. Now, this may seem like a giant *no-duh*, but when you consider that Sulu, Chekov, and Uhura are *not* in every single episode of *The Original Series*, the notion of who and what constituted the Star Trek ensemble was somewhat retroactive. With *The Search for Spock* and *The Voyage Home*, Nimoy solidified who was part of the core family and who wasn't. In this way, he doubled down on the character-oriented focus established by *The Wrath*. This doesn't mean *The Search for Spock* is a great or perfect Trek film, but if you watch roughly the middle of the movie—starting with the moment when Kirk and Sulu break Bones out of a Federation prison—you'll think you're watching the greatest Star Trek movie ever. Kirk walks into Bones's cell, flashes the "live long and prosper" hand salute, and says, "How many fingers am I holding up?" Outside, Sulu flips a security guard over his shoulder like a martial-arts badass. Next, in order to surreptitiously beam Kirk, Sulu, and Bones off Earth and onto the *Enterprise*, Uhura briefly pulls a phaser on a cocky young upstart who tries to tell her how to do her job. This character, known only backhandedly as "Mr. Adventure," incredulously asks Uhura, "Have you lost your sense of reality?" Her response sums up why this "trilogy" of Trek films connected to such a huge mainstream audience. "This isn't reality!" Uhura rasps. "This is fantasy!"

Some might say *The Search for Spock* is the most anti-science and pro-mysticism film in the entire Trek canon—more fantasy than science fiction. Nimoy was keenly aware of this, and was worried about it, too. The Genesis Planet, which rejuvenated Spock's body, was a science fiction concept. But the idea that Spock stuck his soul into Bones's brain was a little more spiritual. On top of that, the failure of the Genesis technology is ultimately revealed to be the fault of Dr. David Marcus,[5] Kirk's son, a young scientist who acted too quickly without doing enough research.

"I thought we had better tread carefully there," Nimoy revealed, noting his "concern" over the David Marcus story line because "we were accusing a scientist of prematurely finishing an experiment with which he had become impatient. I checked with some very important scientists on this subject, and they told me it happens all the time. So, we went ahead with that plot development, which I felt was a very valuable and well-placed story point."

That story point also killed off Kirk's son, who had just been introduced in the previous film. Kirk's moment as an actual father was short-lived, and Merritt Butrick's excellent performance in both *The Wrath* and *The Search* became a footnote in Trek history. Why was David killed off? To prove a point about a scientist who had gone too far? Maybe. But the real motivation seems obvious. While Nicholas Meyer had fought for a hug between estranged father and son at the end of *The Wrath*, Bennett and Nimoy knew the general public just kind of wanted to see the *Enterprise* crew, together,

---

5 David Marcus isn't David Kirk because David kept his mom Carol's name, Marcus. Also, Carol didn't tell David that Jim Kirk was his dad until *The Wrath of Khan*.

kicking ass, unburdened by families and kids, even if those kids were grown-up.

"Truthfully speaking, we didn't know what to do with the character," Harve Bennett said. "We discussed the matter and thought that he might best serve the needs of the story by being killed off. And that's what happens." The translation is pretty clear: There were simply too many characters in the mix now, and Nimoy and Bennett just wanted to get the band back together. It's not *unrealistic* per se that David is killed by Klingons, but it's barely dwelled upon, and only really justified in a literary sense three films later, in *The Undiscovered Country*, when Kirk's bigotry toward Klingons is explained by their having murdered his son. In terms of fan outrage, though, the destruction of the Starship *Enterprise* in *The Search for Spock* was more controversial than the downright arbitrary murder of Kirk's son. Having been burned by the controversy over trying to keep Spock's death a secret during *The Wrath*, Bennett and Nimoy just stuck the destruction of the *Enterprise* in the trailer. The next time somebody tells you protecting spoilers is essential to the success of a big film series, remind them of the Trek films of the '80s. Spock's death was spoiled by Roddenberry. The destruction of the *Enterprise* was spoiled on purpose because the Trek franchise was confident enough that people go to movies for reasons other than to be surprised by random explosions.

Numerous film series borrow from this era of Trek films, specifically in the structure of how you do sequels. After Spock died in *The Wrath* and then came back in *The Search*, several other genre films learned the same trick. Some of these similarities can't be proven as intentional homages (*The Dark Knight* and *The Dark Knight Rises* really feel like *Star Trek II* and *III* to me), but the most successful film franchise of all time, the mega-huge Marvel

Cinematic Universe (MCU), revels in, and freely admits, its Trek cinematic ties. Marvel Studios creative director Kevin Feige has many times overtly acknowledged the influence of the Star Trek franchise on the various Marvel films. In 2017, he revealed that in *Captain America: Civil War*, *Iron Man 3*, and *Thor: Ragnarok*—all the third sequels in their respective series—something sacred was "blown up" or "shattered," and that pattern was derived from the destruction of the *Enterprise* in the Star Trek movies.

"In every part three we can, we do it," Feige explained. "It's what happens in *Star Trek III: The Search for Spock*. They blow up the *Enterprise*. That's where we got it." In 2016, while talking about the rebirth of Baby Groot (who died in the first *Guardians of the Galaxy*) Feige also noted this specific death-and-rebirth arc was directly connected the '80s Trek movies. Baby Groot wasn't a totally new character, but instead, the same character who just underwent a huge metamorphisis. "[Baby Groot] is not mentally a baby. He is still Groot . . . I sort of equate it to Spock circa the end of *Search for Spock* and *The Voyage Home*."

In 1986, Nimoy described the rebirth of his famous Vulcan as resulting in "a kind of growing-up process" for Spock, making the character more "bemused . . . charming and funny" than he'd been in *The Original Series*. Whereas the Spock of *TOS* would have rolled his eyes and used his stoicism as a weapon to shut down the illogical Kirk or Bones, the reborn, post–*Wrath of Khan* Spock is more accepting. After years of everybody wondering how Spock would figure out how to fit in with these zany humans, he kind of just shrugs his shoulders and goes with the flow. Spock of *The Voyage Home* is not exactly Baby Groot, but in *Star Trek III* he is a child, and then an adolescent, for most of the film. By *The Voyage Home*, he's more innocent, more idealistic perhaps than Spock had ever been before. Mirroring that, the story line for *The Voyage Home* departed from the death and destruction of the previous two films to send the crew on their most humanistic journey ever. If there's one way Star Trek can prove itself superior to several other kinds of adventure fiction, it's simply that it's not exclusively reliant on evil characters to create conflict.

"I felt strongly that the films shouldn't be a series of us, good guys, against them, bad guys," Nimoy said in 1986. The result was the story for *The Voyage Home*, which Nimoy claimed was more of a "personal statement" than *The Search for Spock*. Nobody is punched in the film. There are no starship battles and Kirk only uses a phaser as a makeshift door lock. The result was the most critically and finically successful Star Trek film up to that point, a record that was held until the J. J. Abrams *Trek* reboot of 2009. Released Thanksgiving weekend in 1986, *The Voyage Home* found the crew of the *Enterprise* heading back in time to find a couple of humpback whales. In the rosy future of Trek, the humpback whales have gone extinct by the twenty-third century, but now, an alien probe (imagine a Tootsie Roll version of the monolith from *2001*) wants to talk to a few whales, and if it doesn't get an answer, it will *accidentally* destroy Earth. Nimoy describes this conflict as a "problem created by misunderstandings."

After an Eddie Murphy–centric screenplay was dropped, Nicholas Meyer was hired to rewrite the middle of the script. He had "missed" his Trek collaborators anyway: Leonard Nimoy and Harve Bennett. Plus, Meyer was able to retool certain elements of his time-travel romance film, *Time after Time*, in which H. G. Wells had found himself in a present-day 1970s San Francisco. Meyer's funniest contribution is probably when Spock uses the Vulcan nerve pinch on a stereotypical punk—complete with a cartoonish mohawk. The punk is blasting a comically over-the-top song called "I Hate You," written specifically for the film by character actor Kirk Thatcher, who also plays the punk. Years later, Star Trek fanboy Kevin Feige got Thatcher to reprise his role as the *same* punk in the 2018 Marvel/Sony movie *Spider-Man: Homecoming*, proving once again just how deeply the Trek films have ingrained themselves in the zeitgeist of twenty-first-century pop art.

Between *The Voyage Home, Peggy Sue Got Married*, and *Back to the Future*, the late '80s were jam-packed with time travel. But *The Voyage Home* stands apart because, on top of being hilarious, it may have significantly shifted the public perception of how much everyone should be worried about endangered species, specifically, whales. *The Voyage Home* was not the number one movie of 1986, but it was in the top five, which is quite the accomplishment when you consider it came out in the fall, and it had to compete with *Top Gun* and *Aliens*. The number of people this movie reached was unlike any previous Trek film, and it was the rare example of a twentieth-century science fiction film that contained a strong, deeply progressive message that also made some money. In the climax of the movie, Kirk takes the stolen Klingon ship—renamed the HMS *Bounty*—and puts the ship directly between the whales they are protecting and the harpoon of whalers. Nimoy described this as a direct "homage to Greenpeace," because "putting the spaceship between the whaling ship and the whales and being hit by the harpoon has Greenpeace roots . . . Greenpeace used to go out in rubber rafts in front of the Russian ships to try to prevent them from firing their harpoons, and that's where that idea came from."

In 1986, Greenpeace praised *The Voyage Home*, even while

noting that a few pieces of information in it were factually incorrect. In '86, the humpback whale was very much on the endangered species list, but, in terms of classification, it wasn't close to extinction. Endangered and close to extinction are not the same thing.

"Had this been a Jacques Cousteau documentary, it would be unforgivable," said Peter Dykstra, a media director for Greenpeace, in 1986. But Dykstra noted that considering *The Voyage Home* was a Hollywood movie capable of changing the hearts and minds of millions of previously disinterested people, "the message was right on the money." Nimoy even admitted that despite the movie being a personal statement, he didn't intend to create an overtly political movie. "It's a piece of entertainment in which there are some ideas," Nimoy said about the Greenpeace influence. This single denial from Nimoy represents a lot of Star Trek's so-called political idealism. Even in one of its most pivotal and political moments, Trek still defaults to being a piece of commercial pop art *first* and a political animal second.

"Art is not just the history of cut and paste," Nicholas Meyer tells me. "It is also a commercial enterprise. The Globe Theatre was a money-making operation. There is a *Henry IV Part 1* and *Part 2*. There's *Henry VI Part 1, Part 2, Part 3* . . ."

The Voyage Home begins with a tribute from the "cast and crew" of *Star Trek* honoring the tragic deaths of the crew of the Space Shuttle *Challenger*, which exploded in January 1986, just ten months before the release of the film. One of the astronauts who died was Ron McNair, one of the first group of Black and female recruits who joined NASA. Judith Resnik, the first Jewish woman in space, also died on board the *Challenger*; she, along with McNair, was part of the group of astronauts trained after Nichelle Nichols's recruitment drive.[6] While Star Trek was thriving as a permanent and enduring popular art form, its most measurable impact on the real world—the diversification of the space program—had taken a serious hit.

Nimoy, Bennett, and Meyer didn't have a huge sweeping plan for the trilogy of films that ended with *The Voyage Home*. But had *The Voyage Home* been a more violent and action-oriented film, like its two predecessors, there's a real chance the perception of the franchise might not have developed into the politically enlightened media brand we think of today. Again, these moves were not calculated, but had the film centered around political assassinations in space—as in *The Undiscovered Country* in 1991—and had this been the Trek movie that honored the *Challenger* crew, the tribute would have rung hollow or, at the very least, less than sincere. *The Voyage Home* was the only Trek film that could have pulled off this tribute tastefully, which is partly an accident, but also a testament to both Nimoy's insistence on creating a nonviolent Trek film, and Nichols's historic recruitment blitz.

In the 1980s, if the Star Trek brand was selling anything other than movie tickets and merchandise, it was the idea that people wanted to see movies that were a little more optimistic. Out of the thirteen existing Trek feature films, there isn't another movie that can be compared to *The Voyage Home* in any way, shape, or form.

---

6 Resnik herself was pushed into applying by Angel G. Jordan, though the Astronaut Corps group she was in was a direct outgrowth of Nichols's efforts.

That said, several episodes of the various TV series that followed did come close to this film. Or perhaps that's backwards; maybe *The Voyage Home* was more like a good episode of the TV that would follow a year later in 1987: *Star Trek: The Next Generation.* What *The Voyage Home* did was to present a ponderous science fiction premise with huge stakes in an interesting way that was also hilarious and fun without relying on action clichés to get the point across. In *The Original Series,* those gunslinger western tropes were still present, no matter how enlightened Trek tried to be. And so, up until *The Voyage Home,* those tendencies were there, too. But this was the moment where Star Trek walked the walk it claimed to always have been walking in terms of promoting progressive values and nonviolence, and managed to get everyone to love it. And, despite the persistence of the Cold War, *The Voyage Home* was the first Star Trek film to be shown in the Soviet Union, in June 1987. Which Nimoy said, at the time, "encouraged" him that the "response to the film" could have real-world impacts. Nimoy, whose parents emigrated from Isiaslav, Ukraine, also said, "My parents come from [the former USSR] and it's been a long dream to come here and get a feeling of what my roots are really all about."

In terms of game-changing shifts for genre films, pundits tend to cite the first Star Wars trilogy as a moment when science fiction broke through to mainstream. But that viewpoint isn't global. With *The Voyage Home,* Star Trek beat Star Wars to Russia. Although *The Voyage Home* debuted just three years after *Return of the Jedi,* Star Wars films were banned by the USSR, and it wasn't until 1988 that *The Empire Strikes Back*—released in 1980 in the US—was screened at a diplomatic function. Again, even in Soviet Russia, Star Trek had to clear the way for Star Wars.

"People think that Star Wars movies and Star Trek movies are sort of the same, but they're not," Nicholas Meyer tells me. "George Lucas wanted Star Wars to pay tribute to *Flash Gordon* and *Buck Rogers* and all that stuff, which is fine. I love all that. But that's not what Star Trek is, or not what it aspires to be. Those aspirations are there. They may get mushed around sometimes, but Star Trek is about the perfectibility of the human species. Can we fix ourselves? That's what Star Trek seems to me to be about at its best."

The Voyage Home is the most crowd-pleasing of all Trek films, perhaps almost to a fault. Stuffed with scenery-chewing broad comedy, the film's ending puts all the Star Trek toys back in the same place they were before *The Motion Picture*. A new Starship *Enterprise* has been conveniently built (offscreen!) and Admiral Kirk is mercifully demoted back down to *Captain* Kirk once more. Just for that moment, what happened next in those adventures didn't require a sequel. The crew all stood in their familiar places, on the slightly generic new bridge of a pretty much identical *Enterprise*, ready to do . . . whatever. Nothing could ever be this good again for this crew, but for that moment, it was okay.

Meanwhile, back in the past, it seems possible that the *Enterprise* crew actually did change the course of human history. Originally, the Star Trek timeline told us that humpback whales would go extinct by the twenty-first century if we didn't change our ways. And the data in 1986 seemed to (mostly) corroborate this. But then, something strange happened in the real twenty-first century. In 2016, exactly thirty years after the release of *The Voyage Home*, most varieties of humpback whales were removed from the endangered species list. Eileen Sobeck, an assistant administrator for fisheries at the National Oceanic and Atmospheric Administration, said that the return of the humpbacks was "a true ecological success story."

Spock would almost certainly disapprove of directly linking the humpback whale comeback with the popularity of *The Voyage Home*. After all, real policy work, actual activism, and tenacious nonprofit public awareness campaigns all contributed, and directly resulted in humpback whales coming off the endangered species list. Star Trek did not literally save the whales. And yet. Were there other *equally popular* pop culture narratives saying the same thing about whales? Did Tom Cruise turn to the camera in *Top Gun* and say, "I've got the need for speed . . . and also . . . the desire to get whales off the endangered species list"? We all know the answer. No other money-making media empire has been as preoccupied with cramming progressive and humanistic messages into its narratives.

In late 1986, Greenpeace noted that "donations increased" around the time *The Voyage Home* hit theaters. So, Star Trek didn't directly save the whales. But *Star Trek IV* is still the coolest environmental blockbuster of all time. And because it was so popular, saying that Leonard Nimoy's "personal" film about saving the planet didn't sway at least some part of the general population toward a more ecological point of view would be . . . illogical.

CHAPTER 8

UNDISCOVERED GENERATIONS

The saga of the three Saaviks and the desperate need for *The Next Generation*

When Kirstie Alley was a kid, she was so immersed in the magic of Star Trek that she told herself "I should play Spock's daughter." While religiously watching *The Original Series*, she wrote dialogue for herself just in case Spock asked her a question. In 1981, when she auditioned for the role of Saavik in *The Wrath of Khan*, she revealed that "I did all my Spock routines from when I was a kid, with the arched eyebrow and everything." Of all the humans to play a Vulcan or a Romulan,[1] Alley is the only Trek actor who kept their existing eyebrows on-screen.

---

1 In the script and all the promotional material for *The Wrath of Khan*, Saavik is identified as half-Vulcan and half-Romulan, even though it's never mentioned in the actual film. There's a grainy deleted scene you can find fairly easily online in which Spock tells Kirk that Saavik is an unconventional Vulcan because of her mixed Romulan heritage. This detail is unintentional foreshadowing because Spock's big character arc in *The Next Generation* crossover ("Unification" parts I and II) would be focused on him reunifying the feuding pointy-eared Romulans and Vulcans back into one culture. In *Star Trek: Discovery*

She loved her prosthetic ears from *The Wrath* so much that she told director Nicholas Meyer that she even wore them while she was sleeping.

Of all the new elements introduced in *The Wrath of Khan*, Spock's young protégé, Saavik, was the most future facing; a new character played by an emerging young talent, seemingly poised to replace Spock as the first of a next generation of new Trek heroes. In 1982, even the most casual fan expected big things for Saavik after Spock's death. But it didn't last. Just like Kirk stopped being a dad after *The Search for Spock*, by the end of *The Voyage Home* in 1986, Saavik had been downgraded from up-and-coming badass to Spock's secret baby's mama.

"They pretty much kicked Saavik to the Vulcan curb," Robin Curtis tells me, talking about Saavik's abrupt departure in *The Voyage Home*. "The message seemed fairly clear at that time—she's not coming back."

Across three Star Trek films of the 1980s—*The Wrath of Khan* (1982), *The Search for Spock* (1984), and *The Voyage Home* (1986)— the character arc of Saavik, first played by Kirstie Alley, then Robin Curtis, represents a microcosm in what rapidly was becoming a nostalgia-fueled film series that both desperately needed new characters but was noncommittal when the time came to have characters retire and actually hand over the space reins—something that had to happen eventually, even after the triumph of *The Voyage Home*.

In *Star Trek V: The Final Frontier* (1989), Bones says, "Other people have families," to which Kirk replies, "Other people, not us."

("Unification III"), this eventually happens in the far future; Vulcans and Romulans living together without mass hysteria.

It's tempting to agree with both of them. If you squint, the story of the original *Trek* crew is about chosen family.[2] And yet, for Kirk, wearing a flannel shirt and drinking whiskey in the middle of the woods mere months after barely getting his old job back, pretending like he doesn't have real family[3] scans as creepy rationalization. Most Star Trek films reinforce the idea that we're all going to have a lot more fun in the final frontier if we just stick with the old gang—seven childless people,[4] all in middle age. Now I'm not saying there's an inherent virtue in being a parent. There's not. It's just that when you consider that Star Trek is supposed to be about the future, the classic feature films send a pretty damn confusing message about posterity thanks to an unsettling habit of getting rid of young people as fast as possible.

At the end of *The Motion Picture*, the only two new young cast members—Ilia (Persis Khambatta) and Decker (Stephen Collins) were basically killed off.[5] Conversely, *The Wrath of Khan* starts off

---

2 The premise of a chosen family in Star Trek is also done with more intentionality in both *Deep Space Nine* and *Discovery*. In those shows, the idea that the crew becomes a chosen family is methodically developed on purpose, and not used to hide the actual families of the characters.

3 Kirk also *probably* has a living nephew at this point: Peter Kirk (Craig Hundley). In the *TOS* episode "Operation: Annihilate!" Shatner played the dead body of Sam Kirk, a guy who looked exactly like Jim Kirk, only he had a mustache. Sam was Peter's dad. Peter was orphaned in "Operation: Annihilate!" when *both* his parents were killed by flying space parasites that look like misshapen pancakes. Kirk doesn't have a family? What about his orphan nephew?

4 In *Star Trek: Generations* (1994) it was revealed that Sulu had actually been a parent for quite some time. He had a grown-up daughter named Demora Sulu (Jaqueline Kim) who becomes the helm officer for the *Enterprise-B*. Kirk says to Scotty, "Sulu? Where did he find time for a family?" Come on, Jim!

5 "Basically killed off," a phrase that here means "one character was turned into a robot-starship probe, and the other, transmuted into a being of pure energy, both of whom exploded in an *uplifting* flash of light, but were 100 percent *not* coming back in another movie, like *ever*."

by telling us that everyone on the *Enterprise* is a young student, and Spock is their teacher. His star pupil is Saavik (Alley), a brilliant and cocky Vulcan woman who is every bit Kirk's equal in brashness, and Spock's equal in cool logic and analysis. She lacks only experience. Part of the reason *The Wrath* works is because we get to see Kirk and Spock fuck up and be awesome simultaneously, all through Saavik's eyes. The movie literally begins with Saavik in the captain's chair, sending the message that if you're looking for the next generation of Trek, there she sits! For Nicholas Meyer, *The Wrath* was a movie about "friendship, old age, and death," but it's funny that the *Enterprise* is filled with a "boatload of children," and the two youngest characters—Saavik and Kirk's son, David—who survive the movie, very clearly scan as younger analogs of the two leads, but with inverted roles. Kirk's son, David, is the scientist, while Spock's successor, Saavik, is training to become a starship captain. If the way these movies turned out wasn't ingrained into the brains of many Trekkies, it's easy to watch *The Wrath* with fresh eyes and see David and Saavik as the new Kirk and Spock.

Plus, in deleted scenes David and Saavik's budding romance would have been made clear, and if you snagged the ongoing 1984 Star Trek comic books, published by DC Comics, you'd find a story line that picked up right after *The Wrath* in which Saavik had essentially replaced Spock.

"They negotiated with me for the part of Saavik for not only *Star Trek III*, but *IV*, *V*, and *VI* were all negotiated at the same time," Robin Curtis, the second Saavik actress, tells me. "That certainly was a signal to me that perhaps there was a lot more in store for this character."

After *The Wrath*, Kirstie Alley didn't return to the role of Saavik. There are *a lot* of rumors and hearsay as to why she didn't—

including a possible rift with Shatner—but it seems like it mostly came down to money. In 1986, in a feature for *Starlog* titled "She Isn't Saavik, I Am," Kirstie Alley said: "They offered me less money than they did for *Star Trek II*, so I figured they weren't very interested in me for Saavik." But Nimoy claimed it was Alley's team that made a deal impossible, saying that the actress's agent "quoted a price that was so far beyond our reach that it left me slack-jawed." Nimoy also said that whatever this super-high salary request was, it was higher than what DeForest Kelley had been paid during his entire tenure as Bones. In 2016, when Alley appeared at the annual, huge Star Trek convention in Las Vegas, she alluded to having had poor negotiating tactics at the time, but also that the final decision not to include her in the film was "still a mystery . . . it's an anomaly in my career. You don't always know the real reason for certain things."

There are few contemporary interviews with Kirstie Alley on this subject, but when I spoke to documentarian Brian Volk-Weiss—who interviewed Alley for his Trek documentary *The Center Seat*, he told me this: "I just have a feeling she . . . she just pissed off Shatner; Nimoy didn't want to deal with it. And they kind of used the money as an excuse to recast her."

"I don't know if Kirstie Alley did *or did not* want to work with Bill Shatner again," Nicholas Meyer tells me. "Had she stayed as Saavik, would things have gone differently? These are theoretical questions . . . it's not like I've got all the answers at the back of the math book."

One person who doesn't mind saying exactly how much she got paid by Star Trek is Robin Curtis. "It was $30,000 for the first film [*The Search for Spock*], which to me, it was like, I'd won the lottery. I was a rich woman," Curtis says, laughing. "But then, for the sequel

[*The Voyage Home*] I was supposed to make $75,000." Eventually, Saavik's role in *The Voyage Home* was reduced only to a few scenes, which means Curtis filmed with the rest of the cast for just four days. "I guess they fired me," Curtis tells me. "Because they only paid me $10,000 for *Star Trek IV*, Paramount saved themselves $65,000. That's the bottom line."

So, what's the big deal? Movie studios are notoriously mercurial. Actors' salary negotiations break down all the time. Characters are recast in sequels and TV shows often. There are two Jennifers in the Back to the Future movies (Claudia Wells and Elisabeth Shue) and '80s kids barely noticed. Don Cheadle replaced Terrence Howard in the Marvel movies. You get it. Why is the saga of Saavik so damn important to the history of Star Trek? Why should you care?

Two reasons. Moving Saavik from the A-squad and then leaving her "kicked to the Vulcan curb," was a moment where the Trek franchise resisted *hard* against the inevitable need for new characters. Second, the erasure of Saavik is sexist as hell.

In what Curtis describes as a "provocative storyline," Spock is reborn teenage-Groot-style in *The Search for Spock* and becomes RAGING HORMONES SPOCK. This means he undergoes the infamous pon farr, the Vulcan mating cycle in which Spock must fuck—or die! In *The Original Series* episode "Amok Time," Spock was able to get out of this[6] because of his love for Kirk. But in *The Search for Spock*, when teenage Spock hits pon farr, Saavik (Curtis) realizes she has to briefly become Mrs. Robinson and have sex with Spock in order to save his life. This single plot point is the riskiest thing in all of the theatrical *Trek*s, and fans almost never talk about

---

6 Vulcans are always trying to find workarounds for their inherent biological need to have actual sex. In the *Voyager* episode "Body and Soul," when Tuvok (Tim Russ) hits pon farr, the eventual solution is that he has sex with a hologram of his wife. Classy.

it, probably because it's *weird*, but also because, as directed by Nimoy, it's almost too subtle.

Curtis tells me that she "enjoyed working with all the Spocks," but that she and her co-star Stephen Manley, who played the teenage version of Spock, "were very anxious about the Vulcan foreplay . . . we were both really invested in making sure this had solemnity and the pathos that it deserved and that it wasn't some Vulcan sex scene. This was a rite of passage in the Vulcan tradition, and it needed to take place. I'd like to think we brought some sobriety to it."

With G-rated, but suggestive, stroking of the fingers—first glimpsed in "Journey to Babel" and "The Enterprise Incident"—the idea that Saavik is about to have sex with Spock as a young man can go right over your head if you're a kid. There's not even a shoulder's worth of nudity and there's certainly not a kiss. Saavik and teenage Spock touch their fingers gently, and Saavik nods, letting him know that it's gonna be okay. Curtis is pretty hard on herself about her performance as Saavik, telling me many times that she doesn't think she quite "got it" when it comes to playing a Vulcan. And yet, there are some very deft and touching choices Curtis makes as an actor that really sell a strange and messy new link between Saavik and Spock. When the Klingons roll in and rough up David, Saavik, and Spock, we're clearly seeing the morning after. Spock and Saavik are having a cuddle by the campfire. Saavik is sleeping while holding Spock's hand, and when the Klingons grab him and pull him up, her protective response conveys their new complex relationship. She just helped this guy lose his virginity (again?) and she's not about to let some Klingons kill him. In *The Wrath*, Saavik is learning about life from Spock, but in *The Search*, she teaches him about the birds and the bees. Curtis's

Saavik might be slightly less popular with the fans than Alley's. But that's hardly fair. Curtis had the heavier lifting. In *The Wrath*, Saavik's emotional stakes are run-of-the-mill coming-of-age stuff, while in *The Search*, she's a woman whose entire life is turned upside down by Spock coming back from the dead.

For Curtis, this idea that Spock and Saavik were now connected somewhat romantically was solidified in the final moments of *The Search*. After Spock's *katra* (soul) has been put back in his newly regenerated body, his rapid aging has conveniently made him look like Leonard Nimoy circa 1984 again. Producer Harve Bennett has often likened the ending of *The Search* to the film *The Miracle Worker*, insofar as the entire premise rests on one character suddenly being able to say something they've been struggling to utter. In this case, it's when Spock says, "Your name is Jim," to Kirk. But, before that, as Spock walks by the entire crew, unspoken looks of recognition spark between all the characters—Uhura, Scotty, Chekov, Sulu, and, tellingly, Saavik. Kirk/Spock fanfic aside, the only person in this group that Spock has had sex with is her.

"Before we shot that, Leonard leaned in a little closer than usual," Curtis reveals. "His mouth was in my ear, and he said, 'Robin, I want you to think if you were to encounter a former love, someone you had been intimate with, on a New York City street; you're suddenly face-to-face, how would you feel?' And in that nanosecond, I was flushed with the intimacy of the question, and such admiration for him as a director, and a desire to articulate a response of the magnitude of the moment and how much it meant to me. I guess I just looked him in the eye like, 'Oh my God, that would be awesome for that to happen, but it would be bittersweet.' I looked down and I looked back up again, and he said, 'That's it. That's what I want in that moment.' The best directors do that. They just get you out of your own way and they trick you."

Other than various young Spocks[7] in *The Search*, Robin Curtis is the only Vulcan actor to be directly cast by Leonard Nimoy. In the '80s, critical praise tended toward favoring Alley's portrayal as Saavik, but in terms of the Trek brand, Curtis is much more visible as the "real" Saavik. From the lush paintings that adorn Star Trek novels and comic books, the visage of Saavik in nearly all tie-in media was—and still is—Robin Curtis.

In *The Next Generation* episode "Sarek," Captain Jean-Luc Picard mentions he was at the wedding of Sarek's son, which in the 1999 novel *Vulcan's Heart*—written by Josepha Sherman and Susan Shwartz—was revealed to be a "bonding" between Saavik and Spock. For the most part, almost nothing in the various Trek books "counts" in terms of the real Star Trek canon. But there's often nothing to contradict the events of the books and comics either, and sometimes these sorts of things find their way into the films and TV shows eventually, like Sulu's first name, "Hikaru," from the Vonda McIntyre novel *The Entropy Effect*. So, right now, there's nothing that says Saavik and Spock *didn't* eventually get married. And, if a certain scene in *The Voyage Home* had actually made it into the movie, there would have been every reason for Spock and Saavik to end up together.

Though not stated outright on-screen, the reason Saavik stayed on Vulcan was because she was pregnant with Spock's child. Early in the process of returning for *The Voyage Home*, Curtis got a

---

7 In *The Search for Spock*, in order of appearance—from child to twentysomething—Spock was played by: Carl Steven, Vadia Potenza, Stephen Manley, and Joe W. Davis. Spock is also played by an unidentified *baby* in a flashback scene in *The Final Frontier*.

telegram from Harve Bennett which read cheerily: "Be sure to visit the Vulcan obstetrician!" If you go watch the movie right now, you won't find a scene in which Spock talks to Saavik about dropping by and visiting her while she has his baby. In fact, you're meant to think that whatever it is Saavik is trying to tell Spock, he's totally unaware of her discomfort. Saavik *does* tell Kirk that she is proud of David, and that with David's death, "he saved Spock, he saved us *all*." This single line is the only surviving shred of evidence that Saavik was trying to tell Kirk she was pregnant with Spock's baby. "He saved us all" implies a group of people outside of just Saavik and Spock. "Us all" is the sly way that Saavik is clueing Kirk in that yes, she's staying on Vulcan to have Spock's baby, but shhhh don't tell anyone.

"It was written, and we didn't shoot it," Curtis says, and after showing me her telegram from Bennett—complete with the Vulcan obstetrician joke—"There was clearly a suggestion that she was with child, and that was obliterated from the script and the shoot."

This would never happen now. You can't imagine a big sci-fi franchise introducing a new female heroine, setting her up as a replacement for the most famous character in that respective franchise, and then slowly walking back that decision in the subsequent sequels, ending with the reason for her departure being to secretly have a baby. Imagine *The Force Awakens* taking all the trouble to introduce Rey, kill Han Solo, and then, in the next movie, bring Han Solo back from the dead and send Rey to go live on Tatooine.[8] This analogy is imperfect, but if you picture any popular

---

8 Arguably this is *exactly* what happened to Kelly Marie Tran's Rose Tico after *Star Wars: The Last Jedi*. But, in Star Wars terms, the erasure of Saavik would have been like if Rose had been *recast* in *The Rise of Skywalker* AND she was suddenly having Poe or Finn's secret baby.

fantasy/sci-fi/superhero franchise—including contemporary Star Trek—casually getting rid of a strong female character like Saavik, *directly after* a story line where the main male character was implied to have had sex with her, people would, correctly, freak out. This being the progressive Star Trek[9] future, we want to believe that the reason why Saavik didn't get an abortion is because she wanted to keep the baby. But that single-mom agency was forced upon Saavik by a script which was mostly trying to make sure Spock had enough time to go hang with his drinking buddies. To be fair, Spock might *not* be a deadbeat dad. It's certainly possible that right after *The Voyage Home* (fictional year 2286) and in the years leading up to *The Undiscovered Country* (2293), Spock totally got his parenting shit together. But, for some weird reason, there's just not a lot of fanfic about Spock being a good dad.

As the crew departs the surface of Vulcan in their stolen Klingon ride, Saavik stands shoulder to shoulder with Spock's human mom, Amanda (Jane Wyatt). Just a few scenes earlier, Amanda told her son that the *Enterprise* crew flipped the script on Spock's favorite axiom—"The needs of the many outweigh the needs of the few"—by making everything about him. By *The Voyage Home*, the needs of the many don't outweigh the needs of the few. As Amanda tells Spock, "the needs of the one," specifically Spock, are seemingly more important than anything.

The state of the Trek film franchise before the dawn of *The Next Generation* was similar. After *The Wrath*, nearly every plot element—through *The Final Frontier* in 1989—was doggedly

---

9 In 1968's *The Making of Star Trek*, Gene Roddenberry claimed birth control in Starfleet was compulsory. At the time, this claim scanned as feminist because birth control was just entering the mainstream. Obviously, required birth control is not an idea that has aged well, and there's no on-screen version of Star Trek that corroborates this idea.

obsessed with keeping the classic crew firmly in their familiar positions. Remember how Spock was a teacher and everyone was facing down retirement in *The Wrath*? The message of the four films that followed, was . . . never mind! The successful Star Trek "film trilogy" accidentally proved what Ebert had inadvertently predicted in 1979; the deep nostalgia for the old crew distracted from Star Trek's ability to ever really do anything new on a character level. Of all the Trek films, *The Wrath of Khan* is considered the most classic. But this is because of the twisted way nostalgia works in pop culture; a piece of pop art that was successful for being transgressive will always become the new standard and *thus* a "classic." This has the annoying side effect of making everyone forget why the thing was so transgressive in the first place. This is the same reason why people like *OK Computer* more than *The Bends*; both albums are amazing, and both albums are great Radiohead records, but *OK Computer* represents a point of departure, and so did *The Wrath of Khan*. The problem is, and what everyone forgets, is that the *truly* transgressive thing about *The Wrath of Khan* wasn't that Spock died but that the movie floated the premise that he— and the entire original cast—could be replaced.

The more the Trek films blazed a trail through the '80s, the more the stories looked inward. With each subsequent film, one bold status-quo-changing decision would be undone by the next. Spock died, and was reborn in the next film. The *Enterprise* was destroyed, then rebuilt in the sequel. As a series, the films became a time-traveling ouroboros; the snake eats its own tail, but then hops into a time warp and pulls that tail right out of its own mouth. These are introspective films, but also super fun blockbuster buddy comedies with heart and with oodles of nostalgia for the old characters, and barely the time of day for anyone visiting. And yet, it's like the Star Trek films seemed to *know* they needed new, younger characters, and each film is borderline desperate for a next generation to replace Kirk and the gang.

The beginning of Star Trek's next generation, intentionally or not, began in the Trek feature films, but the death of David and the erasure of Saavik made the message of *The Wrath* a false spring. After the death of his son and the derailment of his career, Kirk doesn't really change and grow; he actually becomes *more* like Captain Kirk from *The Original Series*. The William Shatner–directed 1989 film *The Final Frontier* is the best example of this: a movie in which Kirk rides horses, climbs mountains, gets into fistfights, and unmasks a false space god. Tonally, *The Final Frontier* resembles many episodes of *The Original Series*, specifically, "The Apple," "The Return of the Archons," and "Who Mourns for Adonais?" Throughout the original series, Kirk's part-time job was unmasking fake gods, so when Kirk confronts "God" in *The Final Frontier*, saying, hilariously, "What does God need with a starship?" it's pure classic '60s *Trek*. *The Final Frontier* was a back-to-basics Star Trek story that everyone hated. Part of this is because the movie is sloppier than the previous two (Nimoy was the better director), but most of the anger probably comes from the fact that Spock's heretofore unknown brother, Sybok (Laurence Luckinbill) was exactly as unlikeable as he was supposed to be. As we learn, Sybok's whole deal is to get people to join his cause by giving them a mini-therapy session in which he shares their "pain." It's somewhat implied he uses his telepathic mind-meld skills as a Vulcan to make this happen, but whatever. Sybok (again, Spock's *brother*) is recruiting people into a cult to try to steal a nice spaceship and take it to the center of the galaxy and find God. If you've never seen the movie, reading that sentence back will make you think it sounds kind of awesome. But it wasn't. Just not for the reasons people think.

Gene Roddenberry hated this story line, and fought against it, even briefly enlisting Isaac Asimov to try to tell Shatner and Harve Bennett what to do. It didn't work, but Roddenberry and Asimov were wrong, both about what the problem was and how to fix it. The problem with the movie wasn't the story line. The reason why all of this doesn't work isn't because it's not believable or whatever— the crew had acted out of character *many times* in *The Original Series*, for all sorts of kooky sci-fi reasons. In "Amok Time," Spock was so horny he tried to slice Kirk open with a giant Vulcan ax, and that's considered one of the greatest episodes ever! No, the reason why Sybok's come-to-Jesus style of brainwashing is distasteful is that it isn't fun to watch. Imagine if the Emperor from Star Wars was played by Dr. Phil. Scary! But, again, not fun to watch. This was the problem with Laurence Luckinbill's Sybok. As a delusional religious zealot, he kind of did too good of a job.

Initially, Shatner had really wanted Sean Connery to play Sybok. Connery declined and went on to be the father of Indiana Jones in *The Last Crusade*, a wise career move for Connery, but a bummer for Trek fans. Connery playing Sybok would have saved *The Final Frontier*. Not on a granular level that would have made nitpicking fans happy; instead, on a gonzo, mass-appeal scale, the hyperbolic silliness of Sean Connery's star power would have been a slam dunk precisely because it would have won over a mainstream audience.[10]

---

10 If this hasn't been made clear by now, hard-core Star Trek fans and casual fans don't have *different* opinions when it comes to Trek's greatest hits. The most-loved Trek films and episodes are, for the most part, loved by die-hard Trekkies and casuals alike. The only real difference when it comes to "ranking" Star Trek movies or episodes is that more serious fans are more likely to make an argument for something they think is "underrated." (*The Motion Picture* comes up a lot there.) Nobody thinks *The Wrath* "actually sucks." The only place this

The creepy, brainwashing, religious zealot Vulcan would have been fun to watch. If Spock's freaking brother had been James Bond, *The Final Frontier*'s story line would have been more palatable. Sean Connery is actually perfect for Star Trek because by the '80s, his reputation was a unique cocktail of kitschy ridiculousness and utter honesty, which is exactly like William Shatner's entire career.

The farther you go forward in time, the more Connery and Shatner become caricatures of themselves. When it comes to *SNL* impressions or Priceline commercials, this is mostly not a compliment. But in the case of a troubled 1989 Star Trek film, Connery's presence certainly would have helped. As it stands, poor Laurence Luckinbill is about as effective as, well . . . Benedict Cumberbatch playing Khan. When you've got a David Koresh–style baddie in a Star Trek film, you don't really want realism. *The Final Frontier* is a movie that begins and ends with Kirk, Spock, and Bones sitting around a campfire, singing "Row, Row, Row Your Boat," which should mean that the movie is hip to its own bullshit. But, because the thing with Spock's lunatic brother is played entirely straight, the movie doesn't work. And, in killing off Spock's brother in the end, Kirk's ominous "other people have families" comes across as a grisly self-fulfilling prophecy. "I was truly convinced this was going to be a terrific film," William Shatner recalled. "But by the time it came together, it was not."

After two Saaviks and Spock's half brother Sybok, you'd think by the time of the final feature film with the classic crew, the franchise would stop messing around with guest actors playing Vulcans.

---

gets dicey is when something is *new*. Like, in the '90s, whether or not *Deep Space Nine* was legit good was very debatable. So, right now, finding a consensus on the newer shows like *Discovery* or *Picard* is impossible. OTHER than *The Wrath of Khan*, *The Voyage Home*, *First Contact*, or the 2009 J. J. Abrams reboot, new Star Trek things are almost never instant hits.

But, bizarrely, in the final bow for the old gang—1991's *The Undis-covered Country*—a new Vulcan is once again central to the story line, and just like in *The Final Frontier*, this person has a connection to Spock *and* turns out to be a misunderstood villain.[11] Returning director Nicholas Meyer wanted to bring Kirstie Alley back for *The Undiscovered Country*, and in a huge twist reveal that our beloved Saavik is part of a vast conspiracy to subvert a peace treaty with the Klingon Empire. Meyer has said that "in an ideal world," Kim Cat-trall's brand-new Vulcan protégé of Spock—Valeris—would have been the "stalwart Saavik," which, in his mind "would have sharp-ened the pain of the betrayal." Meyer has said many times that the reason this didn't happen was because Kirstie Alley was unable (or unwilling) to do the movie. But why not bring back Robin Curtis?

"I mean, I get it," Curtis says. "Nicholas Meyer didn't cast me in that part initially. But, God, it's a shame. I would have loved to work with him." Curtis also tells me a slightly different version of how Cattrall's Valeris came to be *not* Saavik. From her understand-ing, Majel Barrett Roddenberry claimed credit for that veto, saying that if the character "wasn't going to be played by me or Kirstie Alley, that they had to create a new character."

As played by Cattrall, Valeris does, at first, feel like a slightly sultrier Saavik, partially because she seems to have the same basic backstory. Like Saavik, Valeris is a young Vulcan who was sup-ported by Spock at Starfleet Academy. Unlike with Saavik, Spock is also super-specific about what he wants Valeris to do. "I intend you to replace me," he says early in the film, again hinting at the notion

---

11 People with pointed ears are the villains in *a lot* of Star Trek movies. You've got Sybok in *The Final Frontier*, followed by Valeris in *The Undiscovered Country*, then the Romulans are big in *Star Trek: Nemesis*, and then in the 2009 J. J. Abrams reboot, Nero, a Romulan (Eric Bana) who—wait for it—has a *personal beef with Spock*—is the main baddie.

that the Trek feature films had been toying with for over a decade: New characters were the future, both in real life and in Star Trek.

"It's the love a teacher has for his student," Kim Cattrall said in 1991, responding to a question as to whether or not there was a romantic interest between Spock and Valeris. Cattrall also takes some credit for the formation of Valeris, including designing the character's headband herself, and giving the character a new name. "They told me they wanted a whole new relationship. We don't want to call her Saavik. We want to go a step further . . . so I renamed the character."

Cattrall's idea was to call Spock's new Vulcan apprentice "Eris" after the Greek goddess of strife. "Val" was added to the front of the name, and the final erasure of Saavik was complete. Cattrall's "Eris" idea also telegraphs the secret that Valeris is working against Spock's desire for peace, and by the end of the film is a traitor who is forced to "confess" via a brutal mind meld. Valeris's motivations for betraying Spock were essentially that she claimed to want to preserve the status quo of Star Trek's version of the Cold War. In the film, we're meant to think Valeris is naive and misguided. But Nicholas Meyer tells me that, analogously, the desire to preserve the Cold War feels less clear now than it did in 1991. "Maybe Valeris was right after all?" he says with a laugh. "I mean, is the world a safer place now?"

In the fantasy of Star Trek's politics, *The Undiscovered Country* allows the classic *Enterprise* to sow the seeds of interstellar peace, partly by Kirk owning up to his own prejudice, but also by stopping yet another young person—in this case, Valeris—from screwing everything up. Just before Kirk's final voice-over at the end of *The Undiscovered Country*, he quotes *Peter Pan*, telling Chekov that the course heading for the ship is "second star to the right, and straight on till morning." The message of the final feature film with the original Trek cast is clear: This is *really* it. Kirk says the history of the *Enterprise* "will become the care of another crew . . . and to them and their posterity will we commit our future." Kirk also corrects "where no man has gone before" by stopping himself at "man" and saying, "where no *one* has gone before," a kind of long-overdue apology from a bygone era.

Still, the *Peter Pan* quote is the most revealing. As much as the first crew is responsible for creating and fostering the dream of Star Trek—both in their characters and behind the scenes—our perception of Captain Kirk is similar to that of Peter Pan. He was the starship captain who longed for eternal youth, which helps to explain why so many young characters didn't stick around in these films. Kirk had his lost boys already.

The power of *The Undiscovered Country* is that it retroactively presented the era of the classic *Trek* as a huge Cold War metaphor that had been lurking there since the start. It flips the assumptions we had about the egalitarian and open-minded nature of Kirk's generation, presenting Jim as a bigot who is, at first, only tolerant of the Klingons because he's *forced* to be. Nicholas Meyer directly confronted the audience about the politics of the twentieth century, and with his film said outright that Kirk was a Cold War boomer and it was time for that kind of thinking to end.

The era of the *Original Series* crew overlapped with *The Next Generation* from the years 1987 to 1991. *The Final Frontier* and *The Undiscovered Country* were an extended farewell tour for the old gang, as a new Star Trek series began to overtake them in both fame and acclaim. And so, as Kirk, Spock, Bones, Sulu, Scotty, Uhura, and Chekov grew older on-screen, it was time for Star Trek to grow up. It was time to leave never-never land behind forever.

CHAPTER 9

YOU WILL BE ASSIMILATED

The Next Generation assumes command

On March 7, 1993, from the stage of Veterans Memorial Coliseum in Phoenix, Arizona, Patrick Stewart called on a young boy with his hand raised. As Stewart told *TV Guide* that same year, "The young man stood up and said 'Mr. Stewart, will you please marry my mother?'" After a wave of adorable *ahhhhhs* and friendly laughter rippled through the crowd, Stewart politely declined, and the boy's mother "bent forward and put her head into her hands." As a voracious fifth-grade *TV Guide* aficionado, when I read the interview just a few months later, I felt rage. I had been at that Phoenix Star Trek convention, but that boy was *not* me. Why hadn't I thought of that? Sitting with my own mother, clad in my one-piece maroon Starfleet jumpsuit, I'd watched helplessly, as two rows over and one row up, that clever kid tried to execute his daring scheme. It was a great plan: Get Captain Picard into your family and then your life would be nonstop Star Trek all the time. Would I have traded my dad for Captain Picard? I loved my dad, but the answer is . . . yes.

Because of course it is. If given a chance to swap out memories of my real father and insert a new childhood with Picard as my dad, I'd do it. Picard was the '90s space dad for millions. In the 2022 *Star Trek: Picard* episode "Assimilation," Dr. Jurati (Alison Pill) even says she wishes Jean-Luc was her dad.

The Next Generation was the second coming of Star Trek, in more ways than one. Unlike the successful feature film franchise, *TNG* heralded the return of the messiah, Gene Roddenberry himself. Strangely, two months before preproduction began on *The Next Generation*, in the autumn of 1986, Roddenberry had been ready to walk away from Star Trek forever. He'd been an "executive consultant" on the three Star Trek feature films after *The Motion Picture* and he was pretty much over it. But, in that fateful fall of 1986, around the time *The Voyage Home* was cleaning up at the box office, Gene Roddenberry changed his mind. And, although Roddenberry taking the helm again wasn't entirely smooth, a new and utterly unprecedented era was born.

From 1987 to 2005, there were a staggering eighteen consecutive years of new Star Trek on TV,[1] an unprecedented run that set the standard by which the whole franchise is still judged. Although *The Original Series* and the subsequent films starring the classic cast embedded themselves into the zeitgeist like no other pop art phenomenon, the actual bulk of Star Trek material watched by

---

1 Because this predated streaming TV and social media, the easiest way to think of these eighteen years is just to call it "the nineties." From an American pop culture perspective, you could argue the true end of the '90s happened sometime right after the release of *Iron Man* in 2008, but before 2011, specifically in the scene in *Bridesmaids* where Kristen Wiig drunkenly protests class division on an airplane by hilariously, and incorrectly, claiming, "this is the nineties."

most people on planet Earth—about 620 hours of TV²—comes from the four distinct Trek series of this era: *The Next Generation, Deep Space Nine, Voyager,* and *Enterprise*. It is the most daring (yet simultaneously the most chaste) stretch of Star Trek history, and this golden age was heralded by the critical and mainstream success of *The Next Generation*. If *The Original Series* had veered toward after-school-special morality written by stoners in the '60s, *The Next Generation* has the reputation of a respectable after-school special for the entire family. "Child, parent, and grandparent would all watch together," John de Lancie, best known as *TNG's* trickster space god, Q, said. "That's the ultimate show."

"*The Next Generation* was this show about these responsible, honest grown-ups. It was *designed* to make you feel safe," *Star Trek: Lower Decks* creator Mike McMahan explains. "It was nice to see these paternal and maternal figures on *Next Gen* who are guiding this ship, which is a surrogate family." For the next generation growing up with *The Next Generation* (McMahan and the author were both born in 1981) the crew of the *Enterprise-D* scanned as squeaky-clean role models, flawless and idealistic to the max. For '90s kids, the *TNG* crew were the coolest and most serious teachers you could imagine. "Riker and everyone had like these perfect

---

2 I'm rounding up a little bit here. When you combine the episode totals from *The Next Generation, Deep Space Nine, Voyager,* and *Enterprise,* you get 624 episodes, which is *seven times* the amount of material in *The Original Series*. I'm calling an episode an hour, which, strictly speaking, isn't quite right, because episode lengths vary, especially with the various contemporary series and the animated shows. Still, in September 2021, the *Star Trek: Lower Decks* episode "We'll Always Have Tom Paris" became the 800th official episode of Star Trek. So, about 75 percent of all Star Trek episodes, *ever,* come from the era which began with *The Next Generation*.

smiles," *Deep Space Nine*'s Nicole de Boer tells me. "In your head, when they smiled it would be like CHING! I loved that optimism."

This new *Enterprise* was a place where people were encouraged to talk about their feelings. Which they did, a lot. Like *a lot* a lot. In some episodes—like the whimsical "Data's Day"—the appeal was about just hanging out in the twenty-fourth century. *The Next Generation* boldly went where no one had gone before, but unlike any science fiction series before, that adventure was mostly internal. Years after the show ended, *Star Trek: Enterprise* producer David A. Goodman said, "*The Next Generation* did make therapy palatable for a whole new generation." In a deleted scene from the *TNG* episode "Relics," Counselor Troi (Marina Sirtis) tries to make a time-displaced Scotty (James Doohan) from *The Original Series* feel welcome in the future. But she's also doing her job, because she's a therapist, and being stuck in a transporter beam for seventy years would drive anyone nuts, much less this heavy-drinking Scotsman. When Scotty finds out the new *Enterprise* has a psychologist he freaks out on Troi, heads to the bar, and starts complaining about how there's no real booze on the ship, only "synthehol." The fact that the scene where Scotty rejects the idea of a therapist was deleted from the aired version of "Relics" is understandable. When you watch it now, it's not a great scene, as filmed. But the scene demonstrates the true power of *The Next Generation*. With *The Original Series*, the allegories were big, loud, and in-your-face. On *The Next Generation*, contemplative waves were happening that were barely perceived. More than any piece of filmed science fiction, *TNG* made a lasting mark on pop storytelling because, repeatedly, the stories valued subtext over context. Marina Sirtis claimed that when reshoots were required of one or two actors, the rest of the "company" would also return, if only to deliver *off-camera* dialogue. To be clear, they could do this dialogue remotely, or in a recording booth later. But they didn't. Like a theater troupe, the *TNG* cast would return to re-create the same conditions that had existed during the initial shoot.

Sirtis said this commitment meant that the cast would even stick around in reshoots for "off-camera *looks*." Now, let's get this clear. That's some Charlie Kaufman–level shit. The *TNG* cast believed so strongly in their art that they valued the artistic integrity of a performance that *wasn't even filmed*. This notion perfectly explains why *The Next Generation* is so adored. What we didn't see and what wasn't said was almost more important than the episodes themselves.

While a single therapist for a thousand spaceship people seems a little off, Troi had some backup.

Our new resident space physician, Dr. Beverly Crusher (Gates McFadden), didn't have time to debate philosophy like Bones did because she was too busy trying to save crew members from sentient tar monsters while also raising her oh-so-precocious teenage son, Wesley Crusher (Wil Wheaton), alone. Fresh from his role in *Stand by Me*, Wheaton was a big star, considerably better known at the time than most of his colleagues. Along with LeVar Burton, who Stewart called "the only famous one," Wheaton was a star before *The Next Generation*. The character of Wesley Crusher was one that Gene Roddenberry said he "identified with" because Wesley was "me at seventeen. He is the things I dreamed of being and doing." This may be true, but just like Spock's gender was possibly unclear at a few points, Wesley Crusher was originally conceived as "Leslie Crusher," a teenage girl on the *Enterprise*. Before casting ever began, D. C. Fontana disabused Roddenberry of this notion, and Wesley became a boy, and a pseudo-cipher for Gene himself.

Despite wearing his shoes untied to the audition, Wheaton won the part, and Roddenberry later teased him: "I let my fourteen-year-old wear his shoes untied." Wheaton and Roddenberry's son Rod Roddenberry are the same age, and so the elder Roddenberry was protective of Wheaton on the set of *The Next Generation*, going so far as to require William Shatner to apologize to Wheaton after Shatner was rude to Wheaton[3] when the filming of *The Next Generation* intersected with *Star Trek V: The Final Frontier*. Wheaton called this "intervention" one of the "wonderful gifts" Roddenberry gave him, and the one he remembers "the most fondly."

Next Gen's first tactical officer was Tasha Yar (Denise Crosby), a character Roddenberry intended to brazenly copy from the space marine Vasquez[4] in *Aliens*, initially naming the character "Macha Hernandez." Tasha's extra muscle was Worf (Michael Dorn), the first Klingon in Starfleet, representing the idea that seven decades after Kirk, the Klingons were not only at peace with the Federation, but our friends. The only hint of a Captain Kirk–like Lothario was Will Riker, played by Jonathan Frakes, a six-foot-three former soap opera actor who had moonlighted as an official Marvel Comics in-person Captain America at comic-cons in the '80s. The ship's navigator, and later, chief engineer was the blind Black man Geordi La

---

3 Wil Wheaton has recounted this story many times, and even performed it live as a monologue. He claims that after William Shatner's apology, the two became "cordial."

4 In *Aliens*, Vasquez was played by Jenette Goldstein, who later played a bridge officer on the *Enterprise-B* in the 1994 film *Star Trek: Generations* and, in 2019, played the voice of the *Enterprise* computer in *Short Treks*. Goldstein even auditioned for "Macha" on *The Next Generation* but didn't get the part.

Forge (LeVar Burton). Geordi's eventual best friend and closest confidant was the android Lieutenant Commander Data, a walking AI who dreamed of becoming fully human. When Data tells Riker of his desire to be *real*, Riker flashes that megawatt smile and says, "Nice to meet you, Pinocchio."

And then, of course, there was Captain Jean-Luc Picard. Conceived initially as a hairy, virile Frenchman by Gene Roddenberry, Picard's first name, on paper, was "Julien" until D. C. Fontana suggested "Jean-Luc." The fact that Jean-Luc Picard rhymes with French auteur filmmaker Jean-Luc Goddard was probably lost on a big chunk of the audience, but it does feel like a subtle message: This *Star Trek* was going to make you work for it.

The casting of Patrick Stewart as Picard is easily the most pivotal moment in post-'60s Star Trek history. And that's because Picard is the perfect Star Trek character. He's a passionate fallible human, who is constantly sticking up for fallible humans with big, heart-stopping speeches. But he's also cold and removed, making him like a human version of Spock. In the *TNG* episode "Unification" Spock meets Picard and says warily, "There's an almost Vulcan quality to the man." In 1994, Nichelle Nichols said that, before *The Next Generation*, Gene Roddenberry had created Kirk and Spock as two sides of one personality. But that with Picard, Nichols believed these ideas were fused: "It was telling that his last starship captain embodied both those characters, but was an older man, whose passions, though tempered by time, were not diminished. That was Gene, too."

The character of Captain Picard may have been exactly what Roddenberry wanted his new *Star Trek* to represent, but up until the last possible minute he vehemently opposed casting Patrick Stewart. "He may have been smart," Stewart remembered. "But he didn't want me on the show." Several other actors were up for the role, including Mitch Ryan, Roy Thinnes, and two former James Bond villains—Yaphet Kotto and Patrick Bauchau. Stewart, meanwhile, was briefly considered for the role of Data. Infamously, producers Bob Justman and Rick Berman fought for Stewart to get the part of Picard, and during one critical audition, this resulted in the totally bald actor being forced to wear a hairpiece. And it worked, although everyone later decided it was better if Stewart went bald. Through pressure from his colleagues, or through the strength of Stewart's late-in-the-game reading, it was enough. Roddenberry was convinced that he'd found the new captain of the Starship *Enterprise*. When Paramount Studios president John S. Pike told Roddenberry that Picard's baldness might seem technologically implausible in the twenty-fourth century, Roddenberry quipped, "In the twenty-fourth century, no one will care." Still, it's important to highlight how radical this idea was. William Shatner—the sexy leading man of *TOS*—wore a hairpiece to hide his baldness. Indiana Jones was not bald. Thomas Magnum of *Magnum P.I.* was not bald. Making the new Star Trek captain a bald guy in 1987 is like if Telly Savalas had been cast as James Bond instead of Blofeld.

In the early days, at least, *Next Generation* was very much Roddenberry's invention, although it wasn't really his choice or his idea, at first. For several generations, the *TNG* crew are, as Marina Sirtis put it, "the last of Gene's children." And yet, at sixty-six years old, he had been "coerced and leveraged" into doing a new Trek TV show in the first place. Longtime Roddenberry associate and Trek archivist Richard Arnold remembered that Roddenberry was "looking forward to retirement in just a couple of months" when, on September 12, 1986, Paramount's John Pike came to Gene Roddenberry with a nine-page proposal for a new Star Trek TV series to be called "Star Trek: The Next Generation."

The series described in this peculiar document—written by Greg Strangis, with input from Jeff Hayes and Rick Berman—bears almost no resemblance to what *TNG* eventually became. To put this in perspective, September 1986 was two months before *The Voyage Home* hit theaters. It was also a year and a month before the eventual debut of the real *Next Generation*. As proposed by Strangis, this series was all about the USS *Odyssey* and, in the first episode, a new Vulcan captain named Captain Rhon (Captain Ron?), who was to be killed by Klingons. But don't worry! Rhon would have *stayed* on the series as a holographic re-creation of himself, sort of like a Vulcan version of Max Headroom. (Ah, the '80s!) Meanwhile, the basic thrust of this show was about the USS *Odyssey* constantly trying to prevent intergalactic war and would depict Starfleet as having just come out of a "ten-year war between the Federation and the Klingon Empire." Roddenberry's response to the proposal memo[5] was curt: "Get rid of it." Essentially, the studio's first stab at *The Next Generation* made Gene Roddenberry batshit furious enough to just try and do it himself. To his mind, this "The Next Generation" looked more like Star Wars than Star Trek. The Strangis-written series would have pushed the Federation and the Klingons *back* to the

---

5 Although much of the proposal reads as laughable and cynical (a character named "Helen Joyce" is described as "painfully beautiful"), various elements of this bizzarro "Next Generation" later seemed to crop up in odd places. *Deep Space Nine*'s earliest scenes begin with the death of the Vulcan captain, while the pilot episode of *Star Trek: Discovery* also focused on a heroic captain dying (Michelle Yeoh's Georgiou), who later returned both as a hologram and a Mirror Universe doppelgänger. It's unlikely that anyone was trying to intentionally pay homage to this canceled version of *TNG*, but the parallels are there all the same.

brink of war, which was only prevented by having various observers for the opposing sides serving on one another's starships.[6]

Though the subtitle "Next Generation" was initially suggested by this document, several other titles were floated by Bob Justman—after the fact—such as "The Second Generation," "Star Trek Beyond the Future," "Final Trek," "Future Trek," "Final Quest," "Star Trek: Beyond Eternity," "Star Trek: The Search for Tomorrow," and "Star Trek: The Eternal Mission." Luckily, although Roddenberry rejected the first idea for "The Next Generation," he did keep the title. It may seem a little basic today, but it also just *works*. It feels unlikely we would have all flipped out for "The Eternal Mission."

———

If the idea of Gene Roddenberry launching a more enlightened version of Star Trek designed to smooth out the rough edges of *The Original Series* sounds familiar, it should. Before *Star Trek: The Motion Picture* became, well, a motion picture, Roddenberry had been hard at work on a different next generation, the never-filmed 1977 TV series "Star Trek: Phase II." According to Trek writer Judith Reeves-Stevens: "Whatever didn't end up in *The Motion Picture* ended up in *The Next Generation*." The fact that Roddenberry had tried to make another reboot Trek series nine years earlier partly explains how he was easily able to pivot from "No thanks, fuck Star Trek," to "You know, I actually have a whole format in mind for this new show." In "Phase II," Spock was going to be replaced with a

———

6 The good-guy Klingon Starfleet officer Worf (Michael Dorn) was perhaps inspired by this idea, but then again, maybe not. Producer Bob Justman takes credit for putting a Klingon on the bridge of the new *Enterprise*, a notion that Roddenberry also fought until being cajoled by Justman.

full-Vulcan character named Xon. But, unlike Spock's predilection for suppressing his human side, the idea with Xon was that he'd be interested in learning to act like a human. Despite casting actor David Gautreaux in the role, Xon never materialized. But the idea of dropping in a reverse Spock—an emotionless character who was obsessed with becoming more human—was reborn in the android character of Data. As "Phase II" experts Judith and Garfield Reeves-Stevens point out, "Just as Xon was an early version of Data, Decker [played by Stephen Collins in *The Motion Picture*] was the forerunner of *TNG*'s William T. Riker."

The iconic opening theme for *The Next Generation*, composed by Jerry Goldsmith, was also recycled from *Star Trek: The Motion Picture*, a fact which almost nobody in the early '90s even noticed because our parents all insisted *The Motion Picture* sucked. That brilliant 1979 score by Goldsmith was nominated for an Oscar in 1980, the only Star Trek score to receive such a nomination. Roddenberry knew he had gold with that bombastic and heroic main title march, and reusing *The Motion Picture* theme for *The Next Generation* was just one example of how the show faked it until it made it.

After dusting off a few of his "Phase II" ideas, Roddenberry enthusiastically hired several of his colleagues from the good old days, including Dorothy Fontana, tribble inventor David Gerrold, and producer Bob Justman. Fontana co-wrote the pilot episode ("Encounter at Farpoint") with Roddenberry, in which the crew is harassed by a flippant all-powerful space deity named Q (John de Lancie) that is intent on proving all of humanity is terrible and needs to answer for its crime of a being a "savage" species. Of all Season 1 *TNG* adventures, this one holds up the best, because as a villain, Q is a deliciously amoral foil to the earnest and utterly moral Picard. *TNG* writer Melinda Snodgrass argued Q was a mischievous god "like Loki," while early script editor Maurice Hurley felt Q was always there to "teach a lesson" to the crew and, by extension, the audience.

By the end of the second season of *The Next Generation*, nearly the entire writing staff had either been fired or had quit. Dorothy Fontana recalled that "the first series [*TOS*] was a great experience. This wasn't." Later she told William Shatner, "Gene was fun, but later, as things were not going well, he got somewhat sour." Nearly every *TNG* writer who quit or was fired during these tumultuous early years blamed the erratic, moody, and unwell Roddenberry or his proxy enforcer, an unscrupulous lawyer named Leonard Maizlish. Whether or not Maizlish was really doing Roddenberry's bidding in the firings and script changes was unclear. By 1989 Roddenberry had had at least two documented strokes, but his health problems had been mounting well before that. Prior to and during the production of *TNG* in 1986, Majel Barrett Roddenberry had repeatedly sent Gene to a La Costa substance abuse clinic in San Diego. Roddenberry's long addictions to alcohol, cocaine, and several prescription medications stretched back to the '60s and seemed to get worse in the '70s and '80s. During the filming of *The Motion Picture* in 1979, Star Trek's greatest NASA friend, Dr. Jesco von Puttkamer, repeatedly "told Roddenberry" that his cocaine habit and heavy drinking would "kill him." In September of 1989, Roddenberry's physicians concluded he had had a series of strokes, which resulted in multiple cerebral infarctions, meaning his brain had been permanently damaged, resulting in impaired walking and aphasia. At a Star Trek convention on June 9, 1991, Gene Roddenberry briefly stood onstage and told the screaming fans that "it's amazing to have so many people wishing you well." But, by October 24, 1991, he had died.

Roddenberry's death happened during the fifth season of *The Next Generation*. But, by the time of his death, during the twenty-fifth anniversary of *The Original Series*, Roddenberry's immortal legacy was secure. His second Star Trek wasn't just a success; by 1991, *The Next Generation* was pulling in an average of 20 million viewers a week. It was no longer a cult curiosity; it was a mainstream hit that had eclipsed *The Original Series*.

It wasn't that *The Next Generation* was better than *The Original Series*. In many ways, in terms of raw artistic originality, it's not. By the time *TNG* got good—in the 1989–1990 third season—it did something *TOS* couldn't have ever done: drop the kitsch. *TNG* may seem goofy in the way all Star Trek seems goofy, but its strength was that it took its characters and situations a lot more seriously than its predecessor. By the 1989 third season, savior *TNG* producer Michael Piller instituted two new polices in the way in which *Star Trek* scripts would be written. First, each episode must be focused on one of the regular characters. "It became a character show," writer Ronald D. Moore explained. "He'd ask: 'Whose show [episode] is it? Is it a Worf show? A Riker show? A Picard show?'"

Piller's second innovation was that *Star Trek* would start taking story pitches from *anyone*, regardless of whether the writer had an agent or not. Ron Moore was the first of those "outside" hired to *The Next Generation* staff based only on the strength of his un-agented spec script, "The Bonding." Moore would later go on to become a producer on *TNG*, and then *Deep Space Nine*. Today, he's likely best known as the guy who rebooted *Battlestar Galactica*, adapted *Outlander*, created *For All Mankind* and a plethora of other superpopular TV projects. Launching the writing career of Ron Moore *alone* is just one huge way that *Star Trek: The Next Generation* changed the pop culture universe of the future. "Because he found me through that [freelance] process, Michael thought this was a great resource to find writers," Moore recalled. "And he threw the door open."

In Moore's first script, "The Bonding," a random crew member named Marla Aster (Susan Powell) is zapped by an off-screen alien explosive, which leaves her young son Jeremy (Gabriel Damon) an orphan on the USS *Enterprise*. In *The Original Series*, people like Marla were a running joke. If some guest character—usually wearing red[7]—beamed down with our regular heroes, you could bet they would die horribly before the episode's end. In "The Bonding," *The Next Generation* flipped the script. Marla wore blue, and she was a guest character, but the episode wasn't about the alien explosive or continuing the zany alien planet adventure. The episode was focused on making her son feel better about his mom's sudden space death. Turns out, poor Jeremy's dad died before this episode happened, so, with tears streaming down his face, Aster tells Picard and Troi, "I'm all alone." In a tragically underrated Patrick Stewart performance, Captain Picard firmly reaches out his hand to the young boy and without a hint of sentimentality says, "On the Starship *Enterprise*, no one is alone." Beat. Chills from the audience. Then, just as firmly, Stewart says again, for emphasis, *"No one."*

Unlike George Lazenby breaking the fourth wall as James

---

7 Plenty of guest-actor folks *not* wearing red die in *The Original Series*, too. Still, the trope of the doomed "redshirt" is so strong in the Trekkie mind that simply putting on red in Star Trek is, arguably, a subtle clue to get worried. Case in point, in *The Wrath*, everyone switched to red all the time, and Spock died. In *TNG*, the command officers swapped gold for red. Were we more worried about Picard and Riker because of the color of their uniforms? Maybe?

Bond,[8] Picard did not turn to the camera and say, "This never happened to the other fellow," because by 1989, when this episode aired, Picard and his crew weren't just the *other Star Trek*. They *were Star Trek*. At the point when Patrick Stewart was getting marriage proposals at Star Trek conventions in 1993, the popularity of *The Next Generation* had made Star Trek and science fiction the most ubiquitous it had ever been in history. "We were a harbinger of things to come," LeVar Burton tells me. "Just look at the universe of entertainment we currently live in. We went on to cement our place in science fiction and pop culture, and that's due, largely, in part, to your generation." The toy aisles at Target and Toys R Us in the mid-1990s were not brimming with Star Wars stuff because the early '80s was long over, and the late-1990s Skywalker comeback hadn't happened yet. This was also true of your local paperback book rack in the supermarket, newsstand, or actual bookstore. At the height of Trek's '90s renaissance, Pocket Books was publishing six different original novels a year, crowding out those slots reserved for Fabio-adorned romance novels in a big way. Over half of these books were focused on *TNG* crew. As a child, I devoured these books, which is somewhat appropriate, because my initial excitement about watching the series was a hundred percent connected to *Reading Rainbow* legend LeVar Burton. Would children of the '80s and '90s have been as pumped to dive into a new *Star Trek* if the trustworthy bookworm LeVar Burton hadn't been part of the crew? It seems impossible.

---

8 In the 1969 film *On Her Majesty's Secret Service*, one-time James Bond actor George Lazenby opened the film by acknowledging he wasn't Sean Connery. Debates about Patrick Stewart and William Shatner in the 1990s were *very similar* to debates about James Bond actors.

"I actually hear that a lot," Burton tells me with a laugh. "I was the gateway drug to Star Trek."

"In my opinion, we got credibility when Whoopi [Goldberg] came on the show in the second season," Brent Spiner tells me with a confident professorial twinkle[9] that's hard to imagine for Data or any of Spiner's other Trek characters.[10] At the start of the second season, the *Enterprise* gained its famous bar/lounge, Ten Forward, and the bartender was the mysterious Guinan (Goldberg), later revealed to be from a race of long-lived aliens who have been visiting other planets since at least the nineteenth century. A huge fan of *The Original Series* and Nichelle Nichols in particular, Goldberg personally petitioned the producers to find her a spot on the show. If Star Trek has an analog for Yoda, a kind of wise sage who gets people to pull their heads out of their asses, it's Guinan. "I think that was a real turning point," Spiner says. "I think there's some good, you know, decent episodes in the first season. We had a Peabody nomination for 'The Big Goodbye,' but there were some bad episodes at the start. Finding our way and stuff like that. But by the time a major movie star—Whoopi Goldberg—wanted to be on the

---

9 Yes, I know Data became an actual twenty-fourth-century professor at Cambridge in the episode "All Good Things . . ." I'm talking about the feeling of scholarly charm and eccentricity. Like the real version of it, not the Data-affected version of it. This is a roundabout way of saying Spiner is an amazing actor. He's nothing like those characters.

10 Of all the Trek regulars, Spiner has easily played the most *different* characters. Starting with "Datalore," Spiner also played Lore, Data's evil twin brother. Later, in "Brothers," Spiner played Data's ailing human father/inventor Dr. Noonien Soong. In the prequel series *Enterprise*, Spiner played Arik Soong, Noonien's ancestor in the twenty-second century. In *Star Trek: Nemesis*, Spiner also played B-4, an early Data prototype and Data's *other* secret robot brother. In *Star Trek: Picard* Seasons 1 and 2, he plays *two* different members of the Soong family. If you expand to all the times Data is *possessed* by random alien gods/crazed scientists/other robots, Spiner's Trek oeuvre gets into the double digits very quickly. And don't even try to start counting holographic Datas/Spiners. You'll lose your mind. Also, please don't ask yourself this question: Does Data *pretending* to be Sherlock Holmes count as a separate character? Madness will ensue. Trust me.

show, I think that was crucial. I think all of a sudden the general public, who maybe didn't watch sci-fi, was like, what's going on with this show? We'd better take this seriously. And more people started to watch it because she was at the height of her power at that time."

In 1992, a *TV Guide* readers' poll voted Stewart "the most bodacious man in TV" and he rocked a leather vest on the cover, next to Cindy Crawford, the other celebrity who received the most votes. For non-fans this might seems nuts, simply because at a glance, Picard scanned as such a low-key, understated hero. But, as all fans of *TNG* know, Stewart imbued Picard with smoldering sex appeal. During the filming of "Encounter at Farpoint"—just before the final scene when Picard says, "Let's see what's out there . . . Engage"— director Corey Allen gave Stewart an influential and hilarious note. As Stewart has recounted more than once: Before saying "Action," Allen "yelled out at the top of his voice" and said: "'Patrick! I WANT YOU TO FUCK THE UNIVERSE!'" Let's get real. It worked.

In 1994, Stewart hosted *Saturday Night Live*, perfectly enunciating the name of the musical guest like no other *SNL* host before or since—"Ladies and gentlemen, Salt-N-Pepa!" This is the moment that perfectly encapsulates the '90s: Salt-N-Pepa side-by-side with Captain Jean-Luc Picard, the greatest co-headliners of any show, ever. In 1988, when Patrick Stewart attended his first Star Trek convention in Denver, Colorado, he admitted that he hadn't expected a large crowd, and upon seeing over 3,000 people waiting to hear him speak, after just *one* season of *The Next Generation*, Stewart said, "I now know what it's like to be Sting."

Finding a pop culture analogy for *Star Trek: The Next Generation* is tricky. Marina Sirtis (Counselor Deanna Troi) said that her husband, the late Michael Lamper, likened it to "being asked to join the Rolling Stones." It's a damn good analogy, but it isn't quite right. The Rolling Stones may have gone through a few different guitarists and various backup singers in their never-ending live tours, but Mick Jagger was always the front man. Is Mick Jagger the Starship *Enterprise*? Who is Charlie Watts in this analogy? Most reboots and sequels of big TV or movie zeitgeist events—like the James Bond movies or *Batman*—tend to focus on old characters played by new actors. At the very least, familiar actors are a constant presence. Even *Saved by the Bell: The New Class* brought Screech and Mr. Belding along for the ride. *The Next Generation* was—and still is—deeply *weird* when you consider how gutsy it was, just as a premise. Yes, we're gonna do Star Trek, but no, we're not going to have a single character from the old show in the cast, and we're going to go out of our way to not mention them *for years*. DeForest Kelley appears as an elderly admiral in the *TNG* pilot, "Encounter at Farpoint," but his character is not named, and his brief (and hilarious) scene with the android Data (Brent Spiner) only lasts for about two minutes. Imagine a series of Fast and Furious movies in which they don't drive their cars nearly as fast, and nobody even mentions Vin Diesel. That impossible thing you just failed to envision is what *The Next Generation* was to *The Original Series*.

"I would argue that *The Original Series* is a darker series than *The Next Generation*," *TNG* writer-producer Ron Moore tells me over the phone. "In between *The Original Series* and the movies, Roddenberry had been kind of told he was this utopian visionary, and I think he kind of bought into that and just took it further. By the time *The Next Generation* came along, his definition of what Star Trek was had shifted. I also think *Next Gen* was a bit of a reaction to *Star Trek II*. He really deemphasized the military and dialed back ambiguity and character conflict and made the Federation and Starfleet even more utopian than what we had seen before."

In the twenty-fourth century of *TNG*, Starfleet officers were forbidden from having high-stakes interpersonal conflicts with each other. There would be no Bones-Spock style bickering on this *Trek*, and the grittiness of *The Original Series* and the violence and action of the feature films were left behind.

When Roddenberry created *The Next Generation,* he was actively revising the way he wanted the philosophical core of Star Trek to be perceived and discussed. And he was 100 percent successful in this revision. When fans debate "Roddenberry's vision," in almost every way they are talking about this idea: the notion that idealistic human beings in the future act like the crew of *The Next Generation*. The funny thing is, the writers of *TNG*, both on staff and freelancers, often pushed back against this edict. Moore always wanted the Federation to be less "goody-goody." Along with other writers (notably Naren Shankar), Moore fought producers Michael Piller and Rick Berman for more conflict between the crew, more fights, and moral "ambiguity." They weren't always successful, but Moore tells me he thinks that the "tension" between the writers and this dogmatic rule was what "defined the show." Still, even though *TNG* was an introspective show—shining a light on the interior lives of intrepid space explorers—most of the literal conflict had to come from without. And when that wouldn't work, the characters themselves had to be transformed. Literally.

"I was always trying to get Picard to act a little more like Kirk," writer Morgan Gendel tells me. Although his career path was different than Moore's, Gendel was also an outsider, and wrote for *TNG* as a freelancer, mostly thanks to the open-door policy. "What makes any good show work is the emotions and the relationships.

When I pitched 'Starship Mine,' I wanted it to be about Picard's relationship to the *Enterprise*. When I pitched 'The Inner Light,' I wanted it to be about this other life. The road not taken."

Gendel's tear-jerker episode "The Inner Light"—co-written by *TNG* staffer Peter Allan Fields—is rightly considered one of the finest moments of *The Next Generation*. Thanks to an ancient telepathic probe, Picard suddenly lives an entire lifetime as a flute-playing family man on a distant, long-dead world. For the crew, only about thirty minutes pass as Picard lies comatose on the floor of the bridge. But Picard experiences an entirely different existence, much longer than thirty minutes—decades pass for him. On a pseudo-agrarian planet, Picard lives humbly, relatively free from technology. In his village, he fights against devastating drought, helps his community, has children, grows to be a frail old man, has grandchildren, and lives to see the launch of a space probe that will eventually find "himself" in the future. Gendel's title, "The Inner Light," was derived from a George Harrison–penned Beatles song of the same name. In the song, George sings that you can "arrive without traveling." This is where *The Next Generation* boldly went the best, into science fiction stories that didn't chart courses through space, but instead created a new and enduring emotional cartography. "I don't really care anymore if fans know it was me who wrote 'The Inner Light,'" Gendel says. "They probably just think the author is Star Trek and that's fine. That's how it should be."

Gendel's suggestion that Star Trek might be perceived as a collective of writers and storytelling ideas is telling, mostly because *The Next Generation*'s most compelling science fiction creation was the unstoppable homogeneous hive-mind cyborg species, the Borg. In his book *The Tyranny of E-mail,* critic and author John Freeman writes, "It's hard to find a more potent metaphor for the dangers of the man-machine melding that we have experienced in the last fifty years." Freeman considers the Borg to be a "countermythology," a sci-fi villain that's more of a growing anxiety rather than a plausible end game for humanity. From the perspective of horror tropes, the Borg are pretty much just tech-zombies. But unlike zombies, the Borg aren't really *dead*, they're just dead inside. Because *The Next Generation* was so obsessed with nurturing the inner lights of all of its characters (even the robot!), the Borg were way more horrifying than Q. When Q dropped by, he was mostly messing with Picard and mocking all the virtue signaling from Starfleet, daring everyone to do better, think harder.

The Borg, on the other hand, didn't care about anything. They just wanted to assimilate, erase personal identity, and create their brand of "perfection" through the elimination of individuality. In "The Best of Both Worlds," when the Borg abducted Picard and turned him into Locutus of Borg—a soulless cyborg spokesperson—*The Next Generation* literally held the soul of Star Trek hostage. The writers had figured out how to create the most high-stakes personal drama by using the existing characters, but also didn't break Roddenberry's rules against Starfleet crew fighting with each other. Picard's mind and body were used against his will by an alien force. And yet, the Borg aren't even evil. They're just an AI that got a little too efficient. Of course, there was another message being sent when the Borgified Picard said coldly, "You will be assimilated . . . resistance is futile." Any Trekkie who still thought *The Next Generation* wasn't legit Star Trek had to give up their hater act. Resistance was futile. *The Next Generation* wasn't just good, it was the biggest syndicated show in history, and "The Best of Both

Worlds" was a summer cliffhanger to rival a summer blockbuster movie.

If you only ever watch two episodes[11] of *The Next Generation*, "The Inner Light" and "The Best of Both Worlds" will probably tell you everything you need to know. Like Spock, Picard became the Picard we loved when he did things out of character. But there's more to it than that. *TNG* didn't just have an inner light, it had an inner flame. Exactly when that flame was going to blow up created all the narrative tension. Saying *TNG* was a sunny, optimistic show does it a disservice, because it was a show with very dark undercurrents, and you kept watching to see when all that tension was going to bubble over. The shit always hit the fan in *TNG*, but the fan was turned on sneakily in the background, and you weren't entirely sure what the shit was until it was spinning out of control.

Basically, when Picard loses his temper it's always a really, really big deal precisely because he's so buttoned-up the rest of the time. Picard yelling at people constitutes 99 percent of all of Patrick Stewart's best performances, and it's always a slow burn. He starts out just saying normal stuff, and suddenly he's shouting at the top his lungs. In the 1996 film *First Contact*, it's "THE LINE MUST BE DRAWN HERE!" But take a look at "Yesterday's Enterprise," and "The First Duty," and yes, even "The Best of Both Worlds"—Picard building up to a big blow-up is part of what makes these episodes so moving, exciting, and, occasionally, much darker than *TNG*'s reputation.

And by the time it reached its zenith, it had redefined what Star Trek could be. "It was in our last season we were nominated as best drama on TV," LeVar Burton tells me, referencing the ground-

---

11 Okay, *three*. "The Best of Both Worlds" is a two-parter.

breaking moment when *TNG* got an Emmy nod. Before *The Next Generation*, a science fiction series had never been nominated for best drama. "That felt good," Burton remembers. "Previous to that, in terms of industry acceptance, we were considered more of a sci-fi fringe thing." At the 1994 Emmys, *The Next Generation* lost to *Picket Fences*, but we all know which show matters more today. *The Next Generation* was, and in many ways still is, the most patient Star Trek. It didn't try to top the bombast of *The Original Series*. From the very beginning, it was playing a different game entirely. Kirk and *The Original Series* were like a Sex Pistols song; it's great, but it's over quick. Picard and *The Next Generation* are like the mega-famous Phil Collins song, "In the Air Tonight." It seems like no big deal at first. But then those drums kick in.

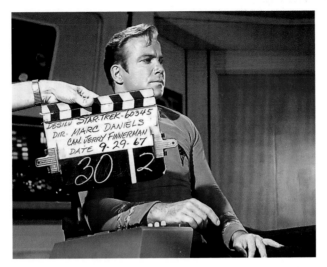

William Shatner as Captain Kirk, filming the *Star Trek* episode "A Private Little War" in 1967. *(Courtesy of Gerald Gurian)*

The cast of *Star Trek: The Original Series* (sans George Takei) in the second season, in 1967: Leonard Nimoy as Spock, Nichelle Nichols as Uhura, William Shatner as Captain Kirk, DeForest Kelley as Dr. McCoy, Walter Koenig as Chekov, and James Doohan as Scotty. *(Courtesy of Gerald Gurian)*

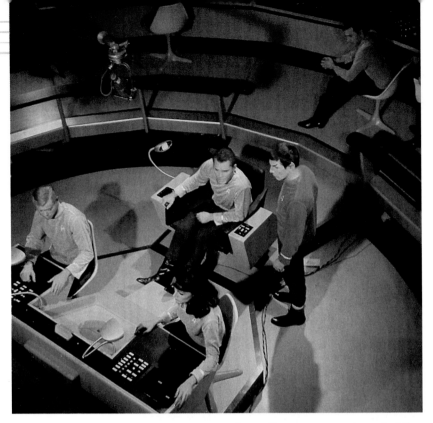

CLOCKWISE FROM LEFT: Peter Duryea as Tyler, Jeffrey Hunter as Captain Pike, Leonard Nimoy as Spock, and Majel Barrett as Number One, filming the first *Star Trek* pilot episode, "The Cage," in 1964. *(Courtesy of Gerald Gurian)*

An early screen test of Leonard Nimoy's Spock hairstyle and eyebrows, with actress Cindy Robbins, from 1964.

(Courtesy of Gerald Gurian)

Nichelle Nichols in her Uhura costume, taking a break from filming *Star Trek* at Desilu Studios in 1966.
(Courtesy of Gerald Gurian)

George Takei as Sulu, filming the *Star Trek* episode "The Naked Time," in 1966.
(Courtesy of Gerald Gurian)

Writer D. C. Fontana (center, seated) poses with fans at a Star Trek convention in the early 1970s. *(Courtesy of an anonymous collection)*

Studio-donated eleven-foot filming model of USS *Enterprise* hanging from the ceiling outside the science fiction exhibit at the Smithsonian National Air and Space Museum in Washington, DC, in 1977.

(Courtesy of Howard Weinstein)

FROM LEFT TO RIGHT: William Shatner, Majel Barrett, and Gene Rodden-berry in 1966 on the set of *Star Trek*.   *(Courtesy of Gerald Gurian)*

SEE THIS TERRIFIC NEW MOVIE

At the end of the universe lies the beginning of vengeance.

STAR TREK II THE WRATH OF KHAN

PARAMOUNT PICTURES presents
STAR TREK II THE WRATH OF KHAN Executive Consultant GENE RODDENBERRY
Based on STAR TREK Created by GENE RODDENBERRY Executive Producer
HARVE BENNETT Screenplay by JACK B SOWARDS Story by HARVE B DD DOLBY STEREO
JACK B SOWARDS Produced by ROBERT SALLIN Directed by NICHO PG PARENTAL

**Week Days—7:32-9:44
Sat & Sun—1:12-3:24-5:31-7:43-9:55**

A newspaper advertisement for tickets to *Star Trek II: The Wrath of Khan*, from June 11, 1982, in the *Ukiah Daily Journal*.
(Courtesy of John and Maria Jose Tenuto)

The ad that was published by the Concerned Supporters of Star Trek in *The Hollywood Reporter* on September 24, 1981, in protest of Spock's death in the motion picture that would become *The Wrath of Khan*.
(Courtesy of John and Maria Jose Tenuto)

Robin Curtis and Leonard Nimoy discuss her casting as Saavik in *Star Trek III: The Search for Spock* during a "lift-off" party at the home of producer Harve Bennett in 1983. *(Courtesy of Robin Curtis)*

Robin Curtis as Saavik, James Doohan as Scotty, Nichelle Nichols as Uhura, Walter Koenig as Chekov, George Takei as Sulu, Kirk Thatcher as the Punk, with hairdresser Silvia Abascal and two unidentified crew members, messing around on the set of *Star Trek IV: The Voyage Home* in 1986. *(Courtesy of Robin Curtis)*

LeVar Burton, Marina Sirtis, Jonathan Frakes, Patrick Stewart, Gates McFadden, Brent Spiner, and Michael Dorn attend Starlight Children's Foundation of Southern California's the Child in All of Us in 1993.

(Ron Galella, Ltd./Ron Galella Collection via Getty Images)

Michael Dorn and LeVar Burton—Worf and Geordi La Forge from *The Next Generation*—at Star Trek Convention Las Vegas on August 2, 2019.

(Courtesy of Nick Duguid)

William Shatner, Kate Mulgrew, Avery Brooks, and Scott Bakula—Captains Kirk, Janeway, Sisko, and Archer—at Destination Star Trek: London in 2012. *(Oli Scarff/Getty Images)*

Avery Brooks—Captain Benjamin Sisko in *Deep Space Nine*—at Destination Star Trek: London on October 22, 2012. *(Xprize Foundation)*

Andrew Robinson, Chase Masterson, and Max Grodénchik—Garak, Leeta, and Rom of *Deep Space Nine*—on stage at Star Trek Convention Las Vegas on August 2, 2018. *(Courtesy of Nick Duguid)*

Whoopi Goldberg with Star Trek fans cosplaying as her *Next Generation* character, Guinan, at Star Trek Convention Las Vegas on August 4, 2016. *(Courtesy of Nick Duguid)*

Jonathan Frakes, Jeri Ryan, and Jonathan Del Arco—Riker, Seven of Nine, and Hugh—promoting *Star Trek: Picard* at Star Trek Convention Las Vegas on August 3, 2019. *(Courtesy of Nick Duguid)*

Chris Pine, Alice Eve, Zachary Quinto, and Zoe Saldaña—Captain Kirk, Carol Marcus, Mr. Spock, and Nyota Uhura—at the London premiere of *Star Trek Into Darkness* in 2013. *(Courtesy of John Hancock)*

Zachary Quinto, Zoe Saldaña, director Justin Lin, Chris Pine, and Simon Pegg attend a *Star Trek Beyond* press conference at Indigo on August 18, 2016, in Beijing, China. *(Visual China Group via Getty Images)*

Emily Coutts, Sara Mitich, and Rekha Sharma—Detmer, Airiam/Nilsson, and Landry—on stage at Star Trek Convention Las Vegas on August 4, 2018. *(Courtesy of Nick Duguid)*

Kenneth Mitchell in 2018.

(Raymond Litster, courtesy of Chase Masterson/ Pop Culture Hero Coalition)

The doctors of Star Trek, Wilson Cruz (Culber on *Discovery*), Alexander Siddig (Bashir on *Deep Space Nine*), Gates McFadden (Crusher on *The Next Generation*), Robert Picardo (The Doctor on *Voyager*), and John Billingsley (Phlox on *Enterprise*), with moderator Scott Matz at Star Trek Convention Las Vegas on August 10, 2019. *(Courtesy of Nick Duguid)*

Sonequa Martin-Green and David Ajala—Captain Burnham and Cleveland Booker—promote *Star Trek: Discovery* at San Diego Comic-Con, 2019.
(Courtesy of Gage Skidmore)

Brent Spiner and Jeri Ryan—Data and Seven of Nine—at San Diego Comic-Con, speaking about *Star Trek: Picard* on July 20, 2019.
(Courtesy of Gage Skidmore)

Producer Alex Kurtzman, Sir Patrick Stewart, and Isa Briones—Jean-Luc Picard and Soji—at San Diego Comic-Con 2019, ahead of the launch of *Star Trek: Picard*.   *(Courtesy of Gage Skidmore)*

Ethan Peck and Rebecca Romijn—Spock and Number One in *Discovery* and *Strange New Worlds*—at San Diego Comic-Con in 2019.

(Courtesy of Gage Skidmore)

FROM LEFT TO RIGHT: Wil Wheaton (Wesley on *The Next Generation*) moderates a panel discussion about *Star Trek: Discovery* with showrunner Michelle Paradise and stars Wilson Cruz (Dr. Culber) and Blu del Barrio (Adira) on September 8, 2021, for a "Star Trek Day" celebration at the Skirball Cultural Center in Los Angeles.   *(Courtesy of Chase Masterson)*

Star Trek Day, September 8, 2021: LeVar Burton speaks about playing Geordi La Forge on *Star Trek: The Next Generation*. Behind him, composer Jeff Russo conducts an orchestra playing musical selections from across the Star Trek franchise.   *(Courtesy of Chase Masterson)*

CHAPTER 10

THE DREAMER AND THE DREAM

Deep Space Nine finally delivers on the promise of *The Original Series*

The two most dangerous words in talking about pop culture are "underrated" and "misunderstood." Like any sweeping generalization about the mood of a majority, you're creating a perpetual value statement that operates outside of the rules of time passing. If you say the band Phish is "misunderstood," you're automatically implying only a select group of smarter people *correctly* understand it. Hard-core Weezer fans are like this, too. But the bigger problem is the way using "misunderstood" and "underrated" freezes discourse. Nobody says Phish *used to* be underrated or Childish Gambino isn't misunderstood *anymore*. When people throw these words around, the implication is This Thing Was, Is, and Always Shall Be Underrated and Misunderstood. Once a pop culture thingamabob is "underrated," its underratedness becomes fixed, and exists outside of linear time. And the strangest case of a thing being called "underrated" is the shape-shifting reputation of Star Trek's "middle child," the political powerhouse series *Deep Space*

Nine, a series that launched with a two-hour episode called "Emissary," about a group of aliens who have no concept of past, present, or future.

In 2018, in the *DS9* documentary *What We Left Behind*, series star Armin Shimerman fumed that it was "hurtful" to continue to endure the "perception that we don't match up [to *The Next Generation* and *The Original Series*]." While sour grapes are a dish best served in deep space, if you were watching *Live! With Regis and Kathie Lee* on the morning of June 7, 1993, you can start to figure out why this guy was still pissed in 2018. Right out of the wormhole, *Deep Space Nine* was treated differently. No other Star Trek cast member before or since Shimerman has been asked (forced?) to appear *in character* on a national talk show in full makeup and costume. Yes, Leonard Nimoy appeared as Mr. Spock on *The Carol Burnett Show* in 1967. But that was cool, and *Star Trek* was already on the air. Armin Shimerman being made to parade around as Quark with Regis and Kathie Lee as a promo for *Deep Space Nine* only succeeded in making *DS9* look like a show for weirdos. Imagine Paul Bettany doing press for *WandaVision* in 2021, wearing his Vision makeup and having Ellen or Jimmy Kimmel refer to him only as "Vision." Nobody would stand for it.[1] But, in 1993, despite the huge mainstream success of *The Next Generation*, somebody thought it was a good idea for Shimerman to do *Regis and Kathie Lee*, not as himself, but as his *DS9* alter ego, the duplicitous, greedy, and creepy alien Ferengi bartender known as Quark. Regis and

---

1 And, in 1987, Patrick Stewart didn't. Infamously, Stewart walked off the set of *The Next Generation*—British pop star style—when *Good Morning America* was filming a weather segment from the bridge of the *Enterprise*, complete with a weatherman wearing a Starfleet uniform. Stewart defended his anger later by saying he thought it was "schtick in our costumes," which he felt was "demeaning" and "disrespectful." Stewart later said he regretted walking off the set, but his statements since then have mostly scanned as *sorry, not sorry.*

Kathie Lee referred to Shimerman as "Quark," the on-screen text identified him as "Quark," and the pair quizzed him about the nature of his species.

"Ferengi are the capitalists of the universe," Shimerman told his hosts. "We think of ourselves as the robber barons, the Carnegies, the Rockefellers." In *The Next Generation*, the Ferengi were initially introduced as the newest, most anti–Star Trek adversary: sexist dudes obsessed with money who looked like big-eared trolls. In the 1987 *TNG* episode "The Last Outpost," Shimerman played one of the first Ferengi ever, and recalled that the director told him and his co-stars to "hop around like monkeys." Then, in 1993, when he returned to play another Ferengi, Shimerman's Quark became a bizarre ambassador for what people liked to call the "dark and gritty" Star Trek. Two decades later, *Deep Space Nine* feels modern and uplifting as hell, and calling it "dark" relative to TV now is kind of a joke. "I bridle when people say *Deep Space Nine* is a 'dark' show," longtime Trek writer Ron Moore tells me. "If anything, it got closer to the feeling of *The Original Series*."

"To me, *Deep Space Nine* is probably the best series next to the original," Star Trek historian Mark A. Altman enthuses. This viewpoint is not uncommon. If you really want to get into it with lifelong, die-hard, and self-styled Treksperts, you'll find that while there's a huge spectrum of debate, almost no one who has seen all seven seasons of *Deep Space Nine* will say it's just kind of okay. Within Trek circles, you either have mad respect for *DS9* or you think it's the greatest Star Trek ever, or you've simply never watched it. There aren't any lukewarm opinions on this series. Also, in spite—or perhaps *because of*—its "underrated" status, *Deep Space Nine* tends to be the Star Trek series offered up to a newbie who has just come to the final frontier by way of the reboot films or the newer twenty-first-century shows. While I was talking to the cast of *Star Trek: Discovery* in late 2021, in *two* separate conversations, young cast members Blu del Barrio and Mary Wiseman *both* mentioned they were bingeing *Deep Space Nine*. "It's definitely my favorite of the older shows," Wiseman told me, while del Barrio said, "*Deep Space Nine* was really ahead of its time."

Outside of newer fans like the *DISCO* cast, older Trekkies who claim *DS9* is the best Trek series are like Weezer fans who say *Pinkerton* is better than the *Blue Album*. It's not wrong. But it's also not controversial, either. There's just always somebody who's gonna say the *Blue Album* is better. And, in this analogy, the *Blue Album* is *The Next Generation*, because of course it is. So, the question is, for those who worked on *Deep Space Nine*, was the popularity of their two other siblings—the eldest child *The Next Generation* and, later, "the baby," *Star Trek: Voyager*—actually all that oppressive? Was *Deep Space Nine* really and truly underrated? And is it anymore?

"On the one hand, yes, it often feels that way still and it often did," Chase Masterson tells me. Masterson played the Bajoran civilian Leeta on *DS9,* a semi-regular who found her way into the hearts of fans, but also into the heart of Rom (Max Grodénchik), the only male Ferengi on the series who rejected the sexist, capitalistic ways of his brethren (and literal brother, Quark). Today, Masterson leverages her *Deep Space Nine* fame into a bullying-prevention organization called Pop Culture Hero Coalition, which she cofounded with child psychology expert Carrie Goldman in 2013. Shirts for the coalition feature an upside-down version of the Starfleet insignia emblazoned with the words "Be Kind." The curriculum of Pop Culture Hero Coalition is called "The Heroic Journey," and is the only social-emotional learning program used by the YMCA. This curriculum draws from various popular narratives in pop culture—not just Star Trek. But still, the *only* social-emotional learning program used by the YMCA came into existence because a former Star Trek actor made it happen. Right now, there are children being taught useful skills around self-esteem and when to recognize and stop emotional abuse, indirectly, because Chase Masterson happened to be a pop culture icon who got involved in social work after *Deep Space Nine*. And because of this work, Masterson has a fair, level-headed, and honest opinion about the perceived neglect of *Deep Space Nine*.

"Look, some of the acclaim that the other casts can get at various events *can* lead us to feel overlooked," Masterson tells me. "However, *Deep Space Nine* was the number one syndicated show in the world when it went off the air [in 1999]. We didn't have the movies like *Next Gen*, and it was a more complicated show. It was more challenging for people to fall in love with it." Masterson's assertion checks out. In 1994, the average viewership for an episode of *Deep Space Nine* was between 13 and 15 million people. A little less than the 20 million *The Next Generation* was pulling in from 1991 to 1994, but still. More people watched *DS9* than you think.

If *The Next Generation*'s success favored a vague, impressionistic notion of plot, *DS9* was the opposite. Story was what mattered, sometimes above all else. The ongoing plot lines were very specific, and what happened in one episode carried over to the next. If you missed an installment, too bad. "When [writers and producers] Ira Behr and Michael Piller brilliantly decided to have the show roll out in a serialized manner, they placed a great amount of trust in the audience," Masterson explains. "And that was because back before Netflix, it was necessary to tune in in real time. So, if the show was syndicated at one a.m. in the morning, that's when you either had to tape it or watch it. And that made it more difficult to follow."

The subtitle *Deep Space Nine* refers to the setting of the series: a space station on the edge of Federation territory sporting that eponymous designation.[2] DS9 is a Federation outpost, politically speaking, but the station itself was constructed by an enemy government, the Cardassians (big, gray lizard necks). To make matters more complicated for your grandmother, or any other person who has never seen Star Trek, the Cardassians have just wrapped up a long and brutal occupation of a neutral planet called Bajor, populated by Bajorans (wrinkly noses). So, DS9 is a space station run by the Federation, constructed by an enemy government, and half-crewed by members of the Bajoran militia, who are *not* Federation members. DS9 is also a center of commerce, which adds even *more* non-Starfleet people into the mix, including the Ferengi Quark, who runs a bar, small casino, and holographic brothel in which people can do . . . *whatever* with holograms. Deep Space Nine is a home away from home for Starfleet crews, Bajoran hustlers, gamblers, and wanderers. The station is sandwiched between the peaceful planet Bajor and a fantastic swirling wormhole—a kind of inter-space superhighway—that can transport spaceships halfway across the galaxy. In a world of warp drive, the wormhole is like warp drive on crack.

The command crew of the station—and later, a tough little starship called the USS *Defiant*—consisted of only four humans: Ben Sisko (Avery Brooks) and his son Jake (Cirroc Lofton); Chief Miles O'Brien (Colm Meaney), who had previously appeared on *The Next Generation* as the guy constantly beaming everyone up; and

---

2 Giving Star Trek space stations the prefix "Deep Space" might seem a little obvious, but this idea originated in the 1967 *TOS* episode "The Trouble with Tribbles," in which the *Enterprise* visited Deep Space Station K-7. Appropriately, the *DS9* crew visited DSK7 in the delightful 1996 crossover episode "Trials and Tribble-ations."

Alexander Siddig as the brash Dr. Bashir. Everyone else in the cast was some kind of alien, and many of them weren't part of Starfleet. Major Kira Nerys (Nana Visitor) was Sisko's Bajoran first officer, and the security chief was a shape-shifter named Odo (René Auberjonois) whose natural state was a puddle of goo. There was the aforementioned Quark, and DS9's science officer, the young Trill Jadzia Dax (Terry Farrell), who, despite looking twenty-eight years old, had a wormy symbiont life-form in her belly that contained nine lifetimes worth of previous experiences.[3]

The supporting cast on *DS9* was huge, including Masterson's Leeta, Grodénchik's Rom, Rom's son Nog (the late Aron Eisenberg), the Cardassian tailor/spy Garak (Andrew Robinson), Sisko's freighter-captain girlfriend Kasidy Yates (Penny Johnson Jerald), DS9's former Cardassian warlord Gul Dukat (Marc Alaimo), and a holographic Frank Sinatra-esque lounge singer named Vic Fontaine (James Darren). By Season 4, *Deep Space Nine* was also permanently given the Klingon Worf (Michael Dorn) from *The Next Generation*. Dorn claims his favorite episodes of Star Trek are not the ones he did on *Next Generation*, but on *Deep Space Nine*.

Even if you understand every single made-up Star Trek word in that paragraph, it's easy to see why keeping up with the Cardassians wasn't always easy, even without serialized storytelling. To this day, *Deep Space Nine* remains the Trek series that is the most in the weeds relative to the complicated franchise continuity. And that's because Quark showing up on *Regis and Kathie Lee* is somehow not the most confusing thing about the show. Series writer Ron Moore once joked that if a Trek-curious viewer casually sat

---

3 For many Trek fans, Dax and the Trill were Star Trek's first real attempt to address trans and nonbinary gender issues. It wasn't entirely successful. This is discussed more in Chapter 15, "The Pride of Starfleet."

down to watch a Season 6 episode of *Deep Space Nine*, they would almost certainly be baffled. "You'd be like 'Really? What's all this? Who are all these people?' . . . If that's your introduction to Star Trek . . . I gotta believe it's almost impenetrable." Out of the eleven existing and distinct Star Trek series, *DS9* is the most inside-baseball show, and that's only partly because characters on the show literally play baseball inside.[4]

"*Fraiser*'s relationship to the show *Cheers* isn't a terrible example of what *Deep Space Nine* is relative to *The Next Generation*," *DS9* writer Robert Hewitt Wolfe tells me. "He was a minor character who goes off from Boston and has a life and adventures in Seattle that are pretty unconnected to what he ever did in *Cheers*. It wasn't that uncommon in television. *Laverne & Shirley* is pretty different from *Happy Days*; and so is *Mork & Mindy*, which people forget is also a *Happy Days* spin-off." Wolfe's point about the complicated spin-off universes of several sitcoms is well taken, but nobody would (or could) ever forget that *Deep Space Nine* was a Star Trek series. For a casual audience, there is no steep hill to climb with *Frasier* or even *Mork & Mindy*; their shared continuity with the series they were spun off from is totally irrelevant for audience comprehension. Every new Star Trek spin-off post-*Voyager* has longed for the simplicity of being the *Laverne & Shirley* to the *Happy Days* of the rest of the franchise; something a casual fan could just dip into without having to understand the rest. But in 1993, *Deep Space Nine* went the opposite direction. It demanded the audience knew

---

4 Sisko's love of baseball is a big part of the *DS9* pilot episode, "The Emissary," but perhaps more famously, the Season 7 banger, "Take Me Out to the Holosuite," in which the crew play a game of baseball in a holographic dugout (inside the space station) against a team of all Vulcans.

what was going on in the Trek universe, and, for complex science fiction and fantasy universes—taking place across multiple shows and feature films—this boldness was unheard of. "I don't think *Deep Space Nine* changed television," Wolfe says. "But I think it was part of a movement that was happening in television that changed the medium."

This "movement" mostly refers to two things: heavy episode serialization combined with the fact that *DS9* was a mainstream drama taking place in a previously established—and absurdly intricate—fictional universe. In the twenty-first century, the Marvel Cinematic Universe makes this kind of layered world-building look easy. But in the '90s, Star Trek did this deep franchise integration first, and boldly. Before the title credits rolled, the cold open for the debut episode of *Deep Space Nine*, "Emissary," was a flashback to the mega-famous *Next Generation* two-parter "The Best of Both Worlds." Picard is a Borg drone, and he's blowing up a bunch of Starfleet ships. Our hero, Benjamin Layfette Sisko (Avery Brooks), isn't a captain, he's a first officer on the tiny USS *Saratoga*, a ship that's getting its ass kicked by the Borgified Picard. In "The Best of Both Worlds," this starship massacre happened offscreen, but *Deep Space Nine* starts here with a very clear message to the audience: What happens to the people who aren't on the *Enterprise*? What is the rest of the galaxy like? When your mission isn't about boldly going, what is everyone even *doing* in the twenty-fourth century? And most important, what happens to those people when the space dust settles?

Sisko's ship is destroyed by the Borg and his wife Jennifer (Felecia M. Bell) dies under a pile of space debris as the traumatized husband barely makes it to an escape pod with his young son, Jake.

We'd all forgiven Picard for blowing up a bunch of spaceships when he was brainwashed by the Borg, but what *Deep Space Nine* presupposed was, maybe we shouldn't have? "I think that was a signal to the audience that this wasn't a safe Star Trek," Wolfe tells me. "The characters were at real risk. When we made those threats, they felt more real. Had we made you think a character on *The Next Generation* was going to die, you might not have bought it. Sure, the stakes of Picard not coming back from the Borg thing felt very real at the time. But, on *Deep Space Nine* we were always ready to do it."

Because *Deep Space Nine* was centered on a widower who was raising his son alone, this set the series apart from anything Star Trek had ever attempted, but it also put it in contrast with most adventure fiction in general. Sisko wasn't a lone man with a phaser against the universe, he had a space station and responsibilities. In January 1994, Brooks said that Sisko "coming to terms with the death of his wife" was a defining and "meaningful" way to start the series because "to go on living after a tremendous loss is one of the greatest human stories." If Picard was the anti-Kirk, then Ben Sisko wasn't even playing the same game. As the first Black actor to lead a Trek series, Brooks also had the dual distinction of being the first *American* to lead a Trek show, too. (William Shatner is Canadian and Patrick Stewart is obviously English.)

"We steeped that character in America," Wolfe explains. "We did that consciously. He's from Louisiana, *specifically*, he's from New Orleans. His dad runs a soul food restaurant on Earth. His middle name is Lafayette, I mean he's named after a Revolutionary War hero. This was very much about an American captain, and the politics of the time."

Sisko was conceived by writer Michael Piller as a "builder" in contrast with the "explorers" of previous Star Trek leads. As Brooks told William Shatner in 2010, he was interested in the part because Sisko was "a man defending humankind to an alien intelligence, while also dealing with loss, and raising a child . . . while also being *brown*." Like the series pilot of *Next Generation*, the pilot of *Deep Space Nine* put our new hero in the position of explaining humanity's whole deal to an all-powerful alien species who are suspicious of our strange ways. In *TNG*'s debut, Picard was arguing against an all-powerful judgment day with biblical implications. In the *DS9* pilot, Sisko had to convince Kurt Vonnegut–esque aliens known only as "the Prophets" that the concept of linear time was what made human life so important and appealing. In *The Next Generation*, the supreme alien intelligence declared itself God, but in *Deep Space Nine*, aliens are *thought* to be gods simply because they exist out of time and make their home inside of an interspatial wormhole, referred to by the native Bajorans as "the Celestial Temple." While *TNG* mocked the idea of God, *Deep Space Nine* was more tender toward spiritualism, and presented characters in the twenty-fourth century as not only pro-science, but pluralistically, sometimes as people of faith, too. When the Bajorans learn their gods are, in fact, aliens, it doesn't change their faith at all. In many ways, it reaffirms it. "In Season 1, it was all about Ben, you're here to get Bajor into the Federation," Ira Behr recalled. "And Bajor said, 'Screw you guys, we're taking your captain and we're making him a god.'"

Still, Star Trek isn't Star Trek unless its lead character is pulling a Kirk and unmasking false gods from time to time. In *Deep Space Nine*'s first season, when *TNG*'s mischievous space god Q (John de Lancie) shows up in the episode "Q-Less," Sisko immediately punches him in the mouth. Genuinely shocked, Q says, "Picard never hit me!" And Sisko fires back, "I'm not Picard."

"I can't believe they let me get away with that line," Wolfe tells me. "I was like, this is a different guy. He does not have patience for Q's nonsense. We were just trying to delineate the differences between this show and *Next Gen*. Sisko is an edgier dude than Picard."

The question of how aggressive Sisko could and *should* be on *Deep Space Nine* was hotly debated in the beginning. Before *DS9*, Brooks was famous for playing the antihero Hawk in the action-crime dramas *Spenser: For Hire* and its short-lived Brooks-centric spin-off *A Man Called Hawk*. Rick Berman and other *Deep Space Nine* producers wanted to distinguish Sisko from Hawk, resulting in a very different look for Brooks than many fans had expected or hoped for. Basically, Brooks wasn't allowed to sport his signature look—a shaved head and goatee—until the fourth season. Fellow *DS9* actor Colm Meaney remembered, "It wasn't an Uncle Tom look but headed in that direction." Author and one-time Star Trek novelist Steven Barnes tells me, "It was fantastic that they cast him in that role. But don't think I didn't notice that they toned him down at first."

Barnes wrote the novelization[5] to what is easily the best-known and correctly praised episode of *Deep Space Nine* ever, the Season 6 episode "Far Beyond the Stars." Although *Deep Space Nine* has a reputation for huge, season-long serialized arcs focused on sci-fi wars and dizzying space politics, the truth of the show's greatest moments is that they are nearly all stand-alone episodes. In "Far Beyond the Stars," Sisko enters a kind of dream world and becomes a 1950s science fiction writer named Benny Russell, writing the

---

5 The teleplay for "Far Beyond the Stars" was based on a story pitch by Marc Scott Zicree, and the teleplay was written by Ira Steven Behr and Hans A. Beimler. All three of those writers were white, while Barnes, who adapted the episode into a stand-alone novel, is Black. The episode was directed by Avery Brooks, who, obviously, starred in it, too.

story of *Deep Space Nine* and trying to sell it to his editor at a pulp magazine called *Incredible Tales*. This fictional magazine did not exist in the age of *Astounding*, but "Far Beyond the Stars" slyly pays homage to what the '60s *Star Trek* owed to the pulp sci-fi that preceded it. Simultaneously, "Far Beyond the Stars" is a brilliant critique *of* the sci-fi culture of the era just before Roddenberry created *Star Trek*. Benny is told he can only get his Captain Sisko story published if he makes the captain of his fictional space station a white man. Benny refuses, and in the episode's heartbreaking finale, Brooks delivers the most powerful and important anti-racist monologue in all of Star Trek, which includes the lines: "You can pulp a story but you cannot destroy an idea. Don't you understand? That's ancient knowledge. You cannot destroy an idea!"

The idea that Benny refers to is, metafictionally, the existence of *Deep Space Nine*, but it's bigger than that. At no other time in its history did Star Trek acknowledge its own armature in such a self-critical way. While in this dream world, most of the rest of the *Deep Space Nine* cast become other science fiction writers—mostly white—who all benefit from their privilege. Even within the closed doors of the brainy, progressive geeks, *DS9* dared to point out that the sci-fi gatekeepers—although maybe well-meaning—were still creating and perpetuating racist viewpoints.

"It's amazing. Star Trek did something amazing in that they were willing to put their brand, their imprimatur, behind Avery Brooks," Steven Barnes tells me. "And that doesn't mean that if they didn't still have problems—which they did—that doesn't mean what they did wasn't remarkable. Nichelle Nichols was a pretty female, so it is easier to get her past that racist line. The primary oppositional forces in racism are males fighting males for reproductive space. So, by the time Sisko came, yes, we'd seen Black people in

Star Trek. But the fact that he was the star was an important fact. A very important fact that a lot of people didn't register."

Far beyond the Trekkie chatter about the "dark" tone of *Deep Space Nine*, or its serializations, this is the true reason why the series was so important. Prior to *DS9*, the depiction of Black families on American TV shows was almost exclusively limited to sitcoms. And when Black families appeared in other mainstream dramas, there was usually some kind of crime angle. Brooks himself turned down a part in a Broadway show because the character he would have had to audition for was simply called "Black dude in a hat."

"Each phase of Star Trek reflected the time it was made in," Travis Johnson tells me. Johnson is one of several prominent Star Trek commentators on *Black Alert*, a podcast that brilliantly and specifically delves into the triumphs and failings of the Trek franchise on racial issues. Johnson's primary focus isn't just to find things to praise about Trek, but to keep our rosy ideas of the franchise in check with a historical context. "Sisko is a fantastic depiction for what the American dream looked like for all of us in the late '90s. *Next Gen* was progressive *for* the '80s. *DS9* was progressive for the '90s. A single Black dad is huge. A single Black professional dad, who is basically the leader of this town, is huge."

Make no mistake. This is the way *Deep Space Nine* pushed the entertainment industry in America toward progressive change. Representation within art isn't just important, it's transformative for the way people think about storytelling itself. Captain Sisko finally delivered on a promise that began with the '60s *Star Trek*, but the difference between this series and the classic show was clear: Sisko wasn't just a token bridge officer. He was the star of the adventure, and a positive Black father figure. Picard was an aspirational and aloof space dad, but Sisko was the real thing. As journalist and critic Angelica Jade Bastién wrote for *Vulture* in 2018, "No series before or since has portrayed a Black father with such complexity, crafting him as a widow, a powerful authority figure, a religious icon, a man whose morals are formed in shades of gray and whose love of his son remained his guiding principle."

Long after people forget what a Cardassian is, or why Odo couldn't shape-shift into perfect replicas of other people, Avery Brooks's Captain Sisko will be remembered. Even if casual fans only watch one episode of *Deep Space Nine*—and that episode is "Far Beyond the Stars"—the positive impact of this series will be greater and more meaningful than a dozen of the best episodes of *The Original Series*. While Walter Koenig believed that the stories told in Star Trek were less important than the symbolism of diversity, *DS9* proved that maybe you could do both. In "Far Beyond the Stars," when Sisko leaves his Benny Russell dreamworld and returns to the present, he's told that he exists as both "the dreamer and the dream"—which is a pretty damn good definition of socially responsible art.

When asked why he took the part of Sisko in the first place, Avery Brooks noted that the fact that he "did not have a prosthetic on my face" was critical. In *Star Trek: The Original Series*, story lines about racism were often turned into metaphors with other aliens, or, very often, about our favorite pointed-eared Vulcan. But in *Deep Space Nine*, the analogies didn't need to be so blurry. *Deep Space Nine* took Star Trek to a place it always claimed it wanted to be. In the crossover episode "Trials and Tribble-ations," Captain Sisko, Dax, and the crew manage to *Forrest Gump* themselves into the 1967 *Star Trek* episode "The Trouble with Tribbles." In a heartwarming scene, Ben Sisko tells 1967 Captain Kirk that "it's been an honor to serve with you."

In real life, though, Sisko is more important than Kirk. Star Trek's honor was to have Brooks embody that character, not the other way around. If a future Star Trek series has Captain Kirk travel into his own future (again), then it would be nice for him to return the compliment to Sisko. Kirk's cool and everything, but of the two captains, Sisko is the one who would make the better baby-sitter. It doesn't seem like Kirk or Picard *like* kids. Sisko does. And, as a role model for children and parents, Sisko is the Star Trek captain that so many of us look up to. The revelation of Sisko isn't that he's an interesting metaphor for humanity, told through a clever sci-fi lens. Despite any "chosen one" vibes we get from Sisko in *Deep Space Nine*, he's the most down-to-earth and *human* Star Trek captain, at least among the male leads. As Avery Brooks said, the fact that Sisko was "brown" sent a hopeful message. But more than that, Brooks felt strongly that it was important that this man of color wasn't hidden beneath any science fiction prosthetics. Before *Deep Space Nine*, Star Trek tended to do its best writing about race through allegory. But with Sisko, that artifice faded, and the so-called hopeful vision of tomorrow became more of a direct reflection of how people really talk, think, and look.

"In four hundred years hence," Brooks said, noting that his face was visible, "I would be completely human. And brown, too."

CHAPTER 11

THERE'S COFFEE IN THAT NEBULA!

Voyager tears down the Starfleet boys' club

On a rainy afternoon in the summer of 1994, Kate Mulgrew took a taxi to Forty-fourth Street in Manhattan to audition for a role she barely understood. She was thirty-nine years old and in "no way" familiar with the "culture of Star Trek." With various guest roles on *Cheers*, *Murphy Brown*, and a two-year stint on the soap opera *Ryan's Hope*, Mulgrew's resume didn't have the fancy gravitas of Patrick Stewart's, but it did prove she knew how to work. While she rode in that taxicab, trying to compose herself for a perplexing audition, she was thinking about her two young sons, while reeling from waves of trauma from her painful divorce, which was then in progress. On top of all that, she was involved in a tumultuous romance with another man. As Mulgrew revealed in her first memoir, she had nothing on her mind but the romantic vortex she was weathering, and so, her first reading for *Star Trek: Voyager* was like putting a starship on self-destruct.

"I delivered an audition so devoid of meaning, so completely inauthentic, stilted, and false, that on several occasions I had to bite my lip to keep from laughing." This was a taped VHS audition, which would be sent to producers Rick Berman, Jeri Taylor, and Michael Piller in LA along with the tapes of several others from "Elizabeth Janeway" hopefuls. Horrified by what she knew was a lifeless, unprofessional performance, Mulgrew ended the audition by looking straight into the camera and saying, "I'd like to apologize . . . [this] is not good work by any stretch of the imagination, but you see I've fallen in love, and I can't concentrate." The producers of *Star Trek: Voyager* watched the audition tape and made their decision. They decided to cast someone else.

Elizabeth Janeway, the captain of the USS *Voyager*, was supposed to be played by the French Canadian actress Geneviève Bujold. Lauded for her roles in David Cronenberg's *Dead Ringers*, Michael Crichton's *Coma*, and most famously as Anne Boleyn in the 1969 classic *Anne of the Thousand Days*, Bujold's casting was a Patrick Stewart–esque coup: a classically trained non-American actor who would, once again, imbue a new Trek series with a kind of international flavor. But, bringing in Bujold was not a "unanimous" decision on the *Voyager* team. Unlike Mulgrew, Bujold did not audition because her representation insinuated it would be beneath her. A *TV Guide* cover story in October 1994 cited several unnamed *Voyager* staffers who referred to Bujold as a spoiled "royal princess."

Like the casting of Jeffery Hunter as Captain Pike in "The Cage" in 1964, it's impossible to really visualize a parallel universe here that turns out well for anyone. The footage of Bujold in her uncompleted pilot of *Voyager* isn't one of those fascinating artifacts of what might have been, it's more like a glitch in the matrix—a pop culture bullet we all collectively dodged. If you've ever seen the cringeworthy screen test with Tom Selleck as Indiana Jones, the footage of Bujold in *Voyager* is way more unsettling. Her performance is so earnestly misguided that you can't even laugh uncomfortably. She's a fantastic actor, but when you watch the handful of scenes Bujold completed for *Voyager* as Janeway, it's like watching an unmemorable guest actor on *The Next Generation*. It's a grim take on the role, and when Bujold says "engage" it sounds like she's picking up her dry cleaning on the way to a funeral. Had she completed filming the pilot episode, *Voyager*—and Trek's first female starship captain—would have been an embarrassment. But fortunately, that didn't happen. After soul-searching with director Winrich Kolbe, Bujold quit just two days into production. Unnamed sources at the time said that when Bujold walked off the set, "no one went running after her."

The demographic optics at the time made things worse, because, apparently, the biggest fans of Star Trek were dude-bros anyway. According to the highly dubious market research, the "prized audience was men between eighteen and forty-nine." But, for *Voyager* producer and co-creator Jeri Taylor, it was essential that the next Trek TV series be led by a woman, and if the dude-bro Trekkies couldn't accept her, well damn the photon torpedoes, full speed ahead. Her collaborators, producers Rick Berman and Michael Piller, were on board, too. Trek had had female captains before, but never one starring in her own series. "The feeling was that the best direction for us to go and to be socially responsible was to go for a female captain," Berman remembered. "And the studio was totally convinced of that." But, after Bujold's walkout, the Paramount executives reversed their support and suddenly worried that *Voyager* wouldn't find its female captain, and so, as Jeri Taylor revealed, "We started to read some men, too."

Into this mess, Mulgrew reemerged and auditioned again, this time in Hollywood, in front of Rick Berman, Jeri Taylor, Michael Piller—and the studio heads of the fledgling United Paramount Network. At the time, UPN had been created by Viacom as a new *fourth* TV network, designed to rival ABC, NBC, and CBS. This meant that *Voyager* had more pressure on it from the beginning than either *TNG* or *DS9*; it wasn't going to be syndicated and, as such, had to be treated more like a mainstream network TV show, arguably the curse of *The Original Series*. But, ignorant of all those machinations, Mulgrew was now determined to get the part. She performed two scenes, one in which Janeway confides in Tuvok (Tim Russ), her trusted Vulcan security chief. The other was a monologue in which Janeway speaks eloquently about her mission. In this version of Star Trek, the Starfleet crew would be going boldly, just not willingly. The in-universe story of *Voyager* is all about one ship stranded on the far side of the galaxy, meaning that even with their nifty warp drive, it will take them seven decades to get back to their home quadrant. This kind of thing happened to the *Next Gen* crew all the time,[1] but in those episodes, the crew always made it back to the regular outer space neighborhood of the Alpha Quadrant within a day or two at most. For the crew of the USS *Voyager*—in the context of Star Trek's rules—they were literally going where no one had gone before.

"*Voyager* was the real deal," Kate Mulgrew tells me in 2021. "A starship literally lost in space, seventy-five thousand light-years from Earth—encountering every possible and conceivable difficulty." *Voyager* was a hard-core remix insofar as it decided to linger on that

---

1 In the *TNG* episode "Q Who" the *Enterprise* is stranded by Q in the Delta Quadrant, where we first meet the Borg. *Voyager* is stranded in that exact same quadrant, which meant the Borg were destined, sooner or later, to be a part of their story. Q shows up on *Voyager*, too, but weirdly, never offers to whisk them home with his space-god magic.

problem, effectively cutting the crew off from the handy assistance of the rest of the Federation. This meant Captain Janeway had to figure out how to apply the high-minded principles of Star Trek to situations that were messier than those in *The Next Generation*. "It brought the Prime Directive into an immediacy," Mulgrew explains. "And that brought a reality to the show that I don't think the [various] other series quite did."

Analogously, this notion of getting thrown to the wolves was perfect, because at the time Mulgrew knew jack shit about Star Trek. "I'm just going to create this character as I see fit," Mulgrew remembered. Because she "had never watched Star Trek" Mulgrew believed she was "therefore not stamped by it." This, she believed, was her "winning ticket." Her monologue promised to get her wayward crew home, Mulgrew got the part, and the universe course-corrected. From that moment, the Bujold version of *Voyager* evaporated, Captain Janeway's first name was changed from Elizabeth to Kathryn, and we all started living in the proper timeline in which Kate Mulgrew boldly went where no woman had gone before.

Mulgrew said that joining the cast of *Voyager* was like "breaking down the door of the boys' club . . . a very successful boys' club, I might add." While that boys' club may have included feminist representation, even the language of Starfleet arguably betrayed latent sexism. In most every iteration of the Trek franchise, members of Starfleet use antiquated paramilitary parlance, addressing female officers like Deanna Troi as "sir" or, in the case of Saavik in *The Wrath,* as "Mister Saavik." This is a strange outgrowth of naval terms like "seamen," which even in 2020 had not been retired by the real-life US Navy.

In *Star Trek: Voyager*'s very first episode, "Caretaker," Captain

Janeway pushes back against this tradition. When Ensign Harry Kim (Garrett Wang) calls Janeway "sir," the captain tells him she doesn't like "sir," to which he hastily replies, "I'm sorry, ma'am." This sets Janeway up for a role-defining dunk: "'Ma'am' is acceptable in a crunch, but I prefer 'Captain.'" Janeway may not have had a bumper-sticker-ready catchphrase like Picard's "Make it so," but of all the Trek captains, Mulgrew's triumph is that she feels the closest to a real boss, and a good one at that. She's obsessed with her black coffee, she misses her dog, and she's more likely to roll her eyes at bullshit than any other Trek leader. As a series, *Voyager* is the blend of what the post–*Next Gen* '90s Trek franchise wanted to do: expand the borders of its fictional galaxy, but make viewers feel warm and optimistic, too. The story of *Voyager*'s success is in how it found longevity by taking two major risks while simultaneously going with the Trekkie flow. If *Deep Space Nine* was the rebellious middle sibling, eager to do the opposite of *The Next Generation*, then *Voyager* was the precocious younger sister, perfectly content to be compared to *TNG* because she believed she was going to do it all better, anyway.

What Bujold's *Voyager* defection revealed is something that often gets lost in discussing all the gravitas and philosophical importance of Trek. The leading actors of each series need a certain kind of panache that's nearly undefinable. If they're too serious and *too* earnest, the illusion is broken. The reason why Kate Mulgrew's Janeway could carry the series, and Bujold's couldn't, is the same reason why it would have been hard to imagine Jeffrey Hunter in every single episode of *The Original Series*. Star Trek captains, even at their most serious, still need a twinkle in their eye, a kind of wink to the audience that the captain is in on the make-believe. For the reality of Star Trek to be convincing, the captain must seem

slightly unreal. When producer Brannon Braga labeled the character of Captain Janeway a "badass," Mulgrew countered, saying that
Janeway is, really, a "good ass."

By today's standards, the amount of sexist garbage Mulgrew
had to endure in her early months as Janeway is staggering. Executives scrutinized her hair, her chest, her legs. Privately, Mulgrew
began to envy Patrick Stewart, a person with no hair, who also
happened to be a man and therefore not subject to the horrible
double standards of so-called beauty forced upon women. "They
probably did this to Stewart, too," she later mused. "For a *second*."
For fans who grew up with *Voyager*, it's somewhat shocking to
think, again, that Kate Mulgrew was *only* thirty-nine years old
while the character of Janeway was seemingly presented as at least
a decade older. In the context of the series, Captain Janeway had
to be a kind of mother figure for her crew, but in real life, Mulgrew
was a young mother being dressed up as an older one. In 2021,
when a hologram of Captain Janeway was created for the Nickelodeon children's series *Star Trek: Prodigy*, Mulgrew told the anima-
tors that they couldn't make this new Janeway simulation "too
beautiful."

Today, Mulgrew charitably describes the sexist scrutiny as
"silly things" which she "acquiesced to" for the larger goal of being
"damn good" at her job of being the first female captain. But, well
into the filming of *Voyager* Season 1, Mulgrew still felt the tendrils
of male ego taking certain decisions out of her hands. Mulgrew
remembers that, early on, she felt her "captaincy" was threatened
by too much meddling from the producers, including Jeri Taylor.
And so, during the filming of the episode "Death Wish"—in which
Next Generation baddie Q (John de Lancie) returns—Mulgrew made
it clear she wanted a say in the way the stories were developed and

more leeway in deciding how she would play her scenes. Just a few years after *Voyager* ended, Mulgrew recalled that after standing her ground during that pivotal episode, Rick Berman told her, "You just go for it. We'll back off now."

In the same way Avery Brooks's Ben Sisko defined *Deep Space Nine* as the first Black person to lead a Trek series, Kate Mulgrew's blend of humor and don't-fuck-with-me command style defined *Voyager*. And even though *Voyager* aired in a contentious and confused time for feminism in the 1990s, Mulgrew's Captain Janeway holds up as a positive and inspiring role model. In 2015, the first Italian woman in space, Samantha Cristoforetti, posted a selfie from the International Space Station, dressed head to toe in the Starfleet uniform of Captain Janeway. When Cristoforetti tweeted her Janeway-tribute selfie, she captioned the photo with the phrase "there's coffee in that nebula"[2] in reference to the *Voyager* episode "The Cloud," in which Janeway's undying love of black coffee is conflated with checking out a possibly game-changing natural resource in a nearby space cloud. The fact that Janeway drank "coffee, black!" and not Picard's stuffy "tea, Earl Grey, hot!" is significant simply because it proves that when it comes to fictional space role models, there's a fine line between affected eccentricity and relatability. Tons of people convince themselves[3] that Earl Grey tastes good because they love Picard, but almost nobody had to convince themselves that they like coffee.

But if you think we're done talking about coffee, strap in. We're

---

2 The complete tweet ended with the phrase "ehm, I mean . . . in that #Dragon" in reference to a SpaceX Dragon capsule.

3 Patrick Stewart also *pretends* to like Earl Grey. On many occasions, he has revealed that although he does like tea, he never drinks Earl Grey.

just getting started. Janeway's preference of black coffee versus Picard's love of Earl Grey tea is the perfect microcosm for understanding why *Voyager* has a greater social and political impact than *Next Gen*, but the coffee-versus-tea thing *also* explains why *Next Gen* is still a little more popular than *Voyager*.

In the context of actual on-screen references to a hot caffeinated beverage choice, Janeway talks about black coffee in *Voyager* waaaaaay more than Picard mentions Earl Grey in *TNG*. Prior to ordering "Earl Grey, decaf!" in the first episode of *Star Trek: Picard*, Jean-Luc only explicitly drinks (or talks about) Earl Grey on ten separate occasions,[4] including the four *TNG* feature films. In the *TNG* episode "Attached," a brief telepathic link between Crusher and Picard reveals he really craves coffee in the morning. Random guess, but I bet most people reading this sentence would agree that if you were in command of a starship, a simple cup of coffee would be easier and more practical than a cup or pot of tea. So, if Picard *doesn't like Earl Grey* as much as his reputation suggests, one difference between Picard and Janeway can be ascribed to affectation. If we assume that Picard probably *pretends* to like Earl Grey, then affectation becomes a huge part of his whole persona. Correlatively, because almost nobody would pretend to like black coffee unless they actually liked it, Janeway is more like a real person that you'd actually be friends with because she drinks coffee. Which is why *Voyager* isn't as mega-popular as *The Next Generation*[5]—its captain

---

4 By my count, Picard drinks or talks about Earl Grey *ten* confirmed times in *The Next Generation* and films. Eleven if you count *Picard* Episode 1, "Remembrance," and the "decaf" joke. On the other hand, Janeway drinks coffee in at least twenty separate *Voyager* episodes.

5 When I say *Voyager* is less popular than *Next Generation*, I'm viewing that through the lens of having watched it when it was new, in 1995. And at *that time*, the *TNG* cast was 100 percent more popular.

isn't as weird. But this is paradoxically why Janeway is more likable, and as the decades pass, her popularity could—and likely will—exceed Picard's. Proof? In 2017, a Netflix survey revealed that of the top ten most *rewatched* episodes of any Star Trek show, *Voyager* had six of those ten slots.

Co-starring Robert Beltran as Chakotay, Tim Russ as Tuvok, Ethan Phillips as Neelix, Garrett Wang as Ensign Harry Kim, Roxann Dawson as B'Elanna Torres, Jennifer Lien as Kes, Robert Duncan McNeill as Tom Paris, and Robert Picardo as the holographic Doctor, the crew of *Voyager* was just as diverse as *Deep Space Nine*, even if the characters were slightly less developed. In this series, the focus was back to a planet-of-the-week and alien-of-the-week style of storytelling. *The Original Series* tried to convince you that the Starship *Enterprise* was out in the wilderness, but in *Voyager*, this was more literal. Because the ship was (initially) cut off from all communication with Starfleet, the crew was more focused and self-contained.

"I thought the work we did was worthy of Star Trek," Tim Russ tells me. "When the episodes were at their best, they were thoughtful and intelligent." In the context of the Star Trek franchise, *Voyager* is the perfect example of what your average Trek show is like, but tellingly, it's hard to argue that this series contains any of Trek's greatest hits. *Star Trek: Voyager*'s stand-out episodes may not be as famous as the greatest hits from *The Next Generation* or *Deep Space Nine*, but like *The Animated Series*, *Voyager*'s median quality is stabler. Outright bad *Voyager* episodes are way more watchable than bad episodes of *TNG*, even if that's a little like saying box wine from the gas station is better than Four Loko.

The best and worst example of this phenomenon is the Season 2 episode "Tuvix," an episode that I would probably not feel compelled to write about if internet memes did not exist. In the episode, the characters of Tuvok (Russ) and Neelix (Phillips) are accidentally fused into the same body. It's a remix of *The Original Series* episode "The Enemy Within" in which Captain Kirk was *divided* into two different people—one positive and one negative—creating the ethical realization that both sides of Kirk were necessary for him to survive. Metaphysically, the rumination in *TOS* was cut-and-dried: Spock and Bones practically look at the camera and say, listen up, everyone, your negative feelings are part of you and you're gonna have to learn to live with that. *The Next Generation*'s "Second Chances," did a slightly kinder version of a transporter-accident episode in which we got two versions of Riker.

But *Voyager*'s take on this is more unforgiving. Once Neelix and Tuvok become the same person—Tuvix (Tom Wright)—this new life-form doesn't *want* to be separated. Whereas previous Trek stories like this would provide a clear path for the heroes, the writing of "Tuvix" puts Janeway in the impossible position of overriding the recommendations of the ship's doctor *and* the request of Tuvix himself. It's one of those weird Star Trek head-scratchers where you're not really sure exactly what they're trying to say. In real life, people don't get merged with other people to create composite life-forms, meaning the analogy isn't applicable to a real thing. It is an ethical dilemma for Janeway, but only because it's written that way. You could easily imagine another version of this episode where the need to separate Tuvix was medically motivated. The "rules" of the ethical dilemma are created by fictional Star Trek science, and nothing else. Getting Tuvixed isn't *like* anything else, and Janeway's choice is only memorable because the internet loves pretending like she's a cold-hearted killer. Some of this is in good fun, but some of it just takes Trekkie analysis too far. And yet, "Tuvix" probably *is* one of the better episodes of *Voyager,* even though it's not really one you'd recommend to someone who has never seen the series. It's not a *fun* episode, but it does communicate what the show is like: Take a "classic" Star Trek premise and make it even weirder.

In the episode "Blink of an Eye," *Voyager* rolls up on a planet where time passes much more quickly below than above. What is only seconds for *Voyager* is entire years for the growing civilization on the planet they're orbiting. Just by *showing up,* the crew accidentally is integrated into the entire history of the culture because they're literally a new star in the night sky. This, at least, is a solid analogy for what *Voyager* is like in real life—a Star Trek series that integrated itself into the culture simply by existing. *Voyager* isn't just greater than the sum of its parts; many of its parts are uniquely compelling. Each time *Voyager* remixed a Trek trope, it did so with a slightly harder edge, even though the series itself feels overly well-mannered. While *TNG* sometimes let Picard off the hook, *Voyager* owned its moral quandaries by showing Janeway making decisions without everyone always agreeing with her.

"One thing I learned watching Janeway growing up is how leadership means being responsible for working through dilemmas [with] no clear answers," Congresswoman Alexandria Ocasio-Cortez said in 2020. "All the easy decisions are made before it gets to the top." AOC ascribes her well-documented Trek fandom to *Star Trek: Voyager* and Janeway specifically. Kate Mulgrew has been a vocal supporter of AOC's political career, and it's easy to see why. The brand of progressive, egalitarian politics espoused by AOC is perfectly in line with Janeway's humanitarian ethics. And, because

AOC was born in 1989, the first version of Trek she saw was the one with the female captain. And, if AOC becomes president before 2040, you can bet Janeway will become a more popular Star Trek captain than Picard. And that's because Janeway's importance, and the importance of *Voyager,* cannot be understated. In 2022, Congresswoman Ocasio-Cortez and astronaut Cristoforetti are the tip of the dark matter iceberg. The inspiration of Captain Janeway is singular not just within Trek, but across science fiction in general.

Although the legacy of *Voyager* is profound, during its third season in 1997, the ratings for the show were not encouraging. Again, because *Voyager* didn't air in syndication like *TNG* and *DS9,* there was considerably more pressure on the series to break viewership records. In some ways, this put *Voyager* in a similar position as *The Original Series*—unfairly scrutinized by a TV network. On top of that, *Voyager* was the *flagship* series for UPN, which, in the end, was a kind of failed experiment. In 2006, UPN eventually merged with the WB (a Warner Bros. network), which later merged with the CW. But before all that happened, in 1997, the studio suits wanted *Voyager* to shake things up. This resulted in *Voyager*'s second-biggest risk, the casting of Jeri Ryan as the former Borg drone Seven of Nine.

In *The Next Generation*'s "The Best of Both Worlds," Captain Picard was turned into a Borg drone for basically an episode and a half. The creation of Seven of Nine postulated something different: What if someone had been assimilated into the hive mind of the Borg collective when they were a little kid? What would it be like to bring that person's humanity out in the open? In *TOS*, Spock was embarrassed by his humanity. In *TNG*, Data wanted to become human. But Seven was something else; she had her humanity *forced* on her by Captain Janeway and Starfleet. Whereas *TNG* and the film *First Contact* repeatedly referenced Picard's assimilation, the scars for Seven run much deeper. Originally known as Annika Hansen, Seven never even uses her human name in *Voyager*, feeling more comfortable with a number than a name. Clearly, if someone had more to complain about relative to the Borg, it would be Seven, not Picard.

"Picard was a poser! You were a Borg for five minutes," Seven actress Jeri Ryan told me with a laugh when we spoke in February 2020. She was joking around, of course, and quickly added, "But, no, I think once you've had those experiences of having your identity taken from you and all of those voices in your head—whether it's a day or most of your life—I think it's enough of a shock to your system, that it would affect you for the rest of your life. She's an amazingly cool—and resilient—character."

However, given Ryan's conventional beauty and skin-tight silver jumpsuit, part of the Trek fan base assumed the addition of Seven of Nine was a ratings ploy to bring in those same male viewers, aged eighteen to forty-nine. "People said we were turning it into *Baywatch*," *Voyager* writer Brannon Braga remembers. "They said: 'Look how desperate they are.'" In 1998, series creator and feminist Jeri Taylor fired back, saying, "We have nothing to apologize for. Sure, we could have put Seven in some dumpy outfit, but what would be served by that? You learn to take it in stride. Star Trek is always under fire for something. If we were the kind of people who ran scared of criticism, we would have gone away a long time ago."

While Ryan's costume and looks occupied a huge amount of the conversation around her character's introduction in 1998, by the end of the series, Seven had become the other star of the *Voyager*. If any Trek series had a triumvirate that re-created the feeling of Kirk-Spock-Bones, *Voyager* came close with Janeway, the Doctor (Robert Picardo), and Seven of Nine. "It was controversial at first," Taylor remembers. "But she became one of the most fascinating characters of the franchise."

When I spoke to Rod Roddenberry, he cited Seven of Nine as one of the best examples of a "Roddenberry" character. When I pointed out to him that Seven was created *after* his father died, Rod told me that was the point. "I loved Data. Data was maybe my favorite. But Seven might be even better than Data." Producer and *Voyager* writer David Livingston echoed the Data sentiment, saying, "She was the Data . . . she was the outside observer. And I think the show really needed that."

Just as Captain Janeway will likely become even more popular in the future than she is now, Seven of Nine's legacy is more important than her origin. In 2020, Jeri Ryan returned to the role of Seven, almost exactly two decades after *Voyager* aired its final episode on May 23, 2001. Although her return as Seven happens in a series called *Star Trek: Picard*, Ryan steals the show in every episode of the new series she's in. In the final moments of the *Picard* Season 1 finale, it's also revealed that Seven has started a relationship with another woman, Raffi, played by Michelle Hurd. In a 2021 essay called "Seven of Nine Was Always Queer," writer S. E. Fleenor points out that although *Voyager* may not have explicitly depicted Seven as queer, "The way she relates to her body and how her body autonomy has been taken from her by both the Borg and the Federation reads like the experiences of many transgender, nonbinary, and queer folks like me."

This is not a minority opinion, and interestingly carries on a beautiful tradition from *The Original Series*. D. C. Fontana told me

Kirk and Spock weren't written as gay, but thanks to fan fiction and fan analysis, a queer subtext between Kirk and Spock is impossible to deny.

"She was coded as queer in some sense, whether that be in her romantic and sexual attractions or in her relationship to her body and identity," S. E. Fleenor tells me over email. "In my mind the key to reconciling the intention of Seven—to put a hottie on-screen to help ratings, which it did—with the impact of her character on many queer and trans viewers is about accepting both. I don't have to pretend that her introduction was all sunshine and rainbows to love Seven. I can acknowledge how she disrupted things I loved about *Voyager* before her arrival while knowing that there is no other character in the totality of Trek that I relate to more."

For many queer fans, Seven of Nine's coming out in *Picard* Season 1 is an eventuality that was baked into the character, whether it was the original intention or not. The interpretation of Seven of Nine's journey as being analogous to the experience of a queer person, or a nonbinary person, or a trans person was, in the late '90s, perhaps accidental subtext for why the character was popular. But, as time passed, that subtext *became* the actual text for contemporary Star Trek.

"It comes from people having been part of these fan bases actually working on the show," critic Jessie Earl tells me. Earl—perhaps better known by their internet handle as "Jessie Gender"—is a popular YouTuber who creates nuanced and fascinating deep dives into LGBTQ+ themes and representation on Star Trek and several other science fiction franchises. Earl is certainly not the only queer Star Trek fan who does this kind of commentary, but their videos are some of the most incisive and comprehensive.

"We are seeing more women and more LGBTQ people getting

jobs in Hollywood, and they have been part of these fandoms, perhaps for their entire lives," Earl continues. "So, they get to do a little bit of their own fan fiction and make it canonical."

Echoing Earl's comments, Fleenor points out that this kind of trend has been happening behind the scenes for a while. "People were right to be suspect of Seven's introduction in 1998," Fleenor tells me. "*Voyager* was the only Star Trek ship and show helmed by a woman and she was decidedly not there for sex appeal. Don't get me wrong, Kate Mulgrew and Captain Janeway are both total babes, but that's not what Janeway was intended to be, nor how she was utilized on-screen."

Because of this perception from female fans at the time—that Seven of Nine's costume and sex appeal were a step backward—Jeri Taylor said that "a lot of the female fans thought I should throw my body in front of this impending disaster and do something about it." But it wasn't a disaster. "For me, it's hard to be frustrated about Seven today," Fleenor admits. "I respect the perspectives and experiences of those who were watching the series when it came out as I'll never be able to go back and have that experience or understand the many political and cultural issues that were happening contemporaneously that impacted people's impression of Seven . . . but that's the real rub: If we didn't have the kind of coding we did with characters like Seven where people could see themselves on-screen—albeit in an indirect and imperfect way—we would have had zero queer or trans representation in Star Trek for decades. Subtext is far from enough, but queer and trans people have always found ways to see and claim space for ourselves in the media, literature, and franchises we love."

Even though Kate Mulgrew botched her first audition, and Jeri Ryan's Star Trek journey began inauspiciously, *Voyager* was the first Star Trek series that, in the end, featured two female lead characters. The ultimate proof that Janeway and Seven are still important to millions of fans isn't just in the ever-increasing retro-popularity of *Voyager*, but in the fact that both Janeway and Seven exist in *contemporary* Star Trek series. Seven of Nine is a regular on *Star Trek: Picard*, and two versions of Janeway—both voiced by Kate Mulgrew—lead the animated children's series *Star Trek: Prodigy*. When one Star Trek podcast invited me to speak about a specific episode from any series, the hosts asked that I *not* choose a *Voyager* episode, simply because *everyone* wanted to discuss *Voyager*. In *Discovery*'s Season 3, when the crew jumps ahead to the thirty-second century, the only other ship with a familiar name they find in the future Starfleet is a new version of the USS *Voyager*. Among Trekkies and casual fans alike, the *Voyager* renaissance is upon us. A fact which Kate Mulgrew tells me she finds utterly unsurprising, saying with dry Janeway wit, "It was only a matter of time."

CHAPTER 12

MAGIC CARPET RIDES

Star Trek's obsession with time travel,
First Contact, and Star Trek's
first prequel—*Enterprise*

In 1977, thanks to the efforts of Carl Sagan and Ann Druyan, NASA's *Voyager* probe was loaded up with the famous "golden record" containing a smattering of media that was supposed to accurately represent humanity. Tragically, even though Carl Sagan's son, Nick Sagan, wrote for *Star Trek: Voyager*—and the *Enterprise* encountered a fictional Voyager 6 probe in *The Motion Picture*—there is no "golden record" that encapsulates all of Star Trek. But, if a Trek golden record did exist, it's easy to imagine what would be on it: a shit ton of time-travel stories. If hypothetical real aliens found an equally hypothetical golden record of Star Trek, perusing the greatest hits would make them very confused as to why the series isn't called "Time Trek."

Although Trek is supposedly about space travel, the most praised, most loved installments of the series prove that time travel is the one sci-fi trope more loved than any other. If *TOS* writer Norman Spinrad is right, and the power of the 1960s *Trek* was that it brought countless science fiction concepts to the masses, who otherwise might not have encountered them, then at the top of that list is the sci-fi subgenre of time travel. Even in *Avengers: Endgame*, when the heroes are listing all the famous methods of time travel, Star Trek gets name-checked, while a series *about* time travel—*Doctor Who*—does not.[1]

The top three most popular *and* critically acclaimed[2] Star Trek feature films have all dealt with time travel: *The Voyage Home* in 1986, *First Contact* in 1996, and the J. J. Abrams film *Star Trek* in 2009. When fans draw up a list of their favorite episodes in each series, it's once again striking how often time travel sneaks in there. The most-praised episode of *TOS*, "The City on the Edge of Forever," gave science fiction the most beloved donut-shaped time portal ever; *TNG*'s fan favorites "The Inner Light" and "Yesterday's Enterprise" both deal with time-skipping shenanigans; *DS9*'s top episodes, "The Visitor" and "Far Beyond the Stars," are about modes of time travel, and the show's most provocative story about social justice and poverty—"Past Tense"—also relies on time travel. *Voyager*'s beloved two-parter "Year of Hell" is ultimately about using time travel to erase a super-depressing 365 days. And using time travel to reset things or fix insurmountable problems is such a com-

---

1 This fact is made doubly strange when you consider that an actress made famous by *Doctor Who*, Karen Gillan, is standing right there in this *Avengers: Endgame* scene in which Star Trek is used as an example of time travel fiction and *Doctor Who* isn't.

2 Technically speaking, *The Motion Picture* (1979) and *Into Darkness* (2013) were successful at the box office. And relative to other Star Trek movies, so was *Star Trek Beyond* in 2016. But none of those movies was *also* considered a critical hit across the board. Of course, *The Wrath of Khan* made money and was a critical hit, too, but its financial success was linked to the fact that it cost *way* less to make.

mon idea in Trek that both the series finales of *The Next Generation* and *Voyager*—"All Good Things . . ." and "Endgame"[3]—use time travel to prevent an unpleasant future.

In 1964's abandoned pilot "The Cage," before Roddenberry and company settled on the terminology of warp drive, Captain Pike refers to the velocity of the *Enterprise* relative to its "time warp factor." When helmsman Tyler (Peter Duryea) speaks to the stranded scientists from the SS *Columbia*, he says "the time barrier has been broken," conflating the idea of velocity with travel through space-time. Speaking pseudoscientifically, this description—the idea that starships are, in fact, traveling in a time/space bubble that allows them to traverse distances "faster"—makes a little more sense than a generalized notion of "hyperdrive." Because, the truth is, even when a Trek episode or movie isn't overtly doing time travel, that is, going faster than the speed of light, *warping* space-time is always messing around with general relativity. Whenever the *Enterprise* pops out of warp and rolls up on a planet, everyone tends to agree that it's the same year. But the only way this is possible is because the *Enterprise* skipped *over* the amount of time it would have taken for the journey to happen conventionally. Warp engines are not called "time engines," but they totally are.

Star Trek's ability to skirt the rules of normal time means the crews of the various shows tend to avoid having to believe in the immortal

---

3 When the title for *Avengers: Endgame* was revealed, *Voyager* fans had a ball. Who did their time heist better? The Avengers or Captain Janeway?

words of the Rolling Stones in "You Can't Always Get What You Want." Often, when something goes wrong in the "present," Star Trek people decide to go back in time and give it another go. Obviously, Trek is not alone in using this extremely seductive plot point to create exciting stakes. Again, consider that *Endgame*, the biggest *Avengers* movie ever, busted out high-stakes time travel for the exact same reasons; the fantasy that our choices can have do-overs is a powerful one, and when you combine that with the inherent decency of most Trek characters, time-travel stories become narrative vehicles for an elevated type of nostalgia. In *Back to the Future*, faux nostalgia for an illusionary version of the 1950s is part of the movie's fish-out-of-water charm. Marty McFly has no idea that sugar-free Pepsi doesn't exist yet, and the idea of Ronald Reagan being president scans as absurd to Doc Brown. The nostalgia in the story works because the audience is also experiencing a sort of time travel, remembering or imagining a *real* time in the past. This is also why moviegoers love the time travel in *Endgame*; revisiting the previous movies is nostalgic in the way looking at photos on your phone from three years ago is fun. When Captain America travels back in time to the '70s and then the '40s, people love that too because the '70s seem "fun" and the '40s seem "romantic."

This is not how time-travel emotion works in Star Trek. In Star Trek, time travel doesn't have to be exclusively reliant on nostalgia. In *The Voyage Home*, the crew is from the future and time-traveling to *our* present, 1986. In a contemporary San Francisco hospital, Bones refers to twentieth-century medicine as "the goddamn Spanish Inquisition." When Star Trek's time-travel stories succeed, they're usually *anti*-nostalgia, and that's generally because there's a bigger narrative goal in mind than everyone wondering "can they fix the timeline?"

In 1995, a year after the first *TNG* feature film—*Star Trek: Generations*—featured Kirk and Picard meeting, thanks to some loosey-goosey time travel called "the Nexus," Rick Berman and the powers that be of the time decided that another time-travel movie was in order, but this time they wouldn't rely on the nostalgia the audience might have had for William Shatner. After pitching a script called "Star Trek: Renaissance," in which Data becomes buddies with Leonardo da Vinci, Berman encouraged writers Brannon Braga and Ron Moore to come up with something else. That film became *Star Trek: First Contact*, a movie in which the Borg travel back in time to Earth's past in an attempt to stop the most important historical event in all of Trek history: our first contact with aliens. Because this happens in the year 2063, there's no nostalgia involved with this time travel, because this period in future history was unfamiliar to the audience at the point at which this movie was made. (And still is!)

The story of the film reboots the inventor of warp drive, a character named Zefram Cochrane (James Cromwell) who had previously appeared—in the guise of actor Glenn Corbett—in a 1967 *TOS* episode called "Metamorphosis," which can best be described as: man falls in love with sentient energy cloud which, in turn, gives him eternal youth. Relative to Star Trek's larger chronology, Kirk, Spock, and Bones meeting eternal youth Cochrane (Corbett) was the character's future while *First Contact* was his past. Most people who love *First Contact* never think about this, and in 2017 the co-writer of the film, Ronald D. Moore, told me that he and Brannon Braga didn't think much about the *TOS* episode either. "We treated him as a totally different character. Where he is in that episode isn't even close to the guy we were writing." As an *Original Series* character being put into a new context in a feature film, the character of Cochrane is nothing like Khan. While the ratio of people who have seen *Wrath of Khan* to people who have seen Khan's first *TOS* episode, "Space Seed," is probably like 10 to 1, the ratio of people who have seen *First Contact* to those who even *think about* the episode "Metamorphosis" is probably something like 1,000 to 1.

Since 1996 was the thirtieth anniversary of the first airing of the first episode of *Star Trek*, although *First Contact* was the first Trek feature film without any of the classic cast, the background of the plot was decidedly a huge tribute to how Star Trek began. By time-traveling back to 2063, and the moment where the Vulcans first met humans, *First Contact* was a low-key Star Trek reboot and, in many ways, overwrote the backstory of the entire franchise. Because the *TNG* crew had to assist Zefram Cochrane in the first human warp flight, Star Trek's future essentially pulled itself up by its own bootstraps. This film also sports the only time the words "star" and "trek" are spoken out loud, in that order, by a character *within* Star Trek. When Cochrane learns that Riker, Crusher, Troi, and Geordi are from the future, he says, "and you're all astronauts, on some kind of star trek."

"I thought the script was remarkable," Borg Queen actress Alice Krige told me in 2021. "It was a stand-alone piece of work that you didn't have to know anything about science fiction to enjoy. I can remember watching it for the first time at the press screening and thinking, wow, this is something that could potentially be in the mainstream of entertainment rather than contained within the genre of science fiction. I thought that it would reach up. And I guess it did."

The climax of *First Contact* was another first for a Star Trek film. When Cochrane, Riker, and Geordi are about to blast off in an archaic-looking rocket, Cochrane suddenly needs to listen to a song. After finding a "futuristic"-looking piece of green plastic, he slams it into his rocket's tape deck and says, "Let's rock and roll!" As the rocket launches over the treetops of Montana, the Steppenwolf song "Magic Carpet Ride" blasts through the cockpit. On the commercial release of Jerry Goldsmith's score for *First Contact*, "Magic Carpet Ride" closed out the album, setting a precedent for the music of Star Trek to start kicking a little more ass.

After *The Voyage Home*, *First Contact* was the most financially successful Star Trek film prior to the J. J. Abrams reboots of the twenty-first century. The knee-jerk reason given for this is that it's a movie in which Picard ends up in a tank top fighting the Borg Queen (Alice Krige). There's also a scene in which Picard wears a tuxedo on the holodeck and shoots up some Borg with an old-timey mobster-style tommy gun. Worf even utters a phrase that many critics came to call "Schwarzenegger-esque" when he bellows, "Assimilate this!" before obliterating some Borg drones with his phaser rifle.

"I always thought we pushed things into the realm of horror with that one," Jonathan Frakes tells me. "That's what I wanted to do as a director, see how far we could push the visual texture without losing the heart."

———————

In 1994's *Generations*, Picard got his ass handed to him by Malcolm McDowell, and so he needed to recruit out-of-shape William Shatner to help him with an old-fashioned beatdown. But in *First Contact*, Picard's the one doing the ass-kicking. Like *The Wrath of Khan*, *First Contact* balanced delicate love for the characters while also giving the general moviegoer a lot of explosions and heroic violence. After *First Contact*, Patrick Stewart insisted that Picard "continue" as an action hero in subsequent films, specifically *Insurrection* (1998) and *Nemesis* (2002). If you have only seen the *TNG* movies, you'd think Picard was picking up a big phaser rifle on the TV series all the time, which, of course, isn't the case at all. The difference between Star Trek on TV and Star Trek at the movies can *possibly* be summed up as the tale of two Picards: the captain on the TV show who was contemplative and reserved, and the guy in the movies who is done with all that shit and is firing phasers all the time. This makes movie-Picard more like Kirk in the TV show, while movie-Kirk is more like Picard in *his* TV show.

When it comes to making a play for big-screen appeal, and an audience that is much larger than a TV audience, Star Trek always plays this game. In order for something to be truly mainstream— like the Marvel movies or Star Wars—the narrative has to contain enough political vagaries that it could be equally loved by right-wingers and progressive liberals alike. Obviously, there's a bigger political spectrum than just that, but overwhelmingly, the Trek TV shows have appealed to people closer to the left of the political spectrum, for reasons that should be pretty obvious if you've been reading all the preceding chapters. When Ronald Reagan visited the set of *The Next Generation* in 1990, Patrick Stewart was not thrilled, saying it was "as grotesque and bizarre as you can imagine." In 2021, the satirical news show *Tooning Out the News* said, "Pundits say the key to winning the new presidential election is gaining support from the all-important demographic of actors who have been in a Star Trek show." Assuming the candidate is left leaning, this isn't far from the truth. With a few exceptions, Star Trek actors and writers are mostly *against* policies that come from the Republican Party.

But again, if you think seriously about how popular movies

work, they must cast a wide net. George Lucas might believe that the Star Wars films are cautionary tales against conservative values, but because those films fetishize weapons of war, it's tough to say that the audience is strictly liberal, progressive, and anti-gun. So, whenever Star Trek has approached this level of mass popularity, it almost always had to fake to the right a little bit. In other words, there's a fine line between Picard kicking more ass and just putting more violence in a story in order to have it appeal to a bigger audience. Trek usually doesn't cross this line, and certainly doesn't in *First Contact*. But after *Voyager* ended in 2001, the franchise started to blur that line—and began faking to the right for almost a decade. Paradoxically, this was probably good for the franchise overall, even if the first fifteen years of the twenty-first century didn't produce the best Star Trek. Being popular is not always right, but with Trek, being popular is *useful*.

After 9/11, the politics of Star Trek changed. Not radically, but noticeably. In 2001, Rick Berman and Brannon Braga created the prequel series *Enterprise*, the first Trek series set *before* the time of *The Original Series*, in the year 2151, in the twenty-second century. The show's mythology also leaned heavily on the then relatively new—and still popular—*First Contact* backstory, specifically the ideas that the Vulcans were helping Earth pull itself out of a long period of disunity and nuclear war. The idea behind *Enterprise* was a laudable one—try to give the world an utterly accessible Trek series featuring human beings who were closer to contemporary. The first scene in the first episode also sported a farmer in a cornfield shooting a Klingon with a shotgun. Get off my lawn, you Klingon!

In a time-travel casting coup, Scott Bakula—beloved for his role on the time-travel drama *Quantum Leap*—was cast as Captain Jonathan Archer, a down-to-earth Trek captain who we're supposed to believe is *really* the person who predated everyone, including Pike and Kirk. The uniforms on *Enterprise* were blue jumpsuits, meant to look more like actual jumpsuits worn by NASA astronauts. Archer even rocks a black baseball cap from time to time, sporting the registry number of this Starship *Enterprise*, NX-01. If you can't get down with an *Enterprise* captain who loves water polo, rocking a baseball cap, nothing about this show will make sense. For the first two seasons, *Enterprise* didn't even have the phrase "Star Trek" in its opening title credits. For brand identification purposes, *Enterprise* was a way of saying "Star Trek" without saying Star Trek.

On top of that, this was also the first—and last—Trek series to use a pop song for the opening title music, rather than an orchestral composition. The song was "Faith of the Heart," written by Diane Warren, and originally performed by Rod Stewart for the soundtrack for the movie *Patch Adams* in 1998. For *Enterprise*, the song was recorded by Russell Watson, a singer who is probably best described as a mash-up of Michael Bublé and one of the famous "Three Tenors." To say that "Faith of the Heart" is *cheesy* is unnecessary. Why a song first sung by Rod Stewart was then re-recorded and selected as the opening title for a new Star Trek series is baffling. The opening title sequence charts the history of human exploration, starting with sailing ships, through the space program (including the real shuttle *Enterprise*) and culminating in warp-speed flights. It's a pretty cool montage, and during various test-footage versions, the production staff used U2's "Beautiful Day" to prove just how awesome and utterly accessible this version of Trek was going to be. If Picard kicking more ass in 1996 was a great decision, everything about selecting a corny pop song for the theme to *Enterprise* was the painful embodiment of a nerd trying way too hard to be cool and only revealing how deeply uncool they really are. *Enterprise* producer Mike Sussman recalled that "in our attempts to modernize the show and make it cool, not only did we lose the fans, but we gained the disdain of the people we were hoping to convert."

In retrospect, "Faith of the Heart" is the perfect theme song for *Enterprise,* because it accurately represents everything good *and* disappointing about the series. At the height of *TNG* popularity in the 1990s, Trek didn't need to try to be cool, it simply was, and the $146 million worldwide box office for *First Contact* in 1996 proved it. But, by 2001, after *two* Trek spin-offs had each run for seven years, the Star Trek brand was exactly like a Rod Stewart cover song: lovely, with a beautiful sentiment, but old-fashioned and out of touch. *Enterprise* initially aired on UPN, but during its four-year run, that network became the CW, and, if you watch the series now, it does, at moments, feel more like a CW drama than a Trek series. Other than Anthony Montgomery as Travis Mayweather and Linda Park as Hoshi Sato, the rest of the cast was all white, including a white male lead in the form of Bakula. In 2001, *Enterprise* should have been a forward-facing Star Trek for a new century, but instead, as a prequel to *The Original Series,* the show felt as if it were aimed at the boomers who had loved Kirk and Spock, and who were vaguely bored and confused by everything post-*TNG.* Like with all things Trek, *Enterprise* has its fans, and like with *Voyager,* there are signs that an entire generation of people who grew up on the show are emerging and saying, loud and clear, that this under-the-radar series is what converted them to Trekdom.

When actor Noah Averbach-Katz was cast as the Andorian Ryn in *Star Trek: Discovery* Season 3, he posted a personal video montage on Twitter, set to "Faith of the Heart," without any irony. A lifelong Trek fan, Averbach-Katz tells me that *Enterprise* was "special" because it "introduced me to this goofy and loving universe." He also revealed that character actor Jeffrey Combs, who played the fan-favorite Andorian Shran on the series, was a huge influence on him as an actor and "one of my personal heroes." Like other diehards, Averbach-Katz feels that *Enterprise* got good just before it was canceled in its fourth season. Jeffrey Combs agrees, citing his work on *Enterprise* as his favorite among various other alien characters he played on Star Trek. And, like Averbach-Katz, Combs thinks *Enterprise* was forced back into space dock before it was really given a chance.

"I feel like *Enterprise*'s sea legs, and its voice, were just starting to happen when it was canceled," Combs tells me in 2021. "It *did* hit its stride in that last season. And I think the same thing can be said for *DS9*, *Voyager*, and maybe *Next Generation*. These things take some time to find their music. They pulled the trigger too fast. I feel strongly about this."

While this may be true, it's still hard to argue that any episodes from *Enterprise* should be put on Star Trek's golden record, even though the show sports a *ton* of time travel, including a memorable Season 4 opener, "Storm Front," in which the *Enterprise* fights German warplanes above the New York skyline in an alternate version of the year 1944. If you just watch the scene where the *Enterprise* has to bob and weave around the Chrysler Building, firing phasers all the way, you might think you've stumbled onto a deleted scene from one of the J. J. Abrams reboots. *Enterprise* very often went very big; the problem was, because of mixed marketing and less-than-stellar critical response, by the time things got interesting, not enough people were watching.

And despite some of the big swings on *Enterprise*, like a lot of Trek on TV, its smaller moments were still, sometimes, the best. My personal favorite episode of the series—"A Night in Sickbay"—is mostly focused on Captain Archer's concern that his beagle Porthos might have picked up a weird alien virus, which seems to be a direct result of Archer bringing his dog down to an alien planet and letting Porthos pee all over the place. *Enterprise* featured the only Trek captain to date who has a dog, which, you'd think, would automatically make it the best one. And, in some bizzarro universe, that might be true. But *Enterprise* also featured that same Andorian referring to *all* humans as "pink-skins" even though a Black man, Travis Mayweather, is standing right there. This isn't to say that *Enterprise* is a racist show. It isn't at all. But it didn't push the envelope in terms of politics the way its predecessors did. Its most provocative episode was a two-part story line called "Terra Prime" and "Demons," in which a xenophobic group of extremists tries to kick all aliens off of Earth. To this end, a madman named Paxton (Peter Weller) has racist scientists create a half-human/half-Vulcan baby in a lab, in order to get *other* racists fired up about crossbreeding. Resident Vulcan officer T'Pol (Jolene Blalock) and lovable Floridian Trip Tucker (Connor Trinneer) find out the baby was made with their DNA, making them insta-parents. Depressingly, by the end of this story line, the cute little pointed-eared baby *dies*, and the audience is left wondering why. The final episode of *Enterprise*— "These Are the Voyages . . ."—aired a week later. Controversially, "These Are the Voyages . . ." framed the finale as a holodeck program being watched by Riker in *The Next Generation*, which would be a little like if the series finale of *Breaking Bad* had revealed that everything was just a dream that Skinny Pete[4] was having after getting too high.

The idea behind "These Are the Voyages . . ." was a noble one. This wasn't just the finale of *Enterprise*; it was intended as a send-off to eighteen years of Star Trek on TV. Rick Berman and Brannon Braga had conceived of the series finale as a "love letter" to the fans, which mostly backfired. Hard-core *Enterprise* fans mostly considered "Demons" and "Terra Prime" to be the real series finale, and "These Are the Voyages . . ." as a strange "it was all a dream"–style episode. Putting Jonathan Frakes and Marina Sirtis back into their *TNG* roles and pretending like this episode of *Enterprise* really took place inside of another episode of *TNG* dialed back the stakes considerably. Years later, in 2020, *Lower Decks* creator Mike McMahan would poke fun at this idea in the episode "No Small Parts," when Riker admits that, yes, yet again he was on the holodeck doing reenactments from *Enterprise*. "These Are the Voyages . . ." is one of the most bizarre moments in television history, in which characters from one TV series essentially *watch* an episode of another TV series, all through science fictional means. It's not exactly Star Trek's version of *Mystery Science Theater 3000*, but it's not far off. Frakes himself was always vocal about his disappointment in "These Are the Voyages . . ." saying in 2011 that his participation in the finale was an "unpleasant memory," and that he felt bad for stealing the thunder on what was, basically, another cast's series.

And yet, the legacy of *Enterprise* lives on in surprising ways. The showrunner of 2022's *Star Trek: Picard* Season 2 is Terry

---

4 I'm not making this Skinny Pete *Breaking Bad* reference for nothing. In the *Breaking Bad* episode "Blood Money," Badger and Skinny Pete have a debate about Star Trek and Skinny Pete comes out as being a huge *Voyager* fan.

Matalas, a writer who cut his teeth on *Enterprise* and is responsible for the excellent episode "Impulse." In that one, a ship full of Vulcan zombies threatens the crew, resulting in an episode that—like *First Contact*—is equal parts horror and Star Trek's brand of soul-searching. Can anything be done to help these Vulcans? What will happen to T'Pol, the resident Vulcan on *Enterprise*? And are Vulcan zombies somehow the secret most scary zombies in all of zombie fiction? This episode, and many others of *Enterprise*, are fast-paced, and almost relentless with their desire to please. Matalas went on to produce the deeply underrated *12 Monkeys* reboot (time travel!) for the SyFy Channel before landing the gig as showrunner for *Picard* Season 2 in 2021.

Both Matalas and Combs think the mixed legacy of *Enterprise* might not be as bad as its reputation. Combs tells me: "I think it holds up quite nicely . . . some of the best episodes of Star Trek are on *Enterprise*." And while Matalas has had a circuitous journey away from Star Trek—from *Enterprise* and now back to *Picard*—he looks at his days as a production assistant, and later writer on *Enterprise*, with humble pride. "My ideas were viable for Star Trek . . . good or bad . . . I don't know. But I was a Star Trek fan. Writing for *Enterprise* was cool. It was very cool."

CHAPTER 13

IT'S SABOTAGE!

The Star Trek reboot films and the redefining of twenty-first-century blockbusters

If humans are still around in three hundred years, there's a good chance people will regard the sick beats of the Beastie Boys as "classical music." At least that's how Spock (Zachary Quinto) and Bones (Karl Urban) describe the Beasties' track "Sabotage" during a tense moment in the 2016 film *Star Trek Beyond*. The Beasties first dropped "Sabotage" in 1994, the same year as *TNG*'s seventh (and last) season, the third season of *DS9*, and the film *Star Trek: Generations*. And even though Gene Roddenberry died three years before the song was released, it's a good bet he would have approved of the way *Star Trek Beyond* weaponized it. In one of the most Star Trek-y climaxes of all time, the crew doesn't defeat the vengeful Krall (Idris Elba) with phasers or photon torpedoes, but instead, with *music*. These alien swarm ships can't handle the discordant vibes of the Beastie Boys, making the case that in the future, pop music—and by extension, pop art—can, and will, win wars. In *The Original Series*, Scotty (James Doohan) always had to figure out where to find the extra power for warp drive. In *Beyond*, Scotty (Simon Pegg) needs extra power for the speakers.

This famous Beastie Boys track is the synecdoche for understanding the entirety of the reboot films. In 2016, having the crew blast "Sabotage" wasn't just a fly needle drop, it was, at that point, a callback to the "first" Star Trek film. And that's because the way the reboot films rewrote Captain Kirk, he was a big fan of the Beasties in his youth.

Played by James Michael Bennett in only one scene of the 2009 film called just *Star Trek*, a tween version of James T. Kirk steals an antique, but very hot, Corvette and drives it off a cliff for kicks. He's having big feelings while blasting "Sabotage," and sticking it to his adoptive (offscreen) stepfather. This first "Sabotage" scene is the most representative of what this era of Star Trek was all about: a contemporary blockbuster about reckless dudes learning to be better people. But this specific blockbuster just happened to be a reboot of a franchise that, in theory, would never have gone this populist. Never mind that it's *impossible* to imagine how the Beastie Boys can exist *within* Star Trek—had Abrams stuck "Intergalactic" into these movies it would have shattered the multiverse since, after all, the Beasties name-check "Mr. Spock" in that one. By not using "Intergalactic," the inclusion of "Sabotage" in *Trek* 2009 represents the audacity and restraint of these films simultaneously. Director J. J. Abrams wanted to ruffle some feathers, but he was being careful, too.

―――――

When producer Damon Lindelof got a call from J. J. Abrams in 2007, Abrams asked Lindelof—his longtime collaborator on *Lost*—one question about doing a new version of *old Star Trek*: "Could we make it cool?"

The idea of making Star Trek *cool* is both totally insulting to the entire franchise but also a billion percent understandable when you consider that post-2005, Star Trek was perceived as unpopular, at least mathematically. This was in an era before streaming TV allowed for niche audiences to make a show targeted for them "a hit." This was before *Doctor Who* blew up Comic-Con International and made all the hipsters think about wearing Chuck Taylors as a statement about time travel. The MCU didn't exist. Even the final installment of the Star Wars trilogy, *Revenge of the Sith*, the last live-action film George Lucas directed,[1] seemed to end with a whimper. When *Star Trek: Enterprise* was canceled, the contemporary explosion of mainstream "geek culture," as we know it, simply hadn't happened. For eighteen years, with a few blips here and there,[2] Star Trek had been, for better or worse, the biggest nerd game in town. And, during that time, it was, essentially, overseen by the same person, Rick Berman. The last series of that era—*Enterprise*—had ended with just an average of 4 million viewers, down from the 20 million viewers at the height of *The Next Generation*. In 2003, *Entertainment Weekly* writer Tom Russo pointed out that audiences weren't just avoiding Trek on TV, but at the box

---

1 To date. As of this writing, George Lucas has not directed a live-action feature film since *Revenge of the Sith*. Maybe he could direct a Star Trek film? Wouldn't that be something.

2 *The Matrix* in 1999 and the rebooted *Battlestar Galactica* (2003–2009) spring to mind. However, *The Matrix* doesn't take place in space, and *BSG* was co-created by Ron Moore, who entered the industry because of his prominent work on Star Trek. There are, of course, dozens and dozens of other "big" science fiction events in this very arbitrary period (*Farscape*). And others that seemed big, but really weren't (*Firefly*). But the truth is, the early mainstreaming of "geek culture" in the very early twenty-first century was focused on fantasy, not science fiction, with the Harry Potter movies and *Lord of the Rings* being the prime examples.

office, too. The last film featuring the *TNG* cast, *Star Trek: Nemesis*, made only $43 million at the box office and, like the *Enterprise* finale, *Nemesis* also ended on a sad moment, the death of Data.

In 2009, just before the release of the 2009 film, J. J. Abrams said, "At a certain point it seems like the Star Trek films and series knew and embraced they were never going to get beyond that core audience." And so, Abrams's whole "make it cool" sentiment can easily be translated into "make it profitable" or "expand the audience."

Around this time, Viacom, the parent company of Paramount, also separated from CBS, effectively putting Star Trek on TV and Star Trek on film into two separate spaces. Had this not occurred, there's every reason to believe that *Enterprise* may have run for seven seasons and, potentially, even staged a comeback. But in this universe, only *two* years passed between the end of *Enterprise* and beginning work on the J. J. Abrams reboot. It feels like a longer stretch of time that Star Trek was "gone," but on some level that speaks to the success of the *Trek* 2009 reboot. The band U2 put out the smash comeback album *All That You Can't Leave Behind* just three years after *Pop*, but when "Beautiful Day" came out in it, it felt like ages since U2 had put out anything good. That's what *Trek* 2009 is. It hadn't *really* been that long since Star Trek had attempted a mainstream prequel, it had just been a while since anyone had cared.

Surprisingly, many from the '90s Trek old guard openly supported the idea of starting over. Ron Moore told me that by the end of writing for *Deep Space Nine*, he found the continuity of Star Trek "crippling," and that the best bet was for the franchise to "totally start over." Even prominent TV producers like *Babylon 5* creator J. Michael Straczynski advocated this approach, going so far as to pen a detailed outline, published online, called "Star Trek: Reboot the Universe." Today, it's easy to think that recasting and remaking all facets of *The Original Series* was super controversial in the early aughts, but the truth is that it was, at the time, the only idea that made any sense. And, from a purely business standpoint, *Star Trek* 2009's goal was identical to that of *Star Trek: Enterprise*: Do Star Trek, but try to attract a mainstream audience. Putting "Sabotage" in a Star Trek movie worked in the same way "Magic Carpet Ride" did in *First Contact*, and the opposite of the way "Faith of the Heart" never worked in *Enterprise*. To be fair, "Faith of the Heart" is probably more honest about what Star Trek is all about, but "Sabotage" is just straight-up awesome. As Oasis songwriter Noel Gallagher said, "You have to be cool to be cool," and it's hard to argue that, conventionally, *Trek* 2009 isn't cool. In several trailers for the film, the sentence "This is not your father's Star Trek" served as a weird takeaway that was both oddly true *and* bizarrely untrue. If the figurative "father" in this marketing analogy were a viewer who only considered Shatner, Nimoy, and *TOS* to be real Star Trek, then strictly speaking, the first Star Trek that "wasn't your father's Star Trek" was, obviously, *The Next Generation*. What *Trek* 2009 succeeded in doing—both in perception and in actuality—was to make the point that *all* Star Trek before it was low-key, inaccessible, and uncool. Because *Trek* 2009 told a story about Kirk, Spock, Uhura, Scotty, Chekov, Sulu, and Bones, its basic elements were much more *my* father's than anything Star Trek had been doing during the previous eighteen years.

The daunting prospect of this movie seems kind of simple: Rebuild Star Trek from the ground up. But if you've been reading these chapters in order, then you know how utterly nuts it was for Abrams and his collaborators to look at four decades of Star Trek material and say, "Nah, let's put most of that to the side." At the time, recasting these roles had never actually happened. It had been considered,[3] but it had never happened. Unlike Batman or Sherlock Holmes, nobody knew if audiences would accept new actors in these roles. The idea that the role of Captain Kirk or Mr. Spock was bigger than Shatner or Nimoy was a *theory*. And, if you think about anyone recasting *The Next Generation* roles in 2022, you might find yourself feeling uncomfortable.[4]

Somewhat controversially, Jim Kirk (Chris Pine) sees the USS *Enterprise* being constructed *on the ground* in Riverside, Iowa. This notion, that the Starship *Enterprise* was something that was made on Earth, just around the corner from a bar that seemed familiar, is core to why the 2009 *Star Trek* movie clicked. And even beyond needle drops, the film's score clues you in very early to the fact that this is just a *movie* that happens to be called *Star Trek*. Composer Michael Giacchino tells me that although he and J. J. Abrams considered using older themes from the other films and shows more heavily, "In the end, we felt that even though the story was about the same characters we knew from the past, this should be treated as a new adventure. We would be inspired by the films that came before but wanted to create something that was distinctive for this new timeline."

J. J. Abrams and Michael Giacchino choosing to open *Trek* 2009 *without* a familiar Star Trek musical theme, and then, after the brief titles, downshift hard into the Beastie Boys is a much

---

3 After *Star Trek V: The Final Frontier* in 1989, producer Harve Bennett pitched an origin story for Kirk and Spock set at Starfleet Academy. The plot was nothing like what *Star Trek* 2009 became, but the basic setup was the same, and Bennett's intention at that time was to recast Kirk and Spock.

4 Then again, in 2021, Brent Spiner told me he thought that Daniel Craig could convincingly play a younger, 1990s-era Patrick Stewart. If you look at photos of Patrick Stewart with a hairpiece, you'll see what he means.

bigger deal than it might seem. Not only was the orchestral *Star Trek* theme distinct and different, but the entire feeling of the film was also a departure, and we haven't even mentioned that J. J. Abrams loves using lens flares in his camera work. If you compare what Abrams did with *Star Trek* in 2009 against what he did in 2015 with *Star Wars: The Force Awakens*, it's almost like you're dealing with two different directors. With *The Force Awakens*, Abrams created a twenty-first-century continuation and homage to the classic Star Wars trilogy that aimed to appease fans at every turn. Although a fantastically thrilling film, *The Force Awakens* would never be accused of transgression or risk. It is, perhaps, the most risk-averse science fiction film of all time. *Star Trek* 2009 is the opposite. Abrams wanted *Trek* 2009 to "reintroduce these characters to a universe of moviegoers who have never seen Star Trek before," while a co-screenwriter, Roberto Orci, said that the "tricky thing was . . . how do we make this movie for everyone?" The short answer is that *Trek* 2009 succeeds at being "for everyone" because it's not actually about anything Star Trek is really known for. It's *only* a character piece, and mostly just about Kirk and Spock. The filmmakers cop to this. Lindelof says the "core" of the movie is about Kirk and Spock "falling in love," like "Butch and Sundance."

What all this bromance meant was that the film wasn't *really* making any kind of big social statement about prejudice. Yes, we got a requisite scene from Spock's childhood in which bullies tease him coldly about his mixed heritage. Spock also ditches the Vulcan Science Academy when the elders refer to his human mother as a "disadvantage." In one of Zachary Quinto's truly inspired moments as Spock, when he coolly turns down the offer to be part of a club that slanders his mom, he says "Live long and prosper" with the same intonation as "Go fuck yourself."

"I loved that guy so much," Quinto said of Nimoy in 2019. "We were so close. We talked not just about the role that we shared on Star Trek, but life, and curiosity. He was endlessly curious at the end of his life." Nimoy believed that *Star Trek* 2009 was "good Star Trek," and it's hard to argue with Leonard Nimoy. And yet, as many fans pointed out at the time, it was hard to locate the *message* within *Star Trek* 2009. The story of that first film wasn't actually about whether or not the Federation is morally justified in existing, and other than the character work with Spock, there are no gestures or big statements made about tolerance.

In fact, in a reversal from the *TOS* episode "Balance of Terror," when Kirk offers a helping hand to the felled Romulan ship, Spock (Quinto) disagrees, and basically tells Kirk to kick the bad guy to the curb. In the 2013 sequel—*Star Trek Into Darkness*—Spock beats the shit out of Khan (Benedict Cumberbatch) while flying on a moving platform straight out of a video game. Then again, *Into Darkness* also features a moment in which Kirk is given a direct order to *kill* Khan via a remote torpedo strike, but instead he defies Starfleet orders, and with Spock's help decides to bring in the fugitive alive. The relationship that the "Abramsverse" films have to the high-minded ideals of the rest of the franchise is slightly inconsistent. This isn't to say these three films aren't good films. And *Star Trek Beyond*, directed by Justin Lin and co-written by Scotty himself, Simon Pegg, was certainly designed to have more of a warm and fuzzy *TOS* vibe. "We were in danger of becoming franchise-weary," Pegg said in 2016. "But it was a different director, a different writer . . . [*Star Trek Beyond*] felt like a breath of fresh air."

Beyond sits at an interesting intersection in Star Trek history. In a sense, it's a soft reboot for the reboots. The film casually establishes that Sulu is gay and has a husband and daughter. The film changes the Starfleet uniforms subtly, and gives Kirk, Spock, and Bones a new reason to come together. It's also the first (and as of this writing *only*) Star Trek film that wasn't directed by a white man. Justin Lin's cinematic skills from working on the Fast and Furious films might seem counterintuitive, but when you consider that *TOS* was mainly an action-adventure series, nearly everything about *Beyond* makes sense. From Captain Kirk riding a motorcycle to a zero-gravity fistfight inside of a space station, *Beyond* feels like the big-screen remake of *TOS* fans had been waiting for. Had a direct sequel to *Beyond* been fast-tracked, it's possible that the reboot crew would continue to dominate the hearts and minds of Trek fans everywhere.

———————

In terms of competently made pieces of cinema, *Star Trek* (2009), *Star Trek Into Darkness* (2013), and *Star Trek Beyond* (2016) are probably better movies, technically, than any of the previous ten films. And, in terms of changing the landscape of sci-fi/fantasy cinema in the twenty-first century, *Trek* 2009 is *the* most important sci-fi movie of the twenty-first century. It remains J. J. Abrams's best film, while making Chris Pine and Zoe Saldaña into household names. When you consider all the films that Pine and Saldaña have done since *Star Trek* 2009, the impact it had on the world is clear right there. No big movies of any kind—from the Marvel films to the DC movies like *Wonder Woman*—would look the way they do if *Trek* 2009 hadn't been a hit.

The brazenness of the film has rarely been as successful in other pop culture franchises. *Trek* 2009 belongs to a strange twenty-first-century blockbuster film phylum—sandwiched between *Batman*

Begins (2005) and *X-Men: First Class* (2011), it was a reboot that *worked*. For a brief period, the 2009 reimagining of the final frontier did for Trek what Daniel Craig did for James Bond with *Casino Royale*. Even if the J. J. Abrams films don't represent the philosophical milieu of the rest of the franchise, *Trek* 2009 does represent a slick version of what the Trek universe should look like if you want to convert someone real quick. While the rest of the Trek franchise kept its phasers on stun, the J. J. Abrams movies are the only time phasers have a default setting of ass-kicking.

"I loved what J. J. did," Jonathan Frakes told me in 2018. Apparently, Frakes is such good buddies with Abrams that they text each other frequently. "I think the J. J. movies kicked open a door for a lot of different styles for Trek. Without those movies we wouldn't have been able to bring Trek back to TV with *Discovery*. We have more colors in the Star Trek palette now because of him."

CHAPTER 14

DISCO INFERNO

Star Trek: Discovery and the twenty-first-century renaissance of Trek on TV

It's all right. It's Saturday night. Wyclef Jean's "We Trying to Stay Alive" is pumping. In a converted cafeteria, rainbow disco lights are flashing, and Mary Wiseman is playing the classic drinking game of flip cup. Everywhere people are dancing, and one of them, Shazad Latif, is wearing a Hawaiian lei of white flowers. Outerspacey green tint on the cups disguises what kind of booze is being tossed back. Everyone is tipsy. There's a great vibe and, for this group, this is a much-needed release. Sonequa Martin-Green stands awkwardly in the corner, confused as to how to act, like a shy kid at their first dance, or like she's a human who was raised by Vulcans. Actually, she *is* a human who was raised by Vulcans. This shindig isn't something that happened in a private party in Hollywood. Wiseman, Latif, and Martin-Green are all in character as crew members of the Starship *Discovery*: Ensign Tilly, Lieutenant Tyler, and Commander Michael Burnham, respectively. This killer party—complete with blasting that Bee Gees remix—is the opening scene to one of the most pivotal Star Trek episodes in the twenty-first century. This party isn't just a part of Star Trek. This party *is* Star Trek. In between sips of her drink, Tilly sidles up to Burnham and says, "So, what's your deal?"

Michael Burnham's deal is that she's Spock's hitherto unknown adoptive human sister. Born to human parents—later revealed to be Starfleet secret agents—Michael Burnham was rescued as a young child by Spock's father Sarek (James Frain) after her family was killed by the Klingons. Spock does not appear in *Discovery* Season 1, but Sarek, Star Trek's most troubled parental figure, does. The backstory reveals not only that Sarek and his human wife, Amanda (Mia Kirshner), adopted Michael Burnham, but that decision also led to Vulcan extremists trying to murder him, his daughter, and his whole family. Right from the start, *Discovery* owned the idea that it was going to be a different type of Trek series, and somewhat tellingly made its main character someone who has been adopted by Star Trek royalty itself. In the *Discovery* pilot, Sarek briefly becomes a kind of Obi-Wan Kenobi figure to Michael Burnham, having telepathically zapped part of his Vulcan *katra* into her mind. "You get a lot of who he is by those actions," James Frain told me in 2017. "He adopted Michael and they tried to kill her and then he gave her a piece of his soul." In 1987, it was gutsy for Roddenberry to bust out an entirely new crew and barely mention the original gang. In 2009, it was equally bold for J. J. Abrams to do the opposite: recast the classic crew as hot, young actors. *Discovery* wanted its *TNG* new-crew cake while feeding off the established Trek continuity, too. The power of nostalgia for Star Trek in 2017 meant that *Discovery* couldn't get away with just having this be another crew on another starship. Perhaps taking a cue from Vin Diesel, *Discovery* decided early on that this series wasn't just going to be about hopping solar systems, it was going to be about *family.*

Starting in 2017, with a piece of Spock's family tucked into its soul, *Star Trek: Discovery* kicked off the ongoing contemporary comeback of Trek on television. And in just a few short years, the *DISCO* era has managed to not only redefine Trek's past, but also create a new road map to its future. The cool kids call it *DISCO*—an abbreviation of the name of the series and the titular starship. This nickname exists in-universe, too, because starting with the episode "Lethe," we see Burnham, Tilly, and other crew members wearing athletic t-shirts with the word DISCO emblazoned on the front. If worn in the wild, these shirts do not scan as Star Trek things. They're just weird, funky post-hipster, post-irony, post-everything statements that signify nothing and everything at the same time. When two people see each other rocking DISCO shirts in public, they nod approvingly.[1] If you know, then you know. In the party episode, "Magic to Make the Sanest Man Go Mad," *DISCO*'s main character, Michael Burnham (Martin-Green) gets stuck in a *Groundhog Day*–style time loop in which she must stop Harry Mudd (Rainn Wilson) from stealing the ship. In *The Original Series*, Harry Mudd was a slimy con man who twirled his mustache and gave Kirk and Spock headaches with his schemes involving anti-aging pills and seriously irritating android duplicates. In *DISCO*, as played by Wilson, Mudd is slightly more dangerous than his 1960s counterpart, but just as ridiculous. After getting his hands on some reality-bending time crystals, Mudd's big idea for time travel is to

---

1 In the *Star Trek: Lower Decks* Season 2 episode "Three Ships," we see Captain Freeman rocking a navy-blue shirt with the word RITOS, an abbreviation of her ship, the USS *Cerritos*. Fans are still wondering if any version of the *Enterprise* crew has off-duty shirts that say PRISE, or ENTER.

use the tech for petty theft. "Khan wants universal domination," Rainn Wilson tells me. "Harry Mudd is just trying to make a dime."

The fact that one of Captain Kirk's goofiest nemeses from *The Original Series* was reborn as Rainn Wilson in 2017 is all because technically, *Star Trek: Discovery* began its life as a roundabout prequel to the classic series. Despite looking like an utterly modern prestige drama, chronologically, *Discovery* is set roughly a decade before the events of *The Original Series*, meaning all the things that happen in the first two seasons of the show—and its spin-off, *Strange New Worlds*—are intended as previously unchronicled Starfleet adventures that all lead to *The Original Series*. DISCO begins in the year 2256, about nine years before the second *TOS* pilot, and chronicles the life of Michael Burnham on two starships, the USS *Shenzhou* and, later, the USS *Discovery*. Although Season 2 takes the crew through the year 2258, complete with a team-up with Spock (Ethan Peck), Captain Pike (Anson Mount), Number One (Rebecca Romijn) and the USS *Enterprise*, by the end of that season, the *Discovery*—led by Burnham—jumps into a space-time wormhole and ends up in the year 3188 *permanently*. Taken as a whole, *Discovery* is rare science fiction whatchamacallit that is both a prequel and sequel simultaneously. On top of all of that, the first and third seasons of the series also spend a fair amount of time in Trek's infamous Mirror Universe, which results in audiences being asked to find room in their hearts for *two* versions of Michelle Yeoh's Philippa Georgiou: one from the "good" universe and one from the "bad" universe. If all of this sounds complicated, it totally is. And yet, *Discovery* is a bizarrely easy place for a first-time viewer to beam into Trek. In case the title didn't make it clear, the whole point of this show is for both the characters and the audience to *discover* what Star Trek is and what it might mean for TV in the twenty-first century.

The creation of Burnham and the crew of the *Discovery* is one of the smartest and boldest Trek revisions to date. After a decade and a half of Scott Bakula and Chris Pine sliding Trek back into white-dude-centric narratives, *Discovery* reawakened the Trek brand to what is arguably its true calling: pushing the envelope with crucially nonmale points of view combined with diverse representation. It's the most diverse Star Trek series *ever*, with most episodes of the series breezily passing the Bechdel test.

"Representation matters," *Discovery* showrunner Michelle Paradise tells me in late 2020. "It matters to see a version of yourself on-screen. It matters there are nonbinary and transgender characters. It matters that there is a Black woman in the captain's chair. It matters that there is a gay couple on our show. We will continue to do that for the show, and the world we live in, but also, to honor the Star Trek legacy."

As the first Black woman to lead a Trek series, Martin-Green's Michael Burnham not only represents a fulfilled promise of diversity in infinite combinations, her character also exists as a philosophical course correction for the entire franchise. Burnham is not just a nifty Easter egg character who exists to fill out Spock's backstory. In *Discovery*, Spock's family fills out *her* backstory. "We were in such a precarious position since the inception of our show because we have to be *new* and yet familiar at the same time," Sonequa Martin-Green tells me. "We happen ten years before *TOS*, which was a decision Bryan Fuller made, and Alex Kurtzman as well. So, because we're right there, you have to see the canon. But you have to see more than just Easter eggs in order to be firmly connected to

The Original Series, in my opinion." Martin-Green talking about *Discovery* co-creator Alex Kurtzman is a telling detail. Today, Kurtzman is the overseer of nearly all that is happening with Star Trek on streaming TV. But he found his way into Star Trek by co-writing the first of the "Abramsverse" reboots. Along with Roberto Orci, Alex Kurtzman wrote both *Star Trek* and *Star Trek Into Darkness.* Meaning, the person who pushed the canon of Trek into an alternate continuity was also the person who brought Trek on TV back into the *old* timeline with *Discovery.*

Naming a woman "Michael" was the result of a collaboration between series creator Bryan Fuller and Season 1 co-showrunner Aaron Harberts. The initial inspiration was a tribute to the female bassist of the Bangles, Michael Steele. Martin-Green later explained that much like boys are often named after their fathers, Michael Burnham is named after *her* biological father, the Starfleet officer Mike Burnham,[2] representing "a very quaint yet powerful symbol of the father-daughter dynamic." The journey of Michael Burnham isn't just meaningful within the context of interplanetary adventure and time-hopping hijinks. Symbolically, she represents a lot of powerful archetypes for various underrepresented demographics. From adopted children who reconnect with their biological families, to women of color in authority roles, to anthropologists, to scientists, and, of course, to women with names that aren't overtly soft or feminine, Michael Burnham contains aspirational multitudes.

"When I was wrapping on *Walking Dead,*[3] I was hoping there

---

2 In *Discovery* Season 2, a flashback reveals papa Mike Burnham in the flesh, played by Martin-Green's real-life husband Kenric Green. He later played the voice of Mike Burnham in the animated *Short Treks* episode "The Girl Who Made the Stars."

3 Martin-Green played Sasha on *The Walking Dead* from Season 3 to Season 6. Her character appears in various cameos and flashbacks after that point. In 2021, Martin-Green shut

was something bright and amazing around the corner," Martin-Green recalled in 2021. "I was not a Trekkie or a Trekker growing up. I had to dive into the deep end." In 2019, Martin-Green told me that when she first began researching the entire Trek canon, she was "overly ambitious" to try and memorize everything there was to know about the Star Trek canon. "In the very beginning I thought I was going to be able to take in everything in a very short period of time. And that wasn't true," she said. "I had to realize that as long as I'm telling this story I'm going to be learning about it. And there's always going to be more that I can learn about this universe. I had to settle that in my heart."

Like Spock, Burnham comes from two worlds, and struggles to reconcile her Vulcan upbringing with her passionate human emotions. Burnham has Spock's intelligence and can do the Vulcan nerve pinch on people. Like many beloved Star Trek characters, she's still an outsider who relies on the found family of Starfleet to define who she is and what she believes in. In the same way Picard was a human manifestation of Spock's cold logic and Kirk's hot-blooded human emotionalism, Burnham is the healthier revision of that revision. "She is the more realistic version of Spock," *Black Alert* podcast host Travis Johnson explains. "A lot of the new shows are doing this—taking Trek to task for the mistakes it's made in the past and trying to do better." To that point, unlike the constant racist teasing Spock got from Bones ("that green-blooded son of a bitch!"), Burnham doesn't get shit for the fact she was raised by a Vulcan dad and a human mom. She also doesn't deny her feelings the way Picard or Spock might have. Instead, the character's

---

down the misconception that she left *The Walking Dead* because of *Star Trek*. According to her, "it was a door closing and another one opening simultaneously."

feelings are the story of the show. The big mood of *DISCO* is that it is a big mood. People cry openly when shit goes down with time crystals. There's a lot of hugging on this show, perhaps more than any Star Trek series to date. When Captain Pike (Anson Mount) temporarily takes over command of the *Discovery* in Season 2, he doesn't describe Starfleet's mission as a scientific quest for pure knowledge. "Starfleet is a promise," Pike says. "I give my life for you; you give your life for me. And nobody gets left behind." Later, in a pep talk he gives himself, Pike says that the defining quality of a Starfleet captain is his belief in love.

There's also a lot of wisecracking on the show, and *DISCO* sports Trek's first f-bomb, which, appropriately, is uttered as a positive affirmation. Burnham's bestie on the ship is Sylvia Tilly (Mary Wiseman), a nonstop chatterbox who, in the episode "Choose Your Pain," says, "This is so fucking cool!" Tilly reminds you of your favorite person and feels plucked from an alternate version of Lena Dunham's *Girls* but a version in which all the characters are nice. Wiseman tells me that "Tilly's not cool and she's not slick. She is goofy, but she's not the fall guy. She's well respected by her peers and well loved. There's not been a female character [in Star Trek] who is so uncool and quirky. That feels contemporary to me." In the Season 3 episode "Far from Home," when Saru (Doug Jones) is faced with a possible first-contact situation with aliens, he decides to take Tilly with him as the ideal representation of human honesty and decency. Because she's a junior officer and a complete goofball, Tilly questions this decision, later asking Saru why he chose her. "We are introducing ourselves to the future," he says. "You, Ensign Tilly, are a wonderful first impression." In the Season 4 episode "All Is Possible," after processing her various outer space traumas, Tilly decides to leave her post on the USS *Discovery* and become a teacher at Starfleet Academy. When I talked to Wiseman about this moment, she said that she's proud that "our show is very mental health focused."

Discovery is constantly having a conversation about the idealism of Star Trek with a self-consciousness that occasionally lays it on a little thick, but sweet. It's also a series that is slightly more on the nose when it comes to social commentary than previous *Treks*. In the Season 3 episode "People of Earth," the crew learns that in the distant future of the thirty-first century, Earth has broken away from the idealistic United Federation of Planets. As an isolationist planet, Earth is beset with paranoia *and* is the victim of constant raids from nearby pirates wearing ridiculous space helmets borrowed from *Spaceballs*. But the denouement of this episode is classic Trek: The alien pirates aren't aliens. They're also humans, forgotten space colonists exiled to Titan, one of the moons of Saturn. For years it was taboo for Roddenberry's future to depict human beings at odds with one another, but what "People of Earth"—and by extension the rest of *Discovery*—does is to say something new. Things in the future *might* get better—but we're going to have to work to make sure they stay that way.

After being forced to jump into the future at the end of Season 2, the *Discovery* crew in Season 3 becomes a relic from an idealistic *past*, suddenly trying to influence a troubled present with their old-fashioned do-gooder notions. This is a powerful metaphor for the desperate need for hopeful fiction in the twenty-first century. Star Trek's 1960s idealism *is* old-fashioned. But that doesn't mean optimism is bad. In the episode "Die Trying," Saru (Doug Jones) convinces Admiral Vance (Oded Fehr) to let *Discovery* continue to serve as a Starfleet ship in a more rough-and-tumble future, mostly because they come from a "revered time," and can help the beaten-down and bedraggled Starfleet of the far future to "look up" with more hope. This isn't subtle. And it's not supposed to be. The function of *Discovery* in Season 3 of the series is the same as its function in real life. Can a series starring Spock's human sister bring in the same kind of upbeat moral philosophy that the first show did over fifty years ago?

"Star Trek, to many people, is a really safe place," Ethan Peck tells me. "It's a beacon of hope. I don't want to say a place of *faith*, but in a *way*, Starfleet represents this ideal notion of unity. And it's a real beautiful sentiment."

Like *The Next Generation*, slowly finding its way through writer turnover and chaos behind the scenes, *Discovery*'s first three seasons are wildly different from one another. Other than the characters and the ship, the biggest plot thread for a casual fan to follow is Burnham's gradual climb into the captain's chair. Starting in Season 1, *DISCO*'s main character wasn't the captain, meaning the story of a Star Trek series was, for the first time, told from the perspective of someone who wasn't making all the big decisions. "I was so appreciative of being the first Black woman to helm the franchises," Martin-Green said. "But *also* knowing that this was a journey to the captain's seat. Being able to see someone slip and trip and fall forward and actually earn their position there. I thought that was dramatic and compelling." Other than Chris Pine's insta-captain character arc in *Star Trek* 2009, this kind of gradual journey to the captaincy of a starship had never really been attempted in Trek before. Intentionally or not, it is a concept left over from some of Gene Roddenberry's earliest notions for *The Next Generation*, when he considered making Riker or "the first lieutenant" into the main character, with the captain a more distant figure.

In *Discovery*, Burnham begins as the first officer of the USS *Shenzhou*, second only to Captain Georgiou (Michelle Yeoh), who tells her she's ready for a ship of her own. This prophecy *eventually* does come true. It just takes three seasons. Following Georgiou's death at the hands of the Klingons, Burnham works for *three* different Starfleet captains. Like the rotating professorship of the Dark Arts at Hogwarts, *Discovery* spent its first three seasons swapping various captains out of its titular starship: Season 1 Captain Lorca (Jason Isaacs), Season 2 Captain Pike (Anson Mount), and Season 3 Captain Saru (Doug Jones). Continuity moved Pike (and his own spin-off series, *Strange New Worlds*) back to the bridge of a pre–Captain Kirk USS *Enterprise*. Saru is still on the series, just no longer the acting captain of the ship. Which means *DISCO*'s most unique captain was its first—Lorca—and the one and only time the resident captain character in a Star Trek series was secretly the villain.

Or, perhaps, *not-so-secretly* the villain. In Season 1, after Captain Georgiou (Yeoh) dies—and before her duplicate from the Mirror Universe arrives—Burnham works for Lorca of the USS *Discovery*, played by former Harry Potter Death Eater Jason Isaacs with scenery-chewing menace and militaristic efficiency. The second that Isaacs was cast in the mysterious role of Captain Lorca, fans began to speculate that maybe—just maybe—the role was hiding a secret spoiler. Then, as the show began airing, Captain Lorca started talking about how much he loved studying warfare, insulted other crew members for not being enough like Elon Musk, and even forgot details about dates he'd had with his old girlfriend Vice Admiral Katrina Cornwell (Jayne Brook). Other than trying to sort out Burnham's angst about losing Captain Georgiou and being labeled a pariah for *sort of* starting a giant war with the Klingons, *Discovery*'s inaugural episodes also telegraphed a twist that would have made almost zero sense to a non-Trekkie, and yet made total sense to the hard-core faithful. Captain Lorca clearly wasn't an upstanding member of Starfleet suddenly hell-bent on winning the war with the Klingons. He had another motive! Ergo, he *had* to be an evil doppelgänger from the Mirror Universe! Many fans suggested this on Reddit or wrote about it on blogs. But there's only one Star Trek fan (to my knowledge) who received a call from CBS Studios specifically asking them to tone it down with all the speculation about Lorca being from the Mirror Universe because, frankly, it was kind of ruining the surprise. That fan—the person who was called on the telephone by the Star Trek spoiler police—was the person writing this sentence.

In the first week of October 2017, just before *Discovery* episode 5 aired, a representative of CBS called me and specifically asked if I could knock off writing too many speculation articles about Captain Lorca being from the Mirror Universe. Again, in fairness, these clues were laid out in the series, but the evidence I was citing in some of the blog posts was extrafictional. Jonathan Frakes— who was directing episodes of the series—had already told fans at a convention that *DISCO* would feature at least one episode dealing with the infamous Mirror Universe. On top of that, a publicity photo of Jason Isaacs had been published in the August 2017 print issue of *Variety* that was *very* revealing. As Isaacs sat barefoot in the captain's chair of the *Discovery*, behind him was an early Easter egg; a plaque that read "ISS *Discovery*" instead of "USS *Discovery*." It couldn't have been a typo. In the evil Mirror Universe, there is no Federation—only the wicked Terran Empire—meaning their starships are not USS (United Starships), they are designated ISS

(Imperial Starships). Captain Lorca was an evil Terran posing as a "good" version of Lorca! I was right! The question was, would I walk back my rampant, weekly speculation, in which I screenshot every single detail that proved Lorca was from the Mirror Universe?

Of course I would! Within the fictional world of Star Trek, there exists a clandestine organization called Section 31, a group of super space spies that often recruits into their ranks people who suddenly know too much. CBS publicity politely calling me out of the blue (I guess my number was easy enough to find?) was the equivalent of being recruited into Section 31. I was on the inside, and if I played my cards right, there was no going back. Now, as a professional entertainment journalist, I have received all sorts of phone calls and worried emails from kind, hardworking publicists. I like publicists, and I like to make them happy, if I can. That said, most journalists don't like being told *what* to write. And, had it come from any of a million other science fiction or fantasy properties or comic book franchises, I would have reacted very differently. If I am ever called by HBO and asked to change the way I write about *Westworld*, I will almost certainly tell them where to stick their robot cowboy hats. Most of the time, when entertainment journalists encounter high-class problems like this one, these things are still *problems*, a barrier to you doing your job and getting those clicks. But this was Star Trek. Not only had I (and *many other fans*) correctly predicted a big plot twist in *Discovery* Season 1, but my reward was also that I was now going to get to talk to everyone about the show *a lot* more. I already liked the series, but this moment made me feel even closer to it.

And as a child who nervously shook Walter Koenig's hand, and marveled at the silver-tipped pen Terry Farrell used to sign an 8x10 glossy, I'd like to think I've come a long way. But I haven't. And I'll blame the singular kindness of Jason Isaacs for the permanent warm feelings I have for the *Discovery* cast in particular.

On January 26, 2018, just forty-eight hours before the episode "What's Past Is Prologue" aired, I waited on hold to be connected with Jason Isaacs to discuss the big reveal from the previous week's episode, "Vaulting Ambition." Although merging calls is accomplished now by touching buttons, I liked to imagine the nice folks at CBS publicity using an old-style switchboard, complete with headsets and wires. It somehow felt appropriate to relate to Jason Isaacs via anachronistic means. And the second we were connected, Isaacs began debating with me about the title of my first book, and whether or not Luke Skywalker had indeed ever read a book. Turns out, while he was being connected, Isaacs had read up on *me*, the *DISCO* spy who cracked the code and prematurely told the world the big secret. And he loved it.

"I feel an enormous relief now that I don't have to lie anymore," Isaacs told me. "Not just to journalists and the public, which is horrible, but also to my friends, my family, everybody. I wouldn't have said yes to just 'being a captain' in the abstract. I also knew it wasn't going to be like any Star Trek captain that had come before. I knew the whole story. It gave me something juicy and fun and very secretive to play with."

Discovery's first season—with its multiple twists and turns, focused on an *evil* captain trying to make the Empire great by murdering his opponents—is a darkly wild ride. When someone tells you that *Discovery* started out as the darkest *Trek*, they are not exaggerating. If *Deep Space Nine* was "hope through darkness," then *Discovery* Season 1 was hope as an abstract concept while also inside a pitch-black room in which the lightbulbs have been broken, and you need to be careful to not step on the glass. Although the overall message of *Discovery* Season 1 concludes with Burnham and Saru standing up for the ideals of the Federation by refusing to carry out a doomsday plan against the Klingons, the beginning of *Discovery* is more violent and frightening than perhaps any incarnation of the franchise to date. Part of this was by design, but part of it was because the tone and concept for *Discovery* was shifting constantly before it aired, after it aired, and while it was airing.

Created by Bryan Fuller—who had cut his teeth writing for *Star Trek: Voyager* in the '90s—the original concept for *Discovery* was to become the *American Horror Story* of the Trek franchise insofar as each season would take place in a new setting with new characters. In a sense, with the proliferation of post-*Discovery* Trek shows, this has kind of happened, just not exactly as Fuller envisioned. He also explained that the idea to cast an Asian woman (Yeoh) and a Black woman (Martin-Green) as the two initial leads for *Discovery* came out of his love and admiration for *The Original Series* and that he "couldn't stop thinking about" George Takei and Nichelle Nichols.

Fuller also had conceived of a longer Mirror Universe arc, which would have put the crew in the evil, inhospitable alternate dimension much earlier. But, after "squabbles" with CBS over budget and creative oversight, Fuller eventually departed *Discovery*, citing his commitment to the series *American Gods*. In his place were co-showrunners Aaron Harberts and Gretchen J. Berg, who changed Fuller's original concept and pulled back on "sending the crew to Mirror" until the midseason finale. As in the early days of *The Next Generation*, the writer turnover in the first two years of *Discovery* is significant. Because neither Berg nor Harberts had a background in Star Trek, there was tension between them and the rest of the writing staff. On top of this, *Wrath of Khan* veteran

Nicholas Meyer had been hired by Fuller as a staff writer, but his role after Fuller's departure was greatly diminished. Ever the gentleman, Meyer won't tell me exactly *why* he asked that his name be removed from the second episode of *Discovery*—"Battle at the Binary Stars"—but simply commented that "when I saw the final episode, I realized what I was concerned about was a real concern." Amid the departure of Fuller, and the tensions between the writers and Harberts and Berg, series co-creator Alex Kurtzman stepped in to try and put *Discovery* on a new, brighter course. "When the writers weren't happy, I couldn't hand the show off to someone else again," Kurtzman recalled. Eventually, this resulted in Kurtzman briefly running *Discovery*, and then firing Harberts and Berg and replacing them long-term with Michelle Paradise, a veteran writer of *The Originals* and a *Vampire Diaries* spin-off, and a former member of that famous improv troupe the Groundlings. And, from the midway point of *Discovery* Season 2 forward, Paradise infused a brighter and gentler tone into the series, continually moving away from the more hard-edged and violent *DISCO* Season 1. By Season 3, *Discovery* feels light-years away from the darker place where it began, and in Season 4 the color-coded *Next Generation* uniform colors returned, too, as if to say, yes, this might be your aging millennial parents' Star Trek after all, and maybe that's a good thing.

From brooding villains to cozy *TNG* vibes to the progressive politics of *Deep Space Nine*, the chimera of *Star Trek: Discovery* endures, partly because it is so different than other shows, and as Martin-Green smartly noticed, "different, but the same."

"Even in our new iteration of Star Trek, it feels like we harken back to *The Original Series* and some of the other great series," Paradise told me in 2020. "Part of what we do is always honoring what gave birth to all of this." The son of Star Trek's Gene Roddenberry, Rod Roddenberry, tells me that the path for *Discovery* had a rocky beginning. But now, he feels like the course is smooth, and true to his father's vision. "I think with Season 3, *Discovery* got Starfleet right," Rod tells me. "I don't want to say they didn't get it right in Season 1 or 2. But in Season 3, they nailed it. *Discovery is real Star Trek now.*"

CHAPTER 15

THE PRIDE OF STARFLEET

Trek's long road to LGBTQ+ representation

On January 5, 2018, two days before *Star Trek: Discovery* first aired the controversial and game-changing episode "Despite Yourself," I'm on the phone with Wilson Cruz talking about the concept of patience. I tell him that I love how his character on *DISCO*, Dr. Hugh Culber, is super patient with some of the fools and villains on the series, and I ask him if that warm, calming presence is part of who he is, too. "I'd like to think so," he says, laughing. "But I do think Dr. Culber has cornered the market on patience. And I do think he learned patience from being in a relationship with a genius." Cruz isn't talking about the fandom having to suffer some inconsistencies from the various geniuses who have written Star Trek over the years, but when you consider how long queer Trek fans had been waiting to be seen on the final frontier, it's a tempting analogy. Star Trek's stop-and-go history with LGBTQ+ progress feels a little like putting up with a well-meaning do-gooder because you love them, even if you're starting to lose your patience.

In our phone call, Cruz wasn't interested in recounting the history of Star Trek; he wanted to talk to me about what was happening in the moment with Dr. Culber, who seemingly dies in the episode we were discussing. For the rest of *DISCO* Season 1, Culber is survived by his husband, mycologist Paul Stamets (Anthony Rapp), and these two are, for all intents and purposes, Star Trek's first openly gay couple. Wilson Cruz tells me Culber learned patience from putting up with the eccentricities and temper of the man who makes the special kind of space travel in *DISCO* possible. Without the genius of Stamets, the spore drive of the Starship *Discovery* couldn't happen. And so, Culber has to wait an entire season and a half to be rescued from an interdimensional realm after getting murdered by a sleeper Klingon agent—a person who we thought was Michael Burnham's secret moody human boyfriend, Ash Tyler (Shazad Latif). While this all sounds zany in a typical Star Trekish way—and the idea of a Klingon agent being disguised as a human was lifted from the goofiest Trek, "The Trouble with Tribbles"—the fact is, killing off one of two gay characters only halfway through the first season of *Discovery* was a big deal. During my call with Cruz, I am already anticipating that a huge chunk of the fandom, will—correctly—be outraged. The episode hasn't even aired yet, and I am worried. We'd just gotten used to Culber and Stamets, and it's concerning that death and violence will *become* the defining quality of the only healthy gay couple in Starfleet. But Wilson Cruz is smarter than me, and like his *Trek* counterpart, intuitive and kind. He isn't exactly on the phone with a journalist to do damage control, but he is going to provide some comfort by broadcasting an advanced spoiler. He wants me and everyone else to know that Culber is not really dead. "You will see Dr. Culber again," Wilson Cruz told me on that phone call in 2018. "This is an epic love story. You will be experiencing highs and lows, triumphs and disappointments. And what we're doing is inviting you to go on the journey of this relationship and the roller coaster ride that it is. This is just one chapter in their story. What we're asking the audience to do now is to trust us. This is not a 'bury your gays' trope."

I was not the only journalist to talk to Cruz about this controversial episode, but I was one of the first. For nearly a year after the episode aired, and before Culber did indeed return in *Discovery* Season 2, Cruz often responded to frustrated fans on Twitter by linking our brief interview. And whenever Cruz or Anthony Rapp would take heat from well-meaning but frustrated fans, I would always feel for them. But I felt for the fans, too. In 2019, ahead of the airing of *DISCO*'s "Saints of Imperfection" and the return of Culber from the ethereal realm of the "mycelial network," Anthony Rapp told me that he understood why fans were pissed, but that he wanted everyone to know that there was never an attempt to "spin" Culber's death.

"Because there was such *understandable* outcry, it became clear that we needed to let people know he [Culber] was coming back. People were upset. Which I can understand," Rapp told me. "But I have *no interest* in telling people how he's coming back and why he's coming back. It was fun for me to keep that secret. Why would they want to know? It would take away from the fun of the story and letting it reveal itself . . . I kept [tweeting] #Patience to people. But people are impatient. Fans are passionate; they want to know. I get that instinct. But at the same time, just *relax*, step back, and trust us."

So, why didn't all LGBTQ+ fans trust the bold, proud course of a gay love story on *Star Trek: Discovery*? Twitter cynicism and genuine concern over the depiction of violence against queer people is part of it, for sure. Popular YouTuber Jessie Earl—known on Twitter as "Jessie Gender"—tells me that "as a fan watching it, it *hurt* to watch that. It felt like it was done for shock value, and they [CBS] had built up so much PR around the first gay couple on Star Trek." Earl's take wasn't unlike those of many LGBTQ+ fans and their allies; everyone wanted to trust the powers that be, but because the death was so brutal, it felt like a betrayal to fans.

"I think fans wanted to trust the show," Earl says. "But at the same time, I remember older queer fans telling me, 'Oh, the show has done this to me before.' They were bitter and resigned. But I was in this middle ground where I was hurt, but I wanted to give it the benefit of the doubt." Earl said part of the way they have reconciled the faux-killing of Culber in *Discovery* Season 1 is because "fundamentally, *Discovery* is a show about trauma. Not just Michael Burnham's trauma, but also the trauma that Starfleet has about the Klingon war in Season 1." Earl also points out that having an LGBTQ story *also* contain trauma is problematic, simply because trauma, historically, defines so much of the queer experience.

So, because of the convoluted way in which Culber returned in Season 2, it's arguable that his faux death wasn't totally necessary, and for critics and fans like Earl, it still sent the wrong message. Culber's death didn't have the gravitas or sense of sacrifice we got from Spock or Data, two characters who, for many fans, were coded as queer anyway. In contrast, Culber was just murdered so a sleeper agent could keep his secret. While his comeback was romantic and genuinely thrilling, one wonders if the death scene needed to be quite so brutal.

Star Trek fandom is made up of several generations, and not all of those generations communicate effectively with one another. "Star Trek Twitter" freely uses the word "Trekkie," even though older Trekkers shame them on that one. Gatekeeping from historical know-it-alls is a problem in Trek fandom, just as much as it is with Star Wars trolls. And often, much of that gatekeeping simply comes from a "get off my lawn" mentality from older generations. But one area the smart Trek fan generations are united in is this: It took way too long for the franchise to get its act together with LGBTQ+ representation, and even the fans who didn't live through those years are aware of that painful truth. The outcry over Dr. Culber's death wasn't just about the possible perpetuation of a harmful trope; it was a collective groan from queer Trek fans who, as a community, had been waiting for healthy, happy gay characters in Star Trek since Gene Roddenberry promised they would appear. In 1986, just after the existence of *The Next Generation* had been made public, fans at conventions started asking whether we'd finally see gay people in Starfleet. At a twentieth anniversary convention in Boston, a representative of a gay Star Trek fan club—the Gaylaxians—confronted Roddenberry directly about the issue. Franklin Hummel, a librarian and member of the Gaylaxians, wanted to know "if there would be a gay character on the new show." Roddenberry gave a half-hearted promise, responding, "Sooner or later, we'll have to address the issue. We should probably have a gay character." Sooner turned out to be later. Much later.

Closeted for much of his early career, George Takei tells a story of Gene Roddenberry swimming toward him at a pool party in Los Angeles, during the run of *The Original Series*. Takei hit him up with the idea of tackling gay rights and, according to the story, Roddenberry was open to the idea but was too afraid of the series getting canceled over a "firestorm."

"'The times will change as we move along,'" Takei remembers Roddenberry saying. "'But at this point, I can't do that.'" Assuming this conversation took place when Takei remembers it happening—sometime between 1966 and 1968, it's notable Roddenberry was talking about this kind of representation at all. Then again, any straight man working in the arts—like Roddenberry—would find himself working alongside gay people. In fact, the man who designed the costumes for *Star Trek*, William Ware Theiss, was gay. That said, we don't really need to pat Roddenberry on the back here too much. Despite what he said to Takei, putting a gay character in *TOS* at all was almost certainly never on the table. But the fact that George Takei even *had* this chat with Roddenberry in the 1960s is saying something. We tend to give Star Trek a lot of credit for pushing racial boundaries on TV, but the truth is, the Civil Rights movement was a very public, massive social movement happening while the show was being produced. The NAACP existed in the 1960s. GLAAD did not. And just to put it in perspective, the Stonewall riots happened on June 28, 1969, three weeks after *Star Trek* aired "Turnabout Intruder," its final episode. So, again, assuming this story from Takei is legit, Takei pushing Roddenberry into a "gay rights" story line was a hundred times edgier than any of the other boundaries *Trek* broke during *TOS*. Roddenberry may have been a risk-taker when it came to race issues on TV, but in the '60s, he was also participating in a movement that was fashionable for white liberals to support. This doesn't detract from the accomplishments of *The Original Series*, but it does make you think about that tricky pop culture sci-fi mirror. Social change can be amplified by pop culture, and in that way, Star Trek is one of the best signal boosters of all time.

Pre-twenty-first-century Star Trek certainly showed a lot of bravery, but when it came time for gay characters to possibly appear in *The Next Generation*, that era of Star Trek failed to provide a meaningful mirror. When Roddenberry launched *TNG*, he promised his writers that writing about AIDS and homophobia would happen on his show. And why not? *Star Trek: The Next Generation* was a syndicated program and, as such, had fewer rules from Paramount about what they could and couldn't do. If a local station didn't want to carry the series because it depicted gay people, that was their business. And yet, with all that freedom, Roddenberry didn't do it. Infamously, "Trouble with Tribbles" writer David Gerrold wrote a script called "Blood and Fire" for *TNG*, which would have depicted gay crew members on the *Enterprise* while also tackling a kind of twenty-fourth-century version of HIV. Although Roddenberry claimed to support the script, the Great Bird of the Galaxy himself seems to be the person who shot it down, allegedly saying the script was "a piece of shit." Gerrold mostly ascribes these viewpoints to Roddenberry's manic behavior and substance abuse during the early years of *The Next Generation*, once recalling that "I don't know how much [Roddenberry] drank because I never saw him sober." Others suggest that Roddenberry's canceling of "Blood and Fire" can be attributed to his aggressive lawyer and puppeteer Leonard Maizlish. When Herb Wright was assigned to rewrite "Blood and Fire," he learned that much of the negative notes supposedly written by Roddenberry originated, more likely, with Maizlish. And in 2014, David Gerrold himself blamed the "clusterfuck" on homophobia deriving from longtime Trek producer Rick Berman.

Still, regardless of whose fault it was, the fact remains that "Blood and Fire," a Season 1 *Next Generation* episode set to depict gay people in the twenty-fourth century, never got made.[1] In the 2003 *Enterprise* episode "Stigma," the Trek franchise asserted a vague HIV analogy; what if mind-melds were considered taboo among Vulcans at a certain point in history? Not only was this episode two decades after the dust-up involving "Blood and Fire," it also failed to portray any gay characters.

In fact, after *The Next Generation* debuted in 1987, across *four* different Trek series for eighteen years, all the way up to the year 2005, there was not one explicitly gay character from "our" universe. In *Deep Space Nine*, it was insinuated that series regulars Kira (Nana Visitor), Ezri Dax (Nicole de Boer), and Leeta (Chase Masterson) were all bisexual. Oh, wait a minute. Their *evil* duplicates from the Mirror Universe were bisexual! In the regular universe, they were not. These bisexual baddies also reinforced negative stereotypes that LGBTQ folks have looser morals, simply by virtue of being not straight. In terms of progress, Mirror Universe bisexual characters were more out, but not exactly good role models in the way other Trek characters are.

Although characters on *The Next Generation*, *Deep Space Nine*, *Enterprise*, and *Voyager* were often coded or read as queer by the fans, none of the Trek series actually managed to depict an overtly non-straight character without some kind of twist or metaphor. Because of this fact, you can start to understand why Trek fans in 2018 felt like they'd had the rug pulled out from under them with

---

1 In 2008, "Blood and Fire" was made as a fan film "episode" by James Cawley's series *Star Trek: Phase II*, later rebranded as *Star Trek: New Voyages*. David Gerrold wrote and directed the piece, which retooled his *TNG* script into a *TOS* setting. In this version, Kirk's nephew Peter Kirk was gay. It enjoyed in-person screenings at Star Trek conventions but existed almost exclusively online as a nonprofit fan film. In 2008, Paramount and CBS had to implement more draconian policies about fan films, meaning "Blood and Fire" probably couldn't have been made today.

Culber's fake-out death. It's bewildering and yet, somehow, predictable that prior to the twenty-first century, Trek *only* used analogies to talk about queerness.

For queer fans like S. E. Fleenor, this meant finding characters that were "coded" as queer. When I asked Fleenor about Seven of Nine's queerness, they pointed out: "We can hold creators, including Gene Roddenberry, responsible for refusing to embrace queer and trans characters and story lines as more than subtext. Their queerphobia and transphobia outside the world of Star Trek had a huge impact on the world created within the narrative." To their point, even with *TNG*, some of the attempts at writing toward gay rights issues ended up sending a mixed message.

Perhaps the most divisive episode of *The Next Generation* is the 1992 episode "The Outcast." Written by Jeri Taylor, the episode introduces a single-gender alien species called the J'naii. On this planet, gender is considered "primitive," and if individuals claim to have gender leanings one way or another, they are required to undergo "therapy," which basically brainwashes them into the cultural norms of the planet. Watching "The Outcast" today is a minefield, partly because Riker admits to the guest character Soren (Melinda Culea) that he can't figure out what pronouns to use if people aren't either male or female. The most overtly heterosexual character on the ship *of course* falls in love with a nonbinary alien who, as it turns out, wants to declare their gender as female, which is forbidden by her culture.

Arguably, Taylor's gay allegory was well-intentioned, but the writing feels directed at heterosexuals. Because a gay allegory was written for a straight audience, many of the queer people in the audience at the time were understandably offended. "We thought we had made a very positive statement about sexual prejudice in a distinctively Star Trek way," producer Rick Berman said in 1992. "But we still got letters from those who thought it was just our way of 'washing our hands' of the homosexual situation." Jeri Taylor went on record saying "The Outcast" was intended as an "outspokenly . . . gay rights story." But was it? Although the contemporary reputation of "The Outcast" is very mixed, the episode has gained some renewed praise in the twenty-first century. Writing for Star Trek.com in 2020, Nitzan Pincu points out, "By giving Soren the chance to rebel against her oppression, the episode voices a queer plea to free sexual 'others' . . . Her reprogramming illustrates the dehumanizing effect of conversion therapy, which was little known outside of the gay community at the time the episode aired." Even when Trek failed to provide real representation, "The Outcast" can be read as a case for allyship. As Pincu mentions, Worf initially presents a bigoted attitude toward the nonbinary J'naii, but by the end of the episode, he's the one who decides to go against orders and help Riker rescue Soren. If the goal of "The Outcast" was to make antigay straight families uncomfortable in 1992 and give kids something to think about that broke through the sexual dogma they'd been taught, then the episode was successful. I was eleven when the episode aired, and I specifically remember it challenging my assumptions about who Riker was allowed to crush on. The episode may not be remotely progressive by twenty-first-century standards, but Jeri Taylor's heart was certainly in the right place. It may not be a moment to applaud, but I dare anyone to find another action-adventure series aimed at families, airing in 1992, that depicted the hunkiest straight dude in the universe falling in love with someone who is clearly queer, and in terms of a contemporary reading, clearly a trans character. Most of Soren's conversations with Riker at the top of the episode are about pronouns. It's clunky in 2022, but in 1992, you'd be hard-pressed to find another big TV show in which characters were having frank conversations about which pronouns they preferred.

When *Deep Space Nine* rolled around in 1993, once again Gaylaxians and straight Trek allies alike had hope for some actual queer representation. From his very first appearance in the episode "Past Prologue," the tailor Garak (Andrew Robinson) is clearly flirting with Dr. Julian Bashir. Of all the regular Star Trek characters in the 1990s, Garak was the only one in which the writers and the actor collaborated to seemingly make the character as openly gay as possible, without ever saying it. Robinson also holds the unique distinction of being the only Star Trek actor to develop a backstory for his character that was so complex that he later published an official tie-in Trek novel—*A Stitch in Time*—which is narrated by Garak in the form of an epistolary story, framed in the second person to his "dear" Julian Bashir.

"I even wanted Garak to have a partner," Andrew Robinson tells me. "Every time they put Garak with a young woman, even though they're in Cardassian drag, it just didn't work. In terms of how I played the character, I played the character as gay. I understand why they were timid, but even he [showrunner Ira Steven Behr] now wishes they were bolder." This is true. In the 2018 *Deep Space Nine* documentary *What We Left Behind*, de facto showrunner Ira Steven Behr admits that although Paramount may have opposed having Garak openly come out as gay, the failure was that "we never asked." Behr thinks Paramount would have probably said no, but feels like it was still a missed opportunity. Robinson tells me that if Garak were to return to a future Star Trek project, he "would certainly hope" that the character's sexuality was finally acknowledged.

While *Deep Space Nine* was still on the air, and Garak was kept firmly in the closet, one Trek character was established as gay. But it happened with very little fanfare, probably because it didn't happen on TV. Decades before he would be known as "the Central Park birder," Christian Cooper was facing another kind of prejudice. Instead of racism, Cooper's writing in comic books collided with homophobia in the form of corporate skittishness. As the head writer for the 1996 Marvel comics series *Star Trek: Starfleet Academy*, Cooper's intention was to have its lead character—the hunky blond Matt Decker, the namesake and descendant of the guy who crashed his starship into "The Doomsday Machine"—come out as gay in the very first issue. "The idea was to do some role reversal," Cooper tells me. "Matt Decker has a problem with Nog being in Starfleet, and [he's] sort of like throwing an eye askance at that—because he can't imagine a Ferengi in Starfleet. And then when Matt comes out as gay, Nog would be horrified because Ferengi came from such a blatantly sexist society. The idea of homosexuality is just absurd to him."

It would be nice to say that this terrific story line is out there in an old issue of a Star Trek comic book you've never read, but the truth is, Paramount told Cooper and his writers they couldn't do it. Matt Decker couldn't be *explicitly* gay, but his roommate, Yoshi, could be. "They [Paramount] perceived Matt Decker as the captain. He was the team leader of Omega Squad. I mean, it's an ensemble comic, but they felt he was equivalent to a captain in one of the series. And they didn't want that ground to be broken by a captain-level character in a comic. If it's going to happen, they wanted it to happen in one of the shows. So they nixed it." Cooper says that although he was disappointed, having Yoshi be openly gay was something, and he still fought to keep Decker's sexuality ambiguous for as long as possible. But, for whatever reason, even in a comic book fairly insulated from the larger events of the interwoven Trek canon of the '90s, the corporate overlords weren't ready for a gay lead character. "The culture hadn't changed yet," Cooper said. "Star Trek was still behind at that time." Bringing gay Star Trek characters out of the closet wasn't just limited to Marvel comics. In *Voyager* novels written by Kirsten Beyer (who would later write for *Discovery* and *Picard*), the character of Icheb is gay. Meanwhile, in Una McCormack's novels, Garak was also depicted as gay. Still, none of this happened on-screen until John Cho's Sulu held hands with his husband in *Star Trek Beyond*. Like so many other moments of half-hearted representation in Trek's history, Sulu being retroactively gay in *Beyond* scanned, to many, as the worst kind of tokenism. As George Takei said in 2016, "Just hugging the baby and arm around the guy . . . and it's over." Clearly, if Trek were going to do anything meaningful for LGBTQ+ representation, we would need to be able to see these characters for longer than fifteen seconds.

Before openly queer or trans characters made their way onto *Discovery*, *Picard*, and *Strange New Worlds*, Trek's most enduring metaphor for the LGBTQ+ community was the alien species known as the Trill. While the Trill were first introduced in the *TNG* episode "The Host," we got to know these folks way better in *Deep Space Nine* in the form of the character of Jadzia Dax. In *DS9*'s very first episode, it's established that although Jadzia Dax (Terry Farrell) has the body of a twenty-eight-year-old woman, her mind is "joined" with a *second* life-form, a centuries-old wormlike Trill symbiont that lives inside of her. The Dax symbiont has had several hosts prior to Jadzia, and the last body was male, a person named Curzon, who was buddies with Ben Sisko when they were both younger. This leads Sisko to refer to Jadzia as "old man," a playful jibe that, at first glance, now scans as misgendering. That said, as Jessie Earl points out, "I have read this as Jadzia allowing *only* Sisko to say 'old man.' No one else is allowed to do so, and it's an acknowledgment of Jadzia's previous 'pretransition' life, something many real-life trans people let a select few close friends of theirs acknowledge."

Like "The Outcast," the legacy of the Trill and Dax specifically on *DS9* isn't one of Trek doing anything offensive on purpose but instead, of making attempts at queer representation with the best of intentions, even though its success was mixed.

In the episode "Rejoined," Jadzia Dax reconnects with Lenara Kahn (Susanna Thompson), who, like Dax, is a joined Trill. When both Dax and Kahn had previous hosts a hundred years prior, they were a heterosexual couple, Torias Dax and Nilani Kahn. But now, having met again, albeit in completely different bodies, Trill society forbids the two women from resuming their love affair. For whatever reason, Trill aren't allowed to reconnect with past loves once the symbiont switches bodies, even though this idea was super contradicted in the first *TNG* Trill episode, "The Host." Once again, Star Trek has a random alien taboo that stands in for discrimination against non-cis people, which occurred again in the *Enterprise* episode "Cogenitor," which imagines a "third sex" in an alien species, one of whom who is driven to suicide. Hardly an aspirational hopeful future there.

That said, while it's easy to be hard on *DS9*'s "Rejoined" for not going far enough, in 1995, lesbian kisses on prime-time TV shows were practically unheard of. The first lesbian kiss for American TV had been only four years earlier on *L.A. Law*. For better or for worse, the Trill became Trek's dominant analogy for exploring same-sex taboos. As Avery Brooks put it, "It was a love story after all . . . It's not about sex or same gender or any of the above, even though, obviously, in our world, that's what people started to look at."

After Terry Farrell left *Deep Space Nine* after Season 6, the character of Jadzia was killed, meaning her symbiont was put into another host, Ezri Dax, played by the younger Nicole de Boer, who tells Sisko right off the bat that he can no longer refer to her as "the old man." Today, de Boer tells me that she not only considers Ezri to be a "feminist icon," but "she was a counselor who was a very brave young person. And, of course, Jadzia was Star Trek's first nonbinary character and Ezri continued with that."

Could Star Trek have introduced its first trans and nonbinary characters without the Trill coming first? In the problematic *DS9* episode "Profit and Lace," we see Quark undergo a sex change, and then back again. This episode gets zero marks for treating this subject seriously, but what it did do was demonstrate that transition was somewhat normalized in the twenty-fourth century.

Still, it wasn't until *Discovery* that Star Trek got real about trans and nonbinary issues. In 2020, *Star Trek: Discovery* added two new regular characters to the cast, a human named Adira (Blu del Barrio) and a Trill named Gray (Ian Alexander). Adira is nonbinary and Gray is trans. And although Adira ends up being saddled with a Trill symbiont (that contains Gray's memories), their path to coming out as nonbinary is not explicitly connected to becoming a Trill. In fact, when Adira first appears, they use she/her pronouns, but by the end of *DISCO* Season 3, Adira comes out to Stamets as nonbinary. This journey was directedly tailored to del Barrio's own experiences in real life.

"I didn't want to be out on-screen as a character who was out until I was," del Barrio explained. "I wanted to wait until I had told my family and my friends. So I kind of came out alongside them [Adira]." Prior to being cast as Gray, Ian Alexander had already starred in a prominent role as a trans character in the sci-fi thriller series *The OA*. Alex Kurtzman, *Discovery*'s producer, said that the reason he wanted to cast Alexander as Gray was because "I was particularly taken by Ian's performance [in *The OA*]. And Ian was the first person that we thought of for the part."

Alexander and del Barrio have charted new territory for Star Trek not just because of what they represent but also who they are. Unlike previously queer-coded Trek characters, Alexander's and del Barrio's gender identities reflect who they are in real life. And in the proud history of many of the franchise's most groundbreaking roles, del Barrio didn't know a whole lot about Star Trek before they joined the cast. "I kind of saw this as a blessing. I had zero experience with Star Trek when I joined," del Barrio tells me in 2021, just ahead of the launch of *Discovery*'s fourth season. "The starting place that gave me, right when I was meant to play Adira, whatever interests I had at that moment, whatever interests I thought Adira might have—where I can now dive into this huge history of a series. Which was really fun. [After being cast] I got really into *Deep Space Nine*." In Season 3 and Season 4 of *Discovery*, Adira also becomes a kind of surrogate child for Stamets and Culber, two gay men looking out for a nonbinary young person. "Throughout LGBTQ existence, we've had to create chosen family units," Wilson Cruz tells me in 2021. "And I love that we're doing that in our own Star Trek way."

Since 2019, in Season 2 of *Discovery*, the crew has also been joined by world-famous lesbian comedian Tig Notaro, who gives this modern *Trek* her own version of a cranky, wisecracking know-it-all character. Notaro claims she just plays herself, or "Tig in space," though longtime Trek fans probably see a lesbian version of Bones fused with Scotty. "I think when I joined the Star Trek world there was a little bit of a feeling from myself and the fans like 'Huh, Tig in *this*?' And then it seemed like it worked out okay," Notaro says with a laugh. But then she gets a little more serious and points out that she would have never even considered doing an action-adventure TV series unless what the show was doing aligned with her values. "It's always such a nice feeling to work on a project that is so positive, that has such a positive view and place in entertainment.

"I always want to come out of the other side feeling like the project lines up with who I am as a person in the world and what my views are," Notaro explains. Two decades ago, it would have been hard to imagine a prominent lesbian comedian joining a Star Trek series alongside openly trans, nonbinary, and gay performers. The fans who searched for coded messages for years no longer have to search. Prominent author and science fiction expert Charlie Jane Anders wrote in 2020, that "*Discovery* has become the queer *Star Trek* I always wanted," and pointed out that the triumph of the series is in doing "what Star Trek does best—what David Gerrold was trying to help it do, back in the '80s. And I'm so glad that Trek is going where far too few television shows have ever gone before." Jessie Earl concurs, telling me that "if we're looking at where we're at now with queerness on the franchise, I think I see a lot of better moves. I feel like they finally learned their lessons."

Thanks to changes behind the camera, Star Trek has started to begin the process for making amends for its negligence on

LGBTQ+ rights. Now, as Notaro tells me, "it feels like Star Trek is right on target." Notaro's optimism is contagious. Still, Star Trek's journey to this point has been troubled, and full of pain. But, if there's any consistent message in the final frontier, it's simply this: We can always do better.

CHAPTER 16

CHOOSE TO LIVE

Picard and Lower Decks flip the script on Star Trek's definition of success

In the final frontier, the hero's journey is overrated. Starfleet's finest aren't wedged into the public consciousness because they follow the rules of an academic mythological theory which was half dreamed up by Carl Jung and hammered into the brains of film critics and professors like Joseph Campbell. If you even dip so much as a toe into critical theories as to why various science fiction or fantasy narratives persist, it won't take long for someone to trot out Campbell's ideas of "the hero's journey." But, crucially, the rejection of so-called traditional hero's journeys is precisely what makes Trek so different. J. J. Abrams notwithstanding, if there's one way in which Star Trek is starkly different than Star Wars, it's simply this: In Star Trek, adolescent tales of heroic quests are mostly backstory. And that's because working adults—complete with regrets and family angst—tend to dominate the narrative. They've gone on the hero's journey already, they've been there, done that, and bought the Starfleet uniform. As Trek has passed into the third decade of the twenty-first century, its version of the hero's journey has calcified as significantly less generic than its sci-fi peers, featuring not-quite heroes, traveling on long and warping roads.

"There's this thing in America, where we tell everyone that they can be the hero and the star. But in other cultures, it's just okay to be good at your job," *Lower Decks* star Tawny Newsome tells me. "I think the whole point of *Star Trek: Lower Decks* is that some people aren't the heroes. I mean, I think Mariner is good at her job, but I don't think she's a hero." Newsome—who is known to non-Trek fans for her comedic contributions to *Comedy Bang! Bang!* and the podcast *Yo, Is This Racist?*—is *probably* the hippest and funniest person ever to be associated with Star Trek. And because her background was primarily in comedy, or playing in a Talking Heads cover band, Newsome always assumed she'd never have a shot at Star Trek, even though she's a lifelong fan. "Everyone comes from a royal academy of real acting and that was never my journey," Newsome tells me. "It wasn't really until Mary Wiseman in *Discovery* popped up that I thought, 'Oh, maybe they do want a little quirky weirdness.'"

In 2020, the Trek franchise expanded into nonheroic territory with two wildly different new TV series, both of which can be described as quirky and weird. On one end of the emotional spectrum, you've got *Star Trek: Picard*, a thematically heavy, tightly serialized novella for TV, which Patrick Stewart favorably compared to his turn in the ultragritty, naturalistic 2017 X-Men film, *Logan*. For the first three episodes of *Picard*, the eponymous retired captain doesn't even leave Earth and spends most of his time sipping wine in his château, trying to solve the mystery around the murder of a young android (Isa Briones). Meanwhile, on the other end of this spectrum, as of 2021 there are two seasons of *Star Trek:*

Lower Decks, an animated comedy for adults (think: *Big Mouth*), focused on the scrappy underdogs of Starfleet, the kind of people we'd usually see in the background, doing menial tasks and boldly going places everyone had gone before.

Both series owe their existence to the continued nostalgia for the *Next Generation* heyday of '90s Trek. Both shows twist the feeling and philosophy of *TNG* into unexpected narratives. And—spoiler alert—both shows sported Season 1 finales in which Will Riker shows up to save everyone's asses. *Picard* and *Lower Decks* might seem like totally different Trekkie beasts, designed for completely disparate audiences, but they're both forms of contemporary, fully sanctioned fan fiction, primarily spun out of *The Next Generation*. One series was co-written and created by a Pulitzer Prize–winning novelist, and the other by a guy who used to write for *Rick and Morty*. What unites both these shows is what makes Star Trek's continued metamorphosis in the twenty-first century so unique: Nobody could have seen either of these shows coming, their individual takes on the canon and characters of Trek aren't remotely safe, and yet, both shows provide the same warm-blanket-on-a-cold-night feeling people *think about* when they *remember* the best of Star Trek.

For children of the '90s, Jean-Luc Picard was the ultimate space dad, but the series *Picard* explores a broken and sad version of that hero, trying not to reclaim his glory days, but simply looking for some closure. So, from that perspective, *Picard* and *Lower Decks* represent what happens when one generation takes the art of a previous generation and then remakes that art for the next generation.

"I see what you're saying. I think that is probably an accurate way of interpreting the content of the show, but I don't think it originated with that kind of intention," *Picard* co-creator Michael Chabon told me when we spoke on March 24, 2020. "That said, the idea of generations, is, I suppose, already built into Star Trek. It's in the title of the second live-action series in the franchise. It's in the title of the feature film that brought those first two series together. And it's wired even more deeply than that in *The Original Series,* in the kind of Kennedy-esque Camelot legacy that was very much present. You can see it in Kirk's haircut! The idea of generational thinking, in terms of a way of thinking about social progress, has been wired into the show from the very beginning. But I don't know if [*Star Trek: Picard*] originated with that kind of intention. It might be an inevitable by-product of something that we did do very consciously, which was to try and build a *Star Trek* series around a seventy-nine-year-old man who is playing a ninety-four-year-old character. It was about thinking about this character, this protagonist, this hero, an acclaimed hero in his own time. Now, he's at a point in his life where all of that is behind him. This is him looking at what he has accomplished, and asking what is left to do."

Uniquely, *Star Trek: Picard*'s fictional time setting mirrors nearly the exact elapsed years since returning *TNG* actors Patrick Stewart, Brent Spiner, Marina Sirtis, and Jonathan Frakes all appeared together in *Star Trek: Nemesis.* That film debuted in 2002 and was set in 2379. *Star Trek: Picard* debuted eighteen years later in 2020 and is set in 2399. As Chabon points out, in the series, Patrick Stewart is playing Picard at least a decade beyond his own age, but what this series reveals is that that's always been the case, even in *TNG.* Harry Treadaway—who played the duplicitous Narek in *Picard* Season 1—tells me that he viewed the entire approach to the show like participating in a Richard Linklater film. "I love the idea that you could keep playing a character, twenty years on; when you see someone who has lived a life, and they're playing the same character. *Boyhood* is amazing like that. And of course, the *Before Sunrise* movies. You can only make that art by waiting that exact period of time."

The concept that an old, crusty hero can be pulled out of retirement for one last big adventure is not remotely new. From way too many *Die Hard* sequels to almost all of Harrison Ford's[1] output in the twenty-first century, the idea that some action badass is "getting too old for this shit" is a trope so tired that pop culture is probably getting too old for this shit, too. Even *The Wrath of Khan* relied on this idea, making Kirk dwell on his usefulness in a similar way that Jean-Luc does in *Picard*. But Stewart coming back in *Picard* isn't like Ford coming back to play Han Solo. Despite the franchise's brief obsession with turning Picard into a cliché blockbuster ass-kicker, the reputation of the character has nothing to do with kicking ass. One early trailer for *Picard* showed Jean-Luc brandishing a sword against a Romulan, while the words "A Hero Never Leaves the Fight" were blasted on the screen. But, in the context of this episode ("Absolute Candor"), Picard actually throws down his sword two seconds later and *refuses* to fight. When his young Romulan companion Elnor (Evan Evagora) slices Picard's would-be assailant's head off, Picard is *furious*. Before swinging his sword, Elnor gives the other Romulan a warning: "My friend, choose to live."

Think about this in contrast to Old Man Han Solo blowing people away with no-look blaster shots in *The Force Awakens*. When Star Wars fandom demanded old Han Solo, J. J. Abrams gave people

---

1 Hilariously, Harrison Ford shares a birthday with Patrick Stewart. Stewart is older, but only slightly. Both were born on July 13, Stewart in 1940 and Ford in 1942.

exactly what they wanted. Stewart's return as Jean-Luc Picard is the opposite. It portrays an older man acting like an older man, not an action hero. And even Picard's muscle Elnor has a code of combat ethics that requires him to ask nicely that the people he's about to fight "choose to live." Somehow, with *Picard*, the phrase "live long and prosper" was turned into a kind of battle cry about avoiding fights. Like saying "phasers on stun!" the phrase "choose to live" is badass but also contains a message of *possible* peace.

As a series, *Picard* is about how, yes, Jean-Luc is getting too old for this shit, and let's talk about that rather than joke about it. But most revealingly, Stewart's return as Picard wasn't simply to set up the adventure of some new youthful Star Trek character. In 2020, Isa Briones told me that Soji was a "boss lady," but the narrative of *Picard* doesn't replace Jean-Luc with Soji.

And so, *Picard* wasn't like what Leonard Nimoy did in *Trek* 2009 or, arguably, what Mark Hamill, Harrison Ford, Carrie Fisher, and Billy Dee Williams did in the Star Wars sequels. *Star Trek: Picard* is like if Disney+ had committed to an open-ended series *only* about sad Luke Skywalker, living on that island, being depressed. *Picard* is the closest the Trek franchise has gotten to playing out like a contemporary literary novel, which makes sense, considering Michael Chabon is the only living author to win both the Hugo and Pulitzer, for a novel (*The Amazing Adventures of Kavalier & Clay*) that blurred the lines of science fiction, comic book narratives, and so-called serious literature. *Picard* is littered with Trekkie Easter eggs, but, like Nicholas Meyer's literary flourishes in *The Wrath* and *The Undiscovered Country*, the series is also chock-full of classic books. The best part of that sword fighting episode isn't a sword fight at all, but instead, the moment we get Patrick Stewart's Picard reading *The Three Musketeers* as a bedtime story.

At least in its initial setup, *Picard*'s first few episodes bear some resemblance to Michael Chabon's 2004 Sherlock Holmes novella, *The Final Solution*. In that book, a very old Holmes is called back into action after World War II while tending to his famous bees in his apiary. Picard's winery is a similar hobby, something to keep him busy and active in his advanced years. As Nicholas Meyer once told me, "All roads lead to Holmes," and the connection between Michael Chabon's love of Holmes, and that impacting Star Trek, circuitously leads back to Nicholas Meyer.

"He was a huge, huge influence on me. I honestly don't think I would be a writer without him," Chabon told me in 2018. "I was a huge Sherlock Holmes fan; one of my first major literary passions was those Sherlock Holmes stories. And then I read [Meyer's] *Seven-Per-Cent Solution* shortly after it came out. I said to myself: Wait a minute; I can write my own Sherlock Holmes story—you can do that? Before that, the first thing that I wrote [as a child] was a Sherlock Holmes story. I loved doing it. But it's not hyperbole; without Nick Meyer and *Seven-Per-Cent Solution*, you know, it wouldn't have happened the way it did."

Chabon was not the only novelist on the writing and creative staff of *Picard*; one of the show's other co-creators is Kirsten Beyer, an executive producer and staff writer on *Discovery*, and someone who got her start writing *Star Trek: Voyager* novels in 2005, four years after the series went off the air. "With *Picard*, I was present from the very first moments the idea of the series began. As always, my Trek knowledge was important, but I was equally involved in the development of the series from day one. And I was blessed with the best possible collaborators in Alex [Kurtzman], Akiva [Goldsman],

and Michael [Chabon]. From the beginning, it was a uniquely egalitarian process. No one's voice was more important than anyone
else's." Beyer tells me that bringing *Voyager*'s Seven of Nine (Jeri
Ryan) into the story of *Picard* was "possibly" her idea, and that the
goal was to "illuminate Picard's character" in new and dynamic
ways. In the episode "Stardust City Rag," we learn that Seven and
Picard haven't actually met, despite the fact they both have a shared
experience of having been assimilated by the Borg. In this episode,
which Jonathan Frakes described as having a "*Westworld*, night
club vibe," Seven of Nine takes revenge on a crime boss who had
killed her surrogate son, Icheb. Beyer admits that the idea of having Seven commit an act of revenge is controversial, because "we
always like to think the best" of our Trek heroes. But, within the episode, Seven deceives Picard into thinking she's taking the high road,
when in fact, she's not. "Somebody's got to have a little bit of hope
out here," Seven says cynically, meaning Jean-Luc Picard can keep
his *Next Generation* idealism, even if the rest of the world can't quite
live up to that standard of moral purity. To his credit, when Seven
asks Picard point-blank if he really felt like he regained his humanity after getting Borgified, he painfully admits, "not all of it."

"I thought that was a really cool moment between those characters," Jeri Ryan tells me. "She's not sure she's going to see him
again. This is her one opportunity to speak with someone who has
had that same experience she has had, or at least some version of
that experience." Ryan also revealed that finding the "voice" for
Seven of Nine decades after the end of *Voyager* "was terrifying."
What Ryan tells me she was "hung up on" was the idea that Seven
spoke so differently now than she had on *Voyager*. How could this
stoic Spockish character suddenly be ordering straight bourbon
and talking like a space cowboy? "Her voice was so specific for

those four years on *Voyager.*" So, after "pacing" and saying she felt "screwed" and unable to play this new, older, and *changed* version of Seven of Nine, Jeri Ryan enlisted the advice of her co-star Jonathan Del Arco, who had also played a Borg named Hugh on *The Next Generation* and also returned for *Picard* Season 1. "Eventually, Jonathan said: 'What if she makes a conscious choice to be as human as possible to survive?' And that was like a little switch going off. That's what I needed as an actor to make it make sense. That was how I could have her speak so much more loosely and casually and in a much more contemporary way."

From Seven of Nine shooting up seedy bars with her phaser rifle, to Picard's new Number One, Raffi (Michelle Hurd), battling drug addiction, to Starfleet admiral Clancy (Ann Magnuson) dropping the f-bomb, *Picard* Season 1 drew plenty of criticism from longtime *TNG* fans who felt betrayed by the darkness of the new show. In one of his Instagram talkbacks following each episode, Michael Chabon countered, saying that the purpose of the show was to delve into characters who lived in the utopian, idealistic world of the Federation "but, for whatever reason, weren't quite *of* that world." This shot of realism is the opposite of what happened with the J. J. Abrams Trek films. The nostalgia the audience has for Jean-Luc Picard and Seven of Nine quickly fades because, in real life, people do change radically over time. And, the journey of these heroes isn't happening when they're young; for Picard and Seven, these life-altering changes are occurring post-middle age. This, if nothing else, might be the most hopeful message twenty-first-century Star Trek has given the world—even if you're over forty, you can still change your ways and turn your life around. Just look at Seven and Jean-Luc!

By the end of *Picard* Season 1, we see Jean-Luc become a

surrogate father to the wayward synth woman Soji (Briones), who, in a roundabout way, is the daughter of Data, our beloved and twice-deceased android. Arguably, *Picard* Season 1 is as much Soji's journey toward selfhood as it is Picard's. To avoid death from a terminal neurological disorder, Jean Luc's soul and mind are placed into the body of an identical android. At that moment he's brought closer to his own humanity and mortality by *becoming* a synthetic life-form. In *TNG*'s critically acclaimed 1988 episode "The Measure of Man," Picard defends Data's right to choose in a court of law, despite the fact that Data is a machine. "We too are machines," Picard says. "Just machines of a different kind." But, in *Picard*, Trek makes the extra leap, and insists all life is "real" life, even the lives of misunderstood robots. Chabon tells me that if *Picard* Season 1 hadn't ended by making Jean-Luc into a nonhuman life-form, "then that meant we were totally chickening out on one of our clear, stated theses of the series—that synthetic life is just as valuable as organic life. If Picard believes that premise, and by extension, we believe it, and the Federation and Starfleet believe it, then the ultimate test and the ultimate proof of that belief can be found in making Jean-Luc Picard a synthetic life-form."

The place *Star Trek: Picard* will eventually hold in the hearts and minds of Trek fans in future generations is, for now, unknowable. But, by literally altering the physiology of Picard, by turning a human character into a nonhuman character while also challenging the audience to *accept* that this is the same person, *Trek* has proven, once again, that the only way to tell new stories with old characters is by making radical changes. When one fan asked Michael Chabon on Instagram if Picard would have a "Ship of Theseus" moment upon seeing his old human body, Chabon quipped, "I would."

Star Trek: Picard Season 2 (2022) also messes with our assumptions about Picard's morality by bringing back that trickster god Q (John de Lancie), to once again guide Jean-Luc through a moral conundrum with space-time-altering implications. Since the beginning of *The Next Generation,* Q has challenged Picard's assumptions about the goodness of humanity, but also about Picard's personal goodness, too. This is why Q is the perfect Star Trek villain, and an ideal figure to harass Jean-Luc well past the end of *The Next Generation.* Q isn't evil at all, he's just confronting us with inconvenient truths. Prior to Jean-Luc fully becoming a synth in the episode "Et in Arcadia Ego Part 2," he rocked an artificial heart for all of *The Next Generation.* In the episode "Tapestry"—*TNG's* near rip-off of *It's a Wonderful Life*—Q gives Picard the opportunity to go back in time and relive a youthful bar fight which would have prevented him from being stabbed through the heart. Ron Moore described this concept as the proof that Jean-Luc was the anti-Kirk, that when he was younger, he was "the wild man." And in "Tapestry," after Picard "fixes" his youthful mistake, he returns to the present to find himself an underling on the *Enterprise.* No longer a captain in Starfleet, Picard is shown another future where he's an underachiever, or, as Jean-Luc says, "a dreary man in a tedious job."

Funnily enough, Q also appears in Season 1 of *Lower Decks,* haunting a quartet of loveable characters who, in some senses, embody Jean-Luc's description of his own personal version of hell. Mariner (Tawny Newsome), Boimler (Jack Quaid), Tendi (Noël Wells), and Rutherford (Eugene Cordero) are all doing the work in Starfleet that nobody wants to do, including—but not limited to— realigning circuits, cleaning elevators, power-washing dirty planetary structures, towing old and busted starships, and cleaning the filter in the holodeck. At the end of the episode "Veritas," when Q bugs Mariner to amuse him, she gets rid of him quickly, saying, "No! We are done with random stuff today! We're not dealing with any of your Q bullshit . . . go find Picard." It's intended as a joke, but the larger implication is wonderful. Picard puts up with Q's bullshit because we think of Picard as an "important" character. But, because the titular lower deckers have way less at stake, and aren't actually making any of the decisions, they can quite literally avoid Q's bullshit. The lesson is clear: Living your life like Jean-Luc Picard might make your life interesting, but it might not make your life cooler.

Inspired by *The Next Generation* episode of the same name,[2] *Lower Decks*, although a comedy, is focused on Starfleet characters who, as series creator Mike McMahan says, "are not at the top of their game"—the characters themselves are not in on the joke. Instead, McMahan insists that "if Star Trek were real, I can't imagine that all these people wouldn't always be talking about all these fucking *amazing* things that happened." For the show, this translates to the characters constantly dropping references to previous iterations of *Star Trek*, which McMahan justifies because the existence of the holodeck proves, to him, that "people on Star Trek watch Star Trek. By letting our Lower Deckers be geeks for Star Trek, it lets the show be geeks for Star Trek and it gets to put it in the canon. Which means *Lower Decks* ends up becoming the Rosetta stone of all the different *Star Treks* . . . This show respects and loves all Star Trek. There is no bad Star Trek to this show. And that's why it's the glue that holds all the other *Star Treks* together."

The success and critical acclaim of *Lower Decks* reveals some-

---

2 The 1994 Season 7 *TNG* episode "Lower Decks" shifts the focus away from the regular crew, and onto four crew members who are junior officers. The episode was written by Ron Wilkerson, Jean Louise Matthias, and *TNG* staffer René Echevarria.

thing everyone always knew, but never admitted: The context of Star Trek is that of a workplace. Sometimes it's a workplace soap opera (*TOS*), sometimes it's like *The West Wing*, a drama where the workplace is about government (*Deep Space Nine*). Before *Lower Decks*, the lead characters on Trek were all portrayed as overachievers, but the other side of that coin is *workaholics*, in danger of burnout. Again, as Chabon admits, the narrative of *Picard* Season 1 is about Jean-Luc trying to find out how to be "useful" again, which he can *only* define through his career. As Kirk famously said in *The Voyage Home*, he's from Iowa, he only works in outer space. And yet, we tend to define these characters by their jobs, something that in real life people actually struggle with all the time. What *Lower Decks* and *Picard* have both done is normalize the idea that you are not your job. Almost zero reoccurring characters wear a Starfleet uniform in *Picard* Season 1 because they're all either retired or civilians or both. In *Lower Decks*, Mariner treats her Starfleet uniform as a joke, constantly rolling up her sleeves and unbuttoning the flap of her jacket. She likes Starfleet, but maybe she doesn't like all the pomp and bullshit that go along with it. In the very first episode, Mariner is dismissive of the bridge of the Starship *Cerritos*, saying, "the bridge is not cool."

Jean-Luc's careerist attitude made him a hero for a time, but nearly left him alone and depressed. Mariner's devil-may-care attitude makes her more realistic than perhaps any Star Trek character before her. Most of us are more like Mariner than Kirk. And, when Tawny Newsome tells me that she thinks Mariner is not a hero, her co-star Jack Quaid chimes in and says, "I'm gonna have to disagree. Because Mariner is totally *my* hero."

CHAPTER 17

THE HUMAN ADVENTURE IS JUST BEGINNING

Strange New Worlds, Prodigy, and the imperfect secret to Star Trek's immortality

In 2018, before he began filming *Star Trek: Discovery* Season 2, Ethan Peck was driving out of Los Angeles on the I-405, "north into the valley," to meet the family of Leonard Nimoy. As he drove, Peck was thinking about all the "qualities I share with Spock." Other than looking like a mega-hot, brooding intellectual, one of those qualities was the pressure of family legacy. While Spock struggles with his status as the son of a famous Vulcan ambassador, Ethan Peck has his own version of expectations that come with his family. He doesn't talk about it a lot, but Ethan Peck is the grandson of Gregory Peck, an actor permanently famous thanks to roles such as Atticus Finch in the 1962 movie version of *To Kill a Mockingbird*. Could Spock have existed without Atticus Finch coming first? Could we believe in fictional characters as idealistic as those in Starfleet if Harper Lee hadn't invented Atticus? When you start to think too hard about literature and Star Trek, you can convince yourself of all sorts of paradoxes, including the idea that Ethan Peck's slick

interpretation of Spock—in *Star Trek: Discovery*, the anthology series *Short Treks*, and, starting in 2022, *Star Trek: Strange New
Worlds*—is proof of a time-travel conspiracy to make sure he got
into Spock's boots. "I thought how serendipitous it is to take on a
burden like this," Peck reflected. "It's the passing of a torch or a
lineage that I think comes with a lot of expectation. In a weird way,
I was prepared for it just by being my grandfather's grandson. Here
I was taking on another legacy. It was really frightening, but in a
way, I've been doing this all my life."

Peck had been cast as Spock four years after Leonard Nimoy's
death, so the family he was driving to see consisted of Nimoy's two
children—Julie and Adam—and their spouses, David Knight and
Deep Space Nine alum Terry Farrell.[1] In order to become Spock,
Peck read *I Am Not Spock, I Am Spock*, and "spent a lot of time with
The Original Series." But he also believed that meeting the Nimoys
would become even more essential to his character research, telling me, "I came away with a deep curiosity for Spock that I might
not have gotten had I not met with them. They really made me feel
worthy of stepping into this role. It brought me instantly closer to
understanding Spock."

Following Zachary Quinto and Leonard Nimoy, Peck was the
third actor to play Spock,[2] at least by most metrics. Before the
supercharged episodic 2022 spin-off *Strange New Worlds* was even
a passing notion, Peck's task was to beam Spock into the pseudo-

---

1 Yes, in real life, Dax is married to Spock's son.

2 If you count all the kids who played Spock in *The Search for Spock*—Billy Simpson, who
did the voice of young Spock in "Yesteryear," AND young Spock actor Jacob Kogan in the
2009 *Star Trek*—Ethan Peck is really the *seventh* actor to play Spock. But he might be the
eighth? Child actor Liam Hughes appears as child Spock on *Discovery* in Season 2, Episode
1, "Brother," well before Peck appears on-screen as adult Spock in Episode 7, "Light and
Shadow."

prequel series *Star Trek: Discovery*, starting to fill in a rough sketch of this tender young Spock from the 1964 pilot "The Cage," and in doing so, remap how everyone's favorite Vulcan became himself. His would be a fractured, less-in-control Vulcan, hanging around on the Starship *Enterprise* in the rowdy, largely unchronicled future decade before *The Original Series*. In this way, he wasn't really the third Spock. Ethan Peck was retroactively becoming *the first* Spock. In his debut *Discovery* appearance—the second season episode "Light and Shadow"—Spock rocks a full beard, is revealed to have been dyslexic as a child, and cries uncontrollably through a "psychotic break." At first green blush, the idea that the super-in-control Mr. Spock would be *crying* uncontrollably might seem wrong. But by now we know better. Sad Spock is classic Spock. From "Amok Time" to "This Side of Paradise," getting at the soul of Spock—and by extension Star Trek itself—is all about the moments when the logical reserve breaks down. "We all love to watch Spock flipping out," Peck tells me. "That makes him exciting. To watch his level of control over himself and his emotions. We realize he is so full of emotion, and to see it burst forth is thrilling."

And yet, despite Peck's delightful take on our favorite sad young literary Vulcan, there were people who weren't having it. In the worst corners of Twitter, Reddit, and YouTube, haters and trolls have scorned the notion of a smiling Spock, spouting the familiar fallacies that Spock shouldn't show this much emotion, and worse, that Spock smiling and singing musical theater in the *Short Treks* "Q&A" would make Gene Roddenberry spin in his grave. In those forums, and sometimes out in the real world, you'll find people who will say that pretty much anything after *The Original Series* isn't *real* Star Trek. Most recently, these complaints contend that the franchise has been *ruined* by everything post-*Discovery*. This phenomenon is not remotely new, and in some ways this cycle of backlash and acceptance not only defines the history of Star Trek, but also presents the real reason why it endures as such a hopeful, and nearly secular, religion. Following the outcry over killing Spock in 1982, various forms of Trekkie backlash reappeared, each one slightly different, yet somehow *exactly the same.*

"When you are a new show and a new character and a new *species* on a new show, it's like you are the country cousin," *Discovery*'s Doug Jones tells me. "They don't trust you until you prove yourself. And I got that vibe at first." Jonathan Frakes sympathizes with Jones. Not only has he directed Jones in some of the most challenging episodes of *Discovery*, Frakes knows exactly what it's like. "You could really feel the resistance at conventions early on," Frakes tells me, speaking to the feeling in the fandom in the late '80s and early '90s. "For years, people didn't really want to accept us [*The Next Generation*]. And then, the same thing happened to all the other casts. To *Deep Space Nine, Voyager,* and *Enterprise.* And I saw it happening to the cast of *Discovery,* too. That cast reminds me of us, of the *TNG* cast."

When *The Next Generation* began, LeVar Burton was aware that his fame from *Roots* and *Reading Rainbow* would be good for the show. Patrick Stewart recalls that Burton is the one who picked up the check at the first cast dinner at a restaurant in Hollywood. Like much of the *TNG* cast, Burton was worried about the financial feasibility of the series, but because he was himself a Star Trek fan, Burton had hope. Specifically, he suspected the naysayers didn't represent the majority. Not even close. "I kind of looked side-eyed at the fans of *The Original Series* who expressed openly and vocally that there was no room in their hearts for another *Trek*," Burton tells me. "As a Trek fan myself, I knew Trek fans—in general—as people who had an open mind. I knew it would change."

Historically, Trekkies have lost their collective Vulcan cool over numerous controversies, great and small. Toxic fandom might seem like a product of the internet age, but this dark underbelly of rage has existed in most fandoms since before the term "fandom" was invented. For angry Trekkies—let's call them Wrekkies—the life-span of Star Trek outrage is actually much shorter than you might think. And that's because the definition of the good old days is always moving into the future.

After the Sherlock Holmes societies that began in the 1930s, the progenitor of all organized, opinionated nerdy fandoms is, without question, the Star Trek fandom. Relative to younger geeky subcultures (like, say, *Buffy* or Harry Potter fans?), there have been several backlash/acceptance cycles spread across half a century. But these aren't the same people. Because so much time has passed, Trek fans of 2022 are literally different people than the fans of 1969. The self-identifying fandom—the people who get excited on Twitter, who cosplay, who go to conventions—is such a significantly different group of people, that comparing the Trek fandom of 2022 to that of 1972 feels intellectually dishonest.

Other fandoms—from Batman fans to James Bond fans to *Doctor Who* fans to Scooby-Doo fans—are all debating the same set of characters and circumstances. For example, in 2019, Scooby-Doo fans—including noted critic Nathan Rabin—were outraged that Matthew Lillard was *not* returning to play the voice of Shaggy for a new reboot of *Scooby-Doo* called *Scoob!* If you were to talk about this in terms of Star Trek post-*TOS*, it would require you to imagine a variety of Scooby-Doo sequels which took place in the same shared universe, featured zero talking dogs, no Velma, Fred, Daphne, or Shaggy, and only *occasionally* featured anyone driving a van called "The Mystery Machine," which, in some versions, may not even be a van. The hypothetical *Deep Space Nine* of an expanded Scooby-Doo universe is a cartoon about kids living in a different city, who don't have a van, who don't solve mysteries, but were visited by Scrappy-Doo in the pilot episode. Now, imagine this hypothetical *Scooby-Doo* spin-off having its *own* fandom inside of "regular" Scooby-Doo fandom. That's right. You can't.

The "rules" of most other fandom backlashes and debates don't apply to Trek fandom controversies because the elements in most other fandom backlashes and debates operate on a fairly predictable spectrum. Take Batman and James Bond. Like Star Trek, certain iterations of this "art" have eclipsed what one generation of fans would consider to be the "original" version of the concept. Some Batman fans still think Adam West was the best version, while '90s kids like me endlessly rep for Michael Keaton. Fans who prefer the comics can get into the Bill Finger/Bob Kane origins, or whether or not Frank Miller's take on bats was made worse by the fact that what passes for edgy in a *Batman* comic book is probably not edgy. Even the derided Joel Schumacher films starring Val Kilmer and George Clooney have been reassessed. Batfleck has his fans. Christian Bale has been hard to top, and Robert Pattinson is the new kid. And through it all, there's generally a somewhat binary criterion that gets turned up or down: Is this version of Batman (or James Bond or Wolverine or Wonder Woman or Sherlock Holmes or Hamlet) *lighter* or *darker* than other takes? Trek fans don't have debates like this, or if they do, those debates are boring. Some of the uglier versions of these Trekkie fights might superficially resemble a Roger Moore fan fighting with a Timothy Dalton loyalist, but the essence of all Trekkie debates is far more abstract. For Star Trek fandom, when a new version of Trek arrives, the stated debate is usually phrased like this: "Is this [insert new Trek show/movie] really Star Trek?" But the meta-conversation is way weirder than people debating about good James Bond movies versus bad ones. Because the real question is: "What is Star Trek?"

Before the debut of *The Next Generation* in 1987, the answer to this question was: "A science fiction series about a spaceship called the USS *Enterprise*, featuring the characters Kirk, Spock, McCoy, and sometimes Scotty, Uhura, Sulu, and Chekov, too." The classic films faked everyone out by killing Spock and blowing up the *Enterprise*, but in 1986, just one year before *The Next Generation* hit the air, the most financially successful Trek film to date at that time—*Star Trek IV: The Voyage Home*—ended by reuniting the classic crew on a new *Enterprise* that looked pretty much exactly like the old one. In the seventeenth century, when the word "nostalgia" was invented by the French doctor Johannes Hofer, it referred to homesickness. This is why when Kirk says, "My friends, we have come home" in *The Voyage Home*, it feels equal parts cheesy and correct.

But then, one year later, *The Next Generation* said, nah, fuck all that. Star Trek was no longer about Kirk and Spock and the *Enterprise*. Picard, Riker, and Data rode on what looked like a funhouse mirror version of Kirk's ship. *TNG* was saying to the kids of the '80s and '90s that this was not their parents' *Star Trek* in the strongest and most convincing possible way: by making it really different. Even the color-coded uniforms denoted different jobs! The fact that Roddenberry was directly involved with *TNG* (as opposed to the films post-1979) mattered less than it should have. "The anti-*TNG* thing was bad with old fans," historian and writer Larry Nemecek recalls. "I remember saying, hang on, wait a second, Gene is involved with this. Let's give it a chance. But it took a while." Fans of *TOS* started letter-writing campaigns. Ron Moore even remembers prominent bumper stickers at conventions saying "I like REAL *Star Trek*. Forget the bald guy."

"Like a lot of Star Trek fans—and I don't think it's particularly admirable—I have this immediate knee-jerk 'uh-oh' whenever I hear about any new *Star Trek*; and that's going all the way back to *TNG*," Michael Chabon tells me. "And when I watched *TNG*, even though I watched it faithfully from the moment it first premiered, I didn't really *like* it. I was not impressed, and it took me a while to get used to it and I think it took the show a lot of time to find its footing. But that sort of typical skepticism has subsequently greeted me when I first heard about *DS9*, about *Voyager*, *Enterprise*, every new series—my first response was like, 'uh-oh.' And I see so much out there with regards to *Discovery*, and with regard to *Picard* and now I get it. I come from the very same place."

Prominent podcaster Kennedy Allen—a founding member of *Women at Warp* and *Black Tribbles*—agrees, saying that she was so suspicious of *Discovery* in 2017 that she didn't even watch the series until 2020. As a Black woman, Allen tells me that the existence of Sonequa Martin-Green on *Discovery* was, eventually, a revelation. "I was a lifelong fan, and even I slept on *DISCO*," she tells me. "I mean, can you imagine not being aware of how wonderful Sonequa Martin-Green was in the year 2017? This fan backlash stuff starts with each of us changing our minds." Chabon believes that this inner change is difficult for fans, but essential. "You are just afraid of change, y'know? You want change for the better. And that's so much harder to imagine sometimes than change for the worse."

So, if fans are inherently conservative and, on some level, hard to please, how did *The Next Generation*—and *Deep Space Nine* and *Voyager* and *Enterprise* and *Discovery*—all eventually find their place in the hearts of Trekkies? How has Star Trek been able to win the fan base over time and time again? It would be easy to say that something about the *message* of Star Trek being *positive* is the reason it's able to continually dig itself out of the toxic fandom pits and render the haters silent and irrelevant. This argument is seductive because we know the result: Over time, a bunch of Wrekkies change their minds about something they previously hated, and slowly that thing (Jean-Luc Picard, *Deep Space Nine*, *Discovery*) becomes something the fandom loves, either because the original haters have changed their minds or are replaced by new people. One prominent presence in the Twitter Star Trek fandom is Heather Rae. She posits that despite some toxicity in the fandom, generational gaps are to be expected.

"Star Trek spans across fifty-five years with fans of all ages; I think there are bound to be generational gaps that affect how we view the shows and interact with one another," Rae tells me. "Star Trek is a series meant to appeal to a broad audience. And it has. It brings together people from all walks of life, from every continent, of all colors, sexual orientation, and genders. I can't think of a better representation of Star Trek's brilliant future than its fandom."

Rae and others are right, of course. The upbeat ideals of Star Trek must play a part in winning out over all this hate. And yet, that only feels like part of the puzzle.

———

According to almost any definition, the pure, original version of any part of Star Trek is hard to find, and hard to define. In the twenty-first century, even watching the first version of the USS *Enterprise* itself requires effort. When you watch *Star Trek: The Original Series* streaming on Paramount+, what you see isn't the same ship that captured the imaginations of several generations of fans in the century prior. The new-old *Enterprise* in the remastered episodes is a simulacrum made from pixels, not plywood. Starting in 2006, when David Rossi, Denise Okuda, and Michael Okuda oversaw the digital remastering of *TOS*, they replaced the grainy analog space shots featuring physical models with cleaner, more dynamic digital starship doppelgängers. According to Denise Okuda, the intention here wasn't "about what we want to change. It's about respecting the original material and thinking about what the artists back in the '60s would have done if they could have done it." To that end, the *Enterprise* doesn't quite do a barrel roll, but in several remastered episodes, the ship looks much more agile and badass than it ever looked in the 1960s.

So, how do you see the real Starship *Enterprise*? Starting in 1976, the original shooting model for the *Enterprise* hung in the Smithsonian's National Air and Space Museum in Washington, DC. It was totally restored in 2015, but that wasn't because that starship model was getting gussied up for a new Star Trek project; it was simply because the model itself was in terrible shape. Then, in 2019, the *Enterprise* was put into semipermanent storage, basically, because the *Enterprise* itself was rotting. In order "to protect the artifact from sunlight as well as temperature and humidity controls to preserve its wooden structure," the *Enterprise* was taken off active museum duty. While the Smithsonian itself was already undergoing renovations, this all resulted in the *Enterprise* model being forced to join "a long list of iconic artifacts that will be off public view for the duration." So, the actual original *Enterprise* is sitting somewhere in a *Raiders of the Lost Ark*–style box, while the original footage of that model, boldly going where no one has gone before, is only available to the public on pre-2006 DVDs, VHS tapes, laser disc, or on carefully selected special features available on the 2016 Blu-rays.

Even the opening music for the remastered *TOS* episodes isn't the same recorded music that aired in the '60s. As conducted by Greg Smith in 2005, new versions of the Alexander Courage *TOS* theme were recorded with "the same sized orchestra, same makeup of woodwinds, brass, and percussion." In a strange bit of time-travel shenanigans, members of this faux-'60s TV orchestra were also musicians who played in orchestras for the '90s versions of Trek, including *The Next Generation, Deep Space Nine,* and *Voyager.* So, when you *hear* the opening notes of the classic Alexander Courage *TOS* theme in the remastered versions of the original *Star Trek,* you're hearing brass and woodwinds from 2005, featuring some talent from people who formerly also played on the score for *The Next Generation.* You can still buy the old scores on CD, and on some used vinyl, but even there you have to be careful not to get the *reissue* records, which are simply music recorded at an unspecified date. Beyond the obvious changes, and hugely divergent films and spin-off shows, *Star Trek* is always replacing itself with other *Star Trek* in almost imperceptible ways. William Shatner was Captain Kirk up until 2009, and then Captain Kirk was Chris Pine *and* William Shatner.

Pop science fiction is inherently less than authentic, but fandoms are notoriously mercurial. Even someone with a passing understanding of Trek's biggest rival—Star Wars—is probably aware of at least one person in their life who is pissed that George Lucas digitally updated his starships and made it just about impossible to see the original 1977 theatrical version of *Star Wars*. The tinkering on those films versus the remastering of *Star Trek: The Original Series* is like comparing apples with Martian avocados, and yet the impact is similar. The revision of the art is what exists to represent the permanent version of the art.

But even before the 2006 remasters, Star Trek's previous revisions have never existed just for the hell of it. Ever wonder why Gene Roddenberry never really wanted to explain why the Klingons looked so different in *Star Trek: The Motion Picture* than they had in *The Original Series*? Simple: What you saw in *TOS* wasn't quite what he wanted. According to at least two sources, Roddenberry claimed he always wanted the Klingons to look differently but was limited by the budget on *The Original Series*. Right there, Roddenberry is saying there is a platonic ideal of Klingons and we're just kind of doing the best we can with what we have here on Earth. Change for the better is baked into the fabric of all of Star Trek, and the reason why Trekkie fan controversies end (relatively) quickly isn't just because Trekkies are primed to embrace change. Star Trek fans also know, deep down, that the perfect version of Star Trek has not yet been made. True fans of Star Trek know that to love Star Trek is to love something that is deeply flawed.

This is something that people who only love Star Wars—and have never loved Star Trek—won't understand. The reason why Star Wars fans get so mad about newer iterations of Star Wars is because both *A New Hope* and *Empire* were pretty damn close to the platonic ideal of what Star Wars "should" be. And so, everything else will always seem like a disappointment, because Star Wars basically got it right the first time around. Star Trek, on the other hand, is defined by its various failures and half triumphs. Again, in "Encounter at Farpoint," in his defense of the entire human race and our various mistakes, Picard tells Q, "We are what we are, and we're doing the best that we can." This is the brutal honesty at the core of all Star Trek. It's not saying it's the best thing ever. It's not even sure it *can be* the best thing ever. But the people who have helped create Star Trek for over half a century are all united in one subliminal belief: After 800 hours of episodes and movies, maybe this time they'll get it right. Maybe this time it will be *perfect*.

––––––––––

When Anson Mount took on the role of Captain Pike for *Discovery*, he told me the goal was to recontextualize Captain Pike's journey "as a victory and not a tragedy." This referred to the idea that in the *TOS* episode "The Menagerie," we know Pike will eventually become unable to speak, trapped in his own body and confined to a mechanized wheelchair. But, in the *Discovery* episode "Through the Valley of Shadows," writers Bo Yeon Kim and Erika Lippoldt flipped this tragedy into a specific *choice* Pike makes. In order to defeat a malevolent AI called Control, Pike needs a time crystal. But there's a catch: The Klingon Timekeeper Tenavik (Kenneth Mitchell) tells Pike that whatever future he sees in that crystal will be a path he's locked on, forever. Of course, what Pike sees is what every fan of *The Original Series* expects, a disaster that robs him of a connection to his own body. Pike, of course, doesn't really have a choice. Like in all of Trek's evolution, a fundamental aspect of a famous character was changed, and made to represent the opposite of what we once believed. Instead of an ableist tragedy born of 1960s sensibilities, Pike's journey now scans as one of acceptance and bravery. The fact that the Trek mythos is this flexible is shocking.

What's more shocking is the way this specific story line eerily creeped into real life. Actor Kenneth Mitchell had appeared as two different Klingons on *Discovery* before his turn as Timekeeper Tenavik. But, during the filming of "Through the Valley of Shadows"— as Tenavik reveals to Pike his tragic fate—Mitchell himself had just learned he had ALS—Lou Gehrig's disease. Essentially, what was going to happen to Captain Pike was going to happen to Mitchell in real life.

"It was one of the roles I did while I was diagnosed," Mitchell tells me in 2020. "To be part of expanding the story of Pike was a really incredible experience. His story of seeing his future and the choices he has to make are very parallel to what I'm going through. It was very meaningful on that level." ALS is a motor neuron disease. It's the reason why astrophysicist Stephen Hawking spoke through a computer. It has no known cure. How does Ken Mitchell turn this tragedy into a victory? "It's certainly hard and created a shift in my focus. I'm more focused on my family than ever before. My kids are my everything. Thinking about them has been the hardest part. I don't want to leave them. But being a part of *Star Trek* keeps me inspired and gives me purpose."

You can tell this last part isn't a lie. For Mitchell, when tragedy struck, his *Trek* community was there. His co-stars visit his home often, and because Mitchell no longer has the use of his legs, Ethan Peck has taught Mitchell's young son to skateboard, generating the nickname "Tony Spock" in honor of skateboarding legend Tony Hawk. "Just the other day, William Shatner sent me a handwritten card," Mitchell tells me in early January 2021. "I thought that was really special. It was so incredibly meaningful."

During this phone call, Ken Mitchell gets real. He tells me his darkest fears as a parent, of not being able to hold his children. He cries. And I cry with him. There are just long pauses for crying. I've interviewed a lot of celebrities, but I've never cried on the phone with one of them. Mitchell's honesty and his willingness to connect is shocking and transformative. He tells me that Shatner's hand-written card made him wish he wrote things down for his family more often, that we "take those things for granted." I immediately become angry at myself for not writing my own daughter more notes. Then we make jokes about how he got sent some Klingon bloodwine and how Klingons really know how to drink.

When the call ends, I'm left with the gift that Mitchell has given me—a gentle reminder that to build the future, you have to live in the present. This gift, this bittersweet perspective is something we all take for granted, but for one afternoon, because I happened to love Star Trek as a child, a brave man reminded me of what matters. The next time I spoke with Ken, in late 2021, it was over a text-message app, because his voice was gone.

In "The Inner Light," Picard says that the most important thing is now. "Seize the time," Picard tells his granddaughter. "Live now. Make now always the most precious time. Now will never come again."

By the end of the current decade, in 2030, at least two more Star Trek series and at least one new feature film will join the ever-expanding Federation family. Fall 2021 saw the debut of the Nickelodeon series *Star Trek: Prodigy*, a series specifically aimed at children over the age of six. It features a crew of orphan teenagers who find a wrecked Starfleet ship called the USS *Protostar*, and like the boxcar children of space, use it to escape to a better life. After watching the debut episode, "Lost and Found," I caught up with some of the younger cast members including eleven-year-old Rylee

Alazraqui, who plays the voice of a friendly rocklike alien named Rok-Tahk. When I asked her whether she felt like it was hard to play a giant rock alien, this young actress didn't miss a beat. "I'm a lot like Rok-Tahk. I'm friendly like Rok-Tahk. I'm loyal. I care about others like Rok-Tahk." To be clear, Alazraqui—who was eight years old when she first started work on *Star Trek: Prodigy*—has seen very little of Star Trek. But clearly, she already gets it. This series may very well be my daughter's first, and perhaps favorite, Trek series of them all.

For the grown-ups, the *TOS* prequel series and *DISCO* sequel *Strange New Worlds* will start streaming on Paramount+ in the US in mid-2022. It will be airing new episodes when the book you're reading first hits the shelves. Featuring new actors playing Uhura (Celia Rose Gooding), Nurse Chapel (Jess Bush), and Dr. M'Benga (Babs Olusanmokun), *Strange New Worlds* is weaving a new ensemble around Spock, Captain Pike, and Number One. It will also feature brand-new characters, including Erica Ortegas (Melissa Navia), La'an Noonien-Singh (Christina Chong), and Hemmer (Bruce Horak), a member of the Aenar, an offshoot of the Andorians, first introduced in the series *Enterprise*.

Because of its diverse ensemble cast, *Strange New Worlds* could be poised to become the *Next Generation* of the twenty-first century: a mix of familiar characters, new characters, all aboard a starship called *Enterprise*. Along with *Lower Decks*, *Prodigy*, and *Discovery*, *Strange New Worlds* might redefine the 2020s of Star Trek, taking us right into 2030. In another decade after that, a spin-off of any of these shows could become the apotheosis of all of Star Trek's achievements, and all of the series and films discussed in these pages could be simply a warm-up. Late 2023 will also see the debut of a very mysterious new Star Trek feature film, directed by Matt Shakman of *WandaVision* fame. This film will be produced by J. J. Abrams with a script from Lindsey Beer and Geneva Robertson-Dworet. This makes it the first Star Trek feature film to be written by women. In the same way the J. J. Abrams films rebooted Trek movies for the masses, this top-secret Trek project could be even wider, and possibly, could reach an even bigger audience well beyond the 2030s and 2040s.

———————

But, in the moments after I got off that phone call with Kenneth Mitchell, I wasn't thinking about the future. The point of all of this boldly going hasn't been about looking into some kind of hazy crystal ball and wondering whether or not warp drive will exist someday or if Trek really predicted the cell phone or whatever. That's not why Star Trek matters. The power of Star Trek is that it teaches you, over and over again, how to live better. How to be a more thoughtful and kinder person. There are other pieces of art that do this, too, of course. There is philosophy. There is religion. There is yoga and meditation and therapy. But in all of that, and perhaps more, Star Trek, I believe, is one of the only phenomena in the world that contains all the benefits of those things, but also mixes the pain and the fun in equal measure.

In *The Final Frontier*, Kirk rants, "I don't want my pain taken away! I need my pain!" I think about this sentence all the time, the raw honesty of how much our failures and tragedies shape our lives, how much our pain guides us into who we are. What we do with our pain is probably the thing that defines whether we live well, or not. How do we live long *and* prosper? How do we turn death into a fighting chance to live? Star Trek has never answered these questions for every situation in our lives, but it has given us, as Picard would say, "powerful tools" like "openness, optimism, and the spirit of curiosity." Perhaps that last one is the key to it all. In order to accept change, in order to sublimate your pain, in order to *prosper* in life, and live in the moment, you have to cultivate curiosity. Because, without that one, tolerance and peace are impossible. In December of 2021 over Zoom, I spoke to William Shatner again and asked him if there were any practical lessons he could give me, as a father, to pass on to my daughter. Having been in space—for real this time—what should we be telling our kids about the future?

"I'm so cognizant of how I know nothing," Shatner told me with a laugh. "Nobody knows anything, especially me. But I am filled with curiosity."

My daughter, like many preschoolers, is, just like ninety-year-old Shatner, a deeply curious person. She's seen only one full episode of the live-action *Trek*, the classic "Trouble with Tribbles." We've also watched a few episodes of *The Animated Series* and she adores "More Tribbles, More Troubles." In fact, my daughter's interest in tribbles is staggering. She loves to ask me questions about tribbles constantly. Like tribbles themselves, her questions multiply as soon as the old questions are answered. Her curiosity becomes like a huge stack of tribbles, falling on Captain Kirk's head, until suddenly, he's chest-deep in those adorable little furballs. As my daughter asks more and more adorable questions about Star Trek ("Where are the tribble's ears?"), she can see that her questions make me laugh. And the more I laugh, the more questions she has. Her curiosity grows. Her adventure is just beginning.

ACKNOWLEDGMENTS

First and foremost, I'd like to thank my patient and wise literary agent Christopher Hermelin, who is perhaps best described as one of those stern Starfleet admirals who gives the captain a reality check from time to time. By extension, this makes Ryan Harbage and the Fischer-Harbage literary agency like Starfleet and the Federation Council. If they didn't exist, I wouldn't be able to boldly go.

Also of paramount importance, my editor, Jill Schwartzman, who stuck to her phasers more than once to make this book much better and more accessible than it would have been without her. As Jean-Luc Picard said of Riker, "You were my strong right arm."

I'm also forever indebted to numerous editors at a variety of publications who have allowed me to write professionally about science fiction—and Star Trek specifically—for fifteen years running. These wonderful editors have empowered me to dive deep into the final frontier over and over again: Irene Gallo, Chris Lough, Andrew Burmon, Nick Lucchesi, Jake Kleinman, Josh Wigler, Gaby Bondi, Jen Glennon, Isaac Feldberg, Jordan Zakarin, Caitlin Busch, Tyghe Trimble, Mike Cecchini, John Saavedra, Julian Gardner, Mark Hill, Matt Berical, Lizzy Francis, Kendra James, and Kayti Burt. This book would not exist without their indulgence and their various talents as editors. Infinite diversity in infinite combinations isn't just about societal peace: It's a good note for writers when you get too precious about your own ideas.

Obviously, this book also wouldn't exist without the scores of amazing humans who have written, produced, and directed Star Trek over the years. Along with the countless millions of Star Trek fans, I would be a lost soul without the hard work of Gene Rodden-berry, Gene Coon, Dorothy Fontana, Bob Justman, Herb Solow, Harve Bennett, Nicholas Meyer, Leonard Nimoy, Rick Berman, Jeri Taylor, Ronald D. Moore, Brannon Braga, Jonathan Frakes, Ira Steven Behr, Manny Coto, J. J. Abrams, Roberto Orci, Alex Kurtzman, Bryan Fuller, Michael Chabon, Kirsten Beyer, Akiva Goldsman, Michelle Paradise, Kevin and Dan Hageman, Terry Matalas, and Mike McMahan, to name just a few.

I'd also like to give a shout-out to some Star Trek scholars and experts, some of whom I'm lucky to be friends with, and others who I'm just lucky that they returned my emails: Ian Spelling, Devra Langsam, Jaqueline Lichtenberg, Ed Gross, Mark Altman, Larry Nemecek, John Tenuto, Anthony Pascale, Heather Rae, Kennedy Allen, Travis Johnson; all the *Women at Warp*; the *Disco Tech* podcast, including Marcie London, Luis Bruzon, and Rachel Amber Bloom; all the Black Tribbles; the *Enterprising Individuals* podcast, the *Discovery Home Companion* podcast; David Mack, Sara Lynn Michener, S. E. Fleenor, Michael Kmet, Maurice Molyneaux, and Marc Cushman. (If I've left anyone off, I'm very sorry!)

Special thanks to all the fans, friends, and professionals who supplied photos: Nick Duguid, Gage Skidmore, Larry Nemecek (again), John Hancock, Howard Weinstein, and—really can't thank this guy enough—Gerald Gurian.

To the friends who don't mind talking, texting, or tweeting about Trek, even at strange hours: Anthony Ha, Colin Cheney, and Justin Lemieux.

I'd also like to thank everyone who works for CBS and Paramount+ publicity. Though this book is not officially affiliated with CBS and Paramount (it's really not!), I nonetheless have, as a journalist, come to rely on the wonderful people who work for publicity at the corporate entity that regulates the beaming in and beaming out of the voices from the future. These people work hard, and hardly anybody ever thinks about it: Jenn Verti, Nikki Kozel, Rachel Voter, Leigh Wolfson, Morgan Seal, and, even though she's not at CBS anymore, Kristen Hall, who called me on the phone and was both professional and nice enough to talk turkey with me about Star Trek spoilers.

I interviewed over one hundred people for this book, and I'd like to thank every single one of them. But, of special note to those who really gave me more of their time than they needed to, either in interviews specifically for this book, or in interviews I initially conducted for shorter articles online: These folks constantly reaffirm my belief that the people who work on Star Trek are a very, very special group of humans indeed. So, an extra thanks to: Doug Jones, Jason Isaacs, Wilson Cruz, Mary Wiseman, Noah Averbach-Katz, Sonequa Martin-Green, Rachael Ancheril, Ethan Peck, Anson Mount, Rainn Wilson, David Ajala, Michelle Hurd, Jeri Ryan, Isa Briones, Michael Chabon (again), Bo Yeon Kim, Erika Lippoldt, Blu del Barrio, Anthony Rapp, Mike McMahan, Jack Quaid, Tawny Newsome, Eugene Cordero, Noël Wells, Brent Spiner, Andrew Robinson, Nicole de Boer, Gates McFadden, LeVar Burton, and Michael Giacchino.

Acknowledgments

A few specific shout-outs among that long list:

To Jonathan Frakes for being one of the kindest people I've ever interviewed (three times total) and for indulging me in some of my rambling questions. He asked me if my beard was a "full Riker," and I've felt challenged to make sure the answer is always *yes*.

To Walter Koenig, who made me laugh, made me think, and insisted that the title of this book remain *Phasers on Stun!* because "that means we don't have to kill each other."

To Robin Curtis, who was infinitely generous with her time and insight. Robin was my favorite Saavik as a kid and that remains truer now than ever before.

To Nicholas Meyer, who took a random email from me over a decade ago and agreed to answer some silly questions about Sherlock Holmes and Spock. The result has been one of the most rewarding series of correspondences and interviews of my life. He's the real deal.

To my friend Chase Masterson: What can I say? You rock. You walk the walk that others talk, and you do it with style, grace, and so much heart.

To my friend Morgan Gendel: You wrote the greatest episode of *The Next Generation*, and we're friends because we both love the Beatles. I look forward to every one of our conversations. Your friendship is just one of the small reasons I'm lucky that this silly space franchise touched so many lives.

And to Kenneth Mitchell: You're an inspiration. I try to be a better father and a better person because of my conversations with you. Thank you.

To my family: my mom and dad, for putting me in front of Star

Trek to begin with. And to my sister Kellie, who didn't throw out the *Enterprise* crew when they invaded the Barbie Dreamhouse.

To my daughter, Randell Elisabeth Britt, the biggest tribble fan on the planet, and the smartest human being I've ever met. I hope if you read this, even twenty years from now, you'll remember that this is what your dad was writing way back when you turned four years old. I love you more and more each day, Randi.

And finally, and most importantly, the person who makes it all possible, my wife, Mary Elisabeth Britt. You wanted to go to a planetarium on a date and look at us now. You prove to me repeatedly that the real final frontier is the human heart. I love you so much and would have never materialized as my truest self without you.

A note on interviews: All quotes from interviews conducted by the author appear in this book, in this form, uniquely. While over half of the interviews for this book were conducted expressly for that purpose, several interviews did initially occur for articles written for Tor.com, Inverse, SyFy Wire, or Den of Geek. In all cases the quotes used appear in entirely different contexts in this book or were quotes not published in the final piece in those publications at all. That said, the author acknowledges that part of the research for this book included quoting from articles which he was uniquely familiar with. The author also strongly suggests that the reader patronize the publications mentioned above.

PROLOGUE
Interviews with William Shatner and Doug Jones, conducted by the author.
"The Stacey Abrams Episode," *The Pod Directive*, October 12, 2020, https://www.startrek.com/news/star-trek-the-pod-directive-the-stacey-abrams-episode.

CHAPTER 1: SPOCK STOLE HIS OWN BRAIN
Interviews with Ethan Peck, Harrison Solow, Rod Roddenberry, Michael Chabon, Mark A. Altman, Nicholas Meyer, Dorothy Fontana, George Takei, Jason Isaacs, Marc Cushman, and Mike McMahan, conducted by the author.
Allan Asherman, *The Star Trek Interview Book* (Pocket Books, 1988).
Marc Cushman, *These Are the Voyages, TOS, Season One* (rev. enl. ed.) (Jacobs/Brown Press, 2013).

Source Notes

Yvonne Fern, *Gene Roddenberry: The Last Conversation* (University of California Press, 1994).

Edward Gross and Mark A. Altman, *The Fifty-Year Mission: The Complete, Uncensored, Unauthorized Oral History of Star Trek: The First 25 Years* (St. Martin's Press, 2016).

Ian Spelling and Ben Robinson, *Star Trek: A Celebration* (Hero Collector Books, 2021).

Edward Gross, "Charting 'Where No Man Has Gone Before.'" *Starlog*, November 1987.

Leonard Nimoy, *I Am Spock* (Hyperion Books, 1995).

Gene Roddenberry and Stephen Whitfield, *The Making of Star Trek* (Ballantine Books, 1968).

Robert Justman and Herb Solow, *Inside Star Trek: The Real Story* (Pocket Books, 1996).

Leonard Nimoy, archived tweet, July 14, 2012: "Often asked: Why did Spock smile and limp in the first ST pilot? Answer: Was told to smile by the director/ to limp by Gene Roddenberry. LLAP" https://twitter.com/the realnimoy/status/224212624903114752?lang=en.

Documentary: *The Captains*. Director: William Shatner. Le Big Boss Productions, 2011.

"Orci and Kurtzman Reveal Star Trek Details in TrekMovie Fan Q&A," Trek Movie.com, May 22, 2009.

"Permission Granted: Boarding Chekov's Enterprise with Walter Koenig," *Inglorious Treksperts*, February 1, 2019, https://www.stitcher.com/show /inglorious-treksperts/episode/permission-granted-boarding -chekovs-enterprise-w-walter-koenig-58531652.

CHAPTER 2: SPACE COWBOYS

Interviews with Marc Cushman, Alec Nevala-Lee, Judy Burns, William Shatner, Dorothy Fontana, Norman Spinrad, Walter Koenig, and Harlan Ellison, conducted by the author.

"50 Best Science Fiction TV Shows of All Time," rollingstone.com, March 12, 2020, https://www.rollingstone.com/tv/tv-lists/best-science-fiction-tv -shows-of-all-time-65434/.

David Gerrold, *The World of Star Trek* (Blue Jay Books, 1984).

Susan Sackett, *Letters to Star Trek* (Ballantine Books, 1977).

Robert Justman and Herb Solow, *Inside Star Trek: The Real Story* (Pocket Books, 1996).

Marc Cushman, *These Are the Voyages, TOS, Season One* (rev. enl. ed.) (Jacobs/Brown Press, 2013).

Early draft of opening narration for *Star Trek*. Internal correspondence at Desilu, August 1966. Retrieved and uploaded by Larry Nemecek for *The Trek Files* on September 8, 2020.

Ian Spelling and Ben Robinson, *Star Trek: A Celebration* (Hero Collector Books, 2021).

Leonard Nimoy, *I Am Spock* (Hyperion Books, 1995).

Edward Gross and Mark A. Altman, *The Fifty-Year Mission: The Complete, Uncensored, Unauthorized Oral History of Star Trek*, volumes 1 and 2. (St. Martin's Press, 2016).

Documentary: *For the Love of Spock*. Director: Adam Nimoy. 455 Films, 2016.

Allan Asherman, *The Star Trek Interview Book* (Pocket Books, 1988).

Star Trek: The Original Series on Blu-ray, commentary on "This Side of Paradise," Disc 6 (CBS Studios, 2016).

Harlan Ellison, *Harlan Ellison's The City on the Edge of Forever: The Original Teleplay That Became the Classic Star Trek Episode* (White Wolf Publishing, 1995).

Gay Talese, "Frank Sinatra Has a Cold," *Esquire*, April 1966.

Alec Nevala-Lee, *Astounding: John W. Campbell, Isaac Asimov, Robert A. Heinlein, L. Ron Hubbard, and the Golden Age of Science Fiction* (Dey Street, 2019).

James Gunn, *Alternate Worlds: The Illustrated History of Science Fiction* (A&W Visual Library, 1975).

CHAPTER 3: INFINITE DIVERSITY, FINITE GENES

Interviews with Ande Richardson, Harrison Solow, Syreeta McFadden, Norman Spinrad, George Takei, Judy Burns, and Walter Koenig, conducted by the author.

Documentary: *Woman in Motion*. Director: Todd Thompson. Shout Studios, 2019.

Allan Asherman, *The Star Trek Interview Book* (Pocket Books, 1988).

Nichelle Nichols, *Beyond Uhura: Star Trek and Other Memories* (G. P. Putnam, 1994).

Nichelle Nichols, "Lost in the Stars," *TV Guide*, October 8, 1994.

Larry Nemecek, "Remembering Gene Coon with Russell Bates," video interview, archived by Trekland, http://larrynemecek.blogspot.com/2008/07/stv-remembering-gene-coon-russell-bates.html.

George Takei, *To the Stars: The Autobiography of George Takei, Star Trek's Mr. Sulu* (Pocket Books, 1994).

David Alexander, *Star Trek Creator: The Authorized Biography of Gene Roddenberry* (Roc Books, 1994).

Joel Engel, *Gene Roddenberry: The Myth and the Man Behind Star Trek* (Hyperion, 1994).

Marc Cushman, *These Are the Voyages, TOS, Season One* (rev. enl. ed.) (Jacobs/Brown Press, 2013).

Gene Roddenberry and Stephen Whitfield, *The Making of Star Trek* (Ballantine Books, 1968).

Edward Gross and Mark A. Altman, *The Fifty-Year Mission: The Complete, Uncensored, Unauthorized Oral History of Star Trek*, volumes 1 and 2. (St. Martin's Press, 2016).

"Star Trek: The Original Series Panel." Archived video on YouTube. Produced by Paramount+, September 8, 2020. https://www.youtube.com/watch?v=gHoqTplqkKM.

Gene Roddenberry, "Star Trek Is . . ." Pitch document, PDF archived via Memory Alpha, 1964. http://leethomson.myzen.co.uk/Star_Trek/1_Original_Series/Star_Trek_Pitch.pdf.

CHAPTER 4: THE TROUBLE WITH TREKKIES

Interviews with Jacqueline Lichtenberg, Devra Langsam, Kirsten Beyer, Della Van Hise, Sonni Cooper, and Larry Nemecek, conducted by the author.

Joan Winston, *The Making of the Trek Conventions* (Playboy Press, 1979).

Joan Winston, Jacqueline Lichtenberg, and Sondra Marshak, *Star Trek Lives! Personal Notes and Anecdotes* (Bantam Books, 1975).

Chuck Klosterman, *Fargo Rock City: A Heavy Metal Odyssey in Rural North Dakota* (Scribner, 2001).

"Obama on Leonard Nimoy: 'I Loved Spock,'" *Deadline*, February 27, 2015.

Jerry Ruhlow, "Protest Against the Possible Cancellation of Star Trek," *The Los Angeles Times*, January 8, 1968, archived by the *LA Times* in 2017:

https://www.latimes.com/visuals/photography/la-me-fw-archives
-1968-protest-against-possible-star-trek-cancellation20170524.

Documentary: *Trekkies 2*. Director: Roger Nygard. Paramount Pictures, 2004.

Documentary: *Trek Nation*. Director: Rod Roddenberry. Roddenberry Entertainment, 2010.

CHAPTER 5: AN ALMOST TOTALLY NEW ENTERPRISE

Interviews with Howard Weinstein, Todd Thompson, Walter Koenig, and Mike Gold, conducted by the author.

Judith and Garfield Reeves-Stevens, *Star Trek, Phase II: The Lost Series* (Pocket Books, 1997).

William Shatner, *Star Trek Movie Memories* (Harper Collins, 1994).

Sherilyn Connelly, *The First Star Trek Movie: Bringing the Franchise to the Big Screen, 1969–1980* (McFarland, 2019).

Mark Evanier, "Star Trek Lives!" *Monster Times*, September, 1973.

Aaron Harvey and Rich Schepis, *Star Trek: The Official Guide to the Animated Series* (Weldon Owen, 2019).

"NASA Unveils the *Enterprise*," *Starlog* no. 3, January 1977.

"*Enterprise* Naming Unpopular," *Starlog* no. 5, May 1977.

Walter Koenig, *Chekov's Enterprise: A Personal Journal of the Making of Star Trek, The Motion Picture* (Pocket Books, 1980).

Documentary: *Woman in Motion*. Director: Todd Thompson. Shout Studios, 2019.

Nichelle Nichols, *Beyond Uhura: Star Trek and Other Memories* (G. P. Putnam, 1994).

CHAPTER 6: KILLING SPOCK

Interviews with Walter Koenig, Alan Dean Foster, Mike McMahan, Nicholas Meyer, Robert Sallin, and Larry Nemecek, conducted by the author.

Walter Koenig, *Chekov's Enterprise: A Personal Journal of the Making of Star Trek, The Motion Picture* (Pocket Books, 1980).

The Longest Trek: *Writing the Motion Picture*: DVD special feature, Paramount Pictures/Paramount Home Video, 2010.

Gene Roddenberry, *Star Trek: The Motion Picture: A Novel by Star Trek's Creator* (Pocket Books, 1980).

Roger Ebert, review of "Star Trek: The Motion Picture," December 7, 1979.

Archived by Roger Ebert.com. https://www.rogerebert.com/reviews /star-trek-the-motion-picture-1979.

Leonard Nimoy, *I Am Spock* (Hyperion Books, 1995).

"Why Is Paramount Deliberately Jeopardizing 28 Million in Revenues?" *The Hollywood Reporter*, September 24, 1981.

Janet Maslin, "New Star Trek Full of Gadgets and Fun," *The New York Times*, June 4, 1982.

Mary Sollosi, "George Takei Reacts to *Star Trek Beyond* Trailer," *Entertainment Weekly*, December 15, 2015.

Nicholas Meyer, *The View from the Bridge* (Viking, 2009).

Allan Asherman, *The Making of Star Trek II: The Wrath of Khan* (Pocket Books, 1982).

William Shatner, *Star Trek Movie Memories* (Harper Collins, 1994).

Star Trek: The Wrath of Khan Official Movie Magazine, Starlog Press, 1982.

CHAPTER 7: COLORFUL METAPHORS

Interviews with Nicholas Meyer, Robert Sallin, and Robin Curtis, conducted by the author.

Leonard Nimoy, *I Am Spock* (Hyperion Books, 1995).

Star Trek III: The Search for Spock Official Movie Magazine, Starlog Press, 1984.

Star Trek IV: The Voyage Home: The Official Movie Magazine, Starlog Press, 1986.

Steven Swires, "Leonard Nimoy: A View from the Bridge," *Starlog* no. 106, May 1986.

David McDonnell, "Searching for Spock by Phone," StarTrek.com, April 10, 2014.

Jamie Lovett, "Kevin Feige Reveals What Marvel Took from Star Trek," comic book.com, November 20, 2017.

Donna Cassata, "'Star Trek IV: The Voyage Home' Spotlights Greenpeace Efforts," *Associated Press*, March 28, 1987.

"Leonard Nimoy," *The Gettysburg Times*, June 30, 1987.

"Star Trek Has Beamed into the Soviet Union," *The Galveston News*, June 30, 1987.

Patrick Hogan, "30 Years Ago, 'Star Trek' Predicted that Humpback Whales Would Die Out. Instead, They're Thriving," Splinter, September 7, 2016.

CHAPTER 8: UNDISCOVERED GENERATIONS

Interviews with Brian Volk-Weiss, Robin Curtis, and Nicholas Meyer, conducted by the author.

"New Faces of the 23rd Century," *Star Trek II: The Official Movie Magazine*, Starlog Press, 1982.

Lee Goldberg, "Kirstie Alley: She Isn't Saavik, I Am!" *Starlog* no. 102, January 1986.

Kirstie Alley speaking at the Star Trek 50th Anniversary Convention in Las Vegas, August 5, 2016. Archived on YouTube. https://www.youtube.com/watch?v=4cFkxknVRCs.

Josepha Sherman and Susan Shwartz, *Vulcan's Heart* (Pocket Books, 1999).

Vonda McIntyre, *The Entropy Effect* (Pocket Books, 1981).

Telegram from Harve Bennett, supplied by Robin Curtis.

Bobbie Wygant interviews Kim Cattrall in 1991, archived on YouTube. https://www.youtube.com/watch?v=Xi_PuyHFHLY.

CHAPTER 9: YOU WILL BE ASSIMILATED

Interviews with Brent Spiner, LeVar Burton, Jonathan Frakes, Ronald D. Moore, Mike McMahan, Nicole de Boer, and Morgan Gendel, conducted by the author.

David Resin, "Patrick Stewart: On Picard, Indecent Proposals and the Perfect Cup of Tea," *TV Guide*, July 31, 1993.

The Sky's the Limit: The Eclipse of The Next Generation: Blu-ray special feature. Director: Roger Lay, CBS Home Video, 2014.

Edward Gross and Mark A. Altman, *The Fifty-Year Mission: The Complete, Uncensored, Unauthorized Oral History of Star Trek*, volumes 1 and 2. (St. Martin's Press, 2016).

Reunification: 25 Years after Star Trek: The Next Generation: Blu-ray special feature. Director: Roger Lay, CBS Home Video, 2012.

Yvonne Fern, *Gene Roddenberry: The Last Conversation* (University of California Press, 1994).

Wil Wheaton, "The William Fucking Shatner Story," WilWheaton.net, archived in 2021. http://wilwheaton.net/2021/03/the-william-fucking-shatner-story.

Joel Engel, *Gene Roddenberry: The Myth and the Man Behind Star Trek* (Hyperion, 1994).

Nichelle Nichols, *Beyond Uhura: Star Trek and Other Memories* (G. P. Putnam, 1994).

Documentary: *William Shatner Presents: Chaos on the Bridge: The Untold Story Behind Trek's Next Generation*, 2014.

"*TNG* Conceptual Work (September 12, 1986)" *The Trek Files: A Roddenberry Star Trek Podcast*, Episode 1-04, uploaded February 13, 2018, https://the trekfiles.libsyn.com/1-04-tng-conceptual-work-september-12-1986.

"*Star Trek* New Show Titles (October 24, 1986)" *The Trek Files: A Roddenberry Star Trek Podcast*, Episode 4-16, uploaded December 31, 2019, https://the trekfiles.libsyn.com/4-16-star-trek-new-show-titles-october-24-1986.

Adam Shrager, *The Finest Crew in the Fleet: The Next Generation Cast On Screen and Off* (Talman, 1997).

Inside the Writers' Room: Blu-ray special feature. Director: Roger Lay, CBS Home Video, 2013.

John Freeman, *The Tyranny of E-mail* (Scribner, 2010).

Larry Nemecek, *The Star Trek: The Next Generation Companion* (Pocket Books, 1994).

CHAPTER 10: THE DREAMER AND THE DREAM

Interviews with Ronald D. Moore, Mark A. Altman, Mary Wiseman, Blu del Barrio, Chase Masterson, Robert Hewitt Wolfe, Steven Barnes, and Travis Johnson, conducted by the author.

Documentary: *What We Left Behind: Looking Back at Star Trek: Deep Space Nine*. Directors: Ira Steven Behr and David Zappone. Shout! Studios, 2019.

"Quark/Armin Shimerman Interview," *Live! with Regis and Kathie Lee*, June 7, 1993. Archived on YouTube: https://www.youtube.com/watch?v= MLpSXOB6ZqQ.

Judith Reeves-Stevens and Garfield Reeves-Stevens, *The Making of Star Trek: Deep Space Nine* (Pocket Books, 1994).

James Van Hise and Hal Schuster, *The Unauthorized and Uncensored Trek Crew Companion* (Pioneer Books, 1994).

The Sky's the Limit: The Eclipse of The Next Generation: Blu-ray special feature. Director: Roger Lay, CBS Home Video, 2014.

Paula Block and Terry J. Erdmann, *The Star Trek: Deep Space Nine Companion* (Pocket Books, 2000).

Deep Space Nine: A Bold Beginning: DVD special feature, CBS Studios, 2003.

Michael Logan, "Avery Brooks: The Private Commander," *TV Guide*, January 15, 1994.

CHAPTER 11: THERE'S COFFEE IN THAT NEBULA!
Interviews with Kate Mulgrew, Jeri Ryan, Tim Russ, Rod Roddenberry, Jessie Earl, and S. E. Fleenor, conducted by the author.
Kate Mulgrew, *Born with Teeth: A Memoir* (Little Brown, 2015).
"Where No Woman Has Gone Before," *TV Guide*, October 8, 1994.
Michael Logan, "Good vs. Borg," *TV Guide*, May 10, 1997.
Michael Logan, "Soul Sisters," *TV Guide*, November 8, 1997.
Braving the Unknown: Season One: DVD special feature (CBS Home Video, 2004).
The First Captain: Bujold: DVD special feature (CBS Home Video, 2004).
Voyager Time Capsule: Kathryn Janeway: DVD special feature (CBS Home Video, 2004).
Ben Robinson and Mark Wright, *Star Trek: Voyager: A Celebration* (Hero Collector Books, 2020).
Edward Gross and Mark A. Altman, *The Fifty-Year Mission: The Complete, Uncensored, Unauthorized Oral History of Star Trek*, volumes 1 and 2. (St. Martin's Press, 2016).
Quote from Alexandria Ocasio-Cortez, archived on Twitter, November 5, 2020. https://twitter.com/aoc/status/1324227680791912454?lang=en.

CHAPTER 12: MAGIC CARPET RIDES
Interviews with Ronald D. Moore, Alice Krige, Jonathan Frakes, Noah Averbach-Katz, and Jeffrey Combs, conducted by the author.
Michael Piller, *Fade In: The Making of Star Trek: Insurrection: A Textbook on Screenwriting from within the Star Trek Universe*. MichaelPiller.net, 2016.
Adam Shrager, *The Finest Crew in the Fleet: The Next Generation Cast On Screen and Off* (Talman, 1997).
Judith Reeves-Stevens and Garfield Reeves-Stevens, *Star Trek: The Next Generation: The Continuing Mission: A Tenth Anniversary Tribute* (Pocket Books, 1997).
Edward Gross and Mark A. Altman, *The Fifty-Year Mission: The Complete, Uncensored, Unauthorized Oral History of Star Trek*, volumes 1 and 2. (St. Martin's Press, 2016).

Simon Brew, "Jonathan Frakes Criticises 'Star Trek: Enterprise' Ending," Den of Geek, November 3, 2011.

"Episode 108—Terry Matalas," *Scripts and Scribes* podcast, May 9, 2016. https://www.scriptsandscribes.com/2016/05/podcast-terry-matalas/.

CHAPTER 13: IT'S SABOTAGE!

Interviews with Jonathan Frakes, Michael Giacchino, and Ronald D. Moore, conducted by the author.

To Boldly Go: DVD special feature on *Star Trek: 3-Disc Special Edition* (Paramount Home Video, 2010).

Tom Russo, "Why the Starship *Enterprise* Is Running on Empty," *Entertainment Weekly,* July 25, 2003. Archived by *EW*: https://ew.com/article /2003/07/25/why-starship-enterprise-running-empty/.

"Simon Pegg Reflects on '*Star Trek Beyond*'—Talks 'Maddening' Process, Critiques Marketing and More," TrekMovie.com, April 4, 2018. Archived by TrekMovie: https://trekmovie.com/2018/04/04/simon-pegg-reflects-on -star-trek-beyond-talks-maddening-process-critiques-marketing-and -more/.

Edward Gross and Mark A. Altman, *The Fifty-Year Mission: The Complete, Uncensored, Unauthorized Oral History of Star Trek*, volumes 1 and 2. (St. Martin's Press, 2016).

Jeff Bond, "Course Change: J. J. Abrams Takes Command of the Star Trek Franchise," *Geek*, May 2009.

CHAPTER 14: DISCO INFERNO

Interviews with James Frain, Rainn Wilson, Michelle Paradise, Sonequa Martin-Green, Aaron Harberts, Mary Wiseman, Doug Jones, Ethan Peck, Jason Isaacs, Gretchen Berg, Nicholas Meyer, and Rod Roddenberry, conducted by the author.

"'Space Jam 2' Star Sonequa Martin-Green on Her Natural Hair Journey in Hollywood," *It's Been a Minute with Sam Sanders* podcast, NPR, July 20, 2021. https://www.npr.org/player/embed/1015459355/1018080402.

James Hibberd, "Bryan Fuller on His *Star Trek: Discovery* Exit: 'I Got to Dream Big,'" *Entertainment Weekly*, July 28, 2017. https://ew.com/tv /2017/07/28/bryan-fuller-star-trek-discovery/.

CHAPTER 15: THE PRIDE OF STARFLEET

Interviews with Wilson Cruz, Anthony Rapp, Nicole de Boer, Anthony Robinson, S. E. Fleenor, Jessie Earl, Christian Cooper, Blu del Barrio, and Tig Notaro, conducted by the author.

Jonathan Kay, "Gay 'Trek,'" *Salon*, June 30, 2001. Archived by Salon: https://www.salon.com/2001/06/30/gay_trek/.

Bob Calhoun, "George Takei: Is 'Star Trek' Fandom Over?" *Salon*, August 5, 2010. Archived by Salon: https://www.salon.com/2010/08/05/george_takei_interview_ext2010/.

Joel Engel, *Gene Roddenberry: The Myth and the Man Behind Star Trek* (Hyperion, 1994).

Brian Drew, "David Gerrold Talks Frankly about TNG Conflicts with Roddenberry & Berman + JJ-Trek & More," TrekMovie.com, September 12, 2014. Archived by TrekMovie: https://trekmovie.com/2014/09/12/exclusive-david-gerrold-talks-frankly-about-tng-conflicts-with-roddenberry-berman-jj-trek-more/.

Larry Nemecek, *The Star Trek: The Next Generation Companion* (Pocket Books, 1994).

Nitzan Pincu, "*The Next Generation*'s Call for Equality," StarTrek.com, June 23, 2020.

Rob Heyman, "Reflections on LGBT Themes in *TNG*'s 'The Outcast,'" TrekCore, July 18, 2014. https://blog.trekcore.com/2014/07/reflections-on-lgbt-themes-in-tngs-the-outcast/.

Paula Block and Terry J. Erdmann, *The Star Trek: Deep Space Nine Companion* (Pocket Books, 2000).

Documentary: *What We Left Behind: Looking Back at Star Trek: Deep Space Nine*. Directors: Ira Steven Behr and David Zappone. Shout! Studios, 2019.

Riley Silverman, "*Star Trek*'s New Non-Binary Star Blu del Barrio Talks Their Debut," SyFy Wire, October 29, 2020. https://www.syfy.com/syfy-wire/star-treks-new-non-binary-star-blu-del-barrio-talks-their-debut.

Charlie Jane Anders, "*Discovery* Has Become the Queer Star Trek I Always Wanted," Happy Dancing, January 11, 2021, https://happydancing.substack.com/p/discovery-has-become-the-queer-star.

CHAPTER 16: CHOOSE TO LIVE

Interviews with Tawny Newsome, Jack Quaid, Michael Chabon, Harry Treadaway, Nicholas Meyer, Kirsten Beyer, Jonathan Frakes, Jeri Ryan, Michelle Hurd, Isa Briones, and Mike McMahan, conducted by the author.

"The First Duty." Audio commentary by Ronald D. Moore and Nareen Shankar, Blu-ray special feature, 2013, CBS Home Video.

CHAPTER 17: THE HUMAN ADVENTURE IS JUST BEGINNING

Interviews with Ethan Peck, Doug Jones, Jonathan Frakes, LeVar Burton, Larry Nemecek, Ronald D. Moore, Michael Chabon, Kennedy Allen, Anson Mount, Kenneth Mitchell, Rylee Alazraqui, and William Shatner, conducted by the author.

Spacelift: Transporting Trek into the 21st Century: Blu-ray special feature, CBS Studios, 2011.

Margaret A. Weitekamp, "The *Enterprise* Model Is Leaving the Smithsonian," StarTrek.com, September 16, 2019.

WHICH STAR TREK IS WHICH?
A BRIEF GUIDE TO ALL THE TREKS, EVER

As of this writing, Star Trek is a science fiction franchise that spans eleven distinct TV series, thirteen films, hundreds of officially licensed comic books and novels, as well as countless games, toys, costumes, and an endless supply of t-shirts, coffee mugs, and bumper stickers, many of which are inside jokes. For the casual fan, that's a lot of Star Trek to keep track of!

If you feel lost in that great sea of stars, here are the basic building blocks of the final frontier.

The TV Shows & Films
STAR TREK: THE ORIGINAL SERIES
(1966–1969)
(Abbreviated as TOS)

This show ran from 1966 to 1969 on NBC. It was not called "The Original Series" during its original nor its syndicated run, because it was the *only* version of live-action TV Star Trek until 1987. The series was created by Gene Roddenberry, produced by Herb Solow, Robert Justman, Gene Coon, and later, Fred Freiberger. The series was bankrolled by Desilu Studios, owned by Lucille Ball. Later, Desilu was purchased by Paramount.

The show focused on the adventures of the USS *Enterprise* during a "five-year mission" of space exploration. It was an episodic show, with self-contained episodes, and there was only one two-part episode in the entire series. Notable writers on the show included: Harlan Ellison, Robert Bloch, Theodore Sturgeon, and Dorothy Fontana, who, in 1966, was the youngest script editor in television history. It starred William Shatner as Captain James T. Kirk, Leonard Nimoy as Mr. Spock, DeForest Kelley as Dr. Leonard "Bones" McCoy, Nichelle Nichols as Lieutenant Uhura, George Takei as Mr. Sulu, James Doohan as Chief Engineer Montgomery "Scotty" Scott, Walter Koenig as Ensign Pavel Chekov, Majel Barrett as Nurse Chapel, and Grace Lee Whitney as Yeoman Rand.

After cancellation, *TOS* ran in syndication from 1969 to the present day.

Chronologically, *TOS* takes place in the twenty-third century, specifically the years 2265–2270, though that was mostly established retroactively. There are 79 episodes of *TOS*.

FIRST (AIRED) EPISODE: September 8, 1966: "The Man Trap"
LAST EPISODE: June 3, 1969: "Turnabout Intruder"

STAR TREK: THE ANIMATED SERIES
(1973–1974)
(Abbreviated as *TAS*)

This animated series ran from 1973 to 1974. It was not marketed as "The Animated Series," but simply as a continuation of the first *Star Trek* series, but as a cartoon. Like the first *Star Trek* series, *TAS* ran on NBC, but not in the evenings. This was a Saturday morning cartoon, which, in theory, was appropriate for children. The show was produced by Gene Roddenberry and Dorothy Fontana, with most episodes directed by Hal Sutherland. For the voice cast, *TAS* featured the return of most of the original cast in voice-over roles, except for Walter Koenig, who later wrote an episode.

Chronologically, *TAS* takes place right after *TOS*, mostly in the year 2270. There are 22 episodes of *TAS*.

FIRST EPISODE: September 8, 1973: "Beyond the Farthest Star"
LAST EPISODE: October 12, 1974: "The Counter-Clock Incident"

STAR TREK: THE NEXT GENERATION
(1987–1994)
(Abbreviated as *TNG*)

This series was the first live-action Star Trek series following *TOS*. It ran from 1987 to 1994 exclusively in syndication, although it was filmed and produced by Paramount. *TNG* was set nearly a century after *TOS* and introduced an entirely new crew on a newer version of the USS *Enterprise*; registry NCC-1701-D, indicating it was the *fifth* version of a starship with this name since the time of Captain Kirk. The series was created by Gene Roddenberry and had several different producers over its seven-year run, including Maurice Hurley, Burton Armus, Rick Berman, Jeri Taylor, Brannon Braga, and Ronald D. Moore, just to name a few.

TNG was one of the most successful syndicated science fiction TV series of all time, with 20 million weekly viewers at the height of its popularity. Like *TOS*, *TNG* was mostly episodic, with self-contained stories. But it had several more multipart stories than *TOS*, and some very pivotal episodes did redefine characters and situations forever. For a story-of-the-week science fiction show, this kind of continuity was relatively new. The regular cast of the series consisted of:

Patrick Stewart as Captain Jean-Luc Picard, Jonathan Frakes as Commander William T. Riker, Brent Spiner as Mr. Data, LeVar Burton as Lieutenant Commander Geordi La Forge, Gates McFadden as Dr. Beverly Crusher, Marina Sirtis as Counselor Deanna Troi, Michael Dorn as Lieutenant Worf, Wil Wheaton as Wesley Crusher, Denise Crosby as Lieutenant Tasha Yar (Season 1 only), and Colm Meaney as Chief Miles O'Brien.

When *The Next Generation* ended in 1994, it was at the height of its popularity. Chronologically within the Star Trek timeline, *TNG* takes place in the twenty-fourth century, specifically from 2364 to 2370. There are seven seasons of *TNG*, with a total of 178 episodes.

FIRST EPISODE: September 28, 1987: "Encounter at Farpoint"
LAST EPISODE: May 23, 1994: "All Good Things . . ."

STAR TREK: DEEP SPACE NINE (1993–1999)
(Abbreviated as DS9)

This Star Trek series was neither a sequel to *TOS* nor *TNG*. Instead, it was a show that took place simultaneously within the same time frame and maintained continuity with the final two seasons of *The Next Generation*, and, when *TNG* ended, simply continued in that *TNG* timeline. Nearly all of *DS9*'s backstory came from *TNG*, but according to many, the series would eventually be the polar opposite of its progenitor in both style and tone. The series was set on the titular space station Deep Space Nine, which was positioned next to a stable wormhole, a passageway through space which provided a quick shortcut to the otherwise distant Gamma Quadrant.

DS9 ran from 1993 to 1999, and like *TNG* was produced by Paramount, but aired entirely in first-run syndication. It was created by Rick Berman and Michael Piller, and later produced by Ira Steven Behr, who is generally considered the showrunner for the series. Other notable writers on *DS9* included Ronald D. Moore, Robert Hewitt Wolfe, René Echevarria, and Naren Shankar.

DS9's regular cast was one of the most diverse Star Trek casts up until that point. Avery Brooks was the first Black actor and first American to lead a Star Trek TV series. The regular cast included: Avery Brooks as Commander Benjamin Sisko (later promoted to captain), Terry Farrell as Lieutenant Jadzia Dax, René Auberjonois as Odo, Nana Visitor as Major Kira Nerys, Armin Shimerman as Quark, Colm Meaney as Chief Miles O'Brien (reprising his role from *TNG*), Cirroc Lofton as Jake Sisko, Alexander Siddig as Dr. Julian Bashir (initially billed as Siddig El Fadil), Michael Dorn as Worf (after Season 4, Dorn reprised his role from *TNG*, when Worf transferred to DS9), and Nicole de Boer as Ezri Dax (Season 7 only). Notable reoccurring characters included: Andrew Robinson as Garak, Max Grodénchik as Rom, Aron Eisenberg as Nog, and Chase Masterson as Leeta.

Like *TNG*, *DS9* lasted for seven seasons, consisting of 176 episodes. Chronologically, the events of *DS9* occur from 2369 to 2375.

FIRST EPISODE: January 4, 1993: "Emissary"
LAST EPISODE: May 31, 1999: "What You Leave Behind"

STAR TREK: VOYAGER (1995–2001)
(Abbreviated as *VOY*)

Voyager was the second spin-off set in the *TNG* era and, like *TNG*, overlapped with *DS9*. However, unlike *DS9* and *TNG*, this Star Trek series aired on network TV, specifically on the new UPN Network, short for United Paramount Network. (UPN no longer exists today.)

That said, *VOY* was produced by Paramount, and shot on the same lot as *DS9*. The series was created by Rick Berman, Michael Piller, and Jeri Taylor; the first Trek series to be co-created by a woman. It was produced by Berman, Piller, Taylor, Brannon Braga, and others. Notable writers included Michael Sussman, Michael Taylor, Bryan Fuller, and Nick Sagan (son of Carl Sagan).

Voyager was marketed as a back-to-basics version of Star Trek, focusing on mostly episodic, self-contained episodes. That said, the premise placed the titular Starship *Voyager* farther away from the familiar characters and situations established by the *TNG* and *DS9* continuity. The overriding premise of *VOY* involved the ship trying to find a quick way back to the familiar Trek neighborhood of the Alpha Quadrant after being suddenly thrust into the Delta Quadrant by a mysterious, all-powerful alien being. Thus, *VOY*'s mission wasn't just to "boldly go" but also, to find a way home.

Led by Kate Mulgrew, *VOY* was the first Star Trek series starring a woman as the lead character. The regular cast also included Robert Beltran as Commander Chakotay, Tim Russ as Tuvok, Roxann Dawson as B'Elanna Torres, Jennifer Lien as Kes (Seasons 1–3, guest starring later), Robert Duncan McNeill as Tom Paris, Ethan Phillips as Neelix, Garrett Wang as Harry Kim, Robert Picardo as the Doctor (Emergency Medical Hologram), and Jeri Ryan as Seven of Nine (Seasons 4–7 only).

Despite being isolated in the Delta Quadrant, the crew picked up some new members along the way, and featured several reoccurring crew members, allies, and enemies, including: the Kazon, the Borg, and Species 8472.

Like *TNG* and *DS9*, *Star Trek: Voyager* continued the tradition of running for seven seasons, from 1995 to 2001. There are 172 episodes of *Voyager*. Excluding time travel episodes, the series takes place from 2371 to 2378.

FIRST EPISODE: January 16, 1995: "Caretaker"
LAST EPISODE: May 23, 2001: "Endgame"

STAR TREK: ENTERPRISE (2001–2005)
(Abbreviated as *ENT*)

Unlike *DS9* and *VOY*, the first Trek series to debut in the twenty-first century (2001) did not take place in the ongoing twenty-fourth-century continuity established by *TNG*. Instead, this series—initially just called *Enterprise* (sans the *Star Trek*) was set before *TOS*, specifically in the twenty-second century. This made it a prequel to *all* existing Star Trek up until that point, a canonical fact which is, more or less, still the case to this day. Like *Voyager*, *Enterprise* was filmed at Paramount Pictures and launched on the UPN Network. By the end of *Enterprise*'s run in 2005, this network would no longer exist.

ENT was created by Rick Berman and Brannon Braga and was the last Star Trek series to be overseen by Berman. When *Enterprise* ended, an unprecedented eighteen years of back-to-back Star Trek on television ended, too. In terms of ratings and critical reaction, *Enterprise* is probably the most derided of the Trek shows, though its reputation and fandom have increased in recent years. It also seems likely that had *ENT* not been caught in the middle of a corporate split at Viacom—Paramount and CBS became separate entities in 2005—the series may have continued in syndicated form, much like its 1990s counterparts.

Enterprise was the only Star Trek series to sport a theme song with vocals, "Faith of the Heart," sung by Russell Watson and written by Diane Warren. Notable writers included: Brannon Braga, Manny Coto (the Season 4 showrunner), Star Trek novelists Judith and Garfield Reeves-Stevens, and Terry Matalas, future showrunner of *Star Trek: Picard* Season 2 (2022).

The regular cast included: Scott Bakula as Captain Jonathan Archer, Jolene Blalock as Subcommander T'Pol, Connor Trinneer as Engineer Charles "Trip" Tucker, Anthony Montgomery as Travis Mayweather, Linda Park as Hoshi Sato, John Billingsley as Dr. Phlox, and Dominic Keating as Malcolm Reed.

ENT ran from 2001 to 2005. Its final episode featured Jonathan Frakes and Marina Sirtis reprising their roles as Riker and Troi from *TNG*, framing one aspect of *Enterprise* as a holographic flashback. There are 98 episodes of *Enterprise* in total.

FIRST EPISODE: September 26, 2001: "Broken Bow"
LAST EPISODE: May 13, 2005: "These Are the Voyages . . ."

STAR TREK: DISCOVERY (2017–PRESENT)
(Abbreviated as DISCO or DSC)

Beginning in 2017, *DISCO* was the first Star Trek TV series in twelve years. It has aired exclusively on streaming, specifically in the US on CBS All Access, which was renamed Paramount+ in 2021. *DISCO* also aired on Netflix in the UK and other global affiliates. As of 2021, *DISCO* began airing on Pluto TV globally, and no longer aired on Netflix. The first episode of the series was broadcast on CBS, a traditional television network, and the first season was rerun on CBS in late 2020, though beyond that, the series, and all twenty-first-century Trek shows that followed, have been exclusively aired on CBS/Paramount streaming services. *Discovery*'s first two seasons were presented as another prequel to *TOS*, taking place roughly a decade before the events of the classic series. This put *DISCO* in the unique position of being the second Trek TV series that was a prequel, but also a direct sequel to the previous series, *Enterprise*. Most of *DISCO* follows the adventures of Michael Burnham (Sonequa Martin-Green), a human raised by Vulcans and adoptive of Spock. We first meet Burnham on board the USS *Shenzhou*, but eventually her path takes her to the titular USS *Discovery*, where she eventually becomes a captain, but not until the very end of Season 3.

DISCO was initially created by Alex Kurtzman and Bryan Fuller. Although Fuller was the showrunner in 2016, by the time the series debuted in 2017, Fuller had left the show, citing scheduling conflicts and creative differences. Since then, the series has been produced and run by Kurtzman, Aaron Harberts, and Gretchen Berg, and, by mid-Season 2 through Season 4, Michelle Paradise. Additional producers include Heather Kadin and Olatunde Osunsanmi, who is also one of the show's frequent directors. Jonathan Frakes of *TNG* fame has also directed several pivotal episodes of *Discovery*. By Season 4, series star Sonequa Martin-Green was also a producer.

Notable *DISCO* writers include Nicholas Meyer, Kirsten Beyer, Bo Yeon Kim, Erika Lippoldt, Sean Cochran, and Kalinda Vazquez.

The regular cast has changed somewhat throughout its four existing seasons, but the core cast includes: Sonequa Martin-Green as Michael Burnham, Mary Wiseman as Sylvia Tilly, Anthony Rapp as Paul Stamets, Wilson Cruz as Dr. Hugh Culber, Doug Jones as Saru, Blu del Barrio as Adira (Season 3 onward), Ian Alexander as Gray (Season 3 onward), David Ajala as Book (Season 3 onward), Michelle Yeoh as Philippa Georgiou (Seasons 1–3), Jason Isaacs as Captain Lorca (Season 1 only), Shazad Latif as Ash Tyler/Voq

(Seasons 1–2), Ethan Peck as Spock (Season 2 only), Mary Chieffo as L'Rell (Seasons 1–2), Rachael Ancheril as Nhan (Seasons 2–3), Oyin Oladejo as Joann Owosekun, and Emily Coutts as Keyla Detmer. Notable guest stars include: James Frain as Sarek (Seasons 1–2), Mia Kirshner as Amanda Grayson (Seasons 1–2), Sonja Sohn as Gabrielle Burnham (Seasons 2–4) and Kenneth Mitchell as Kol, Kol-Sha, Tenavik, and Aurellio.

Discovery's first two seasons were set in the years 2256–2258, but in Season 3, the crew takes a space-time wormhole to the year 3189: 930 years later. This makes *Discovery* the only *Trek* series that is both a prequel to *TOS* and a sequel to *everything* else (including *TOS*) simultaneously. As of this writing there are four seasons of *DISCO*, consisting of 55 episodes.

FIRST EPISODE: September 24, 2017: "The Vulcan Hello"
LAST EPISODE: N/A, series is still airing as of this writing.

SHORT TREKS (2018–2020)

Short Treks is an anthology series of brief vignettes set in the Star Trek universe. It has aired exclusively on CBS All Access, now known as Paramount+. Although initially conceived as a *Discovery*-centric series of shorts, *Short Treks* also has episodes focused on other aspects of the franchise. It is unclear if *Short Treks* will continue in the future. As of right now, episodes of *Short Treks* contain stories set before *The Original Series* in the year 2264 ("Q&A") as well as episodes in the far future, seemingly beyond the scope of *Discovery* Seasons 3 and 4 ("Calypso"). As of this writing, the last episode of *Short Treks* aired was "Children of Mars," a prequel to *Star Trek: Picard*. Considering *Short Treks* to be its own series may not be entirely accurate, since many of the events in these shorts are referenced or expanded upon in other series.

FIRST EPISODE: October 4, 2018: "Runaway"
LAST EPISODE: January 9, 2020: "Children of Mars"

STAR TREK: PICARD (2020–PRESENT)
(Abbreviated as *PIC*)

Created by Alex Kurtzman, Michael Chabon, Akiva Goldsman, and Kirsten Beyer, *Picard* is a direct sequel to *TNG*, *VOY*, and the film *Star Trek: Nemesis*. It also is a sideways sequel to the first *Star Trek* reboot film (2009). The series focuses on the further adventures of Jean-Luc Picard, beginning in the year 2399, roughly thirty years after the end of *TNG*, and twenty years after the final *TNG* feature film. Analogously, the amount of time that passed between Sir Patrick Stewart's last on-screen appearance as Picard and the beginning of this series was also roughly twenty years. Season 1 of *Picard* focuses on a conspiracy involving synthetic life-forms (androids), an ancient Romulan cult, and an abandoned derelict Borg space-craft. Season 2 of *Picard* concerns the reappearance of Q (John de Lancie) from *TNG*, dramatic change in the existing Star Trek timeline, and time travel to the twenty-first century. Because Jean-Luc Picard is no longer a part of Starfleet in this era, he is joined by a "motley crew" of civilians on a non-Starfleet ship called *La Sirena*.

Although there are several guest stars, the core cast of *Picard* consists of: Patrick Stewart as Jean-Luc Picard, Isa Briones as Soji, Evan Evagora as Elnor, Santiago Cabrera as Captain Chris Rios, Michelle Hurd as Raffi Musiker, Alison Pill as Dr. Agnes Jurati, Jeri Ryan as Seven of Nine (reprising her role from *VOY*), and Orla Brady as Laris. This series also features other *TNG* cast members including Jonathan Frakes, Marina Sirtis, and Brent Spiner.

Michael Chabon was the showrunner for *Picard* Season 1. For *Picard* Seasons 2 and 3, the showrunner is Terry Matalas. As of this writing, there are two seasons of *Picard*, consisting of 20 episodes, with a third season planned.

FIRST EPISODE: January 23, 2020: "Remembrance"
LAST EPISODE: N/A, series is still airing as of this writing.

STAR TREK: LOWER DECKS (2020–PRESENT)
(Abbreviated as LDS)

Created by Mike McMahan, *Lower Decks* is an animated comedy for adults set in the post-*VOY* era. Conceived as a tribute to the nineties-era Trek shows (*TNG*, *DS9*, and *VOY*), *Lower Decks* derives its title from a *TNG* episode of the same name, which focused on Starfleet crew members who are not part of the elite "bridge crew." Although presented as a comedy, *Lower Decks* intentionally adheres to the Star Trek canon, and features countless references and Easter eggs to the entire Star Trek franchise. Though the show follows the misadventures of the titular lower deckers, cameos from various Star Trek veterans have been prominent. *Lower Decks* stars Tawny Newsome, Jack Quaid, Noël Wells, Eugene Cordero, Jerry O'Connell, Fred Tatasciore, Gillian Vigman, and Dawnn Lewis.

FIRST EPISODE: August 5, 2020: "Second Contact"
LAST EPISODE: N/A, series is still airing as of this writing.

STAR TREK: PRODIGY (2021–PRESENT)

Produced by Nickelodeon, *Prodigy* is an animated children's series aimed at children roughly of seven years or older. It follows the misadventures of a group of various alien tweens who find an abandoned Federation starship called the USS *Protostar*. It notably features the return of Kate Mulgrew as a hologram version of Captain Janeway.

FIRST EPISODE: October 28, 2021: "Lost and Found"
LAST EPISODE: N/A, series is still airing as of this writing.

STAR TREK: STRANGE NEW WORLDS (2022–PRESENT)

Set after *Discovery* Season 2 but before *The Original Series*, *Strange New Worlds* focuses on the crew of the USS *Enterprise* NCC-1701 before the days of Kirk. Ethan Peck, Anson Mount, and Rebecca Romijn reprise their roles from *Discovery* as Spock, Captain Pike, and Number One, respectively. The series is also notable for recasting other original series roles, including Jess Bush as Nurse Chapel, Babs Olusanmokun as Dr. M'Benga, and Celia Rose Gooding as a younger version of Uhura.

FIRST EPISODE: May 5, 2022
LAST EPISODE: N/A, series is still airing as of this writing.

Star Trek Feature Films

As of this writing, there are thirteen Star Trek feature films. The first six films focused on the original cast:

The Motion Picture (1979)

The Wrath of Khan (1982)

The Search for Spock (1984)

The Voyage Home (1986)

The Final Frontier (1989)

The Undiscovered Country (1991)

After that, there were four films focused on the cast of *The Next Generation*:

Generations (1994)

First Contact (1996)

Insurrection (1998)

Nemesis (2002)

In 2009, the J. J. Abrams films rebooted the *TOS* timeline with an alternate continuity. These films are set in what is sometimes called the "Abramsverse" or the "Kelvinverse" and, as such, don't interact (much) with the timeline of the other *Star Treks*. (Though there is some indication in *Discovery* that this could change.) As of this writing, there are three films in this movie series, the first two directed by J. J. Abrams and the last by Justin Lin. These films star Chris Pine, Zachary Quinto, Simon Pegg, John Cho, Zoe Saldaña, Karl Urban, and the late Anton Yelchin. The films are titled:

Star Trek (2009)

Star Trek Into Darkness (2013)

Star Trek Beyond (2016)

As of this writing, it is unclear if the planned 2023 Star Trek feature film (produced by Abrams) will serve as a sequel to these films or be placed in a different continuity altogether.

Star Trek Chronology

Because the Star Trek franchise consists of crisscrossing timelines, prequels, and alternate dimensions, keeping it all straight can give you a headache. Here's the order in which the films and movies take place, according to the fictional chronology.

2150s–2160s

Enterprise

2250s–2270s

Discovery

Strange New Worlds

The Original Series

The Animated Series

The Motion Picture

2280s–2290s

The Wrath of Khan

The Search for Spock

The Voyage Home

The Final Frontier

The Undiscovered Country

The first fifteen minutes of
Generations

2360s–2390s

The Next Generation

Deep Space Nine

Generations

First Contact

Insurrection

Voyager

Nemesis

Lower Decks

Prodigy

Picard

3189–the future

Thanks to time travel, *Star Trek: Discovery* Season 3 and Season 4 take place in the thirty-second century, with some indications it could go even farther into the future.

What about the Reboot Movies?

Because the reboots happen in an alternate universe, that chronology looks like this:

Star Trek (2009): mostly in 2258, though it opens in the 2230s and features time travel from the 2380s.

Star Trek Into Darkness: 2260

Star Trek Beyond: 2263

Note: Because the reboots involve time travel and crossover from the "prime" universe, there's also a bit of a crossover to the year 2387, which is part of the flashbacks in *Star Trek: Picard*. All of this makes *Picard* a sequel to a prequel/reboot, and *Discovery* a prequel and a sequel at the same time. Isn't Star Trek great?

INDEX

Index

Index

Index

Index

ABOUT THE AUTHOR

RYAN BRITT is the author of *Luke Skywalker Can't Read and Other Geeky Truths* (Plume, 2015). He has written professionally about science fiction, and Star Trek in specific, since 2010. His Star Trek journalism and commentary is frequently published by Inverse, Den of Geek, Syfy Wire, Tor.com, and StarTrek.com. When new Star Trek episodes are airing, you can easily read at least three new articles about those episodes, written by Ryan, every week. Lev Grossman has said about him, "Ryan Britt is one of nerd culture's most brilliant and most essential commentators." His non–Star Trek writing has appeared in *Vulture*, *VICE*, CNN Style, and *The New York Times*. He's also a senior editor at Fatherly.